Psychology *of* Mystical Consciousness

Carl ALBRECHT

Psychology *of* Mystical Consciousness

INTRODUCED AND TRANSLATED WITH ANNOTATIONS BY

Franz K. Woehrer

A Herder & Herder Book
THE CROSSROAD PUBLISHING COMPANY
NEW YORK

A Herder & Herder Book
The Crossroad Publishing Company
www.crossroadpublishing.com

© 2019 by Franz K. Woehrer

Translated from the German edition of *Psychologie des Mystischen Bewußtseins*. Mainz: Matthias-Grünewald-Verlag, 1976 (ISBN 3-7867-0563-1), which is the identical reprint of the original edition published by Carl Schünemann, Bremen, in 1951.

The editor gratefully acknowledges that the publication of this book has been supported by the Austrian Research Association

ÖFG ⫽ ÖSTERREICHISCHE FORSCHUNGSGEMEINSCHAFT

© For the texts of the English translation, the general introduction and the annotations: 2018 Franz K. Woehrer, franz-karl.woehrer@univie.ac.at and Crossroad Publishing Company, New York. All rights reserved. No part of this publication may be reproduced or transmitted in any form or by any means, electronic, mechanical, photocopying or otherwise, without prior permission in writing from both the translator-editor and the publisher.

Crossroad, Herder & Herder, and the crossed C logo/colophon are registered trademarks of The Crossroad Publishing Company.

All rights reserved. No part of this book may be copied, scanned, reproduced in any way, or stored in a retrieval system, or transmitted, in any form or by any means, electronic, mechanical, photocopying, recording, or otherwise, without the written permission of The Crossroad Publishing Company. For permission please write to rights@crossroadpublishing.com.

In continuation of our 200-year tradition of independent publishing, The Crossroad Publishing Company proudly offers a variety of books with strong, original voices and diverse perspectives. The viewpoints expressed in our books are not necessarily those of The Crossroad Publishing Company, any of its imprints or of its employees, executives, owners. Although the author and publisher have made every effort to ensure that the information in this book was correct at press time, the author and publisher do not assume and hereby disclaim any liability to any party for any loss, damage, or disruption caused by errors or omissions, whether such errors or omissions result from negligence, accident, or any other cause. No claims are made or responsibility assumed for any health or other benefits.

The text of this book is set in 11/14 Sabon LT Pro.

Composition and cover design by Sophie Appel

Library of Congress Cataloging-in-Publication Data
available upon request from the Library of Congress.

ISBN 978-0-8245-9954-6 paperback
ISBN 978-0-8245-9955-3 cloth
ISBN 978-0-8245-9956-0 ePub
ISBN 978-0-8245-9957-7 mobi

Books published by The Crossroad Publishing Company may be purchased at special quantity discount rates for classes and institutional use. For information, please e-mail sales@crossroadpublishing.com.

"*I found I had less and less to say, until finally, I became silent, and began to listen, I discovered in the silence, the voice of God.*"
Søren KIERKEGAARD

Noli foras ire, in teipsum reddi;
in interiore homine habitat veritas.
ST. AUGUSTINE (*De vera religione* 39, 72)

ACKNOWLEDGMENTS

It has taken two attempts, and more than thirty years after the first effort, for the project of publishing Carl Albrecht's pioneering study *Psychologie des Mystischen Bewußtseins* in English translation. The first attempt was initiated in the 1980s by the German philosopher Hans A. Fischer-Barnicol, a distinguished scholar of philosophy and comparative religion, and an expert in Chinese and Christian traditions of mysticism. He had a keen interest in the empirical research of the German medical doctor, psychotherapist and mystic Carl Albrecht and became Albrecht's first biographer. He edited Albrecht's letters and literary remains in *Das Mystische Wort* in 1974. The initial project foundered, however, when it became clear that for translating Albrecht's rather intricate subject matter, rendered in rather unconventional, at times idiosyncratic language, replete with neologisms, the bilingual skills of a competent English translator do not suffice. The first attempt ended abruptly in 1999 because of Fischer-Barnicol's untimely death at the age of sixty-nine. The memory of the many inspiring discussions with this brilliant mind and charismatic mentor has remained vivid indeed. This successful second effort to make Albrecht's ground-breaking research accessible to English-speaking scholarship is thus also a late tribute to Hans A. Fischer-Barnicol.

ACKNOWLEDGMENTS

The second attempt to bring out *Psychology of Mystical Consciousness* in an annotated English edition was initiated in 2015. It could be completed successfully thanks to the encouragement, advice and inspiring cooperation as well as financial support by members of the Albrecht family, the owners of the copyright. I am particularly indebted to Adelheid Haas, Carl Albrecht's daughter, for her valuable suggestions, biographical information on her father and her meticulous proof reading over the past two years. Very special thanks are due to Dr. Harald Albrecht, Carl Albrecht's grandson, for his untiring commitment and encouragement. My gratitude extends to all members of the Albrecht family for their financial assistance, unflagging interest in the project and their unwavering trust.

I am also grateful to Simon Peng-Keller, professor of theology at the University of Zurich, for sharing his expert knowledge with the readers of *Psychology of Mystical Consciousness* by contributing a detailed preface. I am moreover especially obliged to Josef Weismayer, professor emeritus of dogmatic theology at the University of Vienna, not only for contributing a preface, but in the first place, for introducing me to Carl Albrecht's studies in a seminar on "Mysticism vs. Pseudo-Mysticism" held by him at the University of Vienna in 1977. Finally, I am thankful to Crossroad Publishing, and to Chris Myers in particular, for their discerning judgment in recognizing the heuristic potential of Albrecht's research, as well as for the excellent cooperation. Crossroad has been the only one amongst the many prestigious academic publishers specializing in spirituality and mysticism in the English-speaking world that have realized the importance of Albrecht's empirical investigations into the nature of mystical consciousness for humanity at large, and acknowledged the relevance of his insights for the cross-cultural understanding of mystical experience across spiritual and religious traditions. Last but not least, I am grateful to the representatives of the Österreichische Forschungsgemeinschaft (Austrian Research Association) who, recognizing the anthropological value of Albrecht's findings, have granted a subsidy in support of publication procedures. My sincere thanks to all of you.

F. K. W.

TABLE OF CONTENTS

PREFACE by Simon Peng-Keller	xi
PREFACE by Josef Weismayer	xix
GENERAL INTRODUCTION by F. K. Woehrer	1
INTRODUCTION by Carl Albrecht	29
PART ONE: PSYCHOLOGY OF 'INTROVERSION'	37
Consciousness	39
Sense Perception	41
Sensory Perception of the Environment	45
Sensitive Perception of the Surroundings	48
Perception of the Vital Functions	49
Experiencing One's Body	55
Feelings Linked to the Vital Functions	57
Emotional Disposition ("Gestimmtheit")	60
First Results	63
Drives	64
The Will	72
Thinking	86
Thinking and 'Introversion'	90
Meditation	94
Processes of Associating	98
The 'I' ("Das Ich")	103
Attentiveness	110
Clarity of Consciousness	113
Dispositional Attitude	119
The Free-Floating Stream of Experience ("Fließendes Erleben")	121
Feelings	126
Pointed Feelings	133

Non-Object-Related Feelings (States of Emotional Awareness)	139
The Second Stage of 'Introversion'	147
The 'Quiet State of Alertness' ("Versunkenheit")	154
'Inner Sight' ("Innenschau")	156
The Concepts of 'Introversion', 'Consciousness of Introversion' and the 'Quiet State of Alertness'	161
Concentration and Recollecting	162
The 'Somnambulist Consciousness'	164
Hypnosis	168
Somatic Processes	172
The Layer Theory of the Personality	177
Outlook	183
PART TWO: EXPERIENCING THE 'QUIET STATE OF ALERTNESS'	**189**
The 'Quiet State of Alertness' Compared to Other States of Consciousness	191
The Focal Points of the Investigation	203
Enhanced Proficiency in the 'Quiet State of Alertness'	205
Psychosomatic Processes	205
Meditative Visualization of Past Experience	208
Thinking in the 'Quiet State of Alertness'	210
Speaking in the 'Quiet State of Alertness'	216
Associating in the 'Quiet State of Alertness'	221
The 'Object Arriving'	224
'Split-Off' Items from the Unconscious (The First Five 'Forms of Arriving')	236
The Self, the Symbol and Self-Understanding	261
A Fragment of the Self Featuring as an 'Object Arriving' (The Sixth, Seventh and Eighth 'Forms of Arriving')	270
The 'Ecstatic Consciousness'	288
Value Judgements ("Die Wertung")	295
Summary of the Findings of Part One and Part Two	303

PART THREE: THE MYSTICAL CONSCIOUSNESS — 307

- The 'All-encompassing' — 309
- 'All-encompassing Calmness' — 324
- The 'Ur' [The Primeval Ground of Being] — 336
- 'Ur-Love' [Primeval Love] — 344
- The 'All-encompassing' as a Persona ["Das Umfassende als Person"] — 353
- The Ninth, Tenth and Eleventh 'Forms of Arriving' — 358
- The Path of Preparation and Conversion — 364
- The Concept of Mysticism — 372

EPILOGUE — 375

BIBLIOGRAPHY — 383

1. Primary Works — 383
2. Works Cited by Albrecht — 383
3. Works Cited in the Prefaces, the General Introduction and Annotations — 387
4. Electronic Sources — 392

INDEX — 393

PREFACE

Simon Peng-Keller

The fact that the first of Carl Albrecht's studies on the nature of mystical experience has appeared in English translation only now, more than half a century after it was first published, is in part probably to be attributed to the rather intricate history of its reception, as well as to the persevering, albeit wavering impact it had at different times on subsequent research. Though the original edition of *Psychologie des Mystischen Bewußtseins* sparked off some lively response also in academe when it was published in 1951, the readership with the most enduring and keenest interest in Albrecht's findings was composed of spiritual seekers amongst the general public whether religious or members of the laity. One of the religious seekers praising Albrecht's achievement was the Jesuit Hugo Enomiya-Lassalle. In his book *Meditation als Weg zur Gotteserfahrung* (1972) he relies on Albrecht's psychology of mysticism in his attempt to explain the differences between Zen and Christian mysticism. In 1973 Enomiya-Lassalle wrote an article (which has remained unpublished) entitled "Carl Albrechts Mystik und Zen", in which he expounds affinities and differences between Albrecht's concept of "Versunkenheit" (translated in this study as 'quiet state of alertness') and the path of Zen. In his introductory paragraph he acclaims Albrecht's achievement, claiming that the German psychologist was the very first scientist who made a genuine and sincere effort to "vindicate the phenomenon of mysticism in the face of rational scientific thinking, and on the empirical basis of words spoken spontaneously during the process of 'introversion' and/or while immersed in the 'quiet state of alertness'. Albrecht has thus opened up a new path for a better understanding of the phenomenon – an achievement that can scarcely be overrated." But is it still possible for us today, more than forty years later, to endorse or share Enomiya-Lassalle's enthusiastic appraisal of Albrecht's achievement? I shall try in the following to give a concise critical assessment of Carl Albrecht's enquiries into the realm of mysticism and the area of meditational practice. In order to facilitate the reading of this book, as well as to provide an incentive for doing so, I will place it in a dual context. First, the book will be related to the context of Albrecht's life, and secondly, Albrecht's place in the history of research into the nature of mysticism and the psychology of meditation of the 20th century will be assessed.

Biographical Background

Carl Albrecht was born in Bremen (Germany) on March 28, 1902 as the eldest son of a prosperous family with a long-standing tradition in commerce and trading. Although his father wanted his son to follow in his footsteps professionally, young Carl had adverse ideas and plans for his life. He pursued his aims despite harsh parental opposition. After a difficult year trying to find his place at the university, involving a change in the subjects of his studies, he finally decided to study medicine. After graduating he continued to specialize as a medical doctor in the field of internal medicine. When working as a medical assistant, he was introduced to the practice of Autogenic Training for the first time. He recognized its potential for psychotherapy and developed this psychosomatic technique further after he had opened his own practice as a medical doctor and psychotherapist. It was this introvertive method of meditative relaxation that opened up to him, albeit only after many years, a personal approach to religious faith and, ultimately, to religious mystical experiences. The very first encounter with the realm of the mystical came to him suddenly and unexpectedly, and had a lasting impact on his life. The initial mystical experience continued to linger, sustained by his ongoing practice of meditation. It also provided succour, consolation and hope in the violent and distressing years of World War II, when Albrecht devoted himself as a medical doctor to the care of the sick and wounded in his native town, Bremen. In 1947 he suffered a severe breakdown from physical and mental exhaustion. In that time of crisis he was also assailed by fundamental doubt as regards the nature of his mystical experiences: he was beset by the question, whether the phenomena that had become manifest during individual sessions of meditative introversion were indeed genuinely mystical ones. The lingering sense of uncertainty and mistrust triggered his desire to establish criteria that could endorse the veridical claims. And this became the starting point and driving force for him to commit himself to long-term empirical enquiries into the nature of mystical consciousness. In a letter he affirms retrospectively the major underlying motive for committing himself to investigations in this field: "For many years I was personally gratified with the experience of a mystical relationship. Like any true and sincere mystic, I was constantly tormented by the question, if my mystical experiences are truly 'genuine'. Considering the fact that I live in the 20th century, and not, like Teresa of Avila, in the 16th century, I thought that I could possibly not – like Teresa – consult my confessor, but rather felt *obliged* to explore and probe into the phenomenon on my own by means of rational thinking." Thus *Psychology of Mystical Consciousness* is the result of a most arduous and painstaking process of self-examination to which Albrecht had been exposed for many years.

On the Current Relevance of a Psychology of Mystical Consciousness

The lasting relevance of Albrecht's research as outlined in his *Psychology of Mystical Consciousness* can be assessed from several perspectives: Historically, as it can be claimed that in the 1940s when Albrecht began his investigations, they were an innovative attempt to explore the borderline areas in which modern psychology, psychotherapy and spiritual practice intersect. Conceptually, this book can be seen – together with Albrecht's later study *Das Mystische Erkennen* (an English translation is currently in progress) – as a significant theoretical and practical contribution to the transdisciplinary study of mysticism. In the following, I will combine the two perspectives and try to demonstrate why it is still worthwhile and illuminating today to study Albrecht's works. In doing so, I will consider some of the scientific research undertaken in the area of meditation and its development over the past fifty years. Like in other areas of psychology, there has also been a tendency in enquiries into the domain of meditation to shift to behaviourist methods and to approaches by neuroscience in recent years. Currently a special focus is put on correlating specific states of meditation to specific functions of neuronal systems and/or the role of particular cerebral areas. Though neuroscientific approaches cannot entirely dispense with data derived from the subject's descriptions of the given states of meditation (however rudimentary), and which have thus been retrieved retrospectively from introspection, behaviourist research does not make use of these subjective accounts, that is to say, they do not consider them as the object of their enquiries. Albrecht's empirical investigations, by contrast, are entirely focussed on the phenomena that become manifest in a subject when immersed in a state of meditation or some other altered state of consciousness.

Whereas the methods of neuroscience are strictly bound to a third-person perspective, Albrecht's method, which is expounded in great detail in *Psychology of Mystical Consciousness*, relies exclusively on introspective observation. This does not mean, however, that a practitioner's personal report is nothing but a subjective account of his/her experience. Even though the personal records quoted in Albrecht's book are tinged and influenced by Albrecht's personal experience, it is also true that within their subjective framework they address and give evidence of phenomena that have claims to general (transsubjective) validity. Albrecht's express intention was to provide a 'strictly' scientific enquiry, and he felt therefore obliged to adhere strictly to the tenets of science, as well as to adopt the stringent terminology and the rather sophisticated jargon of the psychology of consciousness of his time. Already on the first page of the book he admits, however, that his methodological approach precipitated inevitably "a discrepancy between the limited range of scientific concepts at his disposal, which were not always adequate either for denoting certain phenomena and the fullness of mystical life". The intricate style of his book is rather complex but as such consonant with the academic jargon of his time, aiming meticulously at precision and empirical accuracy. However, these linguistic features make reading the book an intellectual challenge to a contemporary reader. The title appears to be ambiguous and can be read in two ways, but the meaning definitely *not* intended by Albrecht is the misconception that the book is an attempt to psychologize mystical experience. Although the study endeavours to provide a systematic phenomenological description of what is encompassed by the umbrella term 'mystical consciousness', it deals to a greater extent with non-mystical phenomena and processes that precede, or prepare for the 'arrival' of mystical states, and which can be clearly identified and differentiated from mystical phenomena proper. That is to say that Albrecht's study offers actually a psychology of the dynamic *consciousness of 'introversion'* ("Versenkungsbewusstsein") and of the *consciousness identified as 'quiet state of alertness'* ("Versunkenheitsbewusstsein"). Albrecht is particularly keen on demonstrating that these two modes of consciousness are distinct, albeit related entities, which do not, as such, qualify as 'mystical' phenomena.

The method of 'introversion', which was developed by Albrecht on the basis of received techniques employed in psychotherapy, assumed a special role in his approach, because he used it regularly in his personal meditational practice as well. As mentioned above, he began to question radically the relevance and veracity of what he had thought to be praeternatural experiences. Read against this biographical background, the book can in some way also be understood as the outcome of a long-term process in self-therapy. As Albrecht claims that the process of 'introversion' and the 'quiet state of alertness' are composed of states of consciousness in which a wide variety of 'objects' become manifest, and thus providing their 'content', he elaborated criteria by which it is possible to distinguish non-mystical states and phenomena from mystical ones. Thus it is not a particular *state* of consciousness per se, but specific *content-related items* that supply the pivotal characteristics by which an experience can be identified as a mystical experience. The state of ecstasy, or the 'quiet state of alertness', each taken by itself, has just as little to do with mystical experience as the sleeping-state, which likewise encompasses modes of introvertive experience. By advancing this kind of approach, Albrecht is able to 'de-mystify', as it were, some of the 'exceptional' states of consciousness which were 're-mystified' only a few years after Albrecht's book had appeared, in experiments with hallucinogenic drugs propagated by several researchers and psychotherapists, notably in the United States.

Although Albrecht is putting into perspective the exceptional states of consciousness, it is the 'quiet state of alertness' that is regarded as a necessary condition for mystical experience. In his view this is the mental state in which mystical phenomena can alone be perceived with ultimate clarity, because the perceiver's mind is most fully alert, emptied and immersed in perfect inner calmness. From this insight he derives his definition of mysticism: "Mysticism is both the experience of an 'All-encompassing' 'arriving' in the 'quiet state of alertness', and the 'ecstatic' experience of an 'All-encompassing'." However, in view of the critical discourse of the 20th century, this definition provokes the critical reservation that it is too narrow and exclusive as it is linked to exceptional states of consciousness. For in empirical reality, we may encounter, after all, varieties of mystical experience that do not occur merely in such altered states of consciousness as the 'quiet state of alertness', or 'ecstasy' – but may happen in daily life: There is, as Johann Baptist Metz insists, such a thing as a "mysticism of open eyes".

The fact that Albrecht in *Psychology of Mystical Consciousness* alludes only in passing to the personal history behind his empirical investigations is however primarily grounded in his endeavour to adhere to the principle of objectivity demanded by science. So he felt obliged to play down the role of his own subjective experience in his empirical research. However, the ultimate ideal of science, the claim to objectivity, is evidently incompatible with a method relying on introspection and 'introversion' and thus depending on empirical data retrieved from subjective experience. From a methodological point of view, Albrecht's *Psychology of Consciousness* can be censured for being impaired by the dichotomy between the scientific claims to objectivity and the subjective nature of the data from which Albrecht's findings and insights are derived. There is no denying that his study is substantially informed by personal experience, the extent of which Albrecht has preferred not to disclose. Despite these epistemological objections, however, Albrecht provides very detailed and meticulous descriptions of the process of 'introversion' and of the mental state of 'quiet alertness', which are all sound and perfectly intelligible, and thus do not require any additional information about his personal experiences and meditational practice.

Albrecht was also reluctant to reveal specific details of the special method of 'introversion' he had developed which enabled him (as well as other practitioners he had introduced to this method) to speak while immersed in the 'quiet state of alertness'. For this reason the uniqueness and originality of this meditational method has almost gone unnoticed, or not been given appropriate acclaim.[1] The process of 'introversion', as outlined by Albrecht, is still marked by the intrusion of scattered thoughts and other disruptions, but when the 'quiet state of alertness' has been achieved, with the mind having become serene, emptied and calm, the subject has inwardly become alert, attentive and receptive to thoughts and words 'arriving' in consciousness. Thus Albrecht's conception of the 'quiet state of alertness' refers to a state of inwardness, in which sense perceptions have been eclipsed almost entirely. But the person absorbed in this state may also assume the role of a spontaneous speaker and is thus placed in a communicative situation. While immersed in the 'quiet state of alertness', the speaker indirectly addresses a listener who writes down what is communicated. Amongst the phenomena encountered and conveyed verbally, the phenomenon termed 'the All-encompassing' by Albrecht may at times become manifest. Thus the 'arrival' of 'the All-encompassing' ushers in a state of consciousness that is framed by language and personal relationships.

Regrettably, Albrecht decided not to hand down all the details relating to the unique method of speaking while immersed in 'the quiet state of alertness', even though he had compiled extensive notes over several years. This method is an advanced, innovative method based on Autogenic Training and on other techniques of meditation and contemplation; it appears that this special method of Albrecht's

---

1 Cf. Albrecht, Carl. *Das Mystische Wort. Erleben und Sprechen in Versunkenheit.* Ed. and introd. Hans A. Fischer-Barnicol. Preface by Karl Rahner. Mainz: Grünewald, 1974.

has not been revived or employed in current research after his death. The methods of meditation widely practiced today are aimed at achieving attentiveness or 'mindfulness' by deepening sensual awareness. The goal of Albrecht's process of 'introversion', by contrast, is the complete elimination of all sensual perceptions and stimuli from consciousness. In the English translation Albrecht's term "Versenkung" is appropriately translated as 'introversion', to indicate that 'turning inward' is its pivotal feature and necessary requirement. But, on the other hand, the English term does not recapture the metaphoric connotation of the German word – the notion of sinking, of experiencing the weight of one's body, which is a vital characteristic in Albrecht's process of relaxation. The person engaged in the process of 'introversion' is gradually removed from the familiar condition of the 'waking consciousness' and feels as if 'sinking', as it were, to the bottom of his/her physical existence until he/she is eventually immersed in the serene and emptied state of inner calm. Albrecht's path of 'introversion' could still be made accessible to contemporary practitioners of meditation. But regardless of whether this is going to happen or not, his approach is yet another example showing the great diversity and transformative potential of meditational practices. These manifold and varied practices are part of the cultural heritage of humanity, and should therefore be valued as part of human consciousness and continue to be creatively developed even further. Albrecht's study explores rare realms of human experience and he endeavours to embrace them, as it were asymptotically, by way of phenomenological description and cognitive conceptualization – but they are realms of experience that are accessible only to the first-person perspective.

Univ. Prof. Dr. Simon Peng-Keller
Chair of Spiritual Care
University of Zurich
Switzerland
15 May 2017

PREFACE

Josef Weismayer

When the German medical doctor and psychotherapist Carl Albrecht (1902-1965) published his study *Psychologie des Mystischen Bewußtseins* in 1951, the interest in mysticism in both academe and the general public was rather slight in Europe and the West. Mysticism was dismissed as esotericism, or was associated with the paranormal and elitist. However, in the second half of the 20th century the interest in mysticism and spirituality revived rather swiftly, in the wake of the Western encounter with Eastern religions and the growing appeal and influence of Eastern spirituality in the West. "In the New-Age-Movement it was not only the borderlines between individual religions that became blurred, but the boundaries between religion, magic, psychotherapy and art also were obfuscated. While the interest in religion was before that one in a religion without church, now the option was offered of a religion without God, or perhaps a religion with a Godhead that, however, had hardly anything in common with the traditional religious conceptions of God."[2] This is the assessment of the Czech theologian Tomáš Halik of the situation towards the end of the 20th century.

---

2 Halik, Tomáš. "Die Religion und der Geistlich Suchende Mensch." Gruen Anselm, Tomáš Halik, and Winfried Nonhoff. *Gott Los Werden? Wenn Glaube und*

Meanwhile publications on mysticism are no longer niche products but have rather occupied centre stage and become the focus of interest. While in English-speaking countries mysticism has been the subject of the ground-breaking scholarly studies of William James and Evelyn Underhill as early as the beginning of the 20th century, it is remarkable that neither James's *Varieties of Religious Experience* (1901), nor Underhill's *Mysticism: A Study in the Nature and Development of Man's Spiritual Consciousness* (1911) were translated into German before the 1970s, thus confirming the lack of scholarly interest in German-speaking countries prior to the final two decades of the 21st century.

Mysticism and spirituality, and the words 'mystical' and 'spiritual' respectively, have in some sense become popular buzzwords and, as a consequence, their meaning has become fuzzy since the original semantic significance has been obscured and become ambivalent. But Tomáš Halik is surely right when he says that "the present interest in spirituality is undoubtedly a sign of the times" (Halik 105). In the light of these developments, the first English translation of Albrecht's *Psychology of Mystical Consciousness* will surely be met by an entirely different readership, one with a more positive approach to mysticism and spirituality than was the case when the book was first published in 1951, and also compared to the time it was reprinted (1976 and 1990). The study of mysticism and spirituality has gained new importance in theology, notably in Roman Catholic theology, from the late 20th century onward. Albrecht's contemporary, the Jesuit Karl Rahner (1904-1984), one of the most eminent theologians of the 20th century, wrote a profound and detailed foreword to Albrecht's research and personal testimonies of mystical experience, published posthumously in a book entitled *Das Mystische Wort. Erleben und Sprechen in Versunkenheit* (1974).[3] In this introductory essay Rahner outlines the basic principles of mystical theology, while conceding that there has so far (i.e. by the early 1970s) been no systematic theology of mysticism in Christian, and

---

Unglaube Sich Umarmen. Münsterschwarzach: Vier-Türme-Verlag, 2016. 103.
3 Cf. Rahner, Karl. "Vorwort." *Das Mystische Wort. Erleben und Sprechen in Versunkenheit.* Ed. and introd. Hans A. Fischer-Barnicol. Main: Grünewald, 1974. vii-xiv.

in particular, in Roman Catholic theology, which has been generally approved.

From the perspective of the history of theology, there was no opposition between systematic theology and mystical experience in the first millennium of Christianity. Reflecting on faith and Christian teaching was closely linked with the experience of the Creator and Redeemer. It was only in the era of High Scholasticism, which was methodologically heavily influenced by Aristotle, that the experiential aspect of faith became subordinate to theological reflection. For the purpose of rendering mystical experience (*cognitio Dei experimentalis*) scholastic theologians resorted often to biblical imagery. It was only in the Late Middle Ages and at the beginning of the Early Modern Era that we for the first time come across attempts at describing psychological states. The writings of Teresa of Avila († 1582) are an important representative example. In both her *Vida* and her major work *Castillo intérior* she gives a detailed account of her experiences during states of mental prayer. She describes indeed states and processes of consciousness that correspond closely to Albrecht's concepts of "Versenkung" ('introversion') and "Versunkenheit" ('quiet state of alertness'). For Teresa, however, mystical experiences and states of mystical ecstasy were not regarded as the ultimate aspirations of religious practice: she insists that the quest for and awareness of God's presence in a Christian's everyday life is what really matters in a truly Christian existence.

The current evaluation of the role of mystical experience in theology is best reflected in Karl Rahner's often quoted dictum: "The faithful believer of tomorrow will be a 'mystic', one who has 'experienced' something, or he/she will be no more."[4] Mystical experience does not supersede faith and the experience of the Spirit of God that is joined to it. Genuine mystical experience is rather a variety of experiencing God's special grace, and thus it has a place in religion and Christianity. Faith and experience are interdependent in the practice of a Christian's life, as Karl Rahner insists: "It seems to me that the task of Christian theology in general, and of Christian theology of

---

4 Rahner, Karl. "Frömmigkeit Früher und Heute." *Schriften zur Theologie VII*. Einsiedeln: Benziger, 1966. 11-31. Quotation: 22.

mysticism in particular, is to show and to render intelligible that the actual core phenomenon of a transcendental mystical experience is also the innermost and essential part (though without being reflected upon) of any pure act of Christian living which is truly informed by faith, hope and love."[5] Thus Rahner states sententiously: "Mysticism is not a 'special event'."[6]

Albrecht, by contrast, as a scientist and psychologist, had to opt for a more limited concept of mysticism: "Mysticism is the 'arriving' of an 'All-encompassing' in the 'quiet state of alertness'."[7] This notion is rooted in what Albrecht has termed the 'mystical Ur-phenomenon' (*PMB* 253). Albrecht's central concern is to explore the empirical domain of mysticism by means of an approach through psychological phenomenology. His investigation is thus a purely scientific and not a theological one (as he insists in several places of his book).

Theology approaches the phenomenon of mysticism in its entirety, conceived as the living encounter with God. Such an encounter is a special 'variety' of perceiving the presence of the Holy Spirit, which is an experience of supreme intensity and ultimately ineffable.

Emer. Univ. Prof. Dr. Josef Weismayer
Institut für Systematische Theologie
Katholisch-Theologische Fakultät
University of Vienna, Austria
15 May 2017

---

5   Rahner, Karl. "Transzendenzerfahrung aus Katholisch-Dogmatischer Sicht." *Schriften zur Theologie XIII.* Zürich: Benziger, 1978. 207-225. Quotation: 210f.
6   Rahner, Karl. "Mystik – Weg des Glaubens zu Gott." *Horizonte der Religiosität. Kleine Aufsätze.* Ed. Georg Sporschill. Vienna: Herold, 1984. 11-24. Quotation: 24.
7   Verbatim in German: "Mystik ist das Ankommen eines Umfassenden im Versunkenheitsbewußtsein" (*PMB,* 254).

GENERAL INTRODUCTION

F. K. Woehrer

"*Die Seele des Menschen ist erwählt, Durchgangsraum zu sein für den Eintritt des Geheimnisses in die Welt*"
["*The soul of man has been chosen to be the passageway for the entrance of the Mystery into the world.*"]
Carl ALBRECHT (Letter of 19 June 1964)

The very first question the critical reader of the English translation of Carl Albrecht's *Psychologie des Mystischen Bewußtseins* (1951) is likely to ask him/herself is whether a study first published sixty-seven years ago can still be relevant for research in this field, considering the fact that the empirical investigations into the nature of human consciousness, on which the book relies, were carried out even before 1951. This critical objection would seem to be persuasive, and is hardly invalidated by the fact that the book was reprinted in 1976 and in 1990. So the scholarly reader of the early 21st century might be inclined to dismiss the study beforehand as outdated. Any serious expert in the study of mysticism and spirituality will surely respond with grave reservations at a study based on empirical data collected several decades ago, and be convinced that the insights into the nature of mystical consciousness provided by it have meanwhile been superseded by the myriad of scientific and scholarly studies published since the 1950s.[8] So the stock response that is likely to be provoked by the English edition of Albrecht's study in academe of the English-speaking world might be phrased in such dismissive terms as: 'an empirical psychological study of this kind can surely be rendered obsolete by recent behaviourist and other scientific enquiries undertaken particularly in the areas of neuroscience and neurotheology.'[9] The answer to the first question is emphatically "yes" – Albrecht's study is as relevant today as it was in the 1950s, and the response to the preconceptions and objections raised above is emphatically "no": The insights of Albrecht's empirical research into the nature of mystical experience are neither "obsolete", nor have they been superseded by more recent empirical enquiries. The following pages, and part three of the book in particular, will persuasively corroborate these seemingly daring claims.

The critical reader prepared to study *Psychology of Mystical Consciousness* without bias will soon realize that the findings provided are indeed ground-breaking, illuminating and relevant for the understanding of the spiritual nature of man across time and cultures. The only disclaimer to be made, though, is that some of the early chapters of the book, dealing with basic aspects of empirical psychology – notably topics from the area of the psychology of sense-perception, feelings, drives, and the 'layer-theory' of the personality – are obviously historically dated and convey the standards of psychology of the first half of the 20th century. However, these elementary issues of empirical psychology are not part of Albrecht's psychological phenomenology of mystical experience as such, but only a methodological point of departure, and therefore only marginally relevant for his conception of mysticism. Thus part one of the book can be said to be to some extent outdated, and of interest primarily for historians of psychology, but this does in no way impair the validity of Albrecht's findings relating to the nature of mystical consciousness, nor does it

---

8   For a representative choice of relevant studies in these disciplines, published between the 1950s and 2017, see the bibliography attached at the end of this book.
9   Cf., for example, Newberg, Andrew, and Mark Waldman. *How God Changes Your Brain*. New York: Ballantine, 2009. Nelson, Kevin. *The God Impulse. Is Religion Hardwired into the Brain?* London: Simon & Schuster, 2011.

affect the significance of his ground-breaking analysis of the mental processes involved in generating altered mental states.

While the German edition of *Psychologie des Mystischen Bewußtseins* won wide acclaim shortly after its publication in 1951 in German-speaking Europe, the book has gone largely unnoticed outside central Europe, mainly because of the language barrier. Scholars and scientists with a keen interest in spirituality and mysticism, who had been alerted to Albrecht's study, have repeatedly expressed the urgent demand for an English translation. Unfortunately, many obstacles had to be overcome before the call for an English edition could be answered, though it had taken nearly seventy years before the project of translating and publishing the book in the United States could be realized. There have been two major reasons why scholars and scientists have insisted that *Psychologie des Mystischen Bewußtseins* should be made available in English: (1) Albrecht's study offers the most comprehensive, most differentiated and most systematic psychological phenomenology of mystical consciousness on the basis of empirical data currently available. (2) Assessed by the criteria of authenticity, reliability and immediacy, Albrecht's findings can be said to be unique as there is no other study in this field as yet available that can claim to rely on first-hand spoken testimonials of subjects transmitted spontaneously *while absorbed in a mystical experience* and/or experiences evoked when they were immersed in other altered states of consciousness, or engaged in the mind-transforming process of 'introversion' ("Versenkung"). That is to say that Albrecht's empirical approach is unique in that, unlike any other empirical enquiry into the varieties of mystical experience currently available, it does not depend on records retrieved retrospectively from the subject's memory or on data derived from 'outside', i.e. behaviourist enquiries. (The only exceptions are a few passages that Albrecht included from the writings of eminent mystics from the Christian and Buddhist traditions to substantiate certain phenomena and to corroborate the authenticity of certain varieties of mystical experience.)

What makes Albrecht's empirical investigation unique is the methodology developed by him. This is the method termed "Versenkung" by him, and translated here as 'introversion'. It is a meditational method, based on Autogenic Training, which allowed a practitioner to speak not only while engaged in the process of relaxation induced by 'introversion', but also when absorbed in any altered state of consciousness, including a mystical state of consciousness. By applying this method Albrecht (or by a confidante when Albrecht was himself the subject) was able to collect numerous authentic records by subjects he had introduced into this technique during his practice as a psychotherapist. The utterances articulated by the subjects during the ongoing process of 'introversion' and/or mystical encounters were recorded by Albrecht and thus he was provided with empirical data of ultimate authenticity and immediacy. He could therefore dispense with any mediated data, i.e. narratives of recorded experience, retrieved in retrospect from memory, and thus inevitably transformed by interpretation. The mystical (as well as non-mystical) phenomena emerging in a subject when immersed in the serene and tranquil state of "Versunkenheit" ('quiet state of alertness'), the final stage of the process of 'introversion', were instantly verbalized aloud. In this way, the ongoing experience became, as it were, immediately incarnate in the spoken word of the practitioner. This is why it can justly be claimed that Albrecht's empirical data are more authentic, more immediate and closer to the 'empirical core' of a mystical experience than any of the data used in scientific enquiries to date. The recorded testimonies of the subjects were compiled by Albrecht over many years prior to 1951 (and he continued his research after 1951 until his untimely death in 1965). The rather voluminous corpus of empirical data furnished Albrecht with invaluable 'raw material' for his systematic phenomenological analysis. His ultimate aspiration was to establish sound scientific criteria by which authentic mystical phenomena could be distinguished from pseudo-mystical ones. Whereas the latter can be traced to the recesses of the subconscious or unconscious, and thus be shown to originate from within the 'sphere' of the subject's 'self', the former are experienced as 'arriving' from *beyond* the confines of the individual consciousness. Only the latter qualify, Albrecht insists, as authentic 'mystical phenomena'. The painstaking task of establishing tangible criteria for distinguishing mystical phenomena from non-mystical, pathological and paranormal phenomena, which may surface in any state of consciousness (e.g. the waking state, night-sleep, somnambulist states, hypnosis, or intermittent higher states of consciousness generated by the practice of 'introversion', or other techniques of meditation), is undertaken by Albrecht in part two of *Psychology of Mystical Consciousness*. Not surprisingly, this part, which provides the pivotal epistemological foundations and detailed practical analyses of empirical records, is twice as long as the final part, which is concerned with the central concern of the book: the portrayal of the phenomenological structure of mystical consciousness and of varieties of mystical experience. Thus part three expounds the results of Albrecht's meticulous empirical investigations, complete with the succinct psychological definitions of mysticism and 'mystical consciousness' derived from them.

Before turning to these definitions, however, it seems necessary to explain briefly the technique of "Versenkung" developed by Albrecht. This technique was first applied by him in his practice as a psychotherapist. He later used and adapted the method for the express purpose of exploring higher states of consciousness, when he had discovered its exceptional potential for probing into the realm of mystical consciousness. "Versenkung" is translated as 'process of introversion' (there is unfortunately no equivalent word in English that has the connotation of 'sinking' attached to the German term). "Versenkung", used as a mind-altering method, is based on the practice of Autogenic Training (as developed by I. H. Schultz in the late 1920s). In essence, this is a psychosomatic technique of calming the mind by shutting out all sense perceptions and intrusive stimuli that might disrupt or interfere in process of overcoming the 'waking consciousness' and advancing towards the tranquil, serene and emptied state of consciousness termed "Versunkenheit" by Albrecht. As there is no adequate word for "Versunkenheit" in English either, the corresponding technical term used here, has been adopted from the American psychologist Roland Fischer:[10] 'quiet state of alertness'. This serene state of calmness is achieved by 'turning inward' and requires – in addition to shutting out all external stimuli – that discursive

---

10   Fischer, Roland. "State-Bound Knowledge: 'I Can't Remember What I Said Last Night, but It Must Have Been Good'." Ed. Woods, Richard. *Understanding Mysticism*. London: Athlone, 1981. 306-311.

thinking is suspended together with any other active function of the mind, including memories and awareness of feelings. All these items of 'content' must be removed from consciousness and temporarily be 'stilled'. The aim of "Versenkung" is thus to advance to the calm, lucid, homogeneous and vacated state of "Versunkenheit". This is a mental state of reduced arousal, but at the same time also a state of increased inward alertness, hence it has appropriately been labelled by Fischer as 'quiet state of alertness'. "Versunkenheit", then, is a lucid and empty state of inner calm and inward alertness, in which the only active function of 'experiencing I' is the capacity of "Innenschau" ('inner sight'). Albrecht summarizes the pivotal characteristics of "Versunkenheit" when he defines it as "... a fully integrated, homogeneous, hyper-lucid and vacated state of consciousness; in it the flow of impressions is slowed down, its underlying, pervasive mood is tranquillity, and the only function remaining in the 'experiencing I', which is otherwise entirely passive, is that of 'inner sight'" (*PMC* 162). Since "Versunkenheit" (the 'quiet state of alertness') is the clearest, most serene and most homogeneous state of consciousness accessible to man, it is the ideal mental setting for perceiving phenomena 'arriving' in the vista of 'inner sight'. Because of this rare and special quality, Albrecht considered it, for methodological reasons, as the only viable mental condition in which mystical phenomena could reliably be identified. This does not apply to the 'ecstatic consciousness', hence to 'ecstatic mystical experience', as he persuasively argues in the final section of the book.

The 'quiet state of alertness' is the perfect medium for perceiving 'incoming' phenomena in 'inner sight', because here the 'object arriving' can be observed in clear juxtaposition to the 'experiencing I'. The clear juxtaposition between the subject and the object perceived enables the subject to discern where the 'object' appearing in 'inner sight' has come from. This means that the 'experiencing I' is unlikely to mistake a phenomenon that has 'arrived' from beyond the sphere of the 'individual self' ("Selbstsphäre") for one surfacing from within the 'sphere of the self'. This safeguard against potential delusion is not given in any other altered state of consciousness since the levels of the degree of clarity, calmness and alertness in the somnambulist state, night-sleep, the waking state, hypnosis, and the state of ecstasy are markedly inferior to that of the 'quiet state of alertness'. However, the method of advancing to and/or generating the serene and emptied state of 'quiet alertness', relying on the practice of Autogenic Training, is obviously not an innovative achievement. The innovative achievement and uniqueness of Albrecht's method is the mental device of 'programming' a 'disposition' in the mind before embarking on the process of 'introversion'; in particular, it was the pre-meditated 'disposition' to speak spontaneously during the ongoing process of 'introversion' and/or while immersed in the 'quiet state of alertness'. This device enables a subject to verbalize his/her inner experience – including mystical encounters – without switching intermittently into the 'waking state', and thus without activating the function of reflective thinking. This methodological approach thus provides access to empirical data thus of paramount authenticity and immediacy. These facts notwithstanding, at present, scholars and scientists are likely to question the significance and validity of Albrecht's research on the grounds that his empirical data have exclusively been derived introspectively, from subjective experience. Considering the fact that contemporary empirical investigations into the nature of mystical consciousness are, as Peng-Keller states in the preface to this book, predominantly behaviourist and/or conducted from a strictly 'objectivist', third-person perspective, the proponents of objective science are likely to censure Albrecht's approach as subjective empiricism, and thus dismiss his insights as subjective and unreliable.

This line of argument, however, provokes the fundamental epistemological question as to what is to be gained by narrowly objectivist enquiries and stringently scientific methodologies in the study of mystical experience. In all fairness to and respect for the scientists who have engaged in empirical research in this field, and by acknowledging their achievements, and in due respect for the heuristic value of strictly objective scientific approaches, the question arises as to what we can really learn about the intrinsic value and the impact of a mystical experience on the life and spiritual development of an individual by strictly scientific behaviourist approaches, such as single photon emission computed tomography (SPECT), or positron emission tomography (PET), or functional magnetic resonance imaging (fMRI)? Though it is true that the underlying intentions of many of the scientists engaging in objectivist empirical research in altered states of consciousness, and the nature of mystical experience, are neither reductionist, nor inherently agnostic, but informed by the sincere endeavour "to help better understand the biological correlates of spiritual experiences" (Newberg 489)[11], the question still remains if it is not more informative and enlightening for humanity at large to learn more about the 'content' and about the impact a mystical experience has on an individual than to establish scientific evidence that certain neurophysiological and cerebral processes correlate in some specific manner with a mystical experience? Though it is surely helpful to supply scientific evidence that a subject's claims to have been gratified with a mystical experience correlate with specific biochemical processes and in specific cerebral areas, and though it is also valuable to learn that distinct neurophysiological and biochemical processes are instrumental in generating altered states of consciousness, 'objective' facts and behaviourist approaches alone can never compensate for the insights gained from authentic first-hand testimonies spoken during a mystical event.

Some of the recent empirical studies carried out by researchers in the natural sciences have won wide public acclaim in the United States, including even footage on television and in prestigious print media. A case in point is Dean Hamer's highly acclaimed book *The God Gene: How Faith Is Hardwired in Our Genes* (2004), which even featured on the cover of the *Times Magazine* on 25 October 2004. Hamer asserts rather audaciously to have discovered a new gene, the "VMAT2 gene" (72 ff.), which he maintains is "to some degree" (215) involved in producing altered states of consciousness, including mystical states. This gene can, he argues, justly be identified as "the God gene" (56). As a geneticist he refrains from transgressing beyond the confines of science, and does not consider aspects pertaining to religion or metaphysics, stating that his "book is about whether God genes exist, not about whether there is a God" (16).

---

11 The reference is to Andrew Newberg's article "Transformation of Brain Structure and Spiritual Experience." *The Oxford Handbook of Psychology and Spirituality*. Ed. Lisa Miller. New York: OUP, 2012. 489-499.

Thus the result of his empirical enquiry is in effect the claim that there is a "God gene", which can be isolated biochemically, and identified as a special component of the human genetic code. The "God gene", Hamer contends, is responsible for the innate human desire for transcendence. This desire is, as he puts it, "hardwired in our genes", and becomes manifest in human beings of all cultures. But however innovative and sensational Hamer's (hypothetical) claim may appear at a first glance, any scholar well read in mystical literature and versed in the study of mysticism and its cultural traditions will not be particularly impressed. The expert reader soon recognizes that Hamer's claims are in fact commonplace, for in effect Hamer is couching in scientific terms an ancient notion addressed up and down mystical lore: The concept of the "divine spark", *scintilla animae* or "Seelenfünklein".[12] The idea that a "divine spark" is ingrained in the human soul can be found, for instance, in ancient Gnostic writings, as well as in the Kabbalah, in Scholastic theology and throughout medieval and modern history of Christian mysticism. Hamer's notion of the "God gene" is also akin to the theological concept of the insatiable "desire for God," which is rooted, or as St. Gregory phrases it, "sown into the heart" of man by the Holy Spirit. But even if we accept that Hamer has established empirical evidence for the existence of "the God gene" responsible for man's inalienable desire for transcendence, such a genetically generated desire for transcendence is as such, from a psychological-phenomenological point of view, only the empirical precondition for mystical experience, but not a mystical state. This means that the "God gene", viz. innate desire for transcendence, is, at best, a trigger for preparing an individual for a mystical event, whereas the mystical experience as such depends inevitably on a response "from the other side". In Albrecht's terms, a mystical experience is inalienably a passive occurrence, thus one that can never be elicited by a subject's desire alone (or by the function of the "God gene", for that matter). Only when intimations of the 'All-encompassing' are experienced as 'arriving' from beyond the 'sphere of the individual self', and only when these 'in-coming'

---

12 Cf. Wilms, Hieronymus, O.P. "Das Seelenfünklein in der Deutschen Mystik." *Zeitschrift für Aszese und Mystik* 12 (1937): 157-166.

phenomena elicit some numinous, noetic, emotional, and cognitive responses in the perceiver which have a long-term after-effect on his life, is it possible to speak of a genuine mystical experience. A genuine mystical experience is moreover always (as Albrecht emphasizes) imbued with a deep sense of 'revelation', by which the 'experiencing self' knows at an instant intuitively, and beyond the flicker of a doubt, to be overwhelmed by a real, numinous transpersonal and 'all-encompassing Otherness', and this awe-inspiring experience can never be confused with any bogus, hallucinatory, psychedelic, pathogenic, or other paranormal experience.

Another recent scientific study to be addressed here is Kevin Nelson's *The God Impulse: Is Religion Hardwired into the Brain?* (2011). Nelson's aim as a neuroscientist is, as he states at the beginning of his book, "to explain the nature of spiritual experience, not to explain it away" (6). But at first glance, he appears to be doing just that, since he tries to explain spiritual experience almost exclusively on the basis of cerebral and neurochemical processes, or by way of comparing mystical experiences with pathological states. Nelson's scientific approach is, however, definitely not reductionist, nor is it inherently agnostic, nor hostile to religion. His endeavour is to probe more deeply into what he acknowledges to be the most highly valued of human experiences. He tries to link objective physiological correlates to mystical states. He claims that mystical states can be related to both specific functions of the limbic system and areas of the brainstem, as well as to neurophysiological causes and neurochemical triggers, such as "psilocybin" (248) and "serotonin-2" (242). He tries to establish affinities and differences between "spiritual states" and "mystical feelings" on the one hand, and "epileptic seizures", drug-induced states and hallucinogenic sensations on the other (93-218). Though he takes a stringently objective scientific approach, he refrains from inferring conclusions from his research that transcend the limitations of the natural sciences. Thus he reiterates the apologetic claim that his motivation for engaging in this kind of empirical research in the field of mysticism and spirituality has been the sincere desire to narrow down the gap between science and religion. By strictly observing the principles of objective empiricism, and sustaining the constraints imposed by its methodologies, Nelson abstains from incorporating subjective experimental data, except for a few descriptions of mystical experiences supplied by acknowledged mystics from Christian and non-Christian mystical traditions (e.g. Plotinus, Teresa of Avila, Eckhart). The lives and accounts of these eminent mystics are, however, merely used by Nelson for the purpose of relating their accounts of unitive mystical states to the function of the thalamus, and for outlining certain parallels between mystical experiences and epileptic fits and near-death experiences.

At the beginning of the 21st century, neurotheology was introduced as a new discipline in the experiential study of mysticism. This new branch of science was established by Andrew Newberg and other neurologists of the University of Pennsylvania. Their methodological approach combines objective empiricist investigation with subjective data recovered from the experiences of practitioners recorded in retrospect from memory. Neurotheology applies neurobiological techniques, notably single photon emission computed tomography (SPECT), and relates these data to the records of personal experience retrieved in retrospect from the narratives of the subjects who had participated in the experiments. Neurotheology, as the term suggests, permits the scientist to read empirical data from a religious (viz. theological) perspective. Its proponents support the epistemological premise that advances in the study of mysticism can only be achieved by a balanced synthesis of both objective empiricist methodologies and subjective data recorded from the subjects' memories.

One of the long-term researches of Newberg and his colleagues was conducted with a group of Franciscan nuns, a group of Tibetan-Buddhist monks, and a group of Pentecostalists. The results were published in several book-length studies, including *How God Changes Your Brain* (2009). All the subjects taking part in the experiment confessed to have been gratified with mystical experiences in their lives prior to the experiment, and several of them affirmed to have experienced brief mystical moments during the testing. Newberg related the 'objective data' from the tomographic images, which illustrate graphically the specific condition of cerebral areas and the changes in the brain at the time when a subject is transported into altered states of consciousness, to the subjects' personal testimonies, which were recorded after the experimental session. In evaluating these post-experiential narratives Newberg is fair enough to admit that they have been assessed from a believer's point of view. His conclusions are thus informed by the dual perspective of the 'objective' neurologist and the subjective view of the believer. In an interview with Steve Paulson,[13] Newberg has conceded the obvious limitations of his methodological approach, admitting that a test subject's avowal to have encountered God at certain moments during the experiment eludes verification. He furthermore acknowledges that the brain-image technology

> ... can tell us what happens in our brain when we have a religious or spiritual experience. For example, in our study of Franciscan nuns during prayer, our brain scans show what happens in the brain if they experience being in God's presence. What those scans don't prove is whether or not that experience was real in some sort of objective sense ... At this point in our technology, that is something we can't answer. (Paulson, 75)

This concise overview of recent developments in empirical research into the nature of mystical consciousness shows quite convincingly that methodological approaches through the natural sciences can at best provide 'objective' cerebral, physiological and biochemical correlates of experiences claimed to be 'mystical'. The methodological strictures imposed by behaviourism and scientific positivism are too narrow to allow access to the 'content' of a subject's personal mystical experience, or to enable conclusive insights into the psychological, cognitive and emotional impact a mystical experience has on the recipient. Considering these methodological and epistemological constraints of empirical scientific approaches in exploring mystical consciousness and/or the nature of mystical experience, a different approach is called for; and one of these is an approach through psychological phenomenology; it can provide a much-needed epistemological reference frame and empirical foundation for neurotheological, neuroscientist and other behaviourist approaches to mystical experience.

---

13 Paulson, Steve. *Atoms & Eden. Conversations on Religion & Science*. New York: Oxford UP, 2010. 73-81.

Before introducing Albrecht's dual definition of mysticism, a brief apologetic and explanatory note on Albrecht's rather idiosyncratic use of language is required. There are various reasons why Albrecht felt constrained to express himself in *Psychologie des Mystischen Bewußtseins* in neologisms, and often rather intricate syntactic structures: On the one hand, he considered it pertinent to use the established scientific idiom and received jargon of contemporary empirical psychology. Moreover, he thought it imperative to define the complex, often elusive, psychological phenomena as accurately as possible. This endeavour resulted, on the whole, in rather involved sentence structures and extended syntactic sequences. On the other hand, however, he considered it necessary to dispense with received concepts from the mystical traditions since many of them were fuzzy, ambivalent or obscure. Hence he introduced innovative terms and tried to define all the novel key-concepts as clearly and unambiguously as possible. Thus he refrains, for example, from adopting a commonplace topos found in both oriental and occidental mystical lore: that of the "inner eye". Albrecht substituted the concept by the descriptive term "Innenschau" ('inner sight'). Over and beyond this, he insisted that an empirical psychological study concerned with mysticism has to operate exclusively with psychological and scientific terms, and must never resort to terminology and concepts from the areas of religion or metaphysics. As a consequence, the words God, Deity, or Divine or any other theologically charged term referring to Ultimate Reality never occur in the *Psychology of Mystical Consciousness*. Whenever the realm of transcendental Reality is referred to, Albrecht resorts to the ideologically 'neutral' neologism "das Umfassende" (translated as 'the All-encompassing'). Albrecht's linguistic idiosyncrasies, together with his innovative terminology, have resulted in a language that makes reading of the German text a rather daunting and time-consuming task and an intellectual challenge even to a native German speaker. The English translation has tried to remove some of the linguistic peculiarities, and to smooth out the style where possible, without affecting the 'subject matter' in any way. Intricate syntactic sequences have often been split up into shorter syntactic units, and several passages with (often inadvertent) semantic ambiguities and some passages in which the meaning is unclear in German have been paraphrased. Occasionally a concise explanatory note has been supplied, either in brackets in the text, or in a footnote to clarify an opaque expression. Despite these linguistic adaptations in the English text, the English text still allows Albrecht's idiosyncratic language to shine through, particularly in the use of his innovative terminology, which had to be rendered adequately into English, an endeavour often resulting in a neologism in English as well.

Turning to Albrecht's dual definition of mysticism: He distinguishes between a 'narrow' and an 'extended concept' of mysticism. The 'narrow' concept is confined to a special mental state, i.e. the state termed "Versunkenheit" by Albrecht ('quiet state of alertness'): "*Mysticism is the 'arriving' of an 'All-encompassing' in the 'quiet state of alertness'*" (PMC 193). The 'extended concept' of mysticism refers to both mystical phenomena becoming manifest in the 'quiet state of alertness', and phenomena appearing in 'ecstatic states of consciousness': "*Mysticism is both the experience of an 'All-encompassing' 'arriving' in the 'quiet state of alertness', and the 'ecstatic' experience of an 'All-encompassing'*" (PMC 193). From a strictly scientific and psychological point of view, Albrecht insists, only the 'narrow' definition applies, because mystical phenomena are unambiguously accessible to introspective observation only when perceived in the 'quiet state of alertness', as it is the most lucid, most homogeneous and most clearly receptive state of consciousness we know. The 'quiet state of alertness' has the highest degree of homogeneity, clarity, emptiness, calmness and alertness accessible to man. And this is the reason why this mental state enables the 'experiencing I' to perceive the 'arrival' of an 'All-encompassing' in the vista of 'inner sight' in the clearest possible manner. However, the moment when the 'experiencing I' is overwhelmed by ecstatic feelings while abiding in the 'quiet state of alertness', and even more so, when the perceiver is transferred into the 'state of ecstasy', the subject's capacity for 'inner sight' is impaired, because the subject-object split is reduced in the process. The capacity of 'inner sight' is finally entirely suspended in the 'ecstatic consciousness', and thus the experience is beyond the grasp of language and reason.

The 'quiet state of alertness' is per se only a formal construct understood to be a specifically lucid and alert state of consciousness in which a mystical experience may occur and be perceived with ultimate clarity. The 'quiet state of consciousness' as such, conceived merely as a mental framework, is thus no mystical state of consciousness. It is transformed into a mystical state only when the 'experiencing self' is passively overwhelmed by the awareness that an 'object' is 'arriving' in the inner field of vision ('inner sight') that is intuitively grasped as coming from *beyond* the realm of the individual self, and perceived to be 'all-encompassing'. This means that an 'object arriving' qualifies as a mystical phenomenon only, when it is part of an experience that exhibits the following characteristics:

1) The 'object' is clearly perceived as 'arriving' from a sphere beyond the individual self; it is thus discerned as something entirely 'foreign'. 2) The 'object arriving' instils spontaneously in the perceiver an unfailing 'sense of revelation', i.e. the intuitive awareness that an unknown and unknowable entity has revealed its presence in the consciousness of the perceiver; the 'sense of revelation' arouses immediately intense 'numinous feelings' in the perceiver (either in terms of a *mysterium fascinosum,* or in terms of a *mysterium tremendum,* or both simultaneously; Albrecht here adopts concepts introduced by Rudolf Otto).[14] 3) The 'object arriving' is perceived as 'all-encompassing', i.e. it is cognitively grasped as something ultimately unfathomable and unknowable. 4) The 'All-encompassing' may become manifest in any of the three modes of self-revelation: It can be experienced as something entirely a-personal (e.g. 'the Ur', 'the Void', 'the Infinite'), or it can be perceived as a 'harbinger' of the 'All-encompassing', i.e. a token such as an intuition, or a locution perceived as having been sent by an unknown 'all-encompassing' Persona (e.g. a word, sound, symbol, image, loving touch, or a flash of intuition). Finally, 5) the 'All-encompassing' can reveal itself in terms of a non-visual awareness of an 'all-encompassing' Persona (e.g. the awareness of the invisible presence of a 'Thou' within and around the perceiver and acting upon and within him/her).

---

14 Otto, Rudolf. *Das Heilige. Über das Irrationale in der Idee des Göttlichen und Sein Verhältnis zum Rationalen.* Breslau: Trewendt, 1921.

There is no need to elaborate on these distinctive characteristics any further at this point as they are explained in detail later in the book. The only exception to be made, however, is the phenomenon of locutions, which needs to be explained here. A 'locution' is a word, or a sequence of words, perceived as a token sent by the 'All-encompassing'. The visual and/or auditory appearance of a single word, or of snippets and sequences of words in the vista of 'inner sight' in the 'quiet state of alertness', or else, in the 'ecstatic consciousness', is classified as one of the special 'forms of arriving' (out of eleven forms) ("Formen des Ankommens") distinguished by Albrecht. In Albrecht's taxonomy this is "the eighth form of arriving". Albrecht deals with this rare and remarkable phenomenon however only briefly in the *Psychologie des Mystischen Bewußtseins*; in fact, his comments are confined to a single page. It is only in his two later studies, *Das Mystische Erkennen* (1958) and *Das Mystische Wort* (published posthumously in 1974), that he elaborates on the phenomenon of 'mystical locutions' in some detail. The gist of Albrecht's explication in these books is that a single word or a sequence of words may suddenly 'arrive' and become manifest visually (and/or auditorily) in the vista of 'inner sight' in the 'quiet state of alertness'. Such a word arouses instantly intense responses in the perceiver: the word is grasped cognitively and elicits the desire to be articulated aloud. It is important to call to mind that the experience of a 'mystical locution' is a special variety of a mystical experience and thus must not be mixed up with the phenomenon of 'speaking during the 'quiet state of alertness' ("Sprechen in der Versunkenheit"), which is only concomitant with altered states of consciousness. The latter phenomenon is thus a verbal utterance, in which subjective feelings and impressions witnessed in an ongoing experience are verbalized while the 'experiencing self' is absorbed in an altered state of consciousness. It refers to an act of speech that is precipitated in the 'experiencing self' by the prior 'disposition' to verbalize subjective experience, which has been 'programmed' in the mind when embarking on a process of 'introspection'. The word, however, that appears visibly or audibly as an 'object' in the 'quiet state of alertness' is perceived as 'arriving' either from within the individual consciousness, or in the case of a mystical event, from beyond the realm of the individual self.

Such a word, or phrase, is experienced as something imparted and as a token conveyed by the 'All-encompassing'. When such a locution occurs, the word infused becomes, as it were, incarnate in the recipient's spontaneous utterance. The important prerequisite for such a mystical locution to happen is, however, that the word revealed is verbalized truthfully; failing that, the word will vanish instantly and the 'experiencing self' is immediately assailed by feelings of unrest by which the 'quiet state of alertness' is terminated and replaced by the 'waking state'.

This succinct outline of the major results of Albrecht's empirical research should be enough to illustrate the significance of his insights and the great epistemological potential and anthropological relevance of his findings across time and space. The claim of the cross-cultural relevance and validity of Albrecht's phenomenology of mystical consciousness may not yet have become sufficiently evident from what has been said so far. There are, however, several passages in *Psychology of Mystical Consciousness* that corroborate that claim – these are the passages dealing exclusively with Buddhist mystical experience, which complement the accounts of Christian mystics and the empirical data gained from Western practitioners of 'meditation' viz. 'introversion'. It is true, however, that the passages relating to the Buddhist experience are relatively short, probably too concise for a critical reader to be able to recognize their ground-breaking value for our understanding of the phenomenological affinities as well as differences between monistic and theistic mystical experiences. For this reason this aspect is given more space in this introduction not least because Albrecht's findings invalidate the commonplace notion widely held that monistic mystical experience (which is inherently a-theistic and entirely a-personal) and theistic mystical experience are entirely incompatible.

When exploring the phenomenological structure of different degrees of the 'quiet state of alertness', Albrecht identified a singular and exceptional borderline phenomenon: The 'quiet state of alertness' can, in a rare liminal event, become itself the exclusive object of 'inner sight'. This means, in Albrecht's phrasing, that the "*'consciousness of the quiet state of alertness' may itself become the 'content' and sole 'object' of 'inner sight' in the 'quiet state of alertness'. This, however, happens only in a rare phenomenological borderline-case"* (PMC 100). Albrecht claims that such a liminal event occurs particularly rarely in a Western practitioner of 'introspection', whereas it can more often be encountered in Buddhist mystical tradition, where this liminal experience is in fact the ultimate goal of the mystical path. In this borderline experience each of the qualities of serenity, homogeneity, calmness and emptiness, which are all integral parts of the 'quiet state of alertness', may feature as the sole 'object' of inner perception. Thus calmness, emptiness and lucidity may individually expand and occupy the entire realm of consciousness and ultimately be perceived as 'all-encompassing'. This is the reason why the phenomenon of 'arriving' is missing in this special experience; it is a borderline event, in which the perceiver is overwhelmed by the awareness that he/she has become fully immersed, and ultimately even 'dissolved' in 'all-encompassing Calmness', 'Nothingness', or the 'Void'. All of these are evidently totally a-personal varieties of mystical experience. The hallmark of the monistic Buddhist's ultimate experience is thus radically a-personal, as Albrecht persuasively demonstrates in the chapter on "All-encompassing Calmness" (PMC 164-171). To prove this point on the basis of a Buddhist text, Albrecht gives a brief outline of the four states of *jhâna* (Albrecht's analysis is not based on primary Buddhist sources, but on excerpts from Buddhist texts as printed in Heiler's study on Buddhist meditation).[15] The Buddhist is required to pass through the four states of *jhâna* on his spiritual path. Albrecht, following Heiler, has the teaching on the four *jhânas* of Theravada Buddhism in mind, notably based on the text of *Sutta Pitaka* of the Pali canon. The ultimate goal of the Theravada Buddhist's meditation is to reach a mental state of perfect tranquillity and emptiness, culminating finally in a state of no-consciousness, in which any sense of self has been dissolved in an experience that is entirely a-personal.

It seems expedient – in view of the subsequent considerations – to outline the pivotal characteristics of the Buddhist path more specifically than Albrecht does in his book. For this purpose an

---

15 Heiler, Friedrich. *Die Buddhistische Versenkung*. 1918. Munich: Reinhardt, 1922.

authentic Buddhist text has been chosen (in English translation): the *Samyutta Nikaya*. In this text the essential psycho-phenomenological characteristics of the Buddhist experience on the fourth *jhâna* stage are depicted in detail. The disciple becomes more and more deeply immersed in the "realm of nothingness", until he arrives at a stage in which any awareness of self is eclipsed and dissolved in the ineffable domain of "unconditioned" being:

> ... what is the fourth jhana? Herein a brother, rejecting pleasure, rejecting pain, by the coming to an end of the joy and sorrow which he had before, enters on and abides in the fourth jhana, which is freed from pleasure, freed from pain, but is a state of perfect purity of balance and equanimity. This is called "the fourth jhana." Now what is the realm of infinite space? Herein a brother, passing utterly beyond the perception of objects, by the coming to an end of the perception of resistance, by not attending to perception of diversity, with the idea of "infinite is space," enters on and abides in the realm of infinite space. This is called "the realm of infinite space." Now what is that realm of infinite consciousness? Herein a brother, passing utterly beyond the realm of infinite space, with the idea: "Endless is consciousness," enters on and abides in the realm of infinite consciousness. This is called "the realm of infinite consciousness." Now what is that realm of nothingness? Herein a brother, passing utterly beyond the realm of infinite consciousness, with the idea of "there is nothing at all," enters on and abides in the realm of nothingness. This is called "the realm of nothingness." Now what is that realm of neither-perception nor-non-perception? Herein a brother, passing utterly beyond the realm of nothingness, enters on the realm where he neither perceives nor perceives not. This is called "the realm of neither-perception nor-non-perception." Now what is that unconditioned consciousness [animitta ceto-samadhi]? Herein a brother, paying no attention to any or all distinguishing marks, enters on and abides in that rapture ... which is without conditions. This is called "the unconditioned." (Woodward 1927, 179-185)

Thus the Buddhist's ultimate aspiration is to probe ever more deeply into the unfathomable "nothingness", until the practitioner's self is extinguished in the boundlessness of unconditioned being. The instruction of the spiritual guide above demands quite clearly that the "realm of perception" must be left behind. Therefore all attentiveness must strictly and exclusively be directed at the final goal of deep-meditation, and no attention whatsoever must be paid to a phenomenon that might 'arrive' in the vista of 'inner perception'. The successful follower of the Buddhist path will thus at some stage be advanced to a peak experience like the one described in the *Samyutta Nikaya* above, whereas any phenomenon that might surface in the practitioner's mind is bypassed and goes unheeded. From these accounts we may infer the hypothesis that Buddhist teaching requires a Buddhist expressly to focus his mind uncompromisingly on the state of "unconditioned consciousness" as the ultimate goal of his path; Buddhist teaching thus imposes limiting parameters on the nature of the experience that the Buddhist seeker aspires to, and eventually has. A person in the West, by contrast, who practices Zen meditation, or varieties of Zen – e.g. apophatic forms of contemplation as was widely practiced, for instance, in medieval Christianity, and is still practiced today for instance in Carmelite, Trappist and Jesuit monasteries, or the variety of Autogenic Training developed by Albrecht – though he may likewise advance to 'the quiet state of alertness' and abide (like the Buddhist practitioner) in the perfectly empty state of consciousness for some time, will hardly ever end up with a purely monistic mystical experience. Whereas in a Western practitioner of meditation the capacity for 'inner sight' is in no way infringed by doctrinal demands, or oriented at the goal of achieving the state of perfect "nothingness", the typical aspiration of the Western practitioner is to advance to the 'quiet state of alertness', which is a state of pure receptivity. The intermediate goal of his spiritual path is thus to become perfectly 'open to receive' and perceive 'in-coming' phenomena. Albrecht has termed this perceptive attitude "Offenstand" – which attitude the Buddhist disciple is particularly exhorted to overcome. The Western practitioner is thus more likely to open up, and respond to any phenomenon that might 'arrive' in the vista of 'inner sight'. When the 'object' that 'arrives' is perceived as 'all-encompassing' it does not matter to him/her whether the distinctive qualities attached to it are personal, a-personal or a combination of both. That is to say that though it is not impossible for a Western practitioner to have a monistic mystical experience, such an event will happen rather rarely.

Albrecht's findings thus suggest the proposition that while monistic and theistic experiences are both generally open to any human being of any cultural and religious tradition, the empirical quality of the mystic event, however, is inevitably co-determined or coloured by the limiting doctrinal and/or religious parameters that the individual mystic brings to the experience. Granting the epistemological premise that every human being is endowed with the capacity of perceiving the 'All-encompassing' in any of the shapes by which it may become manifest (i.e. personal, a-personal, and as a 'harbinger' of the Personal), the doctrinal strictures imposed on the Buddhist disciple function as controlling parameters to the experience he eventually has, or wishes to have. In the Western contemplative, by contrast, the conceptual religious parameters tend to foster the awareness that Transcendental Reality is personal or person-related ("Divine Thou", "Love") rather than an entirely a-personal "Nothingness". Though this suggests that the Western practitioner is predisposed to perceive personal varieties of mystical experience, the fact remains that a-personal experiences are not entirely disclosed to him/her. Yet at close examination, an a-personal experience of a Christian mystic is – unlike that of a Buddhist disciple – never a pure monistic (a-theistic) experience. To demonstrate this, Albrecht refers to records of mystical experience by Meister Eckhart and Johannes Tauler.[16] Albrecht has new perspectives for exploring varieties of mystical experience across cultures and religions and supplied persuasive epistemological foundations not only for an innovative hermeneutics of cross-cultural varieties of mystical experience, but also for the understanding of the spiritual nature of man.

---

16   The Christian apophatic mystical tradition, also known as 'negative theology', originated from the teaching of Pseudo-Dionysius in the 6th c.; it can be traced from the Middle Ages to the present. Meister Eckhart and Johannes Tauler were major representatives amongst the 14th-c. German mystics. Albrecht refers to both to illustrate that the experience of "nothingness" can also be encountered in the context of Christian mysticism. He quotes a passage in which Eckhart describes an a-personal experience of the Godhead in terms of a "soundless desert in which nobody is at home"; similarly, Albrecht quotes a passage from Tauler's works, in which Tauler describes an a-personal experience of the Divine as an encounter with "a vast expanse that has neither image, form nor quiddity" (*PMC* 329 ff.).

Finally, a brief overview of the history of reception of Albrecht's research shall be given to substantiate the claim that his findings are as relevant today as they have been acknowledged to be from the 1950s onward. Chronologically, the first important scholar, theologian and mystic acclaiming Albrecht's achievement was the German Jesuit and Zen master Hugo Enomiya-Lassalle (1898-1990). It is surely no coincidence that one of the most eminent Christian spiritual counsellors of the late 20th century should be the first to recognize the anthropological significance and cross-cultural relevance of Albrecht's psychology of mysticism. Enomiya-Lassalle spent nearly half of his life in Japan, arriving there in 1929 as a Christian missionary. He was familiar with Christian methods of contemplative prayer and acquired first-hand experience in Zen meditation. He was stationed in Hiroshima, where in 1945 he miraculously survived the nightmare of the atomic bomb and its aftermath. He joined a Zen *roshi* and took part in Zen retreats, eventually becoming an enlightened Zen master himself. On one of his visits to Germany after World War II, he happened to come across two of Albrecht's studies: *Psychologie des Mystischen Bewußtseins* (1951) and *Das Mystische Erkennen* (1958). He used these studies as scientific reference frames when dealing with phenomenological aspects of Zen and enthusiastically recommended that his disciples study Albrecht's books. He praised Albrecht's achievement profusely in many of his books, notably in *Meditation als Weg zur Gotteserfahrung* (1972), a book of spiritual guidance addressed to those who wished to embark on the Christian spiritual quest through the practice of Zen.

Enomiya-Lassalle was impressed by the scope and punctiliousness of Albrecht's meticulous empirical investigations, and by the detailed psychological descriptions of the process of "Versenkung" and the state of "Versunkenheit". He was stunned by the many striking affinities between Albrecht's insights gained from empirical research and the teaching of Zen masters and his own experiences with Zen meditation. He realized that both Zen and Albrecht's method of "Versenkung" aimed at achieving a serene state of inner calm, in which discursive thinking (*fushiryo* in Japanese) and all sense perceptions are eliminated.[17] By 1972

---

17 The most recent account of Enomiya-Lassalle's high esteem for Albrecht can be

Enomiya-Lassalle had become a highly respected Zen teacher in Japan and a renowned spiritual counsellor in India and Europe. Though his Zen retreats in Germany, Switzerland and Austria were at that time met with some critical reservations by the Roman Catholic Church, he insisted apologetically that Zen is not incompatible with Christian practices of spiritual prayer, not least because Zen is a method of meditation that is not ideologically charged and thus equally open to Buddhists and non-Buddhists. He claimed, moreover, that Zen, being a mind-transforming meditational technique, has very positive moral, spiritual and psychological after-effects on the practitioner, irrespective of his/her religious beliefs. Zen, he claimed, could over and beyond this serve as a much needed substitute for Christian practices of contemplation, not least because traditional Christian practices of contemplative prayer and meditation had fallen into disuse. In *Zen und Christliche Spiritualität* (1987) Enomiya-Lassalle affirms again that Albrecht has provided "*a concept of mysticism that does not only embrace Christian mysticism and the mysticism of non-Christian religions, but one that can also be accepted by science*" (27).

Enomiya-Lassalle's unequivocally positive assessment of Albrecht's empirical research may have persuaded the eminent Jesuit theologian Karl Rahner to write a preface to *Das Mystische Wort* (1974, vii-xiv), a commented posthumous edition of Albrecht's letters and unpublished writings, edited by the German philosopher Fischer-Barnicol and Albrecht's first biographer. In this preface Rahner affirms that Albrecht's thee books – *Psychologie des Mystischen Bewußtseins* (1951), *Das Mystische Erkennen* (1958) and *Das Mystische Wort* (1974) – "are most valuable contributions to the conception of a theology of mysticism, which has as yet to be developed". Albrecht's insights into the nature of mystical consciousness were acclaimed by Rahner as a much needed empirical foundation for the future conception of a systematic theology of mysticism.

The first full monograph study of Albrecht, dealing with his

---

found in the monograph study of Ursula Baatz, a Viennese scholar and philosopher. She was a long-term disciple of Enomiya-Lassalle's practice of Zen meditation: *Hugo Makibi Enomiya-Lassalle. Mittler Zwischen Buddhismus und Christentum*. Ratisbon: Topos Plus, 2017.

psychological enquiries into the nature of mystical experience, is the doctoral thesis of the theologian Simon Peng-Keller, from the University of Zurich. The doctoral thesis was published as *Gottespassion in Versunkenheit. Die Psychologische Mystikforschung Carl Albrechts aus Theologischer Perspektive* (2003). A concise resume, together with a critical assessment of Albrecht's achievement, is offered by Peng-Keller in his preface to this book.

Two more magisterial studies should be mentioned to furnish evidence of the ongoing interest in Albrecht in European academe. The first book is Eleonore Bock's *Die Mystik in den Religionen der Welt* (1991, 2nd ed. 2009). Bock († 2006) was a doctor of chemistry from the Technological University of Hannover who devoted most of her life to the study of mystical writings from all the major Eastern and Western mystical traditions. In the course of her life she thus acquired encyclopaedic knowledge of a huge canon of mystical writings from Hinduism, Buddhism, Taoism, Judaism, Greek philosophy, Islam and Christianity. Her meticulous scholarship was inspired and endorsed by her practice of Zen in Christian retreats under the guidance of Jesuit monks. One short chapter in her magisterial study is exclusively devoted to Albrecht, entitled "Carl Albrecht: Psychologie der Mystik" (531-544). In this chapter Bock offers a balanced, well-researched appraisal of Albrecht's achievement. She corroborates the view that Albrecht's insights into the nature of mystical experience correspond closely to the testimonies of great mystics and the mystagogical writings of Eastern and Western mystical traditions. In her concluding assessment she states:

> Carl Albrecht's psychological investigations of mystical experiences have confirmed the pivotal issues described by many mystics of all mystical traditions and religions, even though his perspective has been that of a modern Western scientist. This, however, can be seen as another important indication that there is indeed a 'common core' to all varieties of mystical experience across time and space. (543) [English translation provided, FW]

The most recent scholarly study that relies substantially on Albrecht's research is *Sprechakte der Mystischen Erfahrung. Eine Komparative Studie zum Sprachlichen Ausdruck von Offenbarung und Prophetie* (2015), a voluminous monograph by the Polish linguist Alicja Sakaguchi (she has adopted the family name of her Japanese husband). In this long and detailed study Albrecht's works are used throughout as epistemological reference-frame for the interdisciplinary enquiries into the varieties of prophetic and mystical forms of speech. Sakaguchi explores various types of speech-acts can be found in texts of religious revelation and prophecy, including spontaneous utterances elicited during praeternatural and mystical states. It must be added, however, that Sakaguchi does not claim credit for objectivity, and admits that her methodological approach has been influenced not only by her Christian faith, but also by her own mystical experiences (she gives an account of a life-transforming mystical event in the appendix of the book, entitled "My Own Spiritual Experience", 525-531). Given this proviso, Sakaguchi's study is an inspiring and impressive scholarly achievement, in which a massive corpus of mystical texts from several religious and cultural traditions are analysed from an interdisciplinary perspective. Her research is based on methods and epistemological premises derived from several disciplines (including linguistics, theology, philosophy, psychology, history of Christian mysticism and physics), with Albrecht's psychological studies serving as a major source.

Sakaguchi draws extensively on insights derived from *Psychologie des Mystischen Bewußtseins* and *Das Mystische Erkennen* (but does not refer to *Das Mystische Wort*). There are altogether fifteen references to and quotations from Albrecht. In particular, she has adopted Albrecht's proposition that 'ultimate phenomena' ("Urphänomene", or "Phänomenletztheiten", e.g. 'spirit', 'love', the 'mystical relation') are inalienable empirical facts that cannot rationally be 'explained away'. The concept of 'mystical relation' ("mystische Relation") refers to the awareness of the existence of a spiritual bond between an individual and (in Albrecht's terms) the 'All-encompassing' perceived as a Persona, though the latter term is substituted by Sakaguchi with "God" throughout. Like Albrecht, she rejects the traditional notion widely upheld in Christian spiritual theology that the *unio mystica* is the *conditio sine qua non* for a person to be classified as a mystic. Against this view Sakaguchi maintains that it is rather the experience of a living relationship between the self and the Divine

Thou, i.e. the experiential awareness of a living 'mystical relation', and thus the *cognitio Dei experimentalis* that is not necessarily unitive, hence that the experience of a 'mystical encounter' rather than the unitive experience with the Divine in the *unio mystica* is the pivotal criterion for identifying a person as a mystic. The chapter dealing with "Merkmale mystischer und prophetischer (Sprech-) Akte" ["Features of Mystical and Prophetic Speech-Acts"] (Sakaguchi 199-282) is particularly illuminating, as it endorses the findings of Albrecht on the phenomenon of 'mystical locutions' on the basis of a large number of mystical and canonical texts, including the writings of St. Paul, Jacob Böhme or Ibn Arabi. Sakaguchi affirms that in both a mystical and in a prophetic 'speech-act', a word, or a sequence of words, may 'arrive' in the vista of 'inner sight' in the 'quiet state of alertness', which urges the perceiver to articulate it truthfully, i.e. in perfect conformity with the word or locutions infused in the event by the Divine Logos, or Holy Spirit. When a mystic is transported into a mystical state of consciousness, his/her will is in perfect conformity with the will of God, and is thus transformed into a perfect 'channel' or 'medium' of the Divine Logos, thus becoming a participant of "living revelation" ("gelebte Offenbarung", 200). The texts from Christian, Jewish, Arabic, Buddhist and Hindu spiritual traditions analysed by Sakaguchi supply persuasive evidence for the validity of Albrecht's findings, notably for his claim that 'words' arriving in the vista of 'inner sight' is a genuine form of mystical experience.

This concise summary of the history of reception of the German edition of *Psychologie des Mystischen Bewußtseins* can of course not claim to be complete. It was meant to provide a representative choice of the reception of Albrecht's work in contemporary scholarship and science. Thus the concise review does not reflect the entire scope of the reception of Albrecht's works in academe, nor does it indicate the full extent of his influence on recent research in the study of mysticism. Yet however selective this survey, it still mirrors the continuous interest in Albrecht's research over the past sixty years, though this has – because of the language barrier – been largely confined to German-speaking countries. In the United States, however, the country in which interdisciplinary research in the field of spirituality and mysticism has been burgeoning in the past three decades, Albrecht's studies have unfortunately gone largely unnoticed. Only two distinguished scholars in the field could be traced who seem to have studied at least one of Albrecht's works.

One of them, chronologically, is the Jesuit Harvey Egan, now emeritus professor of theology, Boston College. In his *Christian Mysticism: The Future of a Tradition* (1984) Egan, following Karl Rahner, acclaims the value of Albrecht's psychological phenomenology for the study of Christian mystics and the understanding of their experiences, and expresses his regret that "the studies on mysticism by the German psychologist and physician Carl Albrecht" have been "undeservedly neglected" (252). He explicitly acknowledges the heuristic potential and epistemic relevance of Albrecht's studies for probing into the empirical dimension of mysticism. He praises Albrecht's empirical approach in particular, since it is – unlike so many other scientific enquiries conducted in the 20th century – in no way reductionist, though it is inevitably confined – as Albrecht himself insisted – to the exploration of the psycho-phenomenological dimension of mystical consciousness:

> Albrecht's careful phenomenological studies show that mysticism cannot be reduced to intrapsychic processes. Although certain phases of the mystical ascent may involve some regression, neither regression nor pathology explains it. For Albrecht, the mystical consciousness is a 'phenomenological state'. This means that it cannot be reduced to anything else, because it contains an irreducible essence that must be studied in its own right. Although science can and must study this irreducible essence, it demands of its very nature a theological and religious explanation as well. In short, scientific investigation alone cannot do sufficient justice to the mystical consciousness. (Egan 252-253)

The second eminent American scholar, who first came across Albrecht in the 1980s, is Bernard McGinn, professor of historical theology at the University of Chicago (now emeritus professor). McGinn is the doyen of scholars in the history of Christian mysticism, and the most distinguished authority in this field worldwide. He praises Albrecht's achievement in his brilliant four-volume study *The Presence of God: A History of Western Christian Mysticism* (1991).

In volume I, *The Foundations of Mysticism,* he states in the chapter on theoretical approaches to mysticism that "among recent German thinkers [who] have written directly on the meaning of mysticism ... the name of Carl Albrecht, physician, philosopher, and mystic, stands out, though his writing is little known outside Germany" (313). Though McGinn's knowledge and appraisal of Albrecht's research is largely informed by his study of *Das Mystische Erkennen* – as the footnote in his book indicates – rather than by *Psychologie des Mystischen Bewußtseins,* McGinn has recognized the epistemological potential of Albrecht's research for the interdisciplinary and cross-cultural study of mysticism.

Psychology of Mystical Consciousness is now, at long last, and thanks to the discerning judgment of Crossroad Publishing, made available to international scholarship in English translation. In actual fact, the book is not merely a translation, but a commented critical edition of the German work, incorporating the results of most recent scholarship and results of contemporary behaviourist research in numerous annotations. It is hoped that this study will spark off fruitful interdisciplinary and cross-cultural discourse around the globe and provide a fresh impetus to the study of mysticism and the spiritual nature of man for many years to come.

INTRODUCTION

In this study an empirical psychological investigation will be undertaken. Every branch of science endeavours to achieve methodological clarity and precision. Anyone engaging seriously in research in the field of psychology will inevitably have to rely also on its tradition. It is the tradition of psychological research in which the modern psychologist and scientist will find the insights and results of numerous researchers – findings that have subsequently not only influenced the development of psychological methodology, but also resulted in the coining of specific, often even exclusive, psychological concepts. Psychologists have moreover been faced with the pitfall of imposing subjective value judgements and/or ideologically biased notions on to the results of their research on a particular psychological phenomenon. Over and beyond this, psychologists have been entrapped throughout history in the dilemma of having to classify and allocate the immensely wide range of psychic phenomena that can be encountered in empirical reality to a limited systematic and conceptual framework, operating with a rather rigid and inadequate traditional terminology.

Anyone who ventures to embark on a systematic psychological enquiry into the realm of mysticism will inevitably be confronted with a dilemma of this kind as well as with inadequate terminology. Therefore, this study has been inspired, first and foremost, by the sincere desire to open up a new empirical approach into the psychological study of mysticism in which the scientific principles of psychology are strictly observed, and all the concepts used are clearly defined and related to a coherent systematic framework, which is not tinged with notions of and concepts derived from metaphysics, theology and ethics (notwithstanding the fact that the realm of mysticism is inevitably intertwined with theology, metaphysics and ethics). Thus it is, secondly, imperative for anyone who wishes to engage in an investigation of this kind to consider how the gap between the limited range of useful scientific concepts currently at disposal and the great diversity and fullness of the mystical life could best be bridged.

An in-depth psychological investigation into the realm of human consciousness has to differentiate between specific mental states, notably the state of "Versunkenheit" i.e. a *'quiet state of alertness'*,[18] and

---

18 [Note: The term 'quiet state of alertness' was coined by Roland Fischer in "State-Bound Knowledge: 'I Can't Remember What I Said Last Night, but It Must Have Been Good'." *Psychology Today* 10 (1976): 68-72. (Reprinted in Woods, Richard, ed. *Understanding Mysticism*. London: Athlone, 1981. 306-311.) – The term has been adopted in this translation as an appropriate equivalent to Albrecht's term "Versunkenheit", because Fischer's definition of this altered state of consciousness is phenomenologically very close to (if not identical with) Albrecht's concept of "Versunkenheit" – a neologism in German for which there is no adequate word in English. – Fischer has explored the various states of consciousness induced by the practice of meditation; the final goal of meditation is to be advanced to the state of "tranquillity of Zen meditation, where the mind is in a quiet state of alertness." (Woods 308). According to Fischer, "body and mind become progressively more quiescent [in "deeper meditation"] as concentration becomes more focused. At first, the person's attention focuses on a single object. Later the mind seems to merge with the object; there are no other thoughts whatever. Finally, the mind, though alert, is without a single thought, not even the original point of focus" (Woods 308). – This description corresponds closely to Albrecht's definition of the process of 'introversion' ("Versenkung"), which is likewise intended to advance the practitioner to the state of "Versunkenheit" as its final goal. By "Versunkenheit" Albrecht understands (as will be detailed later in the book) a mental state of minimum arousal, emptied of all content; it is a serene and hyper-lucid mental condition permeated by a deep

the mental process termed "Versenkung" [for which *'introversion'* is an equivalent word in English]. The process of 'introversion' ("Versenkung") usually starts in the normal waking state and advances towards the state of perfect inner calm and enhanced inward alertness termed "Versunkenheit", or *'quiet state of alertness'* in English. The latter is thus the ultimate mental condition to which a practitioner may be advance by the *process* of 'introversion'.

The psychological terminology which has been established by a long-standing scientific tradition must necessarily be accepted. Traditional concepts and the usage of received terminology in psychological jargon will provide the basic conceptual tools of the empirical enquiry into the realm of mysticism. However, it will turn out in the course of this scientific investigation that the traditional concepts at our disposal are only useful for exploring the phenomena encompassed by the process of 'introversion', but will prove to be inadequate when probing into the domain of mystical experience. This conceptual deficiency can, to a limited extent, be compensated for when the psychological investigation starts from the initial stage of 'introversion' and its psychological characteristics, which can be used as the psycho-phenomenological reference frame when exploring the realm of mystical consciousness. That is to say, this investigation endeavours quite clearly to open up new perspectives for the study of mysticism through the psychology of consciousness. At first, various states of consciousness that are encompassed by the process of 'introversion' are explored psychologically and phenomenologically by contrasting the phenomena and structural components of

---

and lingering sense of inner calm; it is thus a hyper-alert state of consciousness receptive to in-coming phenomena 'arriving' in the vista of 'inner sight' (i.e. inward perception, termed "Innenschau" by Albrecht), which is the only active function remaining in the otherwise vacated state of consciousness. Albrecht coined the term "Innenschau" (here translated as 'inner sight') to avoid using the traditional metaphor of the 'inner eye', commonly used in the writings of Eastern and Western mystical traditions. When absorbed in 'the quiet state of alertness' the subject is enabled to observe phenomena 'arriving' in the field of vision of 'inner sight'. (The modes of inner perception will be further elaborated below in individual chapters of this study). – FW.]

the consciousness of 'introversion' (specific content- and action-related characteristics) to corresponding phenomena encountered in the normal 'waking-consciousness'. This approach is the only one that enables us to discern the distinctive and unique features of the 'quiet state of alertness'. The realm of 'mystical consciousness', however, can only be fathomed and elucidated when it is juxtaposed to the 'quiet state of alertness'. Distinctly 'mystical' qualities and specific mystical phenomena can only be identified when they are critically compared and contrasted to the pivotal characteristics of the consciousness of 'quiet alertness'. These epistemological foundations must first be established by preliminary psychological enquiries. This procedure is indispensable, not least because some psychologists and scholars have falsely identified certain phenomena which are quite clearly constituent parts of the 'quiet state of alertness' as mystical phenomena. Conversely, some phenomena of consciousness have erroneously been identified as non-mystical though they were endowed with features that were truly mystical: distinctive features of genuine mystical experience have gone unrecognized or have erroneously been attributed to the 'quiet state of alertness' rather than to the 'mystical consciousness'.

This means that we need to gain, first and foremost, insight into the phenomenological structure and specific characteristics of the consciousness encompassed by the 'quiet state of alertness' before we can venture to probe more deeply into the consciousness of a mystic. This means that the domain of mystical consciousness can psychologically be opened up to understanding only if consciousness is explored in relation to, and on the basis of, the phenomenological framework of the 'quiet state of alertness'. It is, after all, an empirical fact that mystical experiences are most frequently encountered in the 'quiet state of alertness' (this claim is neither a value judgement, nor an interpretation of the phenomenon). Now that the basic tenets of the methodology have been outlined, we need to address another requirement that is indispensable to the epistemological foundations of this enquiry: The necessity to assess all the findings of psychological research in this field published to date, systematically and critically. Such a critical review is essential for establishing the current state of research, and for examining the definitions of received concepts. All this is vital for exploring the nature and phenomenology of both the 'waking consciousness' and the process of 'introversion'. Each of the traditional concepts encountered has been systematically attributed to an appropriate terminological 'circle'; and the various 'terminological circles' will function as a yardstick against which individual phenomena pertaining to the stages of 'introversion' and/or to the 'quiet state of alertness' will be tested. This will enable us to classify individual phenomena, and attribute them accordingly to the 'waking state', the process of 'introversion', or to the 'quiet state of alertness'. By applying this contrastive approach, it will be possible to define each concept and each phenomenon unambiguously. It will moreover enable us to judge whether a traditional concept is appropriate or not, and will allow us to discern 'new' distinctive characteristics in phenomena seemingly familiar.

The methodological approach outlined was initially used only for experimental purposes; but the results of the methodological enterprise have turned out to be so astonishing and overwhelming that a critical reassessment of some of the concepts and of the views held by the science of psychology, are called for: The popular claim that conventional mainstream psychology ('school-psychology') is not equipped with the appropriate tools for engaging in experimental investigations into realms of consciousness that are beyond the confines of the 'waking-consciousness', is false and can no longer be upheld. The clear, though limited, terminology of the science of psychology may indeed provide a much better framework than the often vague, though admittedly more elaborate language of 'popular psychology'. But it has to be conceded that the language of scientific psychology is a jargon detached from everyday speech, and employing a rather sparse idiom and vocabulary. Moreover, it is also true that psychological concepts are often inadequate simply because it is not possible for them to adequately recapture empirical reality. This fact aside, the concepts used are not clear-cut and sometimes tend to overlap. It is likewise true that psychological concepts are often merely lexical tools that have no deictic function, or they are only used to highlight a familiar psychological phenomenon. And yet: we are grateful that the consistent endeavour to establish a clearly defined scientific terminology has resulted in a set of logically coherent concepts and systematic classifications. On the basis of these distinct conceptual guidelines, it is possible to steer clear of the pitfalls of deviating into the superficial and inane expressions that we may witness so often in patronising discourses on mystical experience. Shallow, rambling effusions articulated without restraint and sense of responsibility inevitably trivialize the phenomenon of mysticism instead of corroborating its essence. Verbose descriptions can hardly open up new scientific perspectives, nor new orientations. They rather fuel a rapidly growing tendency within the science of psychology, namely, that of propagating theories. I am grateful that the many years of painstaking research have now resulted in this book, which supplies a piece of evidence that empirical psychology has now reached a scientific level by which phenomena can be explored and identified which are per se located in a realm transcending the confines of empirical psychology.

This book contains the results of a detailed, systematic and long-term empirical investigation into the nature of human consciousness. But the book is not a conventional scientific monography, but rather a research-report documenting and commenting on the stages of the progress of the investigations. Several passages are verbatim quotations from a wide variety of sources, while a number of statements summarize views and findings by other authors, to which my own critical reflections and comments have been added. Though all the major sources have been identified and acknowledged in the footnotes, I must confess that it has not always been possible to trace individual sources, or to indicate and acknowledge specifically where a thought, idea or phrase has been taken from. – The intellectual input supplied has largely been the critical analysis of the research data and the systematic classification of these data, resulting in a comprehensive phenomenology not only of the states of consciousness a practitioner will pass through during the process of 'introversion', but also of the phenomena encountered in the 'quiet state of alertness'. The key-concepts of traditional 'school-psychology' have been adopted and acknowledged as a standard. The range of experiences recovered from the spontaneous utterances spoken by a practitioner during the ongoing process of 'introversion', or when he/she has been absorbed in the 'quiet state of alertness', have supplied the empirical raw material for the systematic psychological-phenomenological analysis.

Part one of this study explores in detail the phenomenological structure of the 'quiet state of alertness'. This is a special state of consciousness and the focus of attention in part one. It has to be conceded, however, that in empirical reality it is not possible to separate the mental state of 'quiet alertness' ("Versunkenheit") radically from the mental process of 'introversion' ("Versenkung") by which this mental state is preceded, as the process and the mental state are ultimately intertwined in the final stage. Thus there are phenomena that are integral parts of the 'quiet state of alertness', and which can only be grasped and understood when related and compared to the process of 'introversion'. Secondly, the normal waking-state and the 'quiet state of alertness' are contiguous mental states; they can therefore be explored only on the basis of phenomena encountered during the process of 'introversion'. Most of the essential empirical data have been gained from 'introspection', i.e. from self-observation during the ongoing process of 'introversion'. The method of 'introspection', however, was almost exclusively bound to a mental condition marked by an exceptionally high degree of clarity and inward alertness. However, the issue of the enhanced clarity of consciousness is a phenomenon that can, at this stage of our enquiry, not be accounted for and will be dealt with later in this study. The use of 'introspection' as a method for exploring the psychological phenomenology of 'introversion' is particularly amenable, since it is based on several constituent elements shared with the 'quiet state of alertness', while at the same time some of the characteristics of the waking consciousness continue to persist. This constellation facilitates a comparison between the phenomenological structures of the states of consciousness involved.

From amongst the methods that empirical psychology has at its disposal, we have chosen **the method of psychological phenomenology** [bold print in original]. In order to differentiate the phenomenological method as applied in this study, from the concept of phenomenology as understood in philosophy, I am going to refer to Jaspers[19] and his view on how to distinguish between sane and

---

19 Jaspers, Karl. *Allgemeine Psychopathologie. Ein Leitfaden für Studierende, Ärzte und Psychologen.* 1913. 5th ed. Berlin and Heidelberg: Springer, 1948. 47f.
– [Note: The passage quoted has been translated from the German. – The passage as quoted in *PMB*: "Die Phänomenologie hat die Aufgabe, die seelischen Zustände,

pathological states of the soul: "It is the task of phenomenology *to call visually to our minds* the conditions of the soul actually experienced by people who suffer from a mental illness, and to consider them in their relation to each other, and to *delimit* and *differentiate* them as strictly as possible, and to recapture them in fixed terminological concepts."

> "The word phenomenology was originally used by Hegel to refer to the entirety of manifestations of the Spirit in consciousness, history and thinking. We will use the term for the much more restricted area of individual experiences of the soul. Husserl used the term initially to refer to 'descriptive psychology' and its portrayal of phenomena of consciousness – and in this sense it also applies to our investigations –, though he later applies the word to the notion of 'eidetic vision', which we are not going to apply here."– "Only what is indeed encountered in consciousness is to be considered here, what is not factually given in consciousness is actually not there. We have to push aside received theories, psychological constructs, and everything that is merely interpretation and value judgement; instead, we have to focus exclusively on what we can comprehend, discern and describe as being part of our real existence. This, however, is – as experience has shown – an arduous undertaking." [Translation from Jaspers provided; small print in original.[20] – FW.]

---

die die Kranken wirklich erleben, uns *anschaulich zu vergegenwärtigen,* nach ihren Verwandtschaftsverhältnissen zu betrachten, sie möglichst scharf zu *begrenzen,* zu *unterscheiden* und mit festen Terminis zu belegen." – FW.]

20 [Note: The passage from Jaspers as cited in *PMB,* 9: "Das Wort *Phänomenologie* ist von Hegel für die Gesamtheit der Erscheinungen des Geistes in Bewußtsein, Geschichte und Denken gebraucht. Wir brauchen es für den viel engeren Bereich individuellen *seelischen Erlebens.* Husserl gebrauchte das Wort anfänglich für 'deskriptive Psychologie' der Bewußtseinserscheinungen – in diesem Sinne gilt es für unsere Untersuchungen – später aber für 'Wesensschau', die wir hier nicht betreiben." – – "Nur das wirklich im Bewußtsein gegebene ist nicht vorhanden. Wir müssen alle überkommenen Theorien, psychologischen Konstruktionen, alle bloßen Deutungen und Beurteilungen bei Seite lassen, wir müssen uns rein dem zuwenden, was wir in seinem wirklichen Dasein verstehen, unterscheiden und beschreiben können. Dies ist eine, wie die Erfahrung lehrt, schwierige Aufgabe." – FW.]

PART ONE

Psychology of 'Introversion'

Consciousness[21]

The notion of consciousness has – from the very beginnings of psychological enquiries – been described by imagery derived from visual perception. These images – though originating from everyday speech – were adopted by the science of psychology and became the point of departure for the coining of new psychological terms relating to consciousness, some of which have meanwhile become part of common usage. Thus the trope of the stage, or of the staging platform, representing consciousness has turned out to be particularly apt for describing processes occurring in the normal waking consciousness. Accordingly, the notion of a specific subject matter 'entering' onto the stage of consciousness, and of its 'exiting' is likewise appropriate, and so are the concepts of the 'background' and 'foreground' of the mental stage, which suggest different degrees of clarity. Similarly the metaphor of stage-lighting, which can be adjusted to a given situation, has been used to refer to different aspects of mental lucidity. All these metaphoric expressions denote specific psychological conditions of the mind, and have been acknowledged as helpful and even indispensable for describing [the condition of the waking-] consciousness. In this way we have come to differentiate

---

21 [Note: Albrecht's conception of consciousness is based (as indicated in the footnotes in *PMB*) on the studies of several eminent German psychologists and psychotherapists of that time, including: Elsenhans, Theodor. *Lehrbuch der Psychologie*. 3rd ed. Tübingen: J.C.B. Mohr, 1939; Thomae, Hans. *Bewußtsein und Leben: Versuch einer Systematisierung des Bewußtseinsproblems*. Bonn. Phil. Diss. Leipzig: Akad. Verlagsgesellschaft, 1940 (Archiv f. d. ges. Psychologie, 105); Jaspers, K. *Allgemeine Psychopathologie. Ein Leitfaden für Studierende, Ärzte und Psychologen*. 1913. 5th ed. Berlin and Heidelberg: Springer, 1948; and Gruhle, Hans W. *Verstehende Psychologie*. Stuttgart: Thieme, 1948. – FW.]

between what remains unnoticed and what is noticed, and between what remains unnoticed and what is consciously observed. We also distinguish between different degrees of clarity in consciousness, and between a well-ordered and a disordered state of consciousness. Moreover, we speak of the spotlight of attention, or the impact of the subconscious, and many things more. However, imagery of this kind [though valuable when applied to the waking-consciousness] is neither suitable, nor helpful for defining the 'quiet state of alertness', for the simple reason that in this mental state the capacity of sense perception is entirely suspended.

Another image often applied in this context is that of the 'domain of consciousness'. The word domain is understood to refer to a 'range' of different degrees of clarity. The focus of consciousness is understood to be a clearly illuminated centre; around this centre there are adjacent areas of declining degrees of clarity, ending in a liminal sphere, in which elusive items are grasped as emerging either from the subconscious, or surfacing in a blurred manner from memory, or from what has been perceived accidentally or peripherally, rather than cognitively.

The question I have been asking myself is why this kind of imagery cannot be transferred to the states of consciousness encompassing the process of 'introversion'. This can surely not be explained by the fact that the process of 'introversion' starts on the level of the waking-consciousness; after all, there are in the initial stage sense perceptions and experiences that can be observed as if on a 'stage' in the waking-consciousness and which tend to linger and persevere as the process of 'introversion' continues to advance. The reason is probably that the process of rational reflection on the phenomena encountered during 'introversion' calls for entirely different images and more appropriate forms for its description. Therefore the dimension of the 'depth' of consciousness is indispensable, and the same is probably true of the notion of the 'ground of consciousness'. On the level of experience, consciousness is perceived in terms of a 'space' or a 'chamber', rather than in terms of an area or field. Unlike the person who is rooted in the normal waking-state, the person absorbed in the 'quiet state of alertness' does not perceive consciousness like a 'stage', or an acting arena, but rather as a windowless room, or a secluded 'chamber' shut off from the world outside. Instead of a mental landscape, the person absorbed in the 'quiet state of alertness' perceives an 'atmosphere' rather than a 'background' and becomes aware of a 'ground' or 'base' comparable to the tranquil, rippled surface of a lake, from the 'depths' of which something is expected to surface. The image of the windowless 'space' of consciousness, which is vaulted over a peaceful lake, has been used in accounts of individual practitioners when reporting what they had experienced during the process of 'introversion'.

Sense Perception[22]

The term 'sense perception' cannot be unequivocally defined. Empirical psychology has as yet found no distinctive features that would allow the concept to be clearly differentiated from the notion of the imagination. – Sense perception is a composite psychological phenomenon consisting of several basic phenomena of consciousness. The sequence of sense perceptions described in this section has not been arranged according to the criterion of time, but has been structured on the basis of phenomenological criteria, i.e. by the levels of clarity and intensity. *Sense perceptions* are the empirical raw material, which is, however, linked with items from the *imagination* originating from prior experience. Sense perception and imagination work together in forming a '*Gestalt*', i.e. a distinct form or shape perceived as a whole and which has the characteristics of being self-contained and clearly structured. The 'Gestalt' perceived is the *subject-matter* because it is the subject [i.e. the experiencer] whose teleological act of volition has created it in the act of perceiving. As indicated above, we cannot clearly distinguish between the act of sense-perception and the function of the imagination. However, there

---

22 Cf. Elsenhans, Theodor. *Lehrbuch der Psychologie*. 3rd ed. Tübingen: J.C.B. Mohr, 1939; Rohracher, Hubert. *Einführung in die Psychologie*. 3rd ed. Vienna: Urban & Schwarzenberg, 1948; Kretschmer, Ernst. *Medizinische Psychologie*. 9th ed. Stuttgart: Thieme, 1947; Jaspers, K. *Allgemeine Psychopathologie. Ein Leitfaden für Studierende, Ärzte und Psychologen*. 1913. 5th ed. Berlin and Heidelberg: Springer, 1948.

are other characteristics that provide some assistance here. Objects of the imagination are visual and become manifest in the subject's imaginative realm, and are therefore marked by the quality of [individual] *subjectivity*. Sense perceptions, by contrast, are *physical* and perceived as objects in external space. Sense perceptions are therefore marked by the characteristic of *objectivity*.[23]

Moreover, the term sense perception has remained fuzzy and has suffered from the fact that external sense perception has been juxtaposed to 'inner perception', by which some [psychologists] understand the inward perception of one's own bodily condition. Other psychologists have used the term to refer to a mode of inward awareness, or 'inwardness', and again other scholars understand by 'inner perception' the phenomenon of seeing with one's 'inner eye', which is here termed 'inner sight' ["Innenschau"].

To obviate the hazard of terminological confusion by the use of these concepts, it is necessary first to define these terms and clarify what is meant by them when used in this study:

1. The term perception refers to any type of *sense* perception. – The key concept of 'perception' can be divided into binary supporting concepts: on the one hand, the concept of 'outward perception' [perception of the external world] vs. 'inward somatic perception' [inner perception of bodily phenomena] and, on the other hand, the binary pair of 'sensory perception' vs. 'sensitive perception'.

    In *outward perception* the perceiver's focus of attention is directed at the world outside. In *somatic perception* the focus of attention of the 'perceiving I' is directed at what has been termed his/her own "body schema" ["Körperschema"].[24]

---

23 Cf. Jaspers, *Allgemeine Psychopathologie*, 59.
24 [Note: "Körperschema" is the German translation of the English term "body schema", which was first used in 1911 by the English neurologist Henry Heard in an article published jointly with Gordon M. Holmes: "Sensory Disturbances from Cerebral Lesions." *Brain* 34 (1911): 102-254. Albrecht, however, adopted the concept from Jaspers (1913). – "Body schema" is defined by Head and Holmes as a "postural model of the body", in which "[e]very recognizable postural change enters into

Sensory perception encompasses experiences transmitted in a specific way by the four sense organs referred to below: The eye is the 'photo-receptor', the ear the 'phono-receptor', while nose and mouth are the 'chemo-receptors' for the functions of smelling and tasting. The term *sensitive perception* is mainly used in clinical psychology. It comprises modes of perception that are invariably linked to the autonomous nervous system. Experiences of this kind include the sensations of touch, pressure, temperature and vibration. Perceptions of the outside world are primarily sensory ones, whereas somatic perceptions are mainly sensitive responses elicited by the autonomous nervous system. It is important in the context of our enquiry to refer to the empirical fact that there are both sense perceptions of the world outside, and sensitive modes of perception which are an integral part of somatic experiences. Thus the conceptual spheres of the two terms do not entirely coincide.

2. The word *'inwardness'* ["Innesein"][25] might be replaced by the clearer and linguistically more appropriate term 'inner apperception'. The term 'inwardness' has, however, become widely accepted in the tradition of scientific psychology. But if one wishes to refer explicitly to the process of withdrawing to one's inner world, the expression 'turning inward' ["Innewerden"] is used; but when the mental state is referred to, the term 'inwardness' is

---

consciousness already charged with its relation to something that has gone before [. . .] For this combined standard, against which all subsequent changes of posture are measured before they enter consciousness, we propose the word 'schema'. By means of perpetual alterations in position we are always building up a postural model of ourselves which constantly changes." (Head 186f.) For a critical response and assessment of the relevance of Head's concept for current neuropsychology see Krois, John M. *Bildkörper und Körperschema: Schriften zur Verkörperungstheorie Ikonischer Formen.* Ed. Horst Bredekamp and Marion Lauschke. Berlin: Akademie Verlag, 2011. 257ff.) – FW.]

25 [Note: Albrecht uses the term "Innesein" as defined by Gruhle, Rohracher, Thomae (without giving page references) and Rothacker, Erich. *Die Schichten der Persönlichkeit.* 1938. 4th ed. Bonn: Bouvier, 1948, 68f. – FW.]

employed. – Becoming aware of diverse mental states and processes occurring within is not an experience that qualifies as a sense perception, but is rather one of 'inward awareness'. Thus 'inwardness' is not merely an experience of the psyche, but more than that: it is a mode of awareness that is concomitant with other experiences, or to put it differently, it is a mode of consciousness latently present with mental processes; it is a capacity that is not only very important, but also one that can phenomenologically be clearly defined. During the state of 'inwardness' the 'experiencing I' is able to recognize instantly the subject matters and processes encountered – something that does not apply to the act of rational reflection. The 'experiencing I' grasps intuitively, and recognizes instantly, a given emotional condition. The subject knows instantaneously that he/she is engaged in an act of thinking. Thus 'inwardness' is a spontaneous, non-reflective cognitive state, in which one is aware of one's own doing and suffering.

3. The concept of the 'inner sight' ["Innenschau"] must be clearly distinguished from the concept of 'sense perception' and the concept of 'inwardness'. Elaborating such a differentiation will be one important task of this enquiry, which is why no such definition is provided here.

4. The term 'self-reflection' ["Selbstreflexion"] refers to the deliberate process of focusing one's thoughts on the condition of one's own self. Though 'inwardness' is a prerequisite for engaging in a process of 'self-reflection', it usually is already the object of the 'reflecting I' in the conscious act of self-reflection called self-observation.[26]

---

26 Cf. Jaspers, *Allgemeine Psychopathologie*, 291.

Sensory Perception of the Environment

The perception of one's surroundings occurs generally in the waking-consciousness. As we are now going to explore the special state of consciousness termed 'quiet state of alertness', it will be helpful to consider how the perception of a person's surroundings is modified during the process of 'introversion'. I will try to provide a straightforward description of the experiences generated by sense perceptions, and will refrain from proposing potential answers relating to the phenomena evoked by extra-mental mechanisms, and from offering potential hypothetical answers concerning the nature and provenance of these phenomena.

We know from insights gained from a subject's experiences during the on-going process of 'introversion' *that the world of perception has been emptied to a large extent* [italics in original]. There is in general also a significant decline in the *psychological* susceptibility to sensual stimuli as the process of 'introversion' advances. The responsiveness to external stimuli is constantly declining, until finally, the capacity to respond to external stimuli is almost entirely eroded. For this reason, it might be argued that the given degree of responsiveness to external stimuli could serve as a yardstick for assessing the 'depth' of the given state of 'introversion'. I do not think, however, that such a yardstick is at all practical, and that the degree by which a person has become absorbed in the state of 'introversion' could more appropriately be measured by other criteria. The claim that the responsiveness to external stimuli is suspended when the process of 'introversion' has reached its ultimate stage implies that various other processes, which can all be distinguished from each other, are likewise involved:

1. The detachment from one's surroundings is achieved and initiated by the physical process of shutting off one's sense perceptions. Thus visual stimuli are almost entirely eclipsed by closing the eyes, auditory perceptions are shut out by the person withdrawing to a silent location; the sense of touch is largely suspended because the practitioner of 'introversion' is placed on a bed in a relaxed position so that all muscular activities have likewise

come to an end. It is possible, however, that extra-mental mechanisms of a physiological kind are also involved which reduce the responsiveness of the sense organs, or of centres of the brain. Such extra-mental procedures, however, are phenomenologically to be subsumed under the concept of 'switching' [i.e. changing over into another state of consciousness].

2. Apart from being shielded off physically against external stimuli, there is a mental or psychic process involved as well – and the latter seems to me more important. On the level of experience we need to distinguish the following aspects (an example from the realm of hearing shall serve for illustration):

   a. Sounds, noises or tunes do not reach the individual consciousness at all. The nature of the state of 'introversion' is such that it prevents acoustic stimuli from entering.

   b. Though an acoustic stimulus, e.g. the sound of the doorbell, is noticed subliminally, it does not arouse any response and remains unrecognized; thus the sound is not noticed and can later not be recovered from memory. The sound of the doorbell may linger for a few seconds at the periphery of consciousness, but it is not cognitively responded to, nor identified.

   c. The sound is perceived as an object. It is recognized and related to an external source, which indicates that the sound has in some way been perceived, but it is felt to be irrelevant. The presence or absence of this sense perception has no impact on either the processes of consciousness, or its 'content'. The sound perceived by the person immersed in 'introversion' is as meaningless as a shadow on a wall perceived in passing, and which likewise does not evoke any response.

   d. The sound is not only perceived, but also grasped as a sign of a reality that is intuitively known to be relevant to the person engaged in the process of 'introversion' and/or absorbed in the 'quiet state of alertness'. In this case some meaning is attached to the sound by the 'perceiving I', and, as a consequence, will evoke some response: the sense of being disturbed. The feeling of disturbance triggers instantly some somatic and/or psychic responses. Such an experience of disruption may either be 'stalled', or 'banished', and can thus be quickly removed from consciousness. However, when the sound is powerful, or alarming, or is intuitively grasped as being of vital importance, the response is not stalled and will result in the termination of 'introversion' and effect instantly the interpolation of the waking-consciousness.

This preliminary description of experiences of sense perceptions during the mental process of 'introversion' has to some extent been impaired by the explanations that were considered necessary and by the attempt to transmit these insights systematically. Therefore it is necessary to describe these experiences once more, albeit from a different perspective: the subsequent description provides a representative cross-section of specific occurrences and phenomena of consciousness. The account will resort to pictorial illustration, which seems appropriate considering that the phenomena encountered in the 'quiet state of alertness' are usually perceived in a pictorial manner, and best rendered by the use of visual imagery. It is true, however, that every individual who has become absorbed in the 'quiet state of alertness' has his/her own unique and special way of experiencing this state of consciousness; this means that the experiences of different persons inevitably differ from each other, while sharing certain features at the same time. Thus there is a common pattern of imagery that can be discerned in any person's conception of consciousness: the notion that consciousness is three-dimensional and this is why it is referred to in terms of 'space', 'room' or 'chamber'. Imagery of this kind occurs habitually and universally, and provides what we may call the 'spherical background' ("sphärischer Hintergrund"). The degree of seclusion and detachment of the given 'space' of consciousness from the surroundings and the world of objects, as well as of distractions and sensual stimuli, is aptly expressed by the image of a 'windowless room'. All objects of the outside world, all stimuli and everything that might distract the state of inner calm, has been removed and silenced. Though a few scattered sensory stimuli may at times penetrate the 'wall' [of the 'windowless room'], they are hardly ever strong and persistent enough to trigger a sense perception proper. Though such stimuli may sometimes linger for some time, they are not heeded and, as a consequence, will fade out, or be pushed into the background, and thus stay outside the calm and serene centre of the 'room'. When a stimulus does succeed in intruding into the 'room', it is swiftly removed by a self-generated, autochthonous psychological mechanism. This mechanism, however, functions autonomously and is not part of the ongoing process of 'introversion'.

The fully developed 'quiet state of alertness' is thus a realm of consciousness that is entirely devoid of sense perceptions. Though occasionally some passing notions of the world of sense perception may flash up, they are ignored and have no impact on the ongoing process in which the 'experiencing I' becomes more and more immersed in the calmness of the emptied consciousness. Thus essential prerequisites for the integration of the 'quiet state of alertness' is the screening off of the mind against external stimuli, and adopting an attitude of complete detachment from one's surroundings, if a person wants his/her process of 'introversion' to succeed.

Sensitive Perception of the Surroundings

The term 'sensitive perception' ("sensible Wahrnehmung") does not derive from empirical psychology, but from the disciplines of anatomy and physiology. In the event of a 'sensitive perception', the perceptions of one's surroundings and of one's body are intertwined. The actual experience transmitted by what is commonly called 'sensory perception' (e.g. the sense of touch, the sense of location, temperature or pain) does not only involve the response to a particular external stimulus, but simultaneously also the perception of one's own bodily condition. Over and beyond this, this experience has an emotional component as well which is linked to the given state of well-being. For the current purpose of exploring the nature of the consciousness of 'introversion', it is necessary to split up for methodological reasons what in empirical reality is a coherent whole. We will at first focus on the 'sensitive perception' directed at the surroundings. Hereafter, we will turn to the realm of experience denoted by the concept of the 'perception of the vital functions' ("Vitalwahrnehmung"), though the latter is an integral part of 'sensitive perception' in empirical reality.

In the 'quiet state of alertness' any activity of the organism has come to a standstill. This includes all functions of 'sensitive perception'. This means that a hand no longer touches an object, and the sensitivity of the skin to pain or to temperature has been suspended. The weight of objects is no longer transmitted by receptors in the muscles so that the location of the body and its weight is no longer felt. Thus the practitioner's awareness of his/her sensual relationship to his/her surroundings is [temporarily] extinguished.

The insights gained from the experiences in which the function of 'sensitive perception' has switched into the passive mode are: In the 'quiet state of alertness' sensate experiences of any kind (the feeling of temperature, sensations of touch, pain, vibrations and the like) are eliminated to a remarkably high degree. At the level of 'introversion' in which sounds can still be perceived, the receptivity to temperature (e.g. the heat from a fireplace), or to pain (e.g. when stung by a mosquito), or the susceptibility to movements (e.g. the vibration of an engine) are no longer noticed. The complete cessation of one's response to sensate stimuli, i.e. the complete loss of one's sense-related ties to the environment, can be achieved rather easily by a practitioner who has embarked on the process of 'introversion'. It may happen that he/she is unaware of the ongoing progress of his detachment from the surroundings until he/she has reached the stage in which the world of the senses has become entirely eclipsed.

Perception of the Vital Functions ("Vitalwahrnehmung")

If one wants to investigate to what extent perceptions of the vital functions are part of the various stages of consciousness encompassing the process of 'introversion', it is useful to consider the following aspects:

1. We need to dissect individual components from the entire whole of the perception of the vital functions.

2. The individual perceptions discerned will be analysed by focussing on both the sensory and the sensitive components.

Though sensitive perceptions of the body can often be found in the initial stage of 'self-observation' in the process of 'introversion', we may encounter simultaneously a few *sensory* perceptions which must not go unheeded. There is, after all, such a thing as the smell and the taste of one's body. There are also noises caused by one's body, or the vital functions which are perceived. The three vital functions referred to here are more distinctly perceived when the stimuli of the outside world are shut out and when any muscular activity has stopped. These sensory perceptions do not interfere, however, with the ongoing process of self-observation. Sounds issued by the body, by contrast, may interfere in the ongoing process of 'introversion' and can stall its further progress. But the perception of the taste [of one's own mouth] or of one's own smell cause a disruption in the progress of 'introversion' only when they are symptoms of illness. The sense of taste is usually linked with the sensory 'perception of one's oral cavity' ("Munderlebnis"). This particular sensation tells us something about the condition of the mouth, or cavity, in that it may indicate some somatic change during the process of 'introversion': This may include the relaxing of muscular tension [in the mouth and jaw], the loss of the awareness of one's deglutition reflex, or the awareness of the balanced flow of saliva. – Hearing one's own breath is usually mingled with the awareness of the relaxed condition of one's respiratory muscles, which again results in a composite experience of regular breathing. These descriptions may appear commonplace and of little relevance for our investigation, but they are nonetheless informative as they illustrate the considerable number and the diversity of sensory perceptions that are involved in the experience of one's body during the process of 'introversion'.

The *sensitive* perceptions of the vital functions are diverse and manifold: Every single sense organ conveys an experience that consists of a whole range of components as well as of complex responses to stimuli. If I focus my attention in the stage of 'self-observation', for instance, on my closed eyelids, I may become aware of a certain sensitivity to weight, or pressure, or touch. – The perception of one's arms when one is placed on a bed in a relaxed position, in which all muscular tension is removed, will comprise – apart from the sensations of touch and pressure – the perception of one's location in space, which is commonly called 'sense of location' ("Lagesinn"). – The awareness that one is breathing regularly involves sensations of touch and temperature, as well as of vibration. But none of these sensitive perceptions are really relevant for the current aim of our enquiry, i.e. describing in psychological-phenomenological terms the consciousness termed 'quiet state of alertness', because sensory and sensitive perceptions of this kind are no more encountered in this mental state, or are, if at all, discerned only in passing in the incipient stage of the process of 'introversion'.

In the waking-consciousness a healthy person does not have the immediate awareness that the homogeneous perception of his/her own body contains some features of sense perceptions. During the ongoing process of 'introversion' any sense perception is experienced as interfering in his/her current state of comfort. The individual sense perceptions can, however, be identified only retrospectively on the basis of rational analysis, and be discerned to be a part of the multi-layered structure of the overall experience. For example, when a part of the body is inflamed because of an infection, it will trigger the typical sensation of inflammatory pain. This feeling of pain is however fuelled by several other sensitive perceptions, including temperature, pressure and memories of previous experiences of pain, which together allow the subject to identify and locate the pain in the body. The sensation of the inflamed part of the body becomes an experience of pain,[27] to which the person concerned responds individually with his/her whole being. And this is why we do not call such an experience *'awareness* of pain', but a *'feeling* of pain'. But in empirical reality the awareness and the feeling of pain are inseparably joined in a composite, overall experience of pain. The person concerned comprehends the unique quality of his/her experience of pain in a moment of inwardness. But the feelings and modes of awareness involved are even more complex: A broad range of drives is occupied in it as well, which becomes manifest in a wide variety of desires and impulses. For instance, the desire to withdraw from people or the urge to move about restlessly, are often linked with feelings of fear and

---

27 Cf. Sauerbruch, F. and Wenke, H. *Wesen und Bedeutung des Schmerzes.* Berlin: Junke & Dunnhaupt, 1936.

anxiety, which have animal-like qualities. Moreover, responses of the will are included as well, albeit only in the incipient stage. The experience of sorrows, on the other hand, will interfere in and eventually obstruct the process of 'introversion', and so do acts of volition, the arousal of new, unfamiliar emotions, the upsurge of desires and the surfacing of [intense moral] attitudes. The characteristics outlined here apply equally to cases of organic dysfunction. A healthy heart is hardly ever consciously perceived in everyday life; but a heart that is troubled and afflicted by some disease or malfunction will immediately trigger various feelings and distinct responses. Thus cardiac arrythmia is clearly experienced and identified as a very strong heartbeat, followed by several irregular weaker beats, and accompanied by oppressive feelings of strain and tremors in the chest. The experience of suffering from a 'sick heart' is thus composed of features that are similar to the ones addressed above with the experience of pain.[28]

In the ultimate stage of the 'quiet state of alertness' a person is neither susceptible to the experience of pain, nor to cardiac dysfunction of the kind described above. Fixed patterns of experience like these, which are firmly sustained in the 'waking consciousness', are entirely eliminated during the process of 'introversion', and disappear instantaneously, i.e. without the experiencing person having to govern the process. This is an important insight in view of the aims of our enquiry. The specific nature of events occurring during 'introversion' can be seen as part of the mental processes termed 'detachment from the environment', including the elimination of stimuli

---

28 [Note: The passage printed in small font in *PMB*, 22 ends here. – These rather detailed descriptions of physiological and emotional phenomena are admittedly rather rudimentary and commonplace by the standards of contemporary psychology and physiology. However, the subsequent chapters will show that these considerations are helpful for understanding some typical features of human consciousness. These passages in Albrecht's study demonstrate persuasively his painstaking empirical approach in exploring vital phenomena of consciousness, and, also introduce some of the key-concepts indispensable to the understanding of the mental states of "Versunkenheit" ('quiet state of alertness') and the process of "Versenkung" ('introversion'), which are pivotal to Albrecht's psychological-phenomenological analysis of 'mystical consciousness'. – FW.]

that might intrude upon the person when immersed in the process of 'introversion'. If 'introversion' is to develop accordingly, it is imperative that any item dwelling in consciousness that can become an obstacle, or a disruption, is dissolved. There are, however, patterns of experience that do not disappear automatically, but have to be eliminated by active intervention, i.e. by a function within the process of 'introversion' that isolates and extinguishes disturbing stimuli, as well as any other potentially disruptive items surfacing in consciousness. The psychological method by which this elimination can be achieved is that of a 'dispersing meditation' ["auflösende Meditation", i.e. a meditational practice applied for the purpose of dissolving unwanted perceptions, feelings and disruptive thoughts that are an obstacle to the smooth progress of 'introversion' towards the 'quiet state of alertness'].

In order to be able to understand the meditational technique by which disrupting items are removed from consciousness, we need to know more about the changes caused by it, both in the functions of the ego, the drives, aspirations, desires and emotions. This aspect, however, cannot yet be explored and must be deferred to a later stage of our investigation. We will see later that the awareness of drives, urges, emotions continues to decline, and eventually subsides, when the space of consciousness is permeated more and more by the calmness effected by the process of 'introversion'.

The rather complex experience of pain dissolves gradually when the method of 'dispersing meditation' is applied, until only a dim awareness of pain remains. The intensity and the lingering impact of pain will decrease as 'introversion' advances. This may be due to the fact that the condition of perfect relaxation and muscular inactivity will cause a change in the biological functions, which in turn have an impact on feeling pain, because pain is then deprived of its physiological foundations. Another potential reason for the fact that the feeling of pain undergoes a transformation is changes in the cerebral activities generated by the process of 'introversion': all stimuli are either barred or diverted from certain areas of the brain, and thus from the nervous system and conscious experience. A similar hypothesis has been proposed in psychology for explaining the state of hypnosis and some phenomena of fakirism.

During 'introversion' feelings of pain are more and more shifted to the periphery of consciousness. In the 'quiet state of alertness' pain is either entirely suspended or reduced to a fleeting 'shadow on the wall of consciousness'. Though intense pain and acute functional disorders can impede and even terminate the process of 'introversion', this does not apply to the 'quiet state of alertness', because it is a higher state of consciousness that remains (largely) unaffected by somatic sensations and somatic processes.

Before turning to the description of how one's own body is experienced in 'introversion' ("Leiberlebnis"), and before considering the range of 'perceptions of the body's vital functions' ("Vitalwahrnehmungen"), a few explanations are required concerning the concept of 'vacating' or 'emptying' consciousness entirely from perceptions of the outside world (these comments anticipate later considerations).

1. The process of 'introversion' is based on the conscious predisposition in a practitioner to achieve a state of inner calm; at the same time, this predisposition elicits a chain of associations and governs the gradual removal of mental images and thoughts that might surface in consciousness; in this way, the receptivity to sense perceptions and disturbing stimuli is suspended. There is no longer a sensory basis, neither for stirring emotions, nor for the arousal of object-related feelings, which could disrupt the state of inner calm.

2. It can be claimed (without having to provide supporting evidence) that there is a close link between the given conscious predisposition in a person engaging in the process of 'introversion', and the mental processes involved in 'screening off' the mind from outside stimuli and in removing all sense impressions from consciousness. The interdependence of the two processes is established by the fact that 'introversion' as a whole is based on a pre-determined act of volition.

3. In the incipient stage of 'introversion' we may still find fluctuations in the 'depth' of inner alertness as the condition of consciousness is increasingly filled by inner calm; these fluctuations are caused by accidental intrusions of external stimuli and/or by sense impressions persevering from the preceding 'waking state'.

Experiencing One's Body ("Leib-Erlebnis")

The term 'perception of the vital functions [of the body]' ("Vitalwahrnehmung") is to some extent inaccurate because the actual experience of one's vital functions, including the experience of environment, does not encompass some important features, notably the sense of one's location in space, or feelings that are not related to, or caused by, objects: For instance, the complex experience of 'feeling unwell' may consist of a dim sense of pain, like 'feeling worn out' or 'exhausted', which cannot be related to any object; similarly, such sensations as 'shivering', 'shuddering' or 'being shattered' are marked by features of 'doubtful objectivity'. – Psychology has always acknowledged the elusive and doubtful nature of experiences of this kind.

The term 'perception of the vital functions [of the body]' is not sufficient either as it does not embrace all of the multifarious sensual perceptions of one's own corporeality. For this reason the concept of 'perception' in the context of perceiving one's body has been considered too restrictive, and has therefore been replaced by the broader term 'experience'.

In the fully integrated 'quiet state of alertness' there never occur any experiences that originate from one's body or *part* of one's corporeality. In the course of the preceding process of 'introversion', however, such experiences of corporeality can be encountered and grasped by 'self-observation'. But even then the body is experienced as a single coherent whole; and that is why a single element of one's body-experience is never perceived as something that is separate or foreign to the body. All active functions of the body and all sense perceptions have been stilled when consciousness has been transformed into the perfectly homogeneous 'quiet state of alertness'. All muscles are relaxed and the entire body is in a state of repose, felt to be a still and heavy, albeit spirited mass. This experience of the body is accompanied by the dynamic feeling of warmth flowing evenly through the body. This feeling of warmth is soothing and pleasant – the sense of the heaviness of one's condition is overcome and overwhelmed by a growing sense of inner calm. It seems as if the body has been stretched out beyond its normal size – arms and legs appear to have become more voluminous and lifted up from where they are placed. In this altered state of consciousness the body is intuitively experienced as a singular wholeness in which body and soul are one. This experience may thus be seen as an instance in which the unity between body and soul has become part of empirical reality.

In this state of consciousness body and psyche are so closely joined together that any stirring in the body elicits inevitably a response that affects the 'experiencing self' as a whole. The body is felt to be heavy, solid and 'full of weight' ("sehr gewichtig"). But the body is at the same time felt to be 'hovering', 'relaxed', 'alleviated', 'light' – as if entirely removed from the environment; it is a state of peaceful detachment that is aptly described as 'being-by-oneself' ("Für-sich-Sein"). Since the external space in which the body is located is no longer perceived, the body acquires some space-like quality itself. The body is experienced as if extended in space, and the 'body-schema' experienced is peculiarly harmonious and symmetrical. It is an experience evoking a sense of blissful wholeness and perfect fufilment. Any interference passes unheeded when the person is filled with this deep sense of unified corporeality. The body has become a single harmonious whole, oblivious of any dissonance.

In this mental state the body assumes a heightened 'closeness' to the 'I' ("gesteigerte Ich-Nähe"), which is reflected in the fact that the body as a whole has become, as it were, freely at the disposal of the 'I'. The entire body has been conquered by the 'I'. There is no single element, or 'nook', nor any 'corner' that is not conducive to the spiritual aspirations of the 'I', or that could not be used for advancing the 'I' to achieve these aspirations. This suggests that the body is not experienced as a 'dead amorphous mass' ("tote amorphe Masse"), but rather as matter animated in a most lively manner. In the ultimate stage of 'quiet alertness', the body is felt to be permeated by the soul throughout, and is experienced as a warm, living, reposing, sane primeval substance infused by the soul – detached from its surroundings – being by itself, intertwined and infused by the psyche – relaxed, at ease and motionless – detached from, and unaffected by any stirring of the will, perfectly united with the 'experiencing I', which remains, however, capable of perceiving such a stirring.

Feelings Linked to the Vital Functions

After the detailed analytical description of the phenomenon termed 'experience of one's own body', the focus of our investigation will now be shifted to the area of feelings, in particular feelings related to 'vitality' ("Vitalgefühl"). In doing so, we will enter a domain of the psyche that is governed by the emotions, more specifically, the 'prevailing mood' ("Gemüt") that determines a person's underlying mood or emotional disposition. It is true, however, that a person's basic mood, or state of 'inwardness' ("Innesein"), i.e. 'being in a special way permeated by a particular mood' ("In-bestimmter-Weise-zumute-Sein"), is in part fuelled by the 'vital functions'. It is the feeling of vitality by which a human being experiences something about the current condition of his/her body.

The feeling of vitality can occasionally be reduced; in that case a person's reduced awareness of his/her vitality becomes manifest in such utterances as 'I am feeling weary', 'exhausted', 'frail', 'tense', or 'inhibited', or in a statement like 'I am feeling sick, anguished and depressed'. A normal feeling of vitality, by comparison, finds expression in statements such as 'I am feeling well, comfortable, and healthy'; whereas an enhanced feeling of vitality is expressed such as 'I am feeling alive [energetic], athletic, vigorous or euphoric'. Many of these qualifying attributes convey emotional qualities that are linked to, or associated with, drives. But as we shall see later, drives as such are entirely inactive and silenced in the 'quiet state of alertness'.[29] This means that feelings of vitality related to drives cannot be an integral part of the overall experience in the 'quiet state of alertness'.

Feelings suggesting a *diminished* degree of vitality cannot be part of the 'quiet state of alertness' either. A body that is experienced as

---

29 [Note: In the German text the word used is "Versenkungszustand", which is obviously an error, or a misprint; the context and the clear distinction made by Albrecht between the process of "Versenkung" ('introversion') and the serene state of consciousness termed "Versunkenheit" ('quiet state of alertness') maintained by Albrecht throughout the book elsewhere, suggest that the correct term to be used here is "Versunkenheitszustand". – FW.]

uniform, animated and alive – a body 'occupied' by the soul – can never be felt to be slack, limp or flaccid. A body that is relaxed and at ease will never trigger feelings of anxiety, unease or shyness. Moreover, feelings of ill-health do not surface either, because in the 'quiet state of alertness', feelings that are potentially distracting or disruptive (e.g. sensations of pain, or any distressing emotion) are always dissolved and eventually removed from consciousness.

The words describing an *enhanced* feeling of vitality are of little use for depicting the feelings of vitality that may surface during the process of 'introversion'. Liveliness, vigour and vivacity are expressions denoting quite clearly some activity related to the outside world, or referring to occurrences in one's surroundings. – But even when the experience of my body tells me that it is filled with ineffable vigour and vitality, it is an experience that does not culminate in feelings of elation, since the sense of vigour and vitality is alone rooted in corporeality.

The words used for describing the *normal* feeling of vitality correspond more closely to the body experience encountered in the process of 'introversion'. The body is experienced as healthy, though the expression evoked in a subject when immersed in 'introversion' is more likely to be 'being whole' ("Heilsein"), which conveys more explicitly the sense of harmony and absence of dissonance in the final stage, when body and soul are felt to be one. The word 'whole' ("heil") expresses more intimately the sense of the recovery of a primeval state, which is associated with such an experience. – The expression 'I am feeling well' addresses feelings that accompany drives related to vitality. But this is not the only reason why a person who is immersed in the 'quiet state of alertness' speaks of 'being whole' rather than 'feeling well' when experiencing the peaceful, but vibrant wholeness of the body. Another reason is that a person who is fully absorbed in the 'quiet state of alertness' has been transported into a mental state that is beyond 'weal and woe' ("Wohl und Wehe").[30]

---

30 [Note: Albrecht appears to have opted for this poetic phrase to indicate (as he elaborates later in the book) that a person who is absorbed in the 'quiet state of alertness' is completely detached from the outside world, because all object-related perceptions and feelings, ideas, memories and discursive thoughts have been

I do not think that the complex [multifaceted] experience of one's alert and animated body reposing in calmness, detached from the world outside, and absorbed in the 'quiet state of alertness' can adequately be described by a single term. Expressions like 'I am feeling relaxed', 'I am feeling at ease' suggest a perspective that is too limited and one-dimensional for conveying authentically the many-faceted feelings and degrees of vitality that can emerge during the process of 'introversion'. It is thus a futile effort to search for a suitable singular term to recapture this complex experience. This aside, poetic imagery and metaphoric expressions are much more suitable for conveying this experience adequately and authentically. This can be illustrated by the following examples of spontaneous utterances spoken by a person during the process of 'introversion', when overwhelmed by feelings of vitality and related feelings in his/her own body. These utterances were spoken by a person while 'introversion' was in progress and continued when he/she had reached the 'quiet state of alertness':

> "*The soul encompassing the whole body is pregnant and*
>   *suffused with the*
> *exuberant happiness of perfect oneness.*
> *The soul alert and watchful like a creature,*
> *like a creature of pristine beauty reposing on a green and*
>   *flowery meadow,*
> *so entirely void of any spectre,*
> *so self-assured as a piece of creation,*
> *so full and saturated in her oneness.*
> *Soul and body being one, undivided.*
> *The welcoming mystery is breathing, expanded across its*
>   *domain.*
> *Ripples circling around the reposing oneness.*" [Italics
>   provided][31]

---

removed from conscious awareness. The person involved is transported into a state of perfect inner calm and endowed with the highest capacity of inner alertness, which enables him/her to observe whatever becomes manifest in the vista of 'inner sight' ("Innenschau"). – FW.]

31 [Note: All passages identified as quotations from the 'unmediated utterances'

Emotional Disposition ("Gestimmtheit")

The decision to start this investigation with the description of phenomena pertaining to the area of sense perception and the experience of the vital functions during the process of 'introversion' has resulted in a classification of these experiences. This classification, however, is a theoretical construct imposed on empirical reality. Thus the concept of the 'body *experience*' differentiates between phenomena that are actually not differentiated in empirical reality; in empirical reality these phenomena are more complex and cannot be reduced to single phenomena of the body.

When exploring the 'body experience' we were required – after having isolated the sense perceptions concomitant with it – to provide a description of the 'feeling of the vital functions' of the body. In the course of our investigation we have moved away from the sphere of sense perceptions to the sphere of the emotions. However, the 'feeling of vitality' is still grounded in the vital functions. We will now turn to the concept of 'emotional dispositions' that are inherent in human consciousness in order to complete our enquiry into the 'body experience'.

To begin with, we have to be aware that a person's 'basic mood' does not only originate in his/her current body experience, but is

---

spoken by a practitioner during 'introversion' and/or while absorbed in the 'quiet state of alertness' ("Versunkenheitsaussagen") are printed in italics to set these documentary sections off against the main text, even though the standard font is used for quotations in the German text. These spontaneous utterances are the most authentic empirical 'raw data' on which Albrecht's scientific investigations are based. – Despite Albrecht's disclaimer that this particular utterance has been recovered from an unnamed "person", we may assume that the practitioner was Albrecht himself. We know that Albrecht's own "Versunkenheitsaussagen" were recorded by his wife, and a few by Albrecht's daughter Adelheid; a selection of these private utterances, notably those in which mystical experiences are addressed, was published posthumously by Hans A. Fischer-Barnicol in *Das Mystische Wort. Erleben und Sprechen in Versunkenheit*. Mainz: Grünewald, 1974. – This and other invaluable biographical information has gratefully been furnished by Albrecht's daughter Adelheid Haas, and by Hans A. Fischer-Barnicol (1930-1999). – FW.]

also influenced by drives, emotions, the will and even by the noetic sphere. The concept of 'mood' has been defined as the underlying emotional condition that prevails at a given situation in consciousness. One characteristic feature of a given 'basic mood' is that it tends to stay perseveringly in consciousness, which implies that it is mutable. Because a 'mood' may last only for a limited space of time, it is subject to change, which in turn raises the question if this concept is at all helpful for a systematic classification of phenomena encountered during 'introversion' [and in the 'quiet state of alertness']. Though it is true that the 'basic mood' of a person absorbed in the 'quiet state of alertness' may reveal something of his/her current emotional condition, the given emotional state is always dependent on the progress of 'introversion' [and on the degree of the 'quiet state of alertness' achieved]. But the 'basic mood' experienced in the 'quiet state of alertness' is not determined by a person's character traits and not by his/her temperament and it is not mutable either.

There are, however, difficulties in applying the word 'mood' in the given context, not least because some of the essential emotional states and feelings of which the 'basic mood' is composed are dormant in the process of 'introversion' [and entirely suspended in the 'quiet state of alertness']. Thus the underlying 'mood' of a person absorbed in the 'quiet state of alertness' is in no way affected by drives, thus it is not even 'coloured' by drives, nor by responses to external stimuli. This is the reason why I have substituted the word *'mood'* (*"Stimmung"*) with the term *'emotional disposition'* (*"Gestimmtheit"*) – a neologism that is not burdened by received meanings.

There is indeed a unique 'emotional disposition' inherent in the process of 'introversion': The 'emotional disposition' of [inner] calmness. This means that the prevailing emotional condition that permeates the consciousness of a person immersed in 'introversion', and even more so, when absorbed in the 'quiet state of alertness', is persevering inner calmness. This special 'emotional disposition' is not only evoked by the experience of the body reposing peacefully, but is also released by other conditions, which, however, cannot yet be disclosed at this early stage of our investigation. Therefore it is necessary to explain at this stage of our enquiry some of the distinctive features of the phenomenon of inner calm, not least because it is the pivotal 'emotional disposition' in the final stage of 'introversion', and most importantly in the 'quiet state of alertness'.

Calmness is experienced during 'introversion' in a wide variety of different nuances, different [degrees of intensity], and differences in scope [i.e. calmness may evoke a spatial dimension]. The only epithets that apply here derive more or less from the experience of the body. A person engrossed in the 'quiet state of alertness' may, for instance, describe the special quality of the calmness felt within as 'solid' or 'heavy'. He/she may also perceive the calmness as 'full', or 'soothing', or 'whole', or else as 'supporting', 'self-sufficient' or 'persevering'. All these qualifying expressions have obviously been suggested by the underlying feeling of vitality.

The experience of corporeality can only be rendered adequately, and in the liveliest manner possible, if we consider two aspects: First, the experiencing person needs to know that the calmness is inalienably instilled in the process of 'introversion', and, secondly, that the relaxed and reposing posture of the body is an important prerequisite for calmness to arise within.

In the 'quiet state of alertness' ("*Versunkenheit*") calmness is the underlying emotional condition filling the entire 'space' of consciousness, and the emotional sphere in which all in-phenomena surfacing in consciousness are embedded. In the sequence of mental states encompassed by the *process of 'introversion'* ("*Versenkung*"), inner calmness is the focal point at which all other experiences are directed. It is, however, not possible at this point of our investigation to elaborate further on the 'other experiences' encountered in these altered states of consciousness, because they are too varied and multifarious in their distinctive qualities to be covered here. So we have confined our enquiries above to aspects that could be retrieved from the realm of sense perception. The topic of inner calmness will however be repeatedly addressed in the subsequent chapters, since it is a pivotal phenomenon in both 'introversion' and in the 'quiet state of alertness', and thus the focal point of our subsequent considerations.

First Results

- *The process of 'introversion' is* [essentially a psychoactive technique] *by which a mental state can be achieved that is entirely detached from one's surroundings.*
- *The process of 'introversion' is* [defined as] *a process of emptying the space of consciousness from all 'content' related to the world of objects.*
- *By the process of 'introversion' a transformation of consciousness is achieved that results in a unified, emptied, tranquil and* [homogeneous] *mental state.*

In empirical reality the three processes involved in 'introversion' referred to above, are closely intertwined: Becoming detached from one's environment is a requirement for achieving a vacated mental state. – Emptying the mind from all 'content' is indispensable for consciousness to become unified and homogenous. – Conversely, the unified condition of consciousness is a prerequisite for the processes of vacating the mind, and for becoming detached from one's environment to succeed.

Detachment, emptying and the unifying of consciousness are the after-effects of several mental processes operating in 'introversion'. In the previous section the findings have been established which will enable us to distinguish between phenomena pertaining to the consciousness of 'introversion', and phenomena linked to the 'waking consciousness'. The processes of detachment, of vacating the mind and of calming are distinctive features of 'introversion', whereas they are no typical components of the 'waking consciousness'. The term *detachment* (to be exact, we have to distinguish between physical and psychological detachment) is defined as the deliberate attitude of not responding to any sensory [and other] stimuli for the purpose of screening off the mind against any sense perceptions and sensate phenomena that might intrude and disrupt the process by which the condition of consciousness becomes increasingly calm and homogeneous.

The term *elimination* refers to the entire range of mental strategies intended to eliminate all actions, thoughts and intentions from consciousness that might disrupt or interfere in the process of 'introversion'. Once eliminated these complex experiential patterns do not surface any more during the ongoing process of 'introversion'.

The concept of *dissolving* refers to the mental process of removing disturbing impressions, perceptions and thoughts that might surface while 'introversion' is in progress; dissolving is thus a mental strategy aimed at dispelling and extinguishing phenomena from consciousness which interfere in the process of 'introversion', until the person immersed in 'introversion' is no longer aware of them. A special variety of the process of dissolving disrupting phenomena is the process of *calming* – notably the process by which consciousness is liberated from dissonant emotions and drives, which may surface during 'introversion', and transformed into a state of non-arousal. This is effected by the calmness that emanates from the practitioner's reposing body. There are some more significant processes involved in 'introversion', for instance, those which have been termed 'conversion', 'assimilation' and 'integration' in conventional psychology. What these terms actually signify will be explained in the following paragraphs.

The process of 'introversion' is both coherently structured and pre-determined throughout [i.e. pre-determined by a volitional act before embarking on the process of 'introversion']. This claim, however, has not yet been sufficiently verified by the research results provided so far. But the insights presented in the following chapter will substantiate this claim.

Drives

It has repeatedly happened that the description of certain phenomena has turned out to be flawed or deficient, because we do not yet know enough about the areas of human experience in which they occur. In this chapter I will venture to explore the nature of drives. The reason for this choice is not only the fact that drives can relatively well be inferred and singled out from the complex psychological structure of an experience, but also the fact that drives and urges (as will be shown later) are closely related to the sphere of the body.

But before depicting the characteristics of drives, and their role in the process of 'introversion', some generally valid preliminary remarks have to be made:

1. It is necessary to emphasize once more that the 'quiet state of alertness' has to be distinguished from the process of 'introversion'. It is indeed the central concern of this study to provide a comprehensive phenomenology of the 'quiet state of alertness', which is the ultimate mental state to which the process of 'introversion' can advance. But the process of 'introversion' is itself composed of several dynamic mental states, of which we may identify only a few representative ones. The sample states of consciousness considered here include the '[waking] state', in which the initial resolve to embark on the process of 'introversion' is made, and the intended goal of the process, which is the 'quiet state of alertness' ("Versunkenheit"). The entire process of 'introversion' is governed from the beginning to the end by what Ach[32] has termed 'determinating tendency' ("determinierende Tendenz"). It is the peculiar nature of drives that they can only be identified in the incipient stage of 'introversion', but can no longer be discerned as soon as the person has become fully absorbed in the 'quiet state of alertness'.
2. At the beginning of 'introversion', the ordered psychic activities and typical items contained in the 'waking consciousness' are gradually eliminated. Thus the *process of 'introversion' is* in effect both, a procedure causing the *disintegration of the 'waking consciousness'*, and a procedure launching and advancing the *integration of various new altered mental states, of which the ultimate state is the 'quiet state of alertness', which is the intended final goal of 'introversion'*. When the process of 'introversion' is in progress, the mental framework is transformed and the nature of experiencing significantly changed. Thus, at the end of this process, an entirely new phenomenological constellation of consciousness has been developed. This new mental state differs significantly from the normal 'waking state', and is experienced as a 'marvel' ("Wunderwerk") of perfect harmony. Concerning the function of drives in this process we can say that they are also subject to diverse transformations, such as those termed *'conversion'*, *'assimilation'* and *'integration'*.

---

32   Ach, Narziss. *Analyse des Willens*. Berlin: Urban & Schwarzenberg, 1935.

The term 'drive' is blighted by the fact that it cannot be defined in psychological terms alone, because whenever we refer to drives, we have the unity of body and soul in mind, and thus the entire organism is considered to be something objective. Therefore we cannot define a drive without referring to trans-psychological mechanisms as well, i.e. biological, physiological and biochemical processes.

Traditional definitions of the 'drive' imply the notion that it is related to a disposition. McDougall,[33] for one, distinguishes between a drive conceived as a disposition and a drive experienced as a 'stirring' ("Regung"). The drive that is understood to be a disposition, i.e. a latent tendency, is termed "propensity" [in the original English by McDougall], whereas the latter is regarded as a driving force, hence termed "drive". The German translators [of McDougall's book] have rendered the English word "propensity" as "Triebkraft", and McDougall's "drive" as "Trieb". However, the latter term should better have been translated as "Drang" ('urge'), because this would enable us to use the word 'drive' as a generic term. McDougall states: "Any propensity, once aroused, evoked or elicited, will effect a tendency to act, which may become manifest at any stage on the scale of consciousness." – "Propensity is a disposition, functional unit of the entire psychic organism, that – once having been triggered – generates a tendency, impulse or drive directed at a certain aim or purpose." Rohracher[34] uses a concept as well, and derives it from areas outside psychology, combining it with a biological notion and the hypothesis of a disposition, when he says: "Vital drives are innate, biologically useful urges which surface [in consciousness] without being intentionally activated, and which, after having intruded upon the mind, mobilize the psychic functions so as to achieve their goals by inducing them to act in a manner that will serve to satisfy the drive." Rohracher also states that "drives are by nature dynamic"

---

33 McDougall, William. *Aufbaukräfte der Seele*. Trans. Fr. Becker and H. Bender. Leipzig: Thieme, 1937. – [Note: The original English version of McDougall's book has not been available; this is why this quotation, taken from the German translation of McDougall's study, was re-translated into English. – Quotation: McDougall 93. – FW.]
34 Rohracher, Hubert. *Einführung in die Psychologie*. 3rd ed. Vienna: Urban & Schwarzenberg, 1948. 369, 351.

– "they are vital forces that spur on and coerce". Drives are thus "by nature pathic", i.e. a subject is passively afflicted by them.

This concise survey of concepts conveys thoughts that point beyond the confines of the psychology of consciousness. However, for the purposes of this psychological investigation into the consciousness of 'introversion', considerations of this kind cannot be dispensed with. Single [isolated] experiences of drives are encountered very rarely. Drives rather tend to permeate, affect or flood through, and 'colour' any psychic experience in such a surreptitious manner that they can only be uncovered with the help of approaches from outside the field of the psychology of consciousness.

For our purposes the following definitions are binding: The term *'propensity'* (*"Triebkraft"*) emphasizes the extra-mental dynamic aspect of one's disposition. The term 'drive' emphasizes the unity of body and soul. An 'urge' (*"Drang"*) – the experience of being urged to act – is directed at some goal, but without the subject being aware of the actual object that the urge is directed at.

The concept of 'stirring' (*"Strebung"*), by contrast, refers to complex processes of consciousness thath consist of several [so-called] 'ultimate phenomena of consciousness' (*"Bewußtseinsletztheiten"*): These 'ultimate phenomena of human consciousness' consist of ideas, emotions, intentions, and driving forces (to name only a few; it is not necessary to go into any further detail here). What is important is that a 'stirring' is clearly directed at a conscious goal.

The colourful, heterogeneous nature of drives has suggested the hypothesis that the soul has a 'layered structure' composed of both genetic and psychological 'layers'. This hypothesis has in turn inspired the notion that drives can be categorized hierarchically.[35] In this hierarchical scale, drives related to the body, or affecting corporeality, are ranked lowest; these are drives that originate genetically from the 'animal nature' of man. Other drives, attributed to higher layers, are considered to be supportive to functions of the soul, and these are ranked higher on the scale; drives can be shown to be part of a person's 'spiritual aspirations', and thus they affect also the [highest] layers of the personality.

---

35 Cf. Rothacker, Erich. *Die Schichten der Persönlichkeit.* 4th ed. Bonn: Bouvier, 1948. Lersch, Philipp. *Der Aufbau des Charakters.* 3rd ed. Leipzig: Barth, 1948.

The urge to move is one that is never aroused in the consciousness of a person engaged in the process of 'introversion'. The posture of motionless repose, in which the practitioner is placed from the beginning, appears to disable the entire motoric system and to obviate that the urge to move will enter consciousness. This may even happen before the practitioner's state of consciousness has fully switched from the 'waking consciousness' to the state of 'introversion'. The same applies to drives related to the carnal nature of the body, notably the drive to eat, or to satisfy some sensual 'craving' for pleasure and relish. The feeling of hunger, however, is unlikely to arise, probably because the physiological requirements for feeling hungry are suspended as soon as the person engaged in the process of 'introversion' is no longer governed by the functions of the 'waking consciousness'. Psychologically speaking, any stirring for food is bypassed probably because the awareness that one is detached from one's surroundings signifies that such a craving cannot be satisfied. The situation of being detached from the world outside has evidently a soothing effect on drives, because the prospect that drives can be satisfied in the given context is understood to be futile. This awareness has an impact on the function of social drives as well – in particular, the drive to socialize with other human beings, and the drive to care for others. All these drives belong to the higher layers [of the personality], and they are all transferred into a dormant stage in the ongoing process of 'introversion'. Though in the incipient stage of 'introversion' the stirring to take care of someone may arise, this social stirring is, if it arises at all, much less forceful than it is felt in the normal 'waking state'. In fact, in the serene state of consciousness beyond the 'waking state' such a stirring is scarcely recognized, or identified as a drive. Such a stirring is perceived like the snippet of a thought, flashing through consciousness. All the drives that are related to the environment are assuaged, and finally silenced without the need for the practitioner to intervene in any way. The more deeply individual drives are rooted in one's personality, the more effectively they support the transformation of consciousness during the process of 'introversion'. We will consider two examples of the so-called 'propensity' ("Triebkraft") as a variety of a social drive: the 'propensity' for self-assertion, and, the opposite, the 'propensity' for submission.

The propensity for self-assertion becomes manifest in consciousness in various 'strivings' that are rooted within the individual 'self' ("Selbst"). These include the striving for fame and respect, the striving for power, and the striving for self-esteem. These strivings are all components of the propensity for self-assertion, and may arise while 'introversion' is in progress. Both the striving for power and the striving for fame are related to the outside world. Therefore they are inhibited in the ongoing process of 'introversion', and cannot become *instantly* effective in any of the altered states of consciousness encompassed by 'introversion'. It is possible, however, that the two strivings are part of the motivational force of the person who has embarked on the process of 'introversion'. If this is the case, the practitioner may be aware of this fact, albeit only in the incipient stage of 'introversion'. In the advanced stages, however, the awareness of any of these strivings has disappeared.

The striving for self-esteem, by comparison, does not depend on a person's relationship to the environment. This is probably the reason why this particular striving perseveres for a longer time [in consciousness,] and why it especially surfaces in situations in which the practitioner is concerned about the smooth progress of 'introversion'. The striving for self-esteem can thus be identified as one of the features signalling the potential disruption of the ongoing process of 'introversion'. The more the transformation of consciousness advances towards the 'quiet state of alertness', the less frequently we encounter feelings of concern and anxiety about the progress of 'introversion', and the more unlikely it becomes that a striving is evoked that is disruptive to the initial intention of advancing to the 'quiet state of alertness' as the ultimate goal. Thus the striving, for instance, of aggrandizing one's self-esteem would inevitably interfere with the process, and be incompatible with its smooth progress. This means that we do not encounter the least trace of the propensity for self-assertion in the practitioner any more who has become absorbed in the 'quiet state of alertness'.

The term *propensity for subjugation* has been coined by comparative biology. In the psychology of consciousness, however, the word 'subjugation' is considered inadequate and has therefore been substituted by the term '*submission*' or, alternatively, by '*surrender*'.

The reason for this change in terminology is that in the 'waking consciousness' of a sane human being, the urge to subjugate someone can hardly ever be encountered. But there is a special variety of that urge, namely the desire to surrender to someone or something, i.e. which, however, is rather diffuse and opaque. And this urge can be met more often in the context of 'introversion', though on the whole, this urge is rather unobtrusive, and does not have all the typical characteristics of a drive proper. It is rather marked by the features of a 'disposition' or an 'attitude' ("Gesinnung"). Hence the 'love for something' ("Liebe zu etwas"[36]) is always directed at a specific object. This kind of love is a craving, and as such a multifaceted phenomenon of consciousness, consisting of diverse strivings. "In the experience of the love for something the element of striving is particularly emphasized."[37] Composite elements of the given pattern of strivings include the desire for union, known from the erotic sphere, the propensity to possess something or someone, and in particular, the propensity to surrender, or to abandon oneself to a beloved person, or a situation or an object. Experiences of this kind usually do not persevere in the dynamic consciousness of 'introversion' for a long time. There are two reasons why this is so:

1. Any urge, striving or stirring experienced during the process of 'introversion', which is suffused by inner calm, is inevitably perceived as disturbing, and therefore is eliminated from consciousness. Such an urge or striving encroaching is not linked with other perceptions during 'introversion', and being isolated, it will soon vanish from consciousness.
2. The increasing degree in the state of one's awareness of detachment from the environment obviates the arousal of stirrings or strives for something or someone that is part of the world outside.

The urge for submission can at times be transformed as to be experienced as a desire to surrender or sacrifice one's own existence.

---

36 Lersch, Philipp. *Der Aufbau des Charakters*. 3rd ed. Leipzig: Barth, 1948, 156.
37 Lersch, Philipp. *Der Aufbau des Charakters*. 3rd ed. Leipzig: Barth, 1948, 156.

This kind of a drive-related emotional propensity may linger in consciousness during 'introversion' without conflicting with the basic mood of inner calm. This desire for self-surrender tends to grow and become an integral part of the process of 'introversion', and may continue to abide in the 'quiet state of alertness'. The subject immersed in 'introversion' experiences this inherent willingness to surrender instantaneously. The 'object' at which this desire for surrender is directed has an impact on the quality of the calmness experienced within. The desire to surrender to a process may accompany the entire process of 'introversion'. The 'quiet state of alertness' is [initially] experienced as an undifferentiated, unstructured 'object', and is initially not grasped cognitively ("undurchdacht"). It is experienced as a mental state that advances towards the 'experiencing I', and which overwhelms the 'experiencing I', and triggers the yearning desire to surrender to the serene state of calmness.

These descriptions are admittedly not quite consistent with received psychological terminology and elude psychological classification. But it has been necessary to resort to descriptive accounts of this kind, as there is no other way of recapturing the nature of the transformation of these drives during the process of 'introversion' and in the 'quiet state of alertness'. We may thus summarize the impact that the process of 'introversion' has on the nature of drives: *Drives (urges, strivings, stirrings and propensities) that are connected to the body are 'appeased', i.e. transferred into a latent or dormant state. Drives (propensities) extending into the 'spiritual layer' of the personality become subject to a process of transformation, by which they are deprived of their urge-like characteristics and become integrated into the homogeneous consciousness generated by the process of 'introversion'. The homogeneity of the consciousness of 'introversion' is achieved by ancillary processes such as transformation, integration and assimilation.*

The Will[38]

The expression "I want" originates ultimately from a [so-called] 'ultimate phenomenon of consciousness' ("Phänomenletztheit"); it is, in other words, an instance of what in psychology has been termed 'quality of impulse'. Wanting something is psychologically defined as the *experience of oneself as the cause of something*. "The 'I' is the cause of an action." 'I' am aware that it is me who 'sets a new beginning in motion'. Drives and emotions have 'pathic characteristics', [whereas] the experience of wanting something has clearly active and dynamic features. – The knowledge that I am the cause of something also elicits a sense of freedom. At the centre of an act of the will is thus, phenomenologically speaking, a *decision*. Making a decision is a phenomenon in which the latent capacity of being the cause of something becomes effective and reveals its impulse-like quality. A decision is based on the resolution of the 'I' to resolve a situation of *choice*. Having a choice between several options in a given situation usually triggers the contest between several motives. *Motives* may consist either of experiences generated by a drive, urge, craving or interest, or are based on previous acts of volition, which are recognized to be relevant in the given situation. These preliminary statements do not cover the entire phenomenology of volition. There are at least two more aspects to be added: 1. A deliberate decision requires a mental state that is *alert or wakeful*. Any act of the will requires a lucid and wakeful consciousness. 2. A decision is generally *directed at some specific goal,* which determines the course of action following after a decision has been made. 3. Another important aspect is *willpower*. There is a dynamic element inherent in the

---

38 Cf. Gruhle, Hans W. *Verstehende Psychologie (Erlebnislehre). Ein Lehrbuch.* Stuttgart: Thieme, 1948; Volkelt, Johannes. *Versuch über Fühlen und Wollen.* Munich: Beck, 1930; Ach, Narziss. "Über den Begriff des Unbewußten in der Psychologie der Gegenwart." *Zeitschrift für Psychologie,* 129 (1933): 223-245; Ach, Narziss. *Analyse des Willens.* Berlin: Urban & Schwarzenberg, 1935; Elsenhans, Theodor. *Lehrbuch der Psychologie.* 1912. 3rd ed. Tübingen: Mohr, 1939; Messer, August. *Psychologie.* 1911. 5th ed. Leipzig: Meiner, 1934; Rohracher, Hubert. *Einführung in die Psychologie.* 3rd ed. Vienna: Urban & Schwarzenberg, 1948.

experience of one's own willpower, which is, however, not exclusively a characteristic of a volitional act, but can be found in the 'pathic' experience of 'being driven' as well. It is the dynamic character of drives that justifies the use of the term 'propensity' here, which again is, strictly speaking, not a [scientific] psychological concept but one derived from outside the field of psychology. Another distinctive characteristic of the will (apart from its dynamic nature) is the fact that it is inalienably tied to the 'I' as 'initiator', thus establishing the 'I' as a free agent and the first cause 'positing' a beginning ("Anfang setzendes Ich", *PMB* 38).

In the normal waking consciousness genuine acts of volition, i.e. acts of the will that are phenomenologically fully developed, are surprisingly rare. As maintained by the 'layer theory' of the personality, there are genuine acts of the will that originate in a clear and conscious mind and that are informed by a number of supporting mental processes; but these acts of the will have nonetheless not all the characteristics referred to above; however, irrespective of this fact they are still classified as acts of volition, because of their affinity to genuine acts of the will.

To illustrate this claim, an example from everyday life shall serve for illustration: A friend, for whom I have genuine feelings of affection, has come to visit me; when he is about to leave after a conversation, the impulse that is instantly aroused in me is to accompany him to the door. The 'I' responds to this instant stirring immediately; it perceives and approves of the stirring because it is consonant with the given emotional condition and the principles of courtesy. Thus the action springs immediately from the initial impulse, and the entire reaction – starting from the first inklings of the stirring, and ending in the act of escorting the friend to the door – happens automatically. The initial, emotionally charged response is enough to carry out the action without any delay or interference. Thus a situation of choice, and of making a decision, does not arise, nor is there an occasion for the combat between conflicting motives. Thus the stirring smoothly passes over into an action without the will having been activated. Most of the stirrings that govern our behaviour in everyday life are grounded in some initial impulse, or spontaneous response by the 'I' – rather than by a complex process of decision making. The 'layer theory' claims that the regulating functions of the will are triggered only when the spontaneous, self-governing process is disrupted by some resistance from outside, or by some inner discord. An act of the will is generally a function of wakefulness; this also applies to the function of apperception, which controls the level of attentiveness; both these functions are only switched on in situations when the spontaneous response to external stimuli does not suffice.[39]

The psychology of the will is crucial for exploring the stages of consciousness encompassed by 'introversion'. Our investigation will thus be considerably expanded, and the enquiry can better be placed in a systematic classification, when its focal point is the phenomenon of the will. Two insights can be stated in advance: 1. *The coherently structured process of 'introversion' is initiated by a genuine act of the will*, i.e. 'introversion' is *initiated* by a deliberate decision and is directed at a definite aim; it is moreover based on an underlying intention ['determining tendency']. The 'determining tendency' that directs the progress of 'introversion' is sustained throughout. It should be mentioned, however, that occasionally a process of 'introversion' may start spontaneously, without having been triggered by a conscious decision, and without being governed by some prior determination. This means that a person may be transported into the 'quiet state of alertness' passively and/or be overwhelmed by it. – The deliberate decision to engage in a process of 'introversion' requires several acts of the will and concrete actions arising from these decisions: There is the decision to lie down in a posture of relaxed repose, which again requires the practitioner to close his/her eyes and to ease muscular tension. It furthermore requires him/her to 'abandon himself/herself', i.e. to yield to an attitude in which any desire or stirring is overcome; I wish that from now on, I have no wish anymore. By making such a decision, I will give way to a relaxed mental state and release my readiness to surrender to the autonomous progress of 'introversion'.

---

39 Cf. Rothacker, Erich. *Die Schichten der Persönlichkeit*. 4th ed. Bonn: Bouvier, 1948. Strunz, Kurt. "Über die 'Vertikale' Ordnung der Seelischen Dispositionen. Ein Beitrag zur Psychologischen Schichttheorie." *Zeitschrift für Psychologie* 154 (1943): 103-202.

2. **There are no genuine acts of the will at any stage during the process of 'introversion'.** This is a crucial and infallible criterion by which both the process of 'introversion' and the 'quiet state of alertness' are marked. (The validity of this claim will be tested below on the basis of examples recorded during states of 'introversion' and during the 'state of quiet alertness'.)

The first example utilizes the mental device termed 'focussed observation':[40] The process of 'introversion' is triggered in the 'waking consciousness' and is facilitated by the use of 'focussed observation', in which the practitioner focuses mentally, for instance, on the image of a rose, and then directs the thoughts and impressions to 'revolve around' the object of the rose ("umkreisen"). The practitioner will soon be absorbed by the inner perception of the rose. His/her thoughts, however, tend to remain scattered, moving away from the rose, partly because the attention may have been diverted by disrupting impressions, and partly because he/she is laid astray by ideas and thoughts surfacing in consciousness so that the focus is no longer put on the original object of inner perception. As soon as this aberration is noticed, the original intention will be recalled. This 'calling back' of one's initial attention is an act of concentration, which naturally involves some strain and striving. This act may appropriately be termed a 'deliberate (re)-adjustment of attention'. This act of concentration requires a genuine act of the will, not least because there

---

40 [Note: Albrecht uses the German word "Betrachtung", of which the corresponding technical term in English is 'contemplation'. In English, however, the meaning of the word 'contemplation' is ambivalent, in that it may refer, in its broadest sense, to 'the act of contemplating' an object; however, 'contemplation' is also a traditional technical term in Christian spirituality, which refers to an advanced form of (non-verbal) spiritual prayer, in which a person aspires to be gratified with the gift of the special grace of the mystical contemplation of God, or *cognitio Dei experimentalis*, the experimental knowledge of God. In this translation, the term 'contemplation' is consistently used in the sense of the latter. – In the given passage, the German word "Betrachtung" has clearly a secular meaning, not one related to the direct experience of the Divine, and thus translating it by 'contemplation' would be blatantly wrong and misleading. Hence "Betrachtung" has been translated by the composite term 'focussed observation'. –FW.]

is a clear awareness of the goal that is to be achieved. Moreover, there is also a situation of choice, and most probably, 'a struggle of conflicting motives'. The situation is resolved by deciding to focus the attention again on the image of the 'rose'. This example shows quite convincingly that there is a deliberate act of concentration involved, and this is why the given state of consciousness is not yet one encompassed by 'introversion'. The mind is still repeatedly occupied with acts of the will. There is, however, some affinity between the state of focussed observation and the consciousness of 'introversion'. The main difference is that in the latter the degree of mental absorption in the object is more intense. Though in the practice of 'focussed inward observation' acts of the will are not dispensed with, the acts of volition are transformed while the process of 'introversion' continues to advance: After having passed through intermediate mental states to the intended goal of the 'quiet state of alertness', the practitioner will deliberately 'recall' the intended goal, and he/she will become increasingly aware of his willingness to surrender to the object perceived. But the function of the will is more and more diminished in the course of 'introversion', and there is hardly any 'contest between motives' to be perceived. In the example above, the contest between motives can be said to be one between the wish to succumb to reveries and the 'determining tendency' to adhere to the intended goal of focussing on the image of the rose. In the advanced stage of 'introversion', and in the 'quiet state of alertness' in particular, any impulse to divert the attention away from the object observed inwardly is experienced as an interference rather than as a striving to move away from the focus of attention.

Observations of this kind may help to reveal not just the limitations of some of the traditional psychological concepts but also their phenomenological validity; this applies even to the carefully and exhaustively defined concept of the will. Conventional psychological terms are only helpful if they relate to the area from which they originate, and in which they were coined. That is to say, when features of a subject's conscious relationship to his/her surroundings are at issue, the terminological and psychological reference-frame is inevitably the 'waking consciousness'. Though it is possible to describe the flow of sensations as well as other phenomena that pass through consciousness by resorting to conventional terms, complex dynamic phenomena such as the 'stream' of sensations elude classification. Only very specific phenomena can be inferred individually from this 'stream' of sensations and be attributed to established concepts. The example of the 'rose' has been chosen as it enables us to demonstrate that 'focussed observation' ("Betrachtung") occurs in the 'twilight zone' between the 'waking consciousness' and the consciousness of 'introversion'. It should moreover be emphasized that we cannot speak of a fully integrated consciousness of 'introversion' as long as we may encounter acts of the will in it.

The second example is taken from the practice of 'introversion': I have begun the process of 'introversion'; I am still in the initial stage, in which sensual stimuli – like the sound of the doorbell – can still be discerned. The sound is fully comprehended because a number of other psychological data are transmitted along with it, so that the sound is eventually 'objectified' as that of the doorbell. The emotional responses elicited by this auditory stimulus might be the following: There is someone who wishes to speak to me. – Is this particular sound related to me at all? Other responses that might arise differ considerably from the responses that are triggered by the same event in the normal 'waking consciousness'. The emotional response in a subject who is engaged in 'introversion' is different from the more rational reaction prompted by the doorbell in the 'waking consciousness'. The typical feature of the response to the doorbell in a person immersed in 'introversion' is 'being disturbed'. The following description illustrates how a disturbance is experienced when the process of 'introversion' is in progress: The sound of the doorbell is experienced as a violent intrusion into the space of consciousness. This intrusion is felt to have the shape of a cone, a metaphor evoked by the stimulus declining in intensity and fended off to the periphery of consciousness, and can never penetrate to the centre of consciousness. The crucial issue in the process of 'introversion' is the following: There is a special function operating in this altered state of consciousness that dissolves and eliminates disturbing stimuli and unwanted sensations. (This function has already been outlined in detail above.) In the given example, it is evident that no act of the will is involved. The function of eliminating disturbing stimuli is not preceded by a process of decision-making. This means that the 'I' is not required to intervene actively. The stimulus is eliminated, in other words, by a spontaneous process. The 'experiencing I' has only some dim awareness of what is going on, and affirms intuitively (but not on the basis of an act of reasoning) the spontaneous response of dissolving any intruding disturbance. The nature of the emotional side of this response is reflected in expressions like 'I surrender to what is currently happening by itself'. Or 'I welcome the calmness permeating and inundating my mind'.

Disruptions can not only be caused by the intrusion of sensual stimuli from the world outside; in the incipient stage of 'introversion' there is an inherent propensity to succumb to a wide variety of phenomena surfacing in consciousness. Being removed from the familiar environment, the practitioner will first withdraw to a tranquil location that is conducive to self-reflection. As a consequence, memories may surface which one has not been conscious of before, when the mind was still dominated by the 'waking consciousness'. We are now going to illustrate a case of disruption that occurred during the process of 'introversion' and which was caused by feelings of affliction: A recent incident of grievous carelessness emerges painfully in consciousness, and deeply upsets the person immersed in 'introversion'. The sense of affliction permeates the mind and penetrates to the 'centre of consciousness', which means that the process of 'introversion' is jeopardized and is likely to be terminated, unless the affliction is quickly eliminated from consciousness. This example shows that a disturbance can have a grave impact on the incipient stage of 'introversion', which is still a rather fragile structure, so that 'introversion' cannot develop further; 'introversion' can be terminated, in which case the state of consciousness switches abruptly into the 'waking consciousness'. The process that terminates the progress of 'introversion' is governed by several *psychological* mechanisms. Amongst these, one particular phenomenon stands out: the phenomenon that the body tends to abide in the process of 'introversion' even when the pivotal features of 'introversion' have already disappeared. This phenomenon can be explained by the fact that the 'body at rest' has the tendency to persevere in the altered state of consciousness. Even when the normal psychic functions have been restored, it takes some time before a person absorbed in repose can fully reactivate the motoric functions of the body. The body may thus be compared to a bed, into which one returns after having risen. At the background of the disrupted state of consciousness a sense of calmness remains, however, which originates from the experience of the reposing body. The following example consists of two incidents: I have for some reason failed to keep an important appointment; I had promised a highly esteemed person to visit him the day before and to assist him as he was expected to make a very important decision. During the ongoing process of 'introversion' the agonizing memory of having broken a promise and failed to offer assistance to a dear friend surfaces painfully in consciousness – which was possibly triggered by thoughts and associations aroused by emotions. It is one of the peculiarities of the consciousness of 'introversion' that emotional, affect-laden responses intrude and are experienced in a very forceful manner. Cognitive elements relating to the same experience are, by comparison, sparse, whereas the feelings aroused become even more intense and more upsetting than if this experience had occurred in the 'waking consciousness'. There is even the imminent danger that the 'experiencing I' is overwhelmed by an outpouring of emotions, not least because in the process of 'introversion' the 'experiencing I' is defencelessly exposed to the influx of emotions as long as it is absorbed passively in a receptive attitude. As a result, the 'experiencing I' is overwhelmed by such complex emotions as 'agonizing sorrow', or 'anxious sadness'. As for the role of 'drives': Drives become alive again by such a disruption and are revealed particularly in the person's growing desire to take flight – i.e. the urge of returning to the calmness experienced during the process of 'introversion'. Less obvious is the urge for power that may surface in the event; this urge becomes manifest not only in the desire to be esteemed, but also, conversely, in the painful awareness of shame. These urges are experienced in various degrees of intensity, ranging from a mere fleeting awareness to a clear and agonizing recognition of one's failure. The practitioner's emotional condition is significantly determined by these occurrences. Moreover, there is the urge to surrender, accompanied by a turmoil of emotions – including loving devotion, love, loss of love, deep sadness. This lively response is fuelled by drive-related emotions, urges and feelings, and tends to advance far into the centre space of consciousness. As a consequence, the 'experiencing I' is required to activate the cognitive functions again. This will release verbalized thoughts – such as 'it is too late now to do something about it', or 'the progress of "introversion" will be destroyed by such musings'. The thought 'I have to put up now with this situation' indicates that by now the consciousness of 'introversion' has been substituted by the 'waking consciousness'. The motive of terminating the process of 'introversion' for the purpose of getting some rational apology, or compensation for the (accidental) act of moral transgression, which ultimately originated in drives, is at variance with the original motive of engaging in the process of 'introversion', which was based on a deliberate decision. This illustrates quite persuasively that *the consciousness of 'introversion' is ended as soon as acts of volition are grasped cognitively. Acts of the will and the process of 'introversion' are incompatible and mutually exclusive.* The process of 'introversion' can be resumed only after the deliberate decision to embark on this process has been made anew. This decision may be expressed in such terms as: 'I want to withdraw again into the state of inner calm and revive the functions of "introversion" still effective enough to dispel any potential disruption.' The mental technique applied in the given context is termed 'meditative dissolving of interferences' ("auflösende Meditation"). This is a meditational device by which an object or phenomenon that has intruded into consciousness and disrupted the progress of 'introversion' is targeted, isolated and eventually dissolved and ultimately removed from the realm of consciousness.

A genuine act of the will can never be part of the consciousness of 'introversion', least of all of the 'quiet state of alertness'. This raises the question as to whether the ending of the process of 'introversion' [and/or the 'state of quiet alertness'] does or does not depend on a foregoing act of the will. Over and beyond this, the question arises, if stirrings of the will occur during the 'quiet state of alertness', and if so, when and how. As the 'quiet state of alertness' cannot be maintained for a very long time, it must inevitably be replaced by another mental state, usually the normal 'waking consciousness'. The process of the transformation of consciousness, the switching between different mental states, may at times occur so swiftly that it seems that the 'waking consciousness' has just been switched on again. Normally, however, the transition from the 'quiet state of alertness' to the 'waking state' occurs gradually, and this is also the reason why individual events and phenomena witnessed during this process can clearly be perceived and described (more or less adequately).

There are basically three ways in which the transformation from the 'quiet state of alertness' or the 'consciousness of introversion' to the 'waking state' (and vice versa) may occur:

1. Like in the process effecting the transition from the 'sleeping state' to the 'waking state', the disintegration of the 'quiet state of alertness' can be self-induced, i.e. generated by natural causes rather than by some external stimulus. The process of 'introversion' has a natural function at its disposal, which controls the time-span, and thus terminates the process after some time. (It is not necessary to provide an explanation for this evident empirical fact.) Therefore it can never happen that the normal 'waking consciousness' does not [automatically] switch on again. On the other hand, it is possible that the time-span that a person can stay absorbed in the process of 'introversion' [and/or the 'quiet state of alertness'] may individually be extended. There are several reasons for this: Firstly, when a person engrossed in 'introversion' is overwhelmed and absorbed by a deeply moving experience, the process may last considerably longer; secondly, the case when a person remains immersed in 'introversion' for an unusually long time may have psychopathological causes – e.g. a neurotic predisposition – which affect and take control of the condition of consciousness. None of these causes, however, falsifies the claim that in a healthy human being the process of 'introversion' is, as a rule, terminated by his/her own accord.

2. It is possible to generate a so-called 'determining predisposition' at the beginning of the process of 'introversion', which is intended to co-determine the course of 'introversion' and to release a specific response, or to achieve a particular aim while 'introversion' is in progress. Such a 'determining predisposition' can be created by a deliberate decision, or by an express wish or desire, or by

some visual image. Once established, the 'determining predisposition' will be stored subconsciously in the altered state(s) of consciousness passed through during the process of 'introversion'. The way in which this is achieved can be illustrated by the following example: When a person intends to embark on the process of 'introversion', he/she may agree with the supervising confidant/e (usually a psychotherapist) that the process of 'introversion' shall be terminated by a soft touch by the person attending. As a consequence the person engrossed in 'introversion' does not respond to any other sensual stimulus, whereas he/she will immediately respond to the attendant's gentle touch. This is achieved because this particular cause-effect relationship has been 'programmed' into the mind by a corresponding 'determining predisposition', before he/she embarked on the process of 'introversion'. It is important to add here that the perception of being softly touched and the response evoked by the touch are not triggered by any foregoing act of the will. Volition is not involved in this kind of pre-determined response at all. The 'experiencing I' rather continues to repose 'passively' in the 'quiet state of alertness', and his/her reaction to the touch is spontaneous and performed automatically. At the beginning, the spontaneous response may elicit additional reactions, for instance, an utterance, thoughts and feelings; it is thus a composite response that may be summed up in a verbalized thought like the following: 'What a pity that the 'quiet state of alertness' is coming to a close'. The nature of such a response suggests that the person is aware of his/her state of 'inwardness' – i.e. there is a subconscious cognitive awareness concomitant with the process of 'introversion' by which the person involved is enabled to discern that the transformation of consciousness from the 'quiet state of alertness' to the 'waking consciousness' has begun. The practitioner is aware that now the path of 'introversion' has been reversed. The state of inner calm gradually subsides when snippets of thoughts and stimuli from the outside world begin to intrude upon the mind; these intrusions will increase in number and intensity, though they are perceived at first as rather weak, drab and colourless impressions. It takes some time before these opaque impressions become perceptions proper. The bond to the outside world is gradually restored at several levels, and the thoughts arising are no longer intent on achieving the uniformity of the consciousness encompassed by 'introversion' and the 'quiet state of alertness', until finally ideas and impressions begin to occupy the mind which are evoked by the 'waking consciousness'. The transformation of the consciousness of 'introversion' is first triggered by the instantaneous emotional response in the 'experiencing I'. The response of the body, however, tends to lag behind (as mentioned earlier), because the state of repose tends to persevere. Therefore it is possible that the first true act of the will in this process is the decision to reactivate slowly the one or the other part of the body. In the newly (re-) integrated 'waking consciousness', the body is experienced like a solid substance abiding in repose, which needs to be revitalized by an act of the will. This means that volition starts to operate again only after the 'quiet state of alertness' has disintegrated and been replaced by the 'waking consciousness'.

When observing a person who is immersed in the 'quiet state of alertness', one may notice either changes in the tension of the muscles, or muscular tremors; these are the first symptoms indicating the end of the given altered state of consciousness (i.e. any of the stages of 'introversion' and/or the 'quiet state of alertness'). For example, a finger of the person absorbed in 'introversion' may begin to move, or the relaxed features of his/her physiognomy may be filled again with liveliness. However, none of these corporal changes is initiated by an act of the will. These bodily phenomena are spontaneous somatic reactions elicited by the ongoing process of transformation of consciousness. They indicate that the psychological mechanisms have been activated which will terminate the 'quiet state of alertness' and/or the process of 'introversion'. The spontaneous somatic responses may be seen as evidence of the unity between body and soul. We may thus suggest the hypothesis that these spontaneous somatic responses and the changes in facial expressions in particular are phenomena generated by the deeper, more primeval 'layers' of the personality than the phenomena depending on an act of the will.

3. The process of 'introversion' and the 'quiet state of alertness' can, finally, be terminated forcefully by some violent interference. Since this instance has already been dealt with above, there is no need to repeat this aspect here.

The varieties of acts of volition considered so far were all instances that occurred at the beginning or at the very end of the process of 'introversion'. In the altered states of consciousness that are close to the fully developed 'quiet state of alertness', we hardly ever encounter responses to interferences. In this advanced stage of consciousness the typical reactions of the 'experiencing I' are missing as well. What we are going to explore now is a cross-section of *emerging forms of volition that precede cognitive acts of the will proper* and which can be encountered in any of the states of consciousness encompassed by 'introversion', including the 'quiet state of alertness'.

The term 'emerging form of volition' refers to deliberate acts triggered by such psychological phenomena as 'wishes', 'aspirations' and other varieties of 'longing for something or someone'. This term is however unfortunate and inaccurate, because it is based on controversial hypothetical premises and concepts that elude a clear definition. Thus the term *'wish'* implies that it originates in a clear and conscious mind. We know, for instance, that there are situations in which we know that a wish cannot be fulfilled, or that it is uncertain if or when a wish may be accomplished. This means that a wish is always based on a cognitive judgement. Moreover, a wish does not have any of the distinctive characteristics of an act of the will: There is, for one, neither a situation of choice, nor a deliberate decision to be made. It is possible that phenomena that have wish-like characteristics may be found at the beginning of 'introversion'. In this case, the wish to advance the process of 'introversion' further will prevail over any other wish that might accidentally surface at the time in consciousness, and it is unlikely that the two intentions will collide. The fact that any wish is rooted in the rational capacities of the mind, which are gradually suspended as the process of 'introversion' advances towards the 'quiet state of alertness', may explain why in the advanced state of 'introversion' there are no longer any stirrings that have the typical characteristics of a wish.

The phenomenon of striving for something can – unlike the wish – still be encountered in the advanced states of 'introversion'. There are complex emotional states that embrace both the striving for submission and the striving for resistance. At the beginning of the process of 'introversion' a striving is usually directed at some specific goal, for instance, the striving to achieve a state of inner calm, or the striving not to yield to disturbing stimuli which may intrude from outside. In the advanced stage of 'introversion' emotions tend to prevail. It may happen that a semi-conscious yearning for inner calm is evoked, or the reluctance to respond to a disturbance. The striving to advance to the intended goal, the 'quiet state of alertness', will become more intense and acquire an urge-like quality. Drives are, however (as has been shown in the chapter above), incompatible with the coveted goal of inner calm. In the advanced stages of 'introversion' drives are rapidly extinguished by the prevailing mood of peace and tranquillity, and the only trace of the original stirring remaining is the dim awareness of being directed and moved on to the final goal. In other words, the 'experiencing I' knows intuitively at any time in the process that it is going to advance towards the 'quiet state of alertness'.

It has been necessary to address repeatedly the phenomenon of inner calmness. By this term we understand the singular emotional condition permeating the entire space of consciousness in the 'quiet state of alertness'. It is true, however, that the word 'calmness' evokes the notion that it has object-like characteristics. *The concept 'experience of calmness'* does not only refer to the all-pervasive emotional state permeating the mind of the 'experiencing I' [in the 'state of quiet alertness'] – an experience that can be compared to the state of mourning, or the experience of joy – but it has also some object-like quality, and this is why we prefer to use the objectified term '*the* [state of inner] calm/calmness' instead of just referring to it as 'calmness'.

And indeed, the practitioner of 'introversion' does not just experience [some variety of] 'calmness' within, but he/she is inundated by the [very essence of] calmness; and there is a good reason for this to happen. When we experience our own corporality, we naturally perceive our body as an object. From the perception of the body at rest arises an intense awareness of one's bodily nature, which is closely connected with the feeling of inner calmness. This object-like relationship between the 'I' and the sphere of his/her body continues to be an integral part of the entire emotional condition. The different varieties of calmness experienced by a person immersed in 'introversion' are reflected in verbal expressions such as: 'I am experiencing how calmness is advancing towards me.' – Calmness is advancing, spreading and inundating all the nooks and corners of consciousness – eroding all objects or sensations interfering – and in this way calmness harmonizes the state of consciousness as a whole – and involves the 'experiencing I', as it were, in the process of 'introversion'; calmness supports the 'I' and protects it against any disturbing object in case one should surface. These explanations on the object-like nature of the experience of inner calmness are particularly relevant in view of the comprehensive phenomenological analysis of the altered state(s) of consciousness encompassed by 'introversion', which will follow. We will see that the phenomenon of 'inner calmness' is the pivotal prerequisite for both the capacity of 'inner sight' ("Innenschau"), which in turn is a prerequisite for perceiving 'in-coming' phenomena, i.e. phenomena 'arriving' ("das Ankommende") in the vista of 'inner sight' ("Innenschau"). These complex and often elusive experiences can best be observed in the 'quiet state of alertness'.

Thinking[41]

We began the analysis of experiences encountered during the process of 'introversion' by taking the so-called 'ultimate phenomena of consciousness' ("Bewußtseinsletztheiten") as a point of departure. An 'ultimate phenomenon of consciousness' is an empirical entity that cannot be traced to any other experiential source, and this is its unique distinctive characteristic. Such an 'ultimate phenomenon of consciousness' is, for instance, 'thinking', or more specifically, a 'thought' – and this will be the focus of our critical analysis in the present chapter. To clarify the distinction between 'thinking' and

---

41 Gruhle, Hans W. *Verstehende Psychologie*. Stuttgart: Thieme, 1948; Rohracher, Hubert. *Einführung in die Psychologie*. 3rd ed. Vienna: Urban & Schwarzenberg, 1948; Messer, August. *Psychologie*. 1911. 5th ed. Leipzig: Meiner, 1934; Elsenhans, Theodor. *Lehrbuch der Psychologie*. 3rd ed. Tübingen: J.C.B. Mohr, 1939.

'thought', we should add that the psychological function grounded in the 'ultimate phenomenon' is termed 'thinking', whereas a 'thought' is an 'ultimate phenomenon' revealed in the form of a singular idea surfacing in consciousness.

What we commonly understand by a 'thought' needs to be specified. Before we can do so, we need to differentiate between the concepts of 'thought', 'perception' and 'the imagination'. 'Perception' has been described as a visual representation, more specifically, a pictorial reality marked by physical characteristics. By imagination we understand likewise a visual representation, but one that does not have any physical characteristics. A *thought*, unlike a perception and a mental image, is *a non-visual representation*. For example, when I perceive my son, I see him physically standing in front of me in the room. However, when I imagine my son, a more or less distinct image of his presence will appear in my inner field of vision. It is striking that in linguistic usage the difference between perceiving and imagining is reflected in the fact that the syntactically correct statement is not 'I am thinking my son' but 'I am thinking of my son'. That is to say that I can think of my son even though he is not physically present, and not present in my imagination either. Thinking is, in this sense, equal to assuming; hence it is evident that a 'thought' differs from both perception and the imagination and, therefore, it has unique characteristics.

As stated earlier: Every perception contains thoughts as well as ideas and concepts of the imagination; similarly, any perception of something occurring in the imagination incorporates elements of sense perception and cognition. The entire structure of an imaginative experience is also shaped by the categories of space and time, as well as by cognition, notably the capacity to recognize and identify the object perceived. Only a thought can prevail in consciousness without being sustained by features of perception, or elements of the imagination. There is indeed a way of thinking of somebody that is entirely non-visual, and there is, moreover, a non-visual form of thinking of relations, that is in terms of categories (such as causality), or in terms of relations like in mathematics. This does not mean, however, that at the moment when a thought flashes up in consciousness, visual elements are not involved in some way or other. But what is important in the given context is the fact that *a thought can independently become the object of thinking and be perceived in its pure essence.*

Conveying meaning and signifying a message are [semiotic] markers characteristic of a thought. *Concepts* are thoughts. Concepts deliver meaning and denote something that can neither be sensually perceived, nor imagined in concrete terms. For example, the abstract concept 'creature' is, phenomenologically speaking, devoid of any visual content. It goes without saying that the 'pure thought' expressed by the word 'creature' could hardly ever be stored in a person's individual consciousness on its own. Pure thoughts are thus rarely perceived in a particular empirical event. Psychologically speaking, there is a certain conceptual sphere, or a so-called 'halo' surrounding a single thought, just as the nucleus of a planet is surrounded by a halo.[42] The nucleus is the word that denotes the conceptual core, which is surrounded by the conceptual halo; the halo in turn may be filled, amongst other things, with visual and acoustic impressions, and is usually intertwined with multifarious emotional responses. Moreover, the thought is combined with a word. This synthesis of thought and word is the distinctive characteristic of a concept. Rohracher says:[43] "Concepts are non-visual thoughts which have affiliated themselves with a word by way of association in order to become a fixed unit in everyday experience." – "The word provides the concept with a descriptive characteristic. From the very beginning the visual image of the word and/or the sound of the word are joined to be integral parts of what is called the sphere of the thought." "Thoughts that are not associated with a word or a verbal expression can hardly ever adhere to memory, or if so, only with great difficulty" [Rohracher 331].

Thinking is a process in which relationships are formed. But not every act in which a cognitive relationship is established is necessarily an act of thinking. For instance, images that appear in dreaming are

---

42 [Note: Albrecht appears to have derived this image from the jargon of jurisdiction, in which the metaphor from astronomy is commonly used to distinguish between "Begriffskern" (the 'core of a concept') and "Begriffshof" ('conceptual surroundings' or 'conceptual halo'). According to Bulygin, these legal concepts derive from Heck, Philip. *Begriffsbildung und Interessenjurisprudenz*. Tubingen: J.C.B. Mohr, 1939. 52-53. (Cf. Bulygin, Eugenio. *Essays in Legal Philosophy*. Ed. Carlos Bernal et al. Oxford: OUP, 2015.) – FW.]

43 Rohracher, Hubert. *Einführung in die Psychologie*. 3rd ed. Vienna: Urban & Schwarzenberg, 1948. 330f.

also meaningfully connected, but this connection is not formed by an act of thinking, but by emotional responses. Contrary to the so-called 'catathymic perception of images'[44] which operates in dreams, thinking establishes a relationship on the basis of the categories of order, rooted in the domain of thinking [viz. the cognitive faculties of the mind]. Thus the logical order and the categories of classification are the result of a process of thinking. The simplest act of thinking occurs when a thing that is visually perceived or imagined is objectified. This way of thinking creates meaning spontaneously in a free-floating act. In such a spontaneous cognitive process the 'I' is unaware of how the process has been accomplished. In other words, the feature that the 'I' is actively involved is missing here. The cognitive act of *judging* usually operates in a similar manner. However, a judgement does include features indicating that the process involved is not a spontaneous one. Every judgement is based on the joining of two basic thoughts. For example, when I look at the handwriting in a letter and conclude from it that "the letter has been written by my son", a relationship is established between my son and the handwriting, and this relationship is grounded in a non-visual [intuitive] process of thinking. A judgement, however, has another distinctive feature: its validity can either be affirmed or denied.[45] The question as to whether the handwriting is indeed that of my son is decided on the basis of intuitive evidence. Judgements are thus non-pictorial acts of thinking which rely on both a deictic conjecture and a conscious act in which the conjecture is confirmed or refuted. "Short-term acts of judgement", or free-floating acts of this kind, are intuitive and informed by an unmediated sense of evidence, and acts of this kind are involved in countless processes of our consciousness. However, whenever such a spontaneous process is disrupted by doubt, uncertainty or resistance, the process of forming a judgement cognitively (as described above) is fully "switched on"; and this insight is very important for our future considerations: Any judgement made in the "waking consciousness" inevitably depends on the active function of the 'I', and thus the 'I' is fully conscious of the controlling and

---

44 Kretschmer, Ernst. *Medizinische Psychologie*. 9th ed. Stuttgart: Thieme, 1947. 92.
45 Messer, August. *Psychologie*. 1911. 5th ed. Leipzig: Meiner, 1934.

dynamic progress of thinking. The decision whether a judgement is to be confirmed or denied is made rationally, in a clear state of consciousness, and thus the process of 'judging' is analogous to (albeit not identical with) the process of decision making in the context of volition (as outlined above).

The ability to judge and the capacity of syllogistic reasoning are not the only *dynamic forms of thinking* to be considered here. These forms of thinking are, in fact, only integral parts of what we call the [full] processes of ordered thinking. The typical forms of structured thinking are part of a [complex] whole consisting of non-visual acts of thinking, which are again closely interconnected with genuine acts of the will. For example: If I want to deliver a structured lecture on some topic in a free oral presentation, the voluntary decision to do so will trigger a series of major and minor ideas, which in turn determine the way the chain of associations will advance, because the sequence of associations is governed by a subconscious process of selecting and combining. Moreover, this way of thinking requires a simultaneous process of concentration. A continued, conscious act of concentration is required if one wishes to focus the attention on an intended goal, because acts of the will are again and again called for in order to obviate the tendency of the mind to ramble about or to go astray, and to leave the 'waking consciousness' behind in favour of day-dreaming, or a somnambulist state. Abstract, logical and discursive thinking is thus determined by the intended goal(s) as well as by repeated interventions of the will. Even the process termed 'syllogistic reasoning' – e.g. finding the appropriate word in a crossword puzzle from amongst the torrent of associations surfacing in the mind – is based on both a premeditated goal and a process of concentration focussed on this particular goal.

Thinking and 'Introversion'

It has been necessary to enter the large area of cognitive psychology in order to be able to assess which of the processes of thinking are indeed viable to operate in 'introversion' and in the 'quiet state of alertness'. This enquiry was moreover required for identifying the mental processes that can be ruled out right from the beginning of the process that can be an integral part of 'introversion', because they will have been suspended beforehand. To start with, it is expedient to summarize the results. We have to distinguish between

1. coherently structured processes of thinking, controlled by concentration, which are generated, governed and sustained by genuine acts of the will; and

2. spontaneous processes of thinking which proceed autonomously, and which may include judgements based on a cognitive, emotional or sensual occurrence – and which may even become manifest in 'introversion' in verbalized speech; there are moreover processes of thinking that provide merely the basic cognitive pattern underlying all experience and which endow human experience with meaning and significance.

Before exploring in some detail the varieties of thinking featuring in the process of 'introversion', a few general statements have to be made, in which the significant differences between the modes of thinking in the state(s) of 'introversion' and/or 'the quiet state of alertness', on the one hand, and the ways of thinking in the 'waking consciousness' are outlined:

1. *The modes of thinking mentioned first – i.e. the fully developed dynamic processes of thinking directed at a particular goal – can never be part of the consciousness of 'introversion'.* One reason for this is that these processes are governed by the will, and since any activity generated by volition is barred from the consciousness of 'introversion', deliberate processes of thinking aimed at a goal are forestalled. But there is another reason why concentrative acts of thinking are missing in 'introversion': There is a clash between the ongoing growth of inner calm and the dynamic nature of acts of thinking. During the process of 'introversion' such mental phenomena as tension, strain, concentration and any other conscious activity of the 'I' are eroded; if a cognitive process is triggered at all, it is immediately eliminated again by the calmness increasingly inundating the mind. But if such an incipient process of thinking happens to persevere nonetheless,

for instance, because of some 'obsessive dysfunction', it will be experienced as disruptive and, as a consequence, it will suffer the same 'fate' as any other interference intruding when 'introversion' is in progress: it will either be instantly eliminated from consciousness, or failing that, the process of 'introversion' will come to an end and be replaced by the 'waking consciousness'. There is a third reason why dynamic processes of thinking cannot survive while 'introversion' is in progress: Judgements, understood to be assessments of the validity or non-validity of a given situation or problem, are usually grounded in the desire for knowledge. However, as outlined above, any drive or desire (except for the desire for (self-)surrender) is incompatible with the process of 'introversion'. In the states of consciousness encompassed by 'introversion', and, even more so in the 'quiet state of introversion', we do not encounter any phenomenon that has any of the characteristics of an urge, drive or a stirring.

2. *Processes of thinking that happen autonomously, without any conscious acts of the 'I', may* [still] *be encountered in the incipient stage of the process of 'introversion'.* Whereas the impulse of the 'I' to be the originator of an activity, as well as the dynamic nature of drives and urges, are phenomena that cannot survive any of the stages encompassed by 'introversion', there is one special mode of thinking that may appear in the early stage of 'introversion': These are 'pure' non-discursive forms of thinking that do not directly conflict with the altered states of consciousness during 'introversion'. But these non-discursive forms of thinking are rendered dispensable in the course of 'introversion'. As thinking is just a capacity, or tool that can be utilized by other psychological faculties, it is only subservient to the functions of the human psyche.[46] This means that thinking, when it is not needed, is transferred into a latent state, or stand-by mode. Since the progress of 'introversion' generates altered states of consciousness in which processes of thinking are no longer called for, processes of thinking are suspended.

---

46 Rohracher, Hubert. *Einführung in die Psychologie*. 3rd ed. Vienna: Urban & Schwarzenberg, 1948. 314.

In order to be able to convey the subsequent considerations clearly, we need to split up the process of 'introversion', and consider the different *stages of 'introversion'*. The process of 'introversion' usually starts off in the normal 'waking consciousness'; 'introversion' is meant to advance towards the 'quiet state of alertness', which is its ultimate goal. Between these two distinct 'poles' of consciousness we may discern intermediate mental states, the specific phenomenological characteristics of which can be identified and clearly described. *The first one of these [intermediate] states* is located at the incipient stage of 'introversion'; in this stage we may still encounter some disrupting occurrences originating either in stimuli intruding from the world outside, or distractions surfacing from within the mind [e.g. memory]. The *second intermediate state of the consciousness of 'introversion'* is a more advanced level, in which consciousness has reached a fairly high degree of homogeneity. There are no longer any disturbing occurrences, though we may still find several emotional responses as well as visual images elicited by the imagination. *The 'quiet state of alertness'* is the ultimate and most serene state of consciousness, and the final goal of the process of 'introversion'. Its formal structure can phenomenologically be inferred only indirectly and theoretically from the characteristics of the [adjoining] states of consciousness, which do not entirely elude phenomenological description. In empirical reality the 'quiet state of alertness' is a formal framework of consciousness, which is filled by content, notably by the multifarious processes and attitudes that the person engaged in 'introversion' brings to the process individually. It is necessary to indicate this fact already at this stage of our enquiry, even though these claims cannot yet be substantiated and will be explained later in the book.

On the first stage of 'introversion' we may still encounter numerous processes and other items of content in consciousness that are in some way or other related to, or dependent on, processes of thinking: autonomous, freely floating and persevering streams of thought directed at some particular aim. There are, moreover, individual judgements to be found sustaining the structure of the meditative process, and, furthermore, intrusive snippets of thoughts and random chains of associations surfacing in the mind, which are all experienced as unwelcome digressions and disturbances in the early stage of 'introversion'. This early stage of 'introversion' is still dominated by intrusive forms of thinking. *At the second stage of 'introversion' processes of thinking have been stilled to a large extent because thinking has become dispensable.* There are no sequences of discursive thinking any more, or thoughts aiming at some goal, or thoughts going astray. If we still encounter forms of thinking, these thoughts merely reflect what is currently happening in consciousness. It is only singular thoughts that may surface from within the broad stream of consciousness, which may create a fragile structure for a fleeting sequence of visual images and 'stream' of emotions. Individual words and concepts referring to the present altered state of consciousness may still appear when 'introversion' develops further towards the 'quiet state of alertness'. For instance, the word 'calmness', or the word 'surrender' may emerge, and linger peacefully in the mind for quite some time. And yet: the word 'calm' evoked by an underlying emotional condition does still depend on a thought.

So-called 'modes of awareness', i.e. the spontaneous, intuitive perception of 'knowledge', can often be encountered at various stages of 'introversion'. However, 'modes of awareness' cannot be classified as 'thoughts' proper, as they have different distinctive characteristics.

In the 'quiet state of alertness', processes of thinking can emerge in a new [transformed] shape, when they are released by a predisposition 'encoded' in the mind before embarking on the process of 'introversion'.

Meditation

The range of experiences encountered on the first stage of 'introversion' can be described more specifically, when related to both the process of meditation, and the processes of association released in it. The following description of different stages of meditation will illustrate in an exemplary manner how the experience of undergoing a change in the process of 'introversion' develops from the first stage of 'introversion' towards the second stage.

As soon as the process of 'introversion' has started, the world of sense perception is switched off almost entirely. The calmness arising from the sphere of the body continues to permeate consciousness and thus has a calming impact on any kind of experience. There are no longer any stirrings of the will; and there is no awareness any more of the 'I' functioning as an agent, even though the capacity of thinking has not yet been suspended entirely. However, the given processes of thinking are not actively generated, but arise passively, and are free-floating acts. The 'I' is no longer able to reflect consciously on these free-floating acts, nor are these free-floating thoughts triggered, directed or sustained by an act of the will. It is thus a mode of thinking that is devoid of any mark of activity; it is, in other words, an entirely passive and autonomous development. These autonomous processes of thinking may occur in two varieties: First, as patterns of thoughts perceived as disruptive to the process of 'introversion', and secondly, as integral parts of the processes governing the progress of 'meditation'. We have already given an example of a thought disrupting the progress of 'introversion', above, when a deep and oppressing worry intruded upon the mind of the person engaged in 'introversion'. We have seen in this example that the more deeply the distressing affliction of having inadvertently forsaken a friend penetrates the mind, the more acute and pressing are the patterns of thoughts intruding in consciousness. The great intensity of the disturbance could be inferred from the fact that the agonizing sense of failure even intruded into the realm of verbalized thought.

The fact that any cognitive awareness and any conceptual activity is grounded in thinking, it goes without saying that (spontaneous) thoughts are naturally also involved in disrupting events of lesser gravity than the one referred to above.

Particularly grave disturbances tend to trigger a special function in the consciousness of 'introversion', i.e. the mental technique termed *'meditative dissolution of interferences', or 'meditative elimination'*; that is to say, a function by which a phenomenon interfering in the progress of 'introversion' can be dissolved and removed from consciousness. Any meditative process is coherently structured, and because of this, it can be isolated and identified phenomenologically from the complex of experiences and processes involved in 'introversion'. 'Meditation', as conceived here, is a mental process composed of several (so-called) 'ultimate phenomena'; this process undergoes a transformation as it proceeds towards the 'quiet state of alertness', as 'ultimate phenomena' come more and more clearly into focus. The meditative process does contain genuine processes of structured thinking, which are of crucial importance for identifying the modes of thinking encountered in the incipient stage of 'introversion'.

Meditation, however, cannot alone be defined on the basis of the processes of thinking involved in it. The very special mode of thinking inherent in 'meditation' differs from the process of thinking encountered in the early stage of 'introversion', which is still governed in part by functions of the 'waking consciousness'. 'Meditation' is not an act of concentration. Thinking during the ongoing process of 'meditation' occurs subconsciously, i.e. the 'meditating I' is not aware that he/she is actively engaged in the meditative process, nor does 'meditation' contain any act of the will. Though meditative thinking is not controlled by the will, it is clearly structured throughout, and directed at a particular object or goal. When a meditative process is triggered for the purpose of dissolving a phenomenon disrupting the ongoing process, the 'experiencing I' has some subconscious awareness that the disturbing elements are eliminated, and that the course of meditation is *steered into the right direction*. Moreover, the meditational process is intuitively known to be embedded in the calmness that has 'arrived' in consciousness and that the current mental process is in some way 'meaningful'. The term 'intended goal' is not appropriate for describing this particular kind of subconscious awareness, because the notion of an 'intended goal', as well as the predisposition to achieve the goal generated by it, are not triggered by any act of the will, nor by any other intentional measure. The particular direction the process of 'meditation' is going to take has been encoded in the 'waking state', before the 'meditation' was started, but it proceeds autonomously without involving any conscious choice. The course the process of 'meditation' will take is intuitively approved by the 'meditating I' in a moment of 'inwardness'.

The experiences encountered during the process of 'meditation' are not based on acts of thinking alone. Several other functions of the 'I' are involved as well. Very important are, for instance, emotion-based intentions, for instance, by applying the method of focussing on a disturbing phenomenon meditatively by 'revolving' mentally around it. But this method had better been termed empathy, rather than a method 'dissolving' a disturbing item 'cognitively'. Moreover, judgements are also part of the 'meditation' process, because judgements are often after-effects of moments of emotional inwardness. For instance, in the incidence quoted above in which a person is deeply troubled after having failed to live up to the moral duty owed to a friend, this disturbing event can be eliminated from the centre of consciousness when value judgements become involved: 'This moral failure of mine is irreversible, and as such it is irrelevant to the current process of "introversion".' Judgements of this kind resolving some inner discord are secondary responses to a primary emotional state, which is best (though not quite accurately) expressed by the phrase 'confiding in composure'. This state of 'inwardness' is also marked by a deep sense of being immersed in 'sheltering' calmness. All these experiences resonate with the awareness that the ongoing process of 'meditation' is heading into the 'right' direction.

Acts of meditation have the inherent tendency to substitute processes of thinking with emotional ones. While 'meditation' is in progress, a transformation is effected in consciousness in that the emotional components permeate consciousness more and more, whereas modes of thinking become fewer. Feelings dominate the processes of thinking more and more, so that eventually thoughts are replaced by image-based phenomena. Something similar happens when someone engages in (what might be termed) the 'technique of introversion' ("Technik der Versenkung"). A special variety of this technique is 'Autogenic Training', as developed by I. H. Schultz:[47] After the practitioner has eased all muscular tension, when he/she has been placed in a state of repose, and screened off against the world outside by shutting the eyes, a particular aim that is to be achieved is, as it were, 'programmed' into the mind – for instance, the intention to elicit some somatic change in a particular part of the body by repeating an auto-suggestive phrase or a summons, like for example, "my right arm is heavy", or "I am breathing calmly". Such expressions are essentially judgements, but they also incorporate *a priori* the intention to achieve the special aim addressed, and this is why these iterative formulas become the triggers of the meditative

---

47 Schultz, Johannes H. *Das Autogene Training. Versuch einer Klinisch-Praktischen Darstellung.* Leipzig: Thieme, 1932.

process. The course of 'meditation' initiated in this way is at first still dominated by thinking, but as 'meditation' progresses, the mind becomes increasingly inundated by images and emotions. The overall experience generated by this dynamic process is for quite some time accompanied by perceptions of the body. Thus the range of impressions appearing in consciousness becomes more and more complex; the state of consciousness continues to be transformed, and emotional states eventually dominate over acts of thinking.

Processes of Associating[48]

In processes of thinking, relationships are established. The act of relating things to each other requires some content as a precondition, which is (as it were) the 'substance' in a process of thinking. Thinking is, however, by no means only related to what has been transmitted by sense perceptions. Thinking consists to a considerable extent also of content deriving from the realm of the imagination. Thinking refers primarily to what has previously been a subject matter of thinking. This is the empirical basis for what we call knowledge. Thinking is an encounter between the non-visual acts of guessing and understanding, and the psychic processes termed collectively 'ideation' (i.e. forming an idea; inspiration). The never-ending stream of ideas provides the material for acts of thinking. Ideas (in our context) are memories of what has previously been present in the mind. Ideas may emerge from anywhere and are for this reason experienced as something new. Mental images, verbalized concepts, whole complexes of thoughts, consciously grasped non-visual relationships, and even complete complexes of multifarious experience supply the content of processes of ideation. Psychological theory stipulates that there is a basis for reproduction, which may account for the fact (as its supporters claim) that one is consciously aware of one's ideas and thoughts only temporarily, even though they are potentially available in consciousness

---

48 Kretschmer, Ernst. *Medizinische Psychologie.* 9th ed. Stuttgart: Thieme, 1947. – Rohracher, Hubert. *Einführung in die Psychologie.* 3rd ed. Vienna: Urban & Schwarzenberg, 1948. – Elsenhans, Theodor. *Lehrbuch der Psychologie.* 1912. 3rd ed. Tübingen: Mohr, 1939.

all the time. In the current investigation we cannot dispense with the hypothetical explanations provided by a well-substantiated scientific branch of psychology. The term 'association' suggests that ideas, individual thoughts and sets of complex experiences are linked with each other by a pattern created by natural law; it also suggests that the process of reproduction is understood to occur in an extra-mental process in which individual items are instantly combined. An idea that has become conscious will inevitably evoke additional ideas! We need to know something about these processes of association and the foundations from which they emerge, if we want to delineate intelligibly the processes operating in 'introversion'. Basically, in its simplest form, ideas and thoughts are linked with each other by spatial and/or temporal contiguity: For instance, I may imagine my house and the picture of the tree standing next it; or I can evoke in the imagination the image of a sunset, which may be linked to the notion of the time of leisure approaching after work. The second law of association, which becomes manifest in the latter example, is determined by the principle of similarity. This principle operates most obviously when a person is required to find a suitable rhyming word when composing a poem.

It is possible that complete sequences of content-based associations may trigger each other, elicited by objects or phenomena sharing the same or similar features. For instance, when I imagine the face of my mother, a whole range of memories will be evoked in my mind in which my mother is actively present. In general, it can be stated: Items joined with each other by 'meaning', or by a shared topic, will become conscious step by step, as soon as a single instance has entered consciousness. Why this is so, however, eludes rational explanation.

It is also important to mention that the process of ideation is not exclusively governed by elementary principles of association. There are also complex patterns of experience involved, which are not merely related by images of the imagination, but also by feelings. The same or similar emotional qualities adhering to different objects may become so closely associated with each other that the subsequent complex of experience evoked can become manifest in its entirety.

We are now going to describe a cross-section of phenomena encountered in the incipient stage of 'introversion'. Deliberate acts of thinking are no longer found. The function of 'meditative elimination' includes a free-floating process of thinking so that interferences are still responded to cognitively. The question that arises in this context is, if it is possible that from the process of association, ideas or even acts of thinking may surface which may become the 'content' of an empirical event within the consciousness of 'introversion'.

Psychopathology has coined the term *'flight of ideas'* ("Ideenflucht") to refer to a mode of thinking reflected in a speech act that is typical of patients suffering from manic-depressive disorder. This mode of speech is characterised by a sequence of associations that is logically incoherent. In this kind of disorder any super-ordinated concept is missing, and there is no coherently structured, goal-oriented process of thinking.[49] Only elementary principles of association seem to apply in this case. The sequence of associations operating in a person afflicted by a mental disability typically proceeds like this: 'house – garden – waiting – bank – clock – hall – house – Claus' [the latter refers to a German Christian name that rhymes with the German (and English) word 'house']. *This way of thinking is termed 'flight of ideas'. – It is a mental pattern that cannot be found at any stage of 'introversion'* in a sane person. The peculiar sequence of thoughts witnessed here is determined by a very rudimentary principle of association, caused by 'dissociation' ("Abspaltung"), i.e. some functions of the mind operate autonomously, dissociated from other functions to which they are normally linked. Such instances of 'dissociation', however, occur only when the structure of consciousness has become dysfunctional or fully disintegrated. As long as the consciousness of 'introversion' has not collapsed entirely, the integrity of the entire personality will not be affected. Isolated sequences of association that are not related to the entire whole of the personality are, in general, incompatible with the structure of consciousness at any stage of 'introversion'. But if such isolated processes should still occur in 'introversion', they are instantly experienced as interferences, which disrupt and ultimately destroy the consciousness of 'introversion'. In the incipient stage of 'introversion', however, phenomena may become manifest that can be explained by the principle

---

49 Cf. Kretschmer, Ernst. *Medizinische Psychologie*. 9th ed. Stuttgart: Thieme, 1947. 105 and 111.

of association. For instance, it is possible that *'unexpected thoughts'* ("unvermutete Gedanken") appear in the mind; for instance, the thought: "Peace is the citizen's first obligation". This thought has undoubtedly been triggered by an association rooted in the individual's 'sphere of reproduction'; in this example, not even an emotional relationship appears to have been involved. The intruded snippet of thought is a disturbance, albeit not a particularly intense one. This means that there are disruptions caused by thoughts that are hardly sustained by emotional states or feelings, and which are not accompanied by any image. Hence, we are dealing with a digression of thought that is ephemeral and short-lived – which is indeed the distinctive characteristic of such a thought. Such a thought seems to be flashing through the mind like a falling star. – There is one elementary pattern of associations, however, that can trigger a rather complex response and result in a grave disruption. For instance, when I happen to drift away from the intended goal of achieving the state of inner calm because of an association released by the memory of my father, in a situation when he made a statement on the topic of calmness, and this association evokes affect-laden memories of my father, thus a very grave disruption has been triggered which originated from a single aberrant thought.

By perseverance we understand the persistent recurrence of singular ideas, images or notions that intrude upon the mind and haunt it for some time. Such persevering thoughts and images can also be encountered at the beginning of the process of 'introversion'. I think, however, that this happens rather rarely and that instances of perseverance are quickly bypassed and overwhelmed by the ongoing 'stream of experience'. All disruptions are naturally bound to end and disappear as 'introversion' advances further, and this is why, on the second stage of 'introversion', thoughts cannot be found anymore.

A few remarks have to be added on so-called 'free-floating associations'.[50] There is a special method in psychoanalysis for treating patients who suffer from a psychic disorder that makes practical use of associations. The patient is advised to yield freely to any idea or thought that might arise in his/her mind after having shut his/her

---

50   Kretschmer, Ernst. *Medizinische Psychologie*. 9th ed. Stuttgart: Thieme, 1947. 109.

eyes, suspended discursive thinking and screened off any stimuli from the world outside. The process of 'free-floating associations' tends to release a lively stream of random ideas, thoughts and feelings, which surface in consciousness and are observed by the 'experiencing I' like a spectator who remains entirely passive. Passive processes are phenomenologically to be contrasted to active ones, for instance, discursive thinking. Active processes are ordered in structure and proceed logically. Though the objects appearing in the 'stream' of the imagination are also evoked by associations, they are filtered by active choice, which is in turn governed subconsciously by the intended aim of the current process of 'introversion'. Apart from the principle of active selection, the intended aim of advancing towards a state of inner calm determines the direction 'introversion' will take. Because of this mechanism only ideas and impressions become fully conscious that are consonant with the subliminally governed path of thinking that directs the progress of 'introversion'.

It is reasonable to assume that all active forms of thinking have been stilled before the process of 'introversion' commences, and that the progress of 'introversion' is sustained exclusively by passive modes of experiencing. Observations of patients and/or test-persons have shown that 'free-floating associations' are not essential phenomena in the consciousness of 'introversion'. The 'quiet state of alertness' is the intended final goal of the process of 'introversion'. This final state is a complex mental wholeness, consisting of images from the imagination as well as (non-discursive) thoughts, which determines the progress of 'introversion'. At the beginning, the mental framework is still largely that of the 'waking consciousness', and the final state of 'quiet alertness' is the desired goal. This intended goal has been encoded in the mind before embarking on the process of 'introversion', and is pursued and enabled by the concurrent and persevering impact of the 'thought encoded'. Thus any active control of the ongoing development of 'introversion' by the 'experiencing I' has been rendered redundant and is suspended, so that the course of 'introversion' is determined exclusively by the concurrent subconscious awareness of advancing towards the 'encoded goal'. At the higher stages of 'introversion' the constellation of consciousness is transformed. Passive cognitive processes are more and more replaced by emotional states and emotional responses. The prevailing emotional condition in the 'quiet state of alertness' is calmness, which continues to grow and eventually dwells in consciousness perseveringly. We know that emotional states tend to influence the course of events significantly. Thus amongst the wide variety of ideas, notions and feelings that may surface in consciousness while 'introversion' is in progress, only those are permitted to unfold that are compatible with the prevailing mood of repose. But it is possible that a premeditated (encoded) predisposition affects the nature of the images and impressions arising in consciousness in the course of 'introversion'. This, however, does not impede the progress towards the intended final goal of the 'quiet state of alertness'.

The I ("Das Ich")

The 'I' is an 'ultimate phenomenon of consciousness' ("Bewußtseinsletztheit") that eludes a [conclusive] definition. There is no experience that is not related in some way to the 'I'. Thus any attempt to define the 'I' by an abstract concept is abortive, because any rational reflection on the nature of the 'I' inevitably encompasses features of the 'I' itself. But when some item is stripped off from the 'I', the 'I' is reduced to an [abstract] irrational concept. Thus the 'I' – which is a primeval facticity – defies definition. Psychology, when seriously conceived as a scientific discipline, must avoid using terminology informed by concepts and notions of metaphysics. For this reason it is imperative here to consider the 'I' merely in psychological terms as the 'focal point' of experience. The 'layer theory' avoids talking of a 'layer of the I'. Rothacker[51] states: "The terms 'I-point' and 'centre of the I' are meant to show that the 'I' is not a part of the entire personality in the sense that it has a substance of its own that is endowed with capacities equivalent to the emotional and vital functions of the 'id', but the 'I' is to be seen as a controlling instance rather than a separate layer [of the personality]." On the other hand, nothing is more immediately evident

---

51 Rothacker, Erich. *Die Schichten der Persönlichkeit*. 4th ed. Bonn: Bouvier, 1948. 75.

empirically than the fact that there is such a thing as the 'I'. The consciousness of 'I', the feeling of 'I-hood' and the self-awareness of the 'I' are all aspects of a single entity that eludes differentiation, and this undifferentiated entity is intuitively perceived as something 'given'. The reason why the fundamental concept of the 'I' could not be used as a point of departure of this enquiry into the consciousness of 'introversion' is obvious. The 'I' and its role and significance for elucidating 'introversion' can only be explored when all the functions and capacities pertaining to the 'I' have previously been dealt with. It is now that the time has come to use the psychological concept of the 'I' as a touchstone, or a point of reference for the enquiry into the pivotal features of the phenomena encountered in the consciousness of 'introversion'.

When relating the concept of the 'I' to the process of 'introversion', the deficiencies and paucity of details yielded by current psychological research on the issue of the 'I' become apparent. Though there are numerous statements on the concept of the 'I', which permit us to establish a few important points, the various findings have been pitched together rather incoherently. It seems to me, however, that this incoherence and the great diversity of approaches to the 'I' also reflect, and give evidence of, the great mystery intrinsic to the 'I' as an 'ultimate phenomenon'.

1. One of the established statements on the 'I' is: The 'I' is experienced in the course of time as immutable – the 'I' of the past, the 'I' of the present and the 'I' of the future are one and the same. The identity of the 'I' across time, and its inherent, immutable simplicity are characteristics, however, that are also intrinsic to any other experience in a sane human being. These features apply equally to the 'I' when engaged in the process of 'introversion': The 'I' immersed in the practice of 'introversion' is identical with the 'I' before the beginning and after the end of the process of 'introversion'; similarly, the 'I' of the 'waking consciousness' is identical with the 'I' that experienced events that had happened many years in the past, and identical with the 'I' that will be the centre of experiences in years to come. A 'split personality', or 'divided I', or when the 'I has become alienated' from itself, are cases encountered in psychopathology, and these are clearly instances of mental disorders caused by a pathological disintegration

of the psyche. Yet *in the fully integrated consciousness of 'introversion' we never encounter an instance of a 'split I',* or a split personality.

2. The second approach to the phenomenon of the 'I' is based on the fact that all [conscious] human experience is tied to the so-called 'performance consciousness'[52]. The 'I' attributes, as it were, all the actions performed by it, to itself. All processes of consciousness are related to the 'I', thus every experience has inevitably some quality of the 'I'. Feelings are states of emotion of the 'I' itself. These feelings generate a complex emotional condition that establishes (what may be termed) the 'sphere of the self' pertaining to the 'I'. – All sense perceptions are my own perceptions. Even passive events, as, for example, the surfacing of ideas and impressions from the imagination, are experienced as thoughts and manifestations belonging to the 'I'. The awareness of an occurrence, and a moment of 'inwardness', are experiences pertaining to the 'I'. Any process of consciousness is in some way related to the 'I', though not all of these processes are acknowledged as actions originating from the 'I', or posited by the 'I'. In order to describe experiences witnessed during the process of 'introversion' it is helpful to start from a functional concept in which the 'I' is related to passive experiences encountered in 'introversion': When the 'I' observes ideas, impressions or intuitions surfacing in consciousness, and when perceiving the changing mental and emotional condition, the 'I' is a passive recipient or passive observer.

The 'performance consciousness' is, by contrast, an 'active consciousness' (i.e. it is aware of the 'I' featuring as a performing agent). The 'performance consciousness' accompanies all dynamic and impulse-like activities. Thus one speaks of the 'rational will'

---

52 [Note: Albrecht uses the term "Vollzugsbewußtsein" without quotation marks and without indicating a source. The concept is, however, an established philosophical term, which was coined by Eugen Fink in the late 1920s. In English scholarship the German term "Vollzugsbewußtsein" was translated as 'performance consciousness', which has been adopted in this translation. (Cf. Bruzina, Ronald. *Edmund Husserl and Eugen Fink: Beginnings and Ends in Phenomenology 1928-1938.* New Haven: Yale UP, 2004. – For the meaning of "Vollzugsbewußtsein" and its English translation see Bruzina 124, 197, 566). – FW.]

["Kürwille"][53] of the 'I', which means that the 'I' is perceived as 'the cause of action';[54] the 'I' can act deliberately because of the capacity of volition. One speaks of an act of thinking that is controlled by the 'I', and means by this that the 'I' is able to make use of noetic functions. This approach to the concept of the 'I' is based on the phenomenology of the 'waking consciousness'. The 'I', seen as a controlling, governing, determining and deciding entity, is thus equated with functions encountered in the 'waking state',[55] because the 'waking consciousness' is switched on whenever a free-floating mental process is disrupted by some interference from outside, or by some inner resistance on the part of the 'experiencing I'. This conception of the 'I' is entirely focussed on the 'active mode' and approached from the perspective of the active 'waking consciousness'.

If we transfer these considerations by way of analogy to the consciousness of 'introversion', we have to consider two vital questions: First, "what will happen during the process of 'introversion' to the directing, governing and controlling functions of the 'I'?" And, second, "what is going to happen to the function of observing?" These questions arise because in the consciousness of 'introversion' there is no awareness of an ongoing activity anymore. A characteristic experience of the 'I' in the 'waking consciousness' is the cognitive awareness that the 'I' can initiate a new beginning. This particular aptitude of the 'I' cannot be found in the consciousness of 'introversion'. Therefore we cannot attribute to the 'I' the function of directing or

---

53 [Note: The term 'rational will' is the standard English translation for the German technical term "Kürwille". The term was created by the German sociologist Ferdinand Tönnies (1855-1936). The English translation has been adopted from "Ferdinand Tonnies". *Encyclopædia Britannica. Encyclopædia Britannica Online.* Encyclopædia Britannica Inc., 2016. Web. 25 Jan. 2016 <http://www.britannica.com/biography/Ferdinand-Julius-Tonnies> – FW.]

54 Ach, Narziss quoted in Rohracher, Hubert. *Einführung in die Psychologie.* 3rd ed. Vienna: Urban & Schwarzenberg, 1948. 453.

55 Rothacker, Erich. *Die Schichten der Persönlichkeit.* 4th ed. Bonn: Bouvier, 1948. Strunz, Kurt. "Über die 'Vertikale' Ordnung der Seelischen Dispositionen. Ein Beitrag zur Psychologischen Schichttheorie." *Zeitschrift für Psychologie* 154 (1943): 103-202.

controlling the process of 'introversion'. This means that in 'introversion' the 'I-point' cannot 'slip into' the noetic dispositions anymore, whereas this can be achieved in the 'waking consciousness'. The 'I' does not engage actively in acts of the will any longer. An initial stirring to act is instantly perceived by the 'I' as an interference, or as an unfamiliar drive – experiences that cannot survive in 'introversion' because they conflict with the 'encoded predisposition' not to heed to any distraction and to aspire to achieve the state of inner calm. Therefore any stirring that might arise, however slight and transient, is eliminated. Hence we may state: *The controlling and governing function of the 'I' is suspended in the process of 'introversion'.*

We have especially considered the controlling function of the 'I'. As long as the controlling function involves some activity, the given mental state is not yet that of 'introversion'. But if we expand the concept and concede that passive responses of the 'I' are part of the controlling function, we may discern such a function in the incipient stage of 'introversion'. Girgensohn,[56] in his psychology of religion, puts special emphasis on the function of the 'I' with regard to acts of acceptance and rejection. For instance, when an image arises in the mind from the imagination that has some symbolic import in view of the experience of calmness, or when a thought passes through consciousness that is consonant with the progress and the approved goal of 'introversion', these turn out to be occurrences that are not only accepted and affirmed by the 'experiencing I', but also adhered to in some way or other. On the other hand, there are also adverse responses such as turning away from an image, or averting one's eyes, ignoring, or rejecting content that appears in consciousness. It is difficult to say if responses of this kind are appropriately described by the term 'response of the I' ["Stellungnahme des Ichs"]. It rather seems to me that the word response implies some activity, or dynamic reaction. Affirming and denying, approval and disapproval are actually reactions, and as such they are rather akin to 'pointed feelings'. Any approval implies the spontaneous willingness to 'tune in' with the ongoing process of calming and harmonizing the mind, and to participate in the progress of 'introversion' without admitting any

---

56 Girgensohn, Karl. *Der Seelische Aufbau des Religiösen Lebens: Eine Religionspsychologische Untersuchung auf Experimenteller Grundlage.* Leipzig: Hirzel, 1921.

kind of dissonance. These are all feelings, or spontaneous responses that aptly resonate in the German word "Zustimmung", freely translated as 'consonant approval'.[57] These emotional qualities are closely linked with thoughts and visual images, but they are in no way similar to an act of the will, not even remotely so, since these emotional responses are not elicited by a 'decision'. These intuitive responses of the 'I' do not occur at the centre, but at the periphery of consciousness. For instance, I do know that I am approving of a pictorial image that has emerged in consciousness, and I am aware of its acceptance without having reflected on it; this means that I am clearly aware of my instantaneous approval in a state of 'inwardness', and that this knowledge does not result from a conscious act or a deliberate decision. By way of summary we may state on the issue of the controlling function of the 'I' in the process of 'introversion': *In the initial stage of the consciousness of 'introversion' emotional responses of the 'I' signifying approval or disapproval can still be found. In the final stage of 'introversion' responses of this kind, which are the residual vestiges of the active function of the 'I', can no longer be encountered.*

3. The third approach to the experience of the 'I' is based on the fact that the 'I' is diametrically opposed to an object in the event of a concrete experience. This has been termed the 'subject-object split' in philosophy. And this division between subject and object in experiencing is another 'ur-phenomenon'. In the 'waking consciousness' object-related content clearly prevails over emotional states, though the latter are likewise object-like items. As 'inwardness' expands during the process of 'introversion', the mind is increasingly emptied from all objects so that the functions of the 'I' that are linked to an object are eventually suspended. As the state-like condition of the mind continues to expand, the intuitive modes of experiencing become more intense. The propensity of 'turning inward' continues

---

57 [Note: The pun on the German word "Zu-stimm-ung", which plays on the meaning of the lexical root of the word "Stimme" ('voice'), cannot be adequately rendered in English; "Zustimmung" means voicing an approval, to assent to, or agree with something, but the German word also connotes metaphorically the notion of chiming in with a given mood; the expression 'consonant approval' is a near equivalent to the German term. – FW.]

to grow and along with it, the awareness of 'inwardness' continues to expand. The path of 'introversion' can develop this expansive and receptive state of 'inwardness' only when the process of emptying the 'I' from all active functions, except for the ability to perceive one's state of 'inwardness', has been successful.

When the process of 'introversion' continues to develop, the structure of the 'waking consciousness' continues to disintegrate. An impact of the disintegration of the 'waking state' is the transformation of the 'I', which starts already in the 'waking consciousness'. The process of transformation affects in particular the mental condition of the so-called 'I-point' of consciousness, which is gradually loosened, dissolved and eventually eroded. The process of transformation is *one* of the underlying empirical occurrences which, in the context of mysticism, are identified as integral parts of some varieties of 'mystical' experience, notably the phenomena of the 'dissolving of the I', the 'emptying of the I', 'reducing of the I', and the 'annihilation' or 'extinction of the I'. **The reintegration of the 'consciousness of quiet alertness' is enabled by the 'I' switching to the receptive and passive modes of experiencing. In the final stage of the 'quiet state of alertness' the 'I' has not only become unified and endowed with the instantaneous capacity of 'inward awareness', but it has also been transformed into a 'seeing I' (i.e. endowed with the capacity of 'seeing inwardly').**

Two additional remarks have to be added at this point: 1. The function of 'seeing inwardly' cannot yet be specified at this stage of our enquiry. What can be stated at this point, however, is that the 'I', when immersed in the 'quiet state of alertness', is endowed with the capacity of 'inner sight' ("Innenschau") – a concept that will be explained later. 2. The controversial notion of the 'subject-object split' includes the phenomenon termed 'suspension' of the 'subject-object split'. The question as to whether subject and object may ultimately be claimed to be identical is a philosophical issue, and falls outside the discipline of psychology. Mystical expressions such as the 'annihilation of the 'I' or the 'dissolving of the I' have to be examined on the basis of the psychology of mysticism. **Within the scope of the consciousness of 'introversion', however, there is no phenomenon that could be identified or likened to that of the 'dissolving of the 'I'.**

Attentiveness

The concept of 'attentiveness' ("Aufmerksamkeit") has, to date, not been defined unambiguously by the science of psychology. But this deficiency alone is no sufficient reason for questioning the relevance of the concept, or for doubting its usefulness for enquiries into the nature of the consciousness of 'introversion'. There are indeed other reasons why the distinctive features of this concept have to be assessed individually, and why the current conception of 'attention' or 'attentiveness' is not helpful for exploring the incipient stage of the process of 'introversion'. The concept of 'attentiveness' encompasses some characteristics of other concepts, which were elaborated for the purpose of exploring the perception of one's surroundings. These concepts are valid and useful for experimental investigations by the psychology of sense perception ("Sinnespsychologie"),[58] and, in addition, for exploring the nature of self-observation, as they likewise depend on different degrees of wakefulness governed by the 'I'. However, these concepts are abortive when phenomena such as 'immediate inwardness' and 'one-directedness' are at issue. This fact notwithstanding, I must not bypass the concept of 'attentiveness', because the insights gained from a critical analysis of this phenomenon will be required later, when we are going to explore two important phenomena pertaining to the 'consciousness of introversion', i.e. the phenomenon termed 'directedness', and the phenomenon termed 'hyper-lucidity'.

Amongst the many attempts at providing a definition of 'attention' and/or 'attentiveness', the one suggested by Giese[59] appears to be

---

58 [Note: "Sinnespsychologie" is a psychological term in German, which was introduced by Franz Brentano (1838-1917) in *Untersuchungen zur Sinnespsychologie*. Leipzig: Duncker & Humblot, 1907. The literal English translation is 'sense psychology', which is, however, ambiguous; therefore the term has been translated as 'psychology of sense perception'. – FW.]

59 [Note: The reference is to the German psychologist Fritz Wilhelm Giese (1890-1935), who became famous for developing psychological techniques of relaxation and concentration. – Though Albrecht's reference is to Giese, it is a secondary quotation; the actual source is Elsenhans, Theodor. *Lehrbuch der Psychologie*. 1912. 3rd

the one most useful: "Being attentive to something is a basic biological disposition. Attentiveness establishes a connexion between the 'I' and the environment, and is a [particular] biological function, the psychological and spiritual potential of which is most efficiently released when directed by the will." The sense of being directed by the will is, however, not necessarily an integral part of any instance involving 'attentiveness'. For we have to distinguish between two types of 'attentiveness': *Volitional* attention – which is attention directed by the will. This type of attention enables us to select and focus on specific details of the objects emerging from the 'stream of consciousness'. Deliberate acts of attention are marked by strain. And strain is linked with a sense of achievement, notably the one giving evidence of one's tenacity, or of the phenomenon of 'divided attention', i.e. the ability to do several things at the same time by shifting the focus of attention between different objects, and/or by dividing one's attentiveness between a primary and a secondary activity. There is, moreover, the phenomenon of the fluctuating degrees of 'attentiveness'. – We speak of *involuntary* attention, when someone is not inclined to pay attention to inner or outward perceptions, or when a person is compelled by circumstances to respond to sensual stimuli, or to impressions intruding in consciousness.[60] In this case, objects and/or impressions are imposed on the perceiver and 'attract' his/her attention, as it were, forcefully.

Attentiveness provides the empirical foundation for the phenomenon termed 'the narrowness of consciousness'. The power of attention is limited. As stated by Gruhle: "Attention is a volitional alertness related to, and remaining focussed on, a particular object." "It is", however, "neither an ultimate phenomenon, nor a very special or independent one." Apart from the distinctive feature of lucidity, attention consists of "the strong impulse of shutting out everything else for the purpose of focusing exclusively on a single object." This impulse can be described in such terms as 'directing one's focus deliberately on a special goal' ("Sichrichtenauf"), or 'to continue adhering

---

ed. Tübingen: Mohr, 1939. 443. – FW.]
60   Cf. Elsenhans, Theodor. *Lehrbuch der Psychologie*. 1912. 3rd ed. Tübingen: Mohr, 1939. 443.

to what is currently perceived' ("Dabeibleiben").[61]

The first stage of 'introversion' has been described as a level of consciousness in which all active functions of the 'I' have been suspended, including acts of the will and discursive thinking, though stimuli or incidents disrupting the process of 'introversion' can still be perceived. From this follows that 'volitional attention' is likewise incompatible with the incipient stage of 'introversion', and is therefore absent in 'introversion'. This is different, however, from 'involuntary attention': in the early stage of 'introversion' occurrences involving 'involuntary attention' caused by disrupting stimuli or events can still happen. Moreover, some worrying incident may still arise in consciousness from memory and may occupy the attention of the 'experiencing I'. Also thoughts flashing up in the mind can attract the attention of the 'I' for a moment when absorbed in 'introversion'. On the whole, however, the phenomenological characteristics of instances of 'involuntary attention' appearing in the incipient stage of 'introversion' differ significantly from the incidents of 'involuntary attention' witnessed in the 'waking consciousness'. In 'introversion' it is neither disruptive intrusions nor the flicker of objects surfacing in consciousness that may succeed in attracting attention. Such intrusive phenomena are not placed (as it were) in the 'spotlight' of inward perception, which is a precondition for screening off the mind from any other 'content'. Disruptions do not become the focus of the given field of vision. The phenomena, by contrast, which are vital for advancing the progress of 'introversion', remain in the clear 'spotlight' unabatedly. The calmness emanating from the body and the calmness 'arriving' in consciousness are fused and, as a consequence, the calmness experienced assumes a spatial, object-like quality in the advanced stage of 'introversion'. Any of the remaining phenomena that might appear as 'objects' are either residues of items that have not yet been eliminated entirely, or corollaries of peripheral experiences. Even if such intrusive phenomena have a strong impact on the 'experiencing I', the perception of them is always tinged with the awareness that they are something separate and peripheral that

---

61 Cf. Gruhle, Hans W. *Verstehende Psychologie (Erlebnislehre). Ein Lehrbuch.* Stuttgart: Thieme, 1948. 15f.

does not belong to the ongoing process of 'introversion'. Metaphorically speaking, such intrusions are not the focal point of a darkened field of vision, but merely bits and pieces perceived in passing in the 'chamber' of consciousness that is otherwise radiant with lucidity. On the second stage of 'introversion', disruptions are no longer perceived, or rather can no longer penetrate into the stable structure of the 'quiet state of alertness'. There are no objects anymore at which 'involuntary attention' might be drawn. For the second stage of 'introversion' the concept of attention is no longer appropriate. Therefore the phenomenon of 'attention' should be replaced by two special features: the concept of 'clarity [or lucidity] of consciousness' and that of the 'directionality' of consciousness (i.e. the awareness in the 'experiencing I' that the ongoing process of 'introversion' is directed at a specific goal).

Clarity of Consciousness

The term 'clarity of consciousness' ("Bewußtseinsklarheit")[62] enables us to discern if the stages of 'introversion' and the 'quiet state of alertness' are indeed clear and lucid states, or if some of the stages are still blurred, hypo-lucid mental states. The concept of 'clarity' has been derived from phenomena of the 'waking consciousness'. It refers to a clear and serene mental condition; it is lucid and clearly structured. These characteristic features of the 'waking consciousness' need to be juxtaposed to morbid or disturbed mental states, which are generally blurred and dimmed. The term 'clarity of consciousness' refers, secondly, to an enhanced degree of 'alertness' ("Wachheit"). We may distinguish between several degrees of clarity and lucidity, and several degrees of 'alertness'. We speak of states of consciousness that can be arranged in a coherent sequence; the highest state is the consciousness with the highest degrees of clarity and 'alertness', followed by altered states of limited clarity, down

---

62 Gruhle, Hans W. *Verstehende Psychologie (Erlebnislehre). Ein Lehrbuch*. Stuttgart: Thieme, 1948. – Jaspers, Karl. *Allgemeine Psychopathologie. Ein Leitfaden für Studierende, Ärzte und Psychologen*. 1913. 5th ed. Berlin and Heidelberg: Springer, 1948.

to states of impaired clarity and reduced alertness, states of dizziness, and, at the bottom, the hypo-lucid mental condition in which consciousness has become entirely eclipsed, resulting in the state of unconsciousness.

As the concept of clarity is based on the degree of lucidity, the concept of attention is closely associated with it as well. The 'waking consciousness' encompasses not only the entire range of what is consciously perceived, but also what is just noticed accidentally. The scope of attention, by contrast, embraces only what has been observed consciously and with a high degree of clarity. The linking of attention with the degree of the clarity of consciousness has given rise to the view that the 'waking state' is controlled throughout by the function of the 'I'; this proposition suggests that the 'waking state' will intercede, or switch on, whenever the functions that operate automatically (i.e. without any control by the 'I')[63] can no longer maintain the undisrupted progress of 'introversion', because they tend to succumb to disturbing stimuli intruding either from the world outside or the 'world within'. The 'waking state' is thus contrasted to what has been called 'spherical experiences', or 'spherical processes'. The capacity of apperception is an integral part of the 'waking state', but this is the opposite of experiencing by means of sense perceptions. Moreover, another capacity of the 'waking consciousness' is the power of ratiocination, which is not compatible with the mode of 'instantaneous inward awareness' either, which is inherent in the consciousness of 'introversion'. Acts of volition belong to the 'waking state' as well, and so do acts of discursive thinking, which are generally directed at some goal – all of which are active functions of the 'I', which conflict and interfere with the free-floating process of 'introversion'.

The 'dream consciousness' is an integral part of the 'sleeping state', and as such it is a blurred, hypo-alert and hypo-noetic state of consciousness. This is not only because the function of wakefulness is suspended, but also because the 'dream consciousness' is not

---

[63] Cf. Strunz, Kurt. "Über die 'Vertikale' Ordnung der Seelischen Dispositionen. Ein Beitrag zur Psychologischen Schichttheorie." *Zeitschrift für Psychologie* 154 (1943): 103-202. – Rothacker, Erich. *Die Schichten der Persönlichkeit*. 4th ed. Bonn: Bouvier, 1948.

pinpointed at a particular structured centre. From this juxtaposition we may infer another characteristic of the 'waking consciousness': All impressions perceived in it are well-ordered and oriented at some focal point.

It goes without saying that the different ways of approaching the phenomenon of the 'clarity' viz. 'lucidity' of consciousness are likely to provoke several critical objections concerning the nature of the consciousness of 'introversion'. For this reason we have to elaborate further on the phenomenology of 'introversion' by applying alternative methodological approaches.

The function of wakefulness, as outlined above, *does not belong to the realm of the consciousness encompassed by the process of 'introversion'*. This claim, however, does not allow the inference that the consciousness of 'introversion' has a lesser degree of clarity and lucidity. We generally assume that the highest degree of clarity is achieved when a cognitive act of concentration, performed in the 'waking state' by means of a coherently structured process of logical reasoning, is aimed at a specific goal. But it is precisely because any acts of thinking governed by the will are absent in the consciousness of 'introversion' that we are inclined to think that the degree of clarity and lucidity in states of 'introversion' is inferior to that in the 'waking consciousness'. I am 'clearly conscious' when I know which actions are currently carried out, and when I am clearly aware of the nature of the phenomena I am faced with. Understood in this way, it is indeed the consciousness of 'introversion' that has the highest degree of 'clarity'. The entire content encompassed by the mind – that is to say, everything that is embedded in the medium of consciousness – appears indiscriminately with the highest degree of lucidity: This is true of any phenomenon emerging in consciousness, regardless whether this is an incident of disruption, a specific impression, or a thought, feeling or emotional state, notably nuances of experiencing the all-pervasive mood of inner calmness, or whether this is some 'action' – like a meditative process, or a mental disposition directed at some goal. There is no such thing as a 'profile of clarity', but there is a scale of clarity that extends nearly across the entire realm of consciousness. It even seems to me that experiences that we are usually aware of only peripherally are put much more clearly into focus in the consciousness of 'introversion' than in the 'waking consciousness'. The 'sub-consciousness' ("Mit-Bewußtsein"), i.e. anything that is known to be concomitant with conscious modes of awareness, has a close affinity to the clear and lucid condition of the mind. During the ongoing process of 'introversion' I am always aware that I am absorbed in 'introversion' (and/or the 'quiet state of alertness'). I do know that the process of 'introversion' is oriented towards a particular direction and a specific goal. And I am aware that certain impressions are merely peripheral, because they are none of my concern. The fact that *the level of clarity of consciousness is exceptionally high in the states of consciousness encompassed by 'introversion' is a crucial characteristic of this particular consciousness.*

The high degree of 'clarity' is a persevering characteristic and indestructible 'mode' inherent in the consciousness of 'introversion'. As long as the consciousness of 'introversion' endures, it is at no time constrained, i.e. there are no intercessions by impulses to clarify certain issues cognitively, and there are no attempts at piloting the process into a particular direction. When we consider the 'dream consciousness'[64] by juxtaposing it to the 'waking consciousness', we are provided with another approach that enables us to comprehend the exceptional level of clarity of the consciousness of 'introversion'. The 'dream consciousness' is a hypo-lucid, dissociated and fragmented mental state, whereas the 'waking consciousness' is a fully integrated, focalized form of consciousness, which means that most of its processes are oriented at a particular focal point. In the 'dream consciousness' we may encounter independent dynamic clusters of impressions, and a special phenomenon, which has been termed by Kretschmer[65] the 'asyntactic, katathymic conjunction of images' ("asyntaktische, katathyme Bildverknüpfung"). There are no coherently structured cognitive processes in the 'dream consciousness'; instead, we may identify sequences of visual images surfacing at random. These images are either compact symbolic reproductions

---

64 Cf. Chapter 7 in Kretschmer, Erich. *Medizinische Psychologie.* 9th ed. Stuttgart: Thieme, 1947.

65 Cf. Chapter 7 in Kretschmer, Erich. *Medizinische Psychologie.* 9th ed. Stuttgart: Thieme, 1947.

of complex, interlinked emotional and affective processes, or, alternatively, symbolic manifestations generated by drives. The manifestation of phenomena of this kind in the 'dream consciousness' has provoked the conjecture that the consciousness of 'introversion' is not a clear state of consciousness either, as the controlling instance of discursive thinking is suspended like in the 'dream consciousness' and, therefore, it has been assumed that 'introversion' is similarly open to images and visual and emotional phenomena arising from deeper layers of consciousness. However, the fact is that both the 'consciousness of introversion' and the 'waking consciousness' differ significantly from the 'dream consciousness' in that every single impression and phenomenon contained in any of the former mental states is sustained by the concomitant awareness that the ongoing mental process is 'directed at some goal'. 'Introversion' and the 'waking consciousness' are states in which a predetermined disposition has been 'encoded', which directs the chain of associations, and integrates every single empirical occurrence into a coherent whole. We all know: The 'waking consciousness' may be impaired when certain items of experience encroach on it that cause disorder, disarray, or some discord. During the ongoing process of 'introversion' such phenomena may occasionally be witnessed in the incipient stage, but no longer in the advanced stage approaching the 'quiet state of alertness', because the advanced stage of 'introversion' is a fully integrated and coherently structured mental state. The advanced state of 'introversion' is devoid of any discordant stirrings, conflicting ideas and an adverse constellation of 'motives'. *The final state of 'introversion', 'the quiet state of alertness', can thus be claimed to be the most unified, most homogeneous and most clearly structured state of consciousness that we know; these facts corroborate the claim that the degree of 'clarity' in 'the quiet state of alertness' exceeds that of the 'waking consciousness' significantly.*

There is a third approach to the phenomenon of the hyper-clarity and hyper-lucidity of the consciousness of 'introversion'. This approach is incidentally also the point of departure of another misconception of the consciousness of 'introversion'. A basic prerequisite of the progress of 'introversion' is the need to vacate the mind from any content generated by sense perceptions; this might lead to the assumption that this process of emptying the mind may result in a deprived state of consciousness, i.e. a structure of consciousness marked by an impasse or 'narrowness', like the kind of 'narrowness' exhibited, for instance, in situations of extreme emotional turmoil, like in an outburst of hate, or of fury. In such a liminal state the affective emotions are so strong and overwhelming that there is no 'room' in consciousness left for any other 'object' to be perceived. In 'introversion', however, the process of vacating the mind from all perceptions of the world outside is never an instance of the 'narrowness of consciousness', accidentally evoked by an extreme emotional outburst, or triggered by an unduly prolonged practice of 'focalized attention'. The empty, hyper-lucid condition of the 'quiet state of alertness' rather springs from the deliberately initiated process of 'introversion', by which the mind is progressively vacated from any external stimuli, perceptions and object-related feelings. But there is another potential explanation as to how the hyper-lucid state might be generated in 'introversion': the claim that the hyper-lucid state is 'switched on' spontaneously and as such it is a side-effect when a practitioner has unduly extended the practice of 'focalized attention'. However, all of these hypothetical explanations are flawed and incorrect, not least because in the advanced stages of 'introversion' there are no sense perceptions anymore. Though ideas and thoughts may still emerge from memory and/or the subconscious, only such ideas and thoughts are 'admitted' to enter as are consonant with the overall mental condition of calmness. And this is why persons absorbed in the 'quiet state of alertness', along with the mystics, have described the experience in this serene, altered mental state in terms of 'empty clarity', or 'pure emptiness'.

There is yet another phenomenon (the fourth one) that is related to the 'pure emptiness' of consciousness: that of the subjective awareness of the extended time-span by which an object appearing in 'inner sight' in 'introversion' is perceived; this means that pace of inward perception is slowed down, and objects perceived as 'in-coming' in the space of consciousness appear to linger for quite a long time. In particular, the perception of 'calmness' 'arriving' in consciousness is an experience that tends to persevere for a long time in the person absorbed in the 'quiet state of alertness'. And the experience of calmness in the emptied consciousness is an essential precondition that enables the ultimate degree of clarity to develop in the 'quiet state of alertness'.

By way of summary we may state: **The 'quiet state of alertness' is a fully integrated, consistently uniform and emptied state of consciousness, in which all experience is slowed down to near stasis, and resulting from this, 'the quiet state of alertness' is the clearest and most lucid state of consciousness that we know.** And this is the reason why psychologists have termed this state a 'hyper-awake state of consciousness'. As the term 'wakefulness' has already been applied in our investigation, we had to introduce a different term to refer to the clear and 'quiet state of alertness', and this term is that of 'clarity' or 'hyper-lucidity'.

Dispositional Attitude[66]

A dispositional attitude is 'aiming at, or focused on, something'; it is a phenomenon that cannot be traced to any other source and, therefore, can be said to be primordial; it is an integral part of the phenomenon of attention. In order to avoid the concept of 'attention', some psychologists have opted for the term 'disposition' instead. A pivotal characteristic of a disposition is that it is directed at, and focussed on, something, and that it does not require an advanced degree of 'clarity' for a necessary condition. 'Dispositions' have been acknowledged by the psychology of consciousness as crucial phenomena. A 'disposition' is an important requirement for achieving order and wholeness in the psyche. It also provides the stable backdrop amongst the many diverse fluctuating states of our soul. The consciousness of every human being is governed by numerous dispositions, which are generally intertwined and tend to overlap. An enduring disposition may be generated by a deliberate decision or by a temporary task, arise from a person's professional status, or be created by his/her ideal of life.

When analysing a disposition, a distinction has to be made between what is consciously discerned and what is only noticed

---

66 Rohracher, Hubert. *Einführung in die Psychologie*. 3rd ed. Vienna: Urban & Schwarzenberg, 1948.

inadvertently. This means that a disposition has an important function in any process of perception. A disposition furthermore has an impact on the direction the course of associations is going to take. Dispositions are integral parts of our consciousness, not least because there is (as research has shown)[67] such a thing as 'the experience of one's disposition', that is, the awareness of 'being predisposed to something'. In the spherical backdrop of the 'sub-consciousness' there is a concomitant awareness of a given disposition. Something is present in the 'sub-consciousness' of which I know that it is known at any time though the 'experiencing I' does not have to think of it consciously.[68] A disposition is thus a free-floating, ever present component of the 'sub-consciousness', and in this sense the disposition is present only subliminally, though it can be recalled to conscious awareness at any time.

The phenomenon of dispositions is crucial to the understanding of the consciousness of 'introversion': First, because the coherent, goal-oriented progress of 'introversion' depends on a given disposition, and, secondly, because special dispositions can be incorporated or 'programmed' into the process of 'introversion' (as we shall see later). In the 'quiet state of alertness', encoded dispositions can trigger various after-effects. But as we are going to focus at this stage of our enquiry on the psychology of 'introversion' and the 'quiet state of alertness', we shall bypass here the issue of 'encoded dispositions'.

The process of 'introversion' results in the end in a completely uniform, clear, vacated and homogeneous state of consciousness. The uniformity of this state is reflected in the fact that we may no longer find dispositions which are intertwined and hierarchically arranged.[69] The only disposition remaining is the disposition to advance to the 'quiet state of alertness' and to dwell in it; this disposition continues to persevere at the background of consciousness. But it is not easy to

---

67 Strohal, Richard. "Untersuchungen zur Deskriptiven Psychologie der Einstellung." *Zeitschrift für Psychologie* 130 (1933): 1-27.

68 Rohracher, Hubert. *Einführung in die Psychologie*. 3rd ed. Vienna: Urban & Schwarzenberg, 1948.

69 Strohal, Richard. "Untersuchungen zur Deskriptiven Psychologie der Einstellung." *Zeitschrift für Psychologie* 130 (1933): 1-27.

find a suitable term for this particular disposition. – It is a disposition generated by the decision to embark on the process of 'introversion'. At the beginning of 'introversion' one may appropriately refer to it as a 'determining tendency, because it is fuelled and sustained by the determination to proceed towards the state of inner calm. But the pivotal phenomenological characteristics of this 'determining tendency' can more appropriately be described, if we focus on the feature of its 'directedness'. The intended goal of 'introversion' is the 'quiet state of alertness'; thus the person engaged in 'introversion' is predisposed to advance to this calm and homogeneous state. The person's disposition is intent on becoming absorbed in, and permeated by, inner calmness, and this disposition is sustained as long as 'introversion' is in progress. We have referred to the issue of 'directedness' earlier in the context of the desire for surrender. It is this persevering subliminal awareness of being directed at the intended goal that tends to persevere in the ongoing process of 'introversion' and becomes the experiential core of the predetermined disposition. *Although I am not consciously aware of it, I know at any time of the ongoing process of 'introversion' that my disposition is directed by the wish to become immersed by, and to surrender to, the calmness within. This unique and singular disposition controls all processes and occurrences in the ongoing process of 'introversion', and directs the path of 'introversion' towards the 'quiet state of alertness'.*

The [Free-]Floating Stream of Experience ("Fließendes Erleben")

The function of 'wakefulness'[70] shall serve once more as a touchstone for delineating the considerable differences between the consciousness of 'introversion' and the 'waking consciousness'. The 'waking consciousness' is also based on a 'layer' or 'stream' of floating sensations, in which the current experiences are rooted, which are perceived with clarity. The actions and impressions experienced include, for instance, sense perceptions, instances of 'self-awareness'

---

70 Rothacker, Erich. *Die Schichten der Persönlichkeit*. 4th ed. Bonn: Bouvier, 1948.

and 'inwardness', furthermore so-called automatic (spontaneous) responses – i.e. psychic processes floating freely and unrestrainedly through consciousness. Although all of these phenomena are consciously known to occur, they are not reflected on rationally, but merely noticed on a subliminal level. These phenomena are floating through a state of mind that is not particularly lucid, but rather marked by a reduced degree of clarity. That is to say, the function of 'wakefulness' operates only on a subliminal level. But whenever the function of 'wakefulness' is switched on, which may happen at any time instantaneously, individual phenomena and events are instantly highlighted in the 'stream' of consciousness, floating, as it were, in the twilight through consciousness. This happens, for instance, when an unwelcome, free-floating impression appears, and an instant response of 'wakefulness' will prevent it from developing further; the same mechanism applies when some discord is evoked that is not overcome in the course of the free-floating experience. This means that the (so-called) 'I-point' intervenes, and takes control whenever the function of 'wakefulness' is switched on. When the 'waking consciousness' is clear and alert, it tends to interrupt and to particularize, and to pinpoint mental processes. These are characteristics that cannot be found in the consciousness of 'introversion': As pointed out earlier, since all active functions of the 'I' are suspended in 'introversion', no such deliberate intervention in the free-floating stream of life could ever occur in the consciousness of 'introversion'.

At this stage of our enquiry we should also address the most distinctive feature of the consciousness of 'introversion': Whereas in the 'waking consciousness' the stream of experience occurs in a dimmed, hypo-alert condition of consciousness, and only pointed acts of the 'I' are executed in a state of full clarity, the consciousness of 'introversion' is marked out by the fact that all the events and phenomena are perceived in a perfectly serene and evenly lucid state. Thus the phenomenological hallmark of the consciousness of 'introversion' is that it enables the individual to perceive the free-floating stream of consciousness with an exceptionally high level of clarity; in fact it can be claimed to be the highest degree of clarity human consciousness can achieve.

This crucial insight may explain why practitioners of meditation readily agree with the metaphysical claim of Ludwig Klages[71] that deliberate acts of the 'I' are subversive to the progress of meditation, and thus 'adversaries of the soul'. Metaphysics, however, is a domain outside the field of psychology; but this remark, added here in passing, shall demonstrate that practitioners of meditation prefer to speak of the 'soul' rather than the 'I' when referring to the 'experiencing subject', not least because in meditation the free-floating stream of experience is (amongst other things) invariably tied to a state of consciousness imbued with the highest degree of clarity. *Clarity, serene and without any tarnish, and the free-floating stream of experience, undisrupted by any intervention of active functions of the 'I', are both indispensable qualities of the consciousness of 'introversion'.*

Though occasional items of 'content' and some kind of active behaviour can still be found in the incipient stage of 'introversion', the formal (phenomenological) structure of these experiences is marked by the features of clarity, lucidity and the suspension of the active functions of the 'I'. Considering the formal condition of consciousness, it is useful at this juncture to address another formal principle of experiencing in this altered state of consciousness. This is the perception of time during the process of 'introversion': This refers in particular to the 'pace' at which individual phenomena are experienced when they pass through the space of consciousness. Everyone knows that in the normal 'waking state' the 'pace' in which phenomena and perceptions are experienced when passing through consciousness is not always the same. The awareness of the time-span in which objects are perceived as dwelling in consciousness, and the awareness of the length of time taken by actions, differs in individual events, depending on the given constellation of consciousness. For instance, a feeling of hatred may just flare up for a moment on a particular occasion; but it is also possible that in another instance, hate becomes such a powerful emotion that it permeates the entire space of consciousness, and may persevere for a long time. Discursive

---

71 Klages, Ludwig. *Der Geist als Widersacher der Seele.* 4 vols. Leipzig: J. A. Barth, 1929-1932.

thoughts, by contrast, tend to stay in the 'waking consciousness' only for a short time, because they are acts of the 'I' and are therefore by nature short-lived; feelings are likewise usually only fleeting phenomena as they tend to fluctuate in the 'waking consciousness'. This explains why the 'waking consciousness' is generally replete with multifarious, continuously changing phenomena and occurrences.

The 'content' of the consciousness of 'introversion' is, by contrast, much sparser than in the 'waking consciousness', even in the incipient stage of 'introversion'. The structure of the consciousness of 'introversion' is thus much more uniform than that of the 'waking consciousness', even though in the early stage of 'introversion' some impressions may flash up and pass through the mind. Instances of disruption may likewise occur occasionally, which are triggered by the world of sense perception, and occasional snippets of thoughts may appear, flashing (as it were) like meteors across the mind. Moreover, feelings of fear and sorrow may intrude, and sometimes even complex experiences linked associatively to the subject's environment may appear, which are, however, remnants of experiences persevering from the 'waking consciousness'. But phenomena and experiences of this kind can only be encountered in the incipient stage of 'introversion', when the structure of consciousness is in part still intertwined with the 'waking consciousness'. The affinity with the 'waking consciousness' becomes also apparent in the 'pace' by which phenomena are experienced: the 'pace' in which phenomena pass through consciousness is scarcely slowed down, and thus akin to the 'pace' phenomena are experienced in the 'waking consciousness'. As the process of 'introversion' advances, however, the 'pace' of perceiving the stream-of-consciousness decelerates. The slowing down of inward perception becomes apparent in 'introversion' when the images and other items arising in consciousness begin to linger on and persevere in the 'space' of consciousness. Meditative thoughts that circulate around the visual core of inward perception, and even more so, feelings arising in consciousness are no longer subject to fluctuations or rapid change.

The more the process of 'introversion' approaches the final stage of the 'quiet state of alertness', the more 'viscous' and slowed down the stream-of-consciousness becomes. The pivotal conditions for the decelerating of inner perception are the fact that there are no more transitory impressions surfacing in consciousness, and, secondly, the fact that the mind has been completely vacated from any 'content' that typically fills the normal 'waking consciousness'. There is moreover a third feature, and this is the one I consider to be the most important: The fact that the focus of the experience is shifted from object-oriented perception to state-bound emotional awareness. The 'I' becomes aware of the current condition of the 'sphere of the self' ("Selbstsphäre"), when consciousness has been emptied and become perfectly lucid. The sense of inner calm continues to intensify and inundates more and more the 'space' of consciousness, ultimately becoming the sole prevailing 'mood'. The calmness inside fills the entire space of consciousness, absorbing and embedding any other experience, during the time the subject is immersed in the final state of 'introversion'. The rather elusive experiences in the consciousness of 'introversion' elude literal description and can only be depicted metaphorically.

While 'introversion' is in progress, the stream of experience is slowed down more and more. This implies, considering that all active processes have been suspended, that there no indicators any more that are crucial for gauging time. Thus the person absorbed in the 'quiet state of alertness' is temporarily oblivious of time, and has also lost the awareness of being engrossed in a dynamic process, and eventually feels to have reached a state of complete stasis. This liminal state is typically expressed in metaphoric terms such as 'calmness immutable'. The person absorbed in the 'quiet state of alertness' feels to be inundated by calmness, but it is an awareness of a calmness that is no longer expanding, but has come to a standstill and is all-pervasive and unchanging. Owing to such an absorbing experience, it is easy to understand that the sense of time should be (temporarily) suspended. Though the person concerned is inevitably still aware subliminally that there is such a thing as time, and that he/she is subject to time, he/she is so immersed in the immutable and unfathomable experience of the calmness within during the event that any sense of time is suspended for the time being.

The stages of consciousness antecedent to the 'quiet state of alertness' share several distinctive characteristics. Any experience is perceived in a mental state that is perfectly clear, lucid and emptied of (almost any) 'content', while the 'experiencing I' is absorbed by inner calmness and aware that this calmness is immutable and overwhelming. This rather complex experience may abide in consciousness for quite a long time, and at a heightened level of intensity.

Feelings

The concept of 'inwardness' refers to an area of experience that is considered, in genetic terms (as understood by psychologists supporting the 'layer theory'), as an early antecedent of the 'waking consciousness', and thus claimed to be a layer of primeval, non-reflective, free-floating experience. 'Inwardness' has been defined in a broader sense, as well as in a narrow sense. In the broader sense[72] 'inwardness' denotes any sub-conscious awareness, consisting, for instance, of the ever present subliminal awareness of being predisposed to something, or of the underlying spontaneous awareness that is concomitant with any activity; 'inwardness' is an integral part of any occurrence featuring in the peripheral sphere of consciousness. In the narrower, and arguably, more appropriate sense, 'inwardness' means 'to be aware of, and responsive to, feelings'. The emotion-based concept of 'inwardness' suggests that a subject's current emotional condition is instantaneously known and it is known without being reflected on. For example, when I am cheerful, I do know immediately that I am glad without having to think of what 'cheerful' means, and I know at an instant that *I* [italics in the original] am here and now in harmony with myself and in harmony with my surroundings.

The term 'feeling' is the most controversial of all psychological terms, not least because it is one of the (so-called) 'ultimate phenomena of consciousness'. The science of psychology has not yet succeeded in clearly differentiating the realm of feelings from other areas of experience. Definitions of feelings have for the most part merely resulted in theories of feelings. The empirical dimension of feelings

---

[72] Cf. Rothacker, Erich. *Die Schichten der Persönlichkeit*. 4th ed. Bonn: Bouvier, 1948.

is, however, not only indispensable to the description of experiences occurring in 'introversion', but is in many ways also essential for portraying the feelings encountered in the consciousness of 'introversion'. The ambivalence of the psychological concept of feelings, and above all, the inadequate depiction of the many varieties of feelings, would severely impede the further progress of our investigation, if it were not possible to resort to the thesaurus of our language and its great wealth of idioms, vocabularies and phrases denoting emotional experience. Psychology that does not claim to comply strictly with the linguistic standards of science may adopt expressions used in the vernacular, since its idioms and lexical jargon are more suggestive and suitable for recapturing emotional states and feelings than the scientific terminology of psychology. However, we will still rely on the insights gained by scientific psychological research on the topic of feelings and use terms coined by psychology and take them as a frame of reference, even though we are going to offer informal (and more lively) descriptions of the emotional states and feelings encountered in the process of 'introversion'.

In his study *Versuch über Fühlen und Wollen (An Attempt [at a Study] on Feelings and the Will)*,[73] Johannes Volkelt has provided an appealing, vivid and life-like account of what we call feelings. Felix Krueger[74] has suggested a definition but has approached the topic of feelings from an entirely different perspective, i.e. a purely theoretical one. Meanwhile Krueger's concepts have become widely popular and standardized [in German-speaking academe] and been commonly used in psychological enquiries into the nature of feelings. Though I have to refrain here from summarizing Krueger's terms and findings, I will consider some of his concepts later, as they are relevant and illuminating for the phenomenological analysis of the consciousness of 'introversion'.

However, a few statements from Volkelt's study shall be referred to here, since they illustrate clearly why feelings are to be classified as

---

73 Volkelt, Johannes. *Versuch über Fühlen und Wollen*. Munich: Beck, 1930. Cf. in particular 12-15, and 31.

74 Krueger, Felix. *Das Wesen der Gefühle: Entwurf einer Systematischen Theorie*. Leipzig: Akademische Verlagsgesellschaft, 1930.

'emotional states' of the 'I': "Feeling is the immediate self-awareness of the undivided condition of the 'I'." – "The feeling of joy and the feeling of grief originate from a depth that I must call the immediate experience of the I as it is itself in its I-hood." – "Specifically seen, the I does not respond to joy and grief like it does to objects. The I has neither an object, nor is it ever itself the object to be perceived." – "The I does not confront itself, neither imaginatively, nor cognitively." – "Joy is a special way of the I of experiencing and becoming aware of itself." – "We are required to see that in the immediate, undivided and unperturbed condition of the self-inwardness of the I, *consciousness reveals itself as something absolute and ultimate.*" – "The undivided inwardness of our emotional condition is a primeval mode of consciousness, a quality of consciousness that exists only for itself."

Experiences of states of feelings are commonly complex and include several 'ultimate phenomena of consciousness'. Joy is thus more rarely encountered as a singular emotional condition of the 'I' than the feeling of joy that is directed at some object. In *moments of emotional arousal* we may often find the quality of striving for something as well. "One may refer here to hope, fear, love, hate – but in these dynamic feelings we may still discern basically a condition in which the 'I' is embedded." – "A feeling is thus the core and primeval part of a state of emotional arousal. The latter is a complex experience, composed of several 'ultimate phenomena of consciousness'." – In view of the enquiries into the nature of the consciousness of 'introversion', it is necessary to distinguish between pure states of feelings – such as joy, calmness, composure, patience, awe – and feelings affiliated with an inherent striving – such as hope, aversion, or fear. – Very intense feelings, and feelings triggered abruptly, are termed affects.

The phenomenological domain of feelings is considerably more important for elucidating the processes involved in 'introversion' and specific states of consciousness than the psychological features considered previously. The analysis of the process of transformation in the realm of feelings will enable us to discern more closely how the 'quiet state of alertness' evolves from the initial 'waking consciousness'. It is helpful if we examine in the following how diverse feelings operate in successive states of consciousness. The explanations on this issue, I think, can be better understood if I begin by commenting on the process of transformation that feelings tend to undergo while 'introversion' is in progress:

1. *During the process of 'introversion' the depth of the feelings that arise in consciousness is enhanced.* The concept of 'depth'[75] is indispensable to the classification of feelings. The more deeply a single feeling is intertwined with the personality of the subject, the greater is the depth of the feeling experienced. For example, the feeling of joy evoked when one is offered an act of courtesy is not a particularly deep feeling, whereas the joy elicited when a person's love for someone is responded will move him/her deeply, i.e. the experience touches the heart, and hence is a deep emotional experience. Such an experience affects a person's values and dispositions, which establish the stable long-term structure of the personality. During the ongoing process of 'introversion' the depth of feelings grows continuously, because the 'space' of consciousness is increasingly emptied of all object-related 'content'. It would be impossible for the process of 'introversion' to advance any further, if intense adverse feelings, such as some worry or fear, were not instantly removed. The diverse feelings attached to the function of the active 'I', and the miscellaneous feelings accompanying drives, urges and aspirations in the 'waking consciousness', have no longer a 'homestead' in the vacated 'space' of the consciousness of 'introversion'. The emptied space of consciousness has become open to receive passively feelings that are consonant with the state of 'introversion'; these feelings 'arrive' in consciousness and tend to expand in depth. This explanatory comment may appear ambivalent and might be misunderstood; therefore I would like to add that the selective response to feelings that are consonant with the current state of 'introversion' does not imply any value judgement.

---

75 Krueger, Felix. *Die Tiefendimension und die Gegensätzlichkeit des Gefühlslebens*. Munich: Beck, 1931.

2. *As the process of 'introversion' advances, the feelings arising tend to dwell more and more perseveringly in consciousness.* This is the reason why affects (i.e. a gush of intense emotions) as well as short-lived feelings disappear quickly from consciousness, whereas feelings that have a state-like quality tend to persevere. The slowing down of all processes during 'introversion' is undoubtedly caused to a large extent by the prolonged space of time these feelings dwell in consciousness. In the 'waking consciousness', the 'experiencing I' is evidently aware that feelings have an impact on the emotional atmosphere permeating consciousness; moreover, the 'experiencing I' is also aware that feelings are volatile and subject to fluctuations, which will modify a given emotional condition. At the beginning of 'introversion', disrupting events, including intense emotions, or emotion-based incidents, tend to cause some disquiet and thus impede the growth of the (still fragile) mood of inner calm. Towards the end of 'introversion', however, the basic mood of inner calm has become so tenacious and persistent that any feeling conflicting with calmness is absorbed by the overwhelming calmness within, and is in this way dissolved; calmness thus becomes the stable and sustaining ground on which only such feelings are allowed to grow that harmonize with the ongoing process of 'introversion'. This means that such discordant feelings and emotional states as discomfort, fear, sorrow, restlessness and doubt can be found, if at all, only in the incipient stage of 'introversion'. Conversely, consonant feelings like joy, cheerfulness and peace tend to dwell in consciousness and may be an integral part of the advanced stages of 'introversion', which are all deeply embedded in calmness.

3. *In the course of 'introversion' the state-like components of the experience are enlarged, whereas object-related components are reduced and eventually entirely eroded.* The 'quiet state of alertness' is, phenomenologically speaking, a mental state in which a person is clearly aware that his/her current emotional condition is a uniform state of enhanced 'self-inwardness' and (inner) 'calmness'. *The 'quiet state of alertness' is thus the ultimate*

experience of inner calmness. – These statements will be corroborated shortly by some explanatory remarks.

4. *While 'introversion' is in progress, the emotion-based features of the overall experience become more pronounced compared to the empirical components elicited by other 'ultimate phenomena'.* This means that a disruption experienced in the 'waking consciousness' is an entirely different experience from a disruption perceived in any of the stages of 'introversion'. For example, when a person who is hiking on a footpath is suddenly struck by some artificial sensation of light, which appears entirely unfamiliar, the first response will affect the person's emotional condition: Before he/she is able to grasp the light phenomenon rationally, or before he/she is able to identify or assess it, he/she will be aware that an abrupt change in his emotional condition has taken place, which may elicit an exclamation such as "Oh, my gosh!". But when encountering a sense perception of this kind, it is not the emotional response that prevails, but elements of the sense perception and the process of thinking. It goes without saying that in the 'waking consciousness' there are also numerous experiences that are dominated by feelings, but it is commonplace knowledge that, on the whole, the 'waking state' is usually filled with countless objects and processes, which are hardly ever accompanied by feelings.

In the first stage of 'introversion', we usually still encounter diverse distractions caused by thoughts surfacing in the mind, or by other intrusive phenomena that are not necessarily intertwined with feelings. It is true, however, that at the early stage of 'introversion' we may at times discern complex experiences as well, in which the emotional condition is foregrounded. The example referred to earlier, i.e. the episode of a person who has failed to keep a promise to a friend, shows how powerful the feeling of remorse can be: it intrudes forcefully in consciousness and perseveres, and even occupies centre stage for some time. If such an experience occurs in the 'waking consciousness', the feelings of remorse and sorrow, as well as the sense of guilt, are immediately dealt with rationally, supported by acts of the will. Yet this experience is entirely different in the consciousness of 'introversion', in which coping with the given incident occurs in a mental state that has been vacated from all 'content', and the person concerned is passively exposed to the full intensity of grief, sorrow and remorse aroused in consciousness. This example demonstrates once more the great impact that an unwanted intrusion of emotions may have in the incipient stage of 'introversion' on the person concerned; at this early stage the troubling feelings can intrude unimpeded, and are experienced as something 'foreign'. The encounter with these feelings is perceived as a grave interference; this may happen because the basic mood of inner calm is at this stage still vulnerable and not stable enough for the disruptive and dissonant feelings to be absorbed and thus extinguished.

In the example referred to, we may still discern patterns of discursive thinking. It is a characteristic feature of the advanced stage of 'introversion' that complex forms of disruptions can arise that are not accompanied by discursive thinking anymore, but are composed entirely of feelings which are felt to be dissonant with the growing mood of inner calm. In the advanced stage of 'introversion', thoughts and impressions originating from the imagination no longer occur; what arises is a purely emotional response – coming (as it were) from its own sphere. As a consequence, a complex emotional response is elicited, in which the dominant emotions are fear and/or restlessness, though the cause(s) of which elude explanation. The person concerned does not know why he or she has been afflicted by these upsetting feelings.

The importance of feelings for the progress of 'introversion' has already been outlined, and corroborated by the findings of the current investigation: Feelings are probably the sustaining ground by which the progress of 'introversion' is nurtured. We have seen that the transformation of emotional states causes also a change in other processes involved in 'introversion'. At this stage of our enquiry there is no need to deal with any further considerations concerning the general principles by which the transformation of feelings is actually achieved. We will rather focus on the special qualities of individual feelings and examine a cross-section of the phenomena featuring in altered states of consciousness.

In order to be able to carry out these enquiries, we have to begin with a clear-cut *classification of the multifarious emotional experiences.* There is one classification that seems to serve our purpose best: It has been outlined in the study of Philipp Lersch,[76] entitled *Der Aufbau des Charakters* ('The Structure of the Character'). Lersch distinguishes (like other psychologists) between two kinds of feelings: first, feelings that are *pure* conditions of the 'I', and, secondly, *pointed* feelings, i.e. feelings intentionally directed at some object, or triggering some action. The former are "*varieties of emotional states* projected on to the world; they are state-bound emotions reflecting what moves us in this world." The latter are "moving emotional responses, endothymic experiences, in which intimate responses are released by encounters with the world." As regards the classification of 'pointed feelings', we need to remember that "the formation of psychological concepts is based on emphasis, rather than on determining criteria." We distinguish, firstly, between various forms of being moved emotionally, which are related to the 'experiencing I', and, secondly, forms of being moved emotionally related to objects. Examples of the latter include feelings that are directed at a fellow human being, and furthermore, religious, social and ethical feelings of which the 'object' has some 'spiritual' value.

As the process of 'introversion' develops further, consciousness is increasingly vacated from all object-related content. This helps us to understand the following psychological process: Feelings acquire more and more the characteristics of an emotional state, whereas pointed feelings are encountered less frequently. The more pointed feelings are directed at an object, the sooner they tend to disappear from the consciousness of 'introversion'.

Pointed Feelings

We begin the descriptive account of the different stages of 'introversion' by turning first to the emotional responses that have variously been categorised as 'personality-related feelings' or 'spiritual feelings'. They belong to the category of object-related 'pointed feelings'. The

---

76 Lersch, Philipp. *Der Aufbau des Charakters.* 3rd ed. Leipzig: Barth, 1948. See in particular 76ff. and 4.

realm of aesthetic experience and the realm of moral experience have the common characteristic that with them the emotional response is not evoked by objects of sense perception, but by abstract concepts or ideas. The question to be asked at this point is if these spiritual feelings, which are evidently deeply rooted in the personality, can also be found in the process of 'introversion'. Aesthetic feelings, to begin with, are hardly ever encountered in 'introversion', not least because the perception of aesthetic objects (which usually trigger responses like assessing something as ugly, beautiful, attractive, harmonious or disharmonious) is suspended. However, there are a few stages in the process of 'introversion' in which we may still find fleeting traces of aesthetic feelings: The process by which the structure of consciousness is transformed is unique, because the mind is more and more vacated from discord and any object-related 'content', so that consciousness becomes homogeneous and uniform; this process is directed at the ultimate goal of achieving the 'quiet state of alertness'. During this process of transformation, feelings such as pleasure and harmonious calmness can arise. This example illustrates what we shall later be concerned with in more detail: Only those feelings will survive (from amongst the entire range of emotions) and continue to dwell in consciousness for a long time that do not conflict with the ongoing process of 'introversion'.

'Pointed feelings' from the *area of ethical feelings* no longer appear in the consciousness of 'introversion'. Deep-rooted, unsettling emotions such as shame, remorse and other moral feelings are generally not part of the psychological-phenomenological structure of 'introversion'. It is possible, however, that individual ethical feelings may occasionally surface, but when this happens, these feelings are usually remnants of the 'waking consciousness'. This means that the ethical feelings accidentally surfacing in 'introversion' originate from the 'waking state' and have persevered in the incipient stage of 'introversion'. As a consequence, personality-related feelings such as shame, remorse and guilt are only transitory, and felt to interfere in the ongoing development of 'introversion', and will therefore be quickly eroded.

I would not go into so much detail about the moral feelings that are rooted in the individual personality if these considerations did not result in important insights, which will prove to be particularly relevant in the further progress of our investigation: For we may infer from the presence or absence of particular feelings if the person engaged in 'introversion' has become absorbed in the state of 'introversion' with the whole personality. Large areas of emotional states and experiences encompassed by the 'I', in particular feelings of great depth and intensity, will not be aroused unless the transformation of consciousness has advanced beyond the lower levels of 'introversion'.

The second group of object-related, pointed feelings consists of *compassion and empathy*. The feeling of empathy for someone is a 'pointed feeling'. It is (as it were) the present psychic condition of another human being that affects me instantly either with the joy, or with the grief shared between us, and which endures in me and continues to affect my 'inwardness'. The very deepest 'pointed emotions' that a human being may feel for someone else, ideally for a familiar person, or 'Thou',[77] are love and hate. When experiencing love for someone, it is not the state of the psyche of another person that touches us, but his/her very presence as a unique individual that moves us, and affects our own life, and is valued as a treasured being who gives meaning to my own existence.[78] Everybody knows from experience that there are many different ways of expressing

---

77 [Note: The German personal pronoun 'Du' has deliberately been translated here by the archaic English pronoun 'thou', to indicate that it is an intertextual reference to Martin Buber, and the philosophical meaning implied in his dialogical use of 'Thou' in his philosophy. Buber juxtaposes the relationship to a person addressed as 'Thou' to that of an ordinary human being addressed as 'you': the latter refers to a distant, impersonal relationship to the 'other', whereas 'thou' denotes an intimate, empathetic, loving and charitable bond with the 'other', i.e. one in which 'the other' is not regarded as an object or 'it', but as a unique individual with whom one is united by a spiritual (mystical) relationship. The use of 'thou' in lieu of 'you' in the translation can moreover be supported by the fact that Carl Albrecht's use of 'Du' corresponds with Buber's philosophical concept of 'thou'. Albrecht refers to Buber's *Ecstatic Confessions* in *PMB*, and it can be taken for granted that he knew Buber's *I and Thou*, as he had a copy of this book in his private library. (Cf. Buber, Martin. *I and Thou*. 1923. Trans. Ronald Smith. Edinburgh: Clark, 1937.) – FW.]

78 Lersch, Philipp. *Der Aufbau des Charakters*. 3rd ed. Leipzig: Barth, 1948. 105.

compassion and empathy, and in different degrees of intensity. There are superficial and deeply felt varieties of compassion and empathy, which are part of our 'waking consciousness'. But in the process of 'introversion', a person has left the 'waking consciousness' behind, and is not only removed from the 'primordial realities of the spiritual' ("Urwirklichkeiten des Geistigen"),[79] which affect us when we are overwhelmed by aesthetic or ethical experiences, but also from any relationship with a fellow human being. In the consciousness of 'introversion' there is no experience of a relationship to a 'thou' (or 'you' retrospectively) anymore, because the person immersed in 'introversion' is solely absorbed in his/her own 'inwardness'. Therefore we may state as an important finding: *While 'introversion' is in progress, any form of experience becomes 'impoverished', i.e. consciousness is increasingly emptied of all concrete experiences.* The most differentiated and most ramified experiences encountered in the 'waking consciousness' no longer occur in the consciousness of 'introversion'. Even experiences that are sustained by feelings of greatest depth and intensity – i.e. feelings by which we are shattered, aroused, moved or paralysed – are conspicuously absent in 'introversion'. We may therefore propose the provisional claim (without implying any value judgement) that one of the pivotal features of the consciousness of 'introversion" is that it undergoes a transformation leading towards the complete cessation of experiencing.

The claim that the most differentiated and deepest social experiences are no longer found in the consciousness of 'introversion' does not conflict with the earlier claim that all emotional experiences acquire greater depth in the course of 'introversion', because the underlying mood of inner calm, which permeates, embeds and affects all empirical occurrences, does not allow superficial emotions and stirrings to remain in consciousness. Thus cheerfulness is transformed into gaiety, whereas listlessness and moroseness are transformed resulting in a state of sadness. However: the calmness filling the consciousness of 'introversion' keeps its exceptional level of depth throughout the process. The calmness within thus transforms all modes of experience during the process of 'introversion'

---

79 [Note: Albrecht does not indicate the source. – FW.]

as it dissolves and 'silences' all disrupting occurrences and phenomena, and even sets limiting strictures on what is to be experienced. This means that intense negative emotions – such as anger, fear and despair – are entirely banned from consciousness, and so are all positive emotions related to a 'thou'. In the advanced state of 'introversion', the long-term dispositions that have determined our enduring relationship and attitudes to a 'thou' in the 'waking consciousness', and all the attitudes to the values and the meaning of our existence encoded in the 'waking consciousness', are no longer perceived to be relevant while 'introversion' advances. This means that the 'I' of 'introversion' is exclusively referred back to itself. Hence only those 'pointed feelings' can survive in the advanced stage of 'introversion' that are related to the 'I', and known to be of special value for the 'I'.

By the term 'inverted-reference' of 'pointed feelings' we do not understand a cognitive process at all, nor a process of self-reflection. 'Inverted-reference' does not involve any act of thinking, but refers back to one's own self in an attempt to elucidate the 'sphere of the I'; it is an emotional response to an inner state of feeling, i.e. the 'feeling of a person's current state of feeling'. For instance, the practitioner's joy when he/she can feel the calmness within grow in intensity and scope, or the awareness of the benefits of residing in inner calmness, or the awareness of the benefits achieved by the process of calming down, or the feelings of contentment and fulfilment evoked in the event, are all typical emotional responses evoked when the 'experiencing I' is more and more deeply immersed in inner calmness. – The feeling of 'inwardness' in the 'I' is experienced intuitively in that the given state of 'inwardness' becomes (as it were) the object of inner perception, and the source from which the 'feeling of its own state of feeling' originates. The feelings of joy, contentment, as well as the first inklings of rapture induce the 'I' to turn inward spontaneously; and this spontaneous response encompasses the immediate, non-cognitive awareness of the current emotional condition.

In order to be able to fully assess *the importance of the 'inverted reference' of feelings to the subject's self* in 'introversion', we need to bear in mind that the act of turning to one's emotional state within the 'sphere of the self' occurs when the mind has attained a high degree of 'clarity', i.e. a 'clarity' that can never be achieved in the normal 'waking consciousness'. In the advanced stage of 'introversion' the space of consciousness has been emptied entirely from sense perceptions, discursive thinking and pictures of the imagination; this vacated mental state allows feelings and emotional responses to be experienced with a heightened degree of intensity as well as with exceptional clarity. The feelings and emotional responses evoked in this state are the only remaining objects perceived by the 'inner eye'. These emotions do not become the objects of rational reflection, but are the only 'subject matter' observed intuitively in consciousness with ultimate clarity. I specifically emphasize this fact because it will turn out to be important later, when we are going to deal with the phenomenon of 'inner sight' ("Innenschau").

There are many varieties of feelings that can be identified as immediate experiences emanating from the 'sphere of the self'. These feelings include both emotions that are consonant with the ongoing process of 'introversion' and feelings that are incompatible with 'introversion' because they are negatively connoted. The latter include, for instance, sadness, sorrow, anxieties, embarrassment or distrust, and personal feelings of doubt as to whether the current process of 'introversion' will be successful. Negative feelings of this kind are often closely affiliated with the sense of personal inadequacy, i.e. an (apparent) lack of self-esteem. Negative feelings impair, or may ultimately even destroy, the progress of 'introversion'. Conversely, positive emotional responses have the opposite effect: Hope, anticipation, joy and self-confidence produce an emotional setting that is consonant with the inner calmness inundating consciousness.

At the beginning of 'introversion' there is often some dissonance between the calmness emanating from the 'sphere of the self', and occasional disruptive feelings surfacing in consciousness. However, it is a typical feature of the homogeneous structure of 'introversion' that the calmness arising in it tends to elicit only emotional responses of a positive kind. The experience of calmness inundating consciousness embraces also germs of joy, contentment as well as happiness and cheerfulness. On the other hand, negative emotions such as grief, sorrow and shyness, which is often affiliated with a lack of self-esteem, are removed from consciousness as 'introversion' develops. This is achieved in a threefold manner: First, disruptive emotions are progressively eliminated in a person engaged in 'introversion', because he/she is screened off from the outside world, and thus there are no sense impressions, no impressions from the imagination, nor discursive thoughts any longer, which might fuel the person's lack of self-esteem; as a consequence, feelings of unease dissipate and are eventually dissolved. Secondly, the calmness arising within has various nuances, but they all will converge as 'introversion' progresses so that the calmness finally results in an all-pervasive emotional state, which is stable and enduring and absorbs any phenomenon that does not harmonize with it. Thirdly, the person immersed in 'introversion' is intent on achieving the ultimate state of inner calm (determined by the disposition 'encoded' in the mind before embarking on the process of 'introversion'), and this mental predisposition, though experienced at times in terms of a stirring, is yet another 'pointed feeling', albeit one imbued with a rare sense of trust.

We may summarize the insights gained from these considerations as follows: *During the process of 'introversion' a transformation takes place in the area of feelings, in which object-related feelings are removed increasingly from consciousness, whereas pointed feelings, which refer back to the sphere of the self, become more and more predominant at the same time; and, secondly, within the varieties of 'pointed feelings' it is particularly the ones that grow in depth and intensity that are enriching for the subject's individual existence, because they are positively oriented at the future.*

Non-Object-Related Feelings [States of Emotional Awareness] ("Das Zumutesein")

The focus in the following considerations is put on the category of feelings which are, in essence, *emotional states of the 'I'*. These emotional states are evoked spontaneously in a person immersed in 'introversion' after having turned into his/her inwardness. When entirely absorbed in 'inwardness', the 'I' is permeated, infused, overwhelmed and shattered by emotional states surfacing in consciousness. Generally speaking, while 'introversion' is in progress the following may happen to a practitioner: *During the ongoing process of 'introversion' the range of the emotional states inundating the consciousness of the 'experiencing I' continues to grow. The emotional states dwelling in consciousness tend to linger and expand, whereas emotional responses to impressions or phenomena appearing in consciousness become fewer and fewer, and have less and less impact on the overall experience.*

Until now it has been possible to describe the experiences encountered during the process of 'introversion' by the use of scientific language. The complex and multifarious emotional states and experiences emerging in 'introversion', however, can no longer be adequately described by the language of science, which is why we have to adopt the speech of poets and mystics, which is more flexible and elaborate. In the following, passages taken from the spontaneous utterances of a person spoken while absorbed in 'introversion' will be quoted; the passages quoted are put in quotation marks and printed in italics.[80]

I begin the description with emotional states that are strictly speaking not yet part of the experience of the process of 'introversion', since they are incongruous with the state of inner calm that emerges gradually during 'introversion'. In particular, three state-like emotions will be considered, which are helpful for exploring specific features of the consciousness of 'introversion' at greater depth. These emotional states are grief, angst[81] and restlessness.

---

80 [Note: In the German text Albrecht does not use italics; in the translation, however, italics are used throughout for all quotations taken from personal records spoken by practitioners while absorbed in states of 'introversion' to differentiate them graphically from the text of Albrecht's critical analysis of these records. – FW.]

81 [Note: The translation of the German word 'Angst' by the identical German loan-word in English rather than by words 'fear' or 'anxiety' is imperative here, as Albrecht distinguishes explicitly terminologically between 'Angst' and 'Furcht'. He uses these terms as defined by existentialist philosophy, notably by Kierkegaard and Heidegger (Albrecht refers to both philosophers in *PMB*). 'Fear' is thus evoked by a real threat, and this emotion will be removed as soon as the cause of fear has disappeared (e.g. a burglar discovered in one's home will instantly cause fear; but the fear disappears as soon as the burglar has gone or been captured). – 'Angst', by contrast, is an existential emotion that is deeply engrained in human consciousness on a subliminal level, and thus can surface anytime anywhere; it may be released, for instance, in situations involving some moral choice, or when a person is facing the

Grief is an emotion that is diametrically opposed to, and interfering in, the sphere of calmness emerging in the incipient stage of 'introversion'. But as 'introversion' advances, grief is gradually embedded in, and eventually becomes absorbed by the calmness permeating consciousness. This means that grief is transformed in the process, i.e. grief is modified and assimilated to the state of inner calmness, which indicates that the awareness of the particular directedness of grief towards someone or something disappears. The state of grief expands to reach a level of 'depth' and intensity equal to that of inner calm. Grief thus is experienced as an emotional state adhering to the calmness within. Grief finally becomes an integral part of the emotional condition permeating 'introversion' and is fully assimilated to, and eventually extinguished by, the all-pervasive calmness within.

Considering the transformation of grief during the process of 'introversion', we are alerted to a phenomenon that has not yet been explicitly addressed: The tendency of feelings and emotions to persevere in consciousness as the process of 'introversion' progresses. This means that a feeling evoked in the 'waking consciousness' with a particular intensity continues to dwell in consciousness, and will persevere in the incipient stage of 'introversion'. At the beginning of 'introversion' it is particularly feelings and emotional states that have been so dominant in the 'waking consciousness' as to obfuscate any other experience. In the incipient stage of 'introversion' we may therefore still encounter feelings and emotional states such as being worried, feeling genuine concern for someone, or feeling anger, displeasure, frustration or having misgivings about one's own situation, the awareness of one's own negligence or weakness, some harm inflicted by someone, or being overcome by dejection – emotions and feelings of this kind may intrude in consciousness at the outset of 'introversion'. But when 'introversion' progresses, the mind becomes fully screened off against the world outside, and the person engaged

---

'last things', or when someone is suddenly overcome by a sense of the 'meaninglessness' or 'absurdity' of human existence (in the sense of Camus), or by the awareness of the 'eternal abyss'. 'Angst', unlike 'fear' and 'anxiety', is thus a non-directional emotion and hence an 'ultimate phenomenon of consciousness', which has no specific objective cause. – FW.]

in 'introversion' is more and more immersed in inner calmness, until all responses to the world have become eclipsed. What may persevere in the incipient stage is the feeling of nostalgia, i.e. a pensive, melancholy mood may surface, which is however soon enfolded in and harmonized with the prevailing mood of inner calmness. There are two ways in which this melancholy emotion can be harmonized with the calmness within:

The melancholy mood can tune in with qualities of the calmness arising from the bodily sphere. Thus, for example, the heaviness of the body in repose may chime in with the lingering sense of sadness. And there is indeed a variety of calmness that has been described in terms of a 'heavy calmness', or a 'dark, oppressing calmness'. Moreover, the sense of *'being overwhelmed by melancholy in the midst of lucid calmness'*, and the sense of equanimity arising from it, have an emotional quality in which sadness and the sense of gloom become harmonized. From this point in the development, there is one path that leads towards the state of *'empty* calmness', through *'the boundless feeling of silence'*, to the experience of *'silence devoid of any rushing wind'* permeating the final state of 'introversion', resulting in a state of *'poised clarity'*.

The second path by which grief can be dissolved is by means of a meditative technique – that is to say, by applying a specific method of meditation that is aimed at eliminating grief. This can best be illustrated by referring to an authentic report, in which the practitioner focuses on the somatic aspects accompanying the changes in his emotional condition: The calmness arriving in consciousness is in this case permeated by lucidity, cheerfulness and serenity. *"From deep inside arises an abysmal sense of relief and of being (physically) alleviated"* – *"the dark, strong and heavy texture becomes luminescent, transformed into a soft web of clearest luminescence. The cold, bulky mass is transformed into a warm, hovering lightness. Even when some time later some oppressive weight is felt again, the sensation quickly subsides and becomes absorbed by a lightness – [an all-pervasive] sense of ease."* – *"Pure clarity is inhaled and blended with surrender"* – *"the act of breathing freely and cheerfully causes the fetters and the constraining strings around the heart and lungs to melt"* – *"the blood is welling and the body aglow with delight – both are at ease"* – *"joy is flooding in like through soundless gateways"* – *"the sense of being saturated with solid bliss"* – *"the dissolving of a rigid pattern gives birth to calmness"*. From this results a state in which the practitioner is *"standing in silence, full of awe"* – *"a warm sense of reposing within myself"* – *"all painful and melancholy past being gone"* – [*filled by a sense of*] *"wholeness"*.

As 'introversion' progresses, the *"stream of reposeful bliss"* merges with an emotional state that can be best described [by metaphors such as] *"empty calmness"* – *"silent nothingness"* – or *"dwelling in tranquillity serene"*.

The varieties of calmness depicted here are all tinged with perceptions of the vital functions as well as with feelings of vitality; these emotional responses have such a great impact on the subject that the feelings of grief and melancholy, which had previously haunted him/her and intruded from the 'waking consciousness', are entirely removed in the advanced state of 'introversion'.

Before talking about 'angst' and 'restlessness', we have to make some important statements pointing at the way ahead in this investigation:

1. *During the process of 'introversion' the object-like quality of calmness is transformed into a state-like character. Towards the end of 'introversion' calmness has become a pure condition of the 'I' – a serene state of calmness, which is "the only emotion permeating and sustaining experience"*.[82]

2. The experience of calmness in 'introversion' has a core[83] to which an increasing number of impressions and phenomena become attached, which all harmonize with calmness.

3. Having once been evoked, the complex experience of calmness is perceived with great clarity; it becomes ever more easily

---

82 Krueger, Felix. *Das Wesen der Gefühle: Entwurf einer Systematischen Theorie.* Leipzig: Akademische Verlagsgesellschaft, 1930.
83 Störring, Gustav. *Über Grundfragen der Medizinischen Psychologie.* Düsseldorf: Renaissance Verlag, 1948.

accessible, if 'introversion' is practiced regularly. Consecutive sessions of 'introversion' will establish associations and generate automatic physiological [and neuropsychological] patterns, which facilitate the transformation of consciousness from the 'waking state' to the altered states of consciousness encompassed by 'introversion'.

What has been said so far may further be illustrated by referring to visual images: The 'I-point' is the focal point of experience, and the centre or 'ground of consciousness', whereas the space of consciousness surrounding the 'I-point' is almost entirely empty of any 'content' in the advanced stage of 'introversion'. As 'introversion' is advancing, calmness arises first from the sphere of the body and moves towards the 'I-point', which is open to receive it. The calmness is perceived like an object approaching, to which the 'I' is willing to yield entirely. As a consequence, a centre of calmness (which has by now gained state-like quality) will emerge around the 'I', and establish a stable 'sphere of the self' ("Selbstsphäre"). The 'sphere of the self' thus becomes a constant mirror, while the 'ground' around it still abounds with fluctuating impressions and feelings. When reposing in calmness the 'I' becomes a receptive 'inwardness', which, once achieved, can always be taken recourse to, because this condition is stored in memory. The deep sense of 'inwardness' becomes a familiar and intimate haven of confidence, safety and reassurance. And this is what is meant by the expressions "*intimate calmness*" and "*comforting realm of calmness*" in the records quoted.

Angst [dread] and restlessness are different state-like emotions. None of them can ever be entirely dissolved by the basic mood of inner calmness. When these emotions surface in 'introversion', they must either be removed by the meditative process described above, or be in some other way isolated from the ongoing process of 'introversion'. When referring to 'angst', one is inevitably reminded of the philosophical concepts of Kierkegaard[84] and Heidegger.[85] The definition

---

84 Kierkegaard, Søren. *Der Begriff Angst*. 1844. Jena: Diederichs, 1923.
85 Heidegger, Martin. *Sein und Zeit*. 1927. 2nd ed. Halle: Niemeyer, 1929.

of 'angst' provided by Philipp Lersch[86] is likewise a philosophical rather than a psychological one. According to Lersch, 'angst' is "an emotional state of confinement", in which an individual's "personal existence is immediately threatened by the anonymous power termed nothingness." Angst "is an emotional state aroused by the feeling that human existence is just about to be devoured by the anonymous abyss of nothingness."

Psychologically speaking, I wish to emphasize that 'angst' is definitely not a 'pointed feeling', but a state of arousal evoked by an existential mood, which may be intertwined with the feeling of despair, i.e. the sense of being assailed by doubt per se, hence a condition in which all confidence and self-assurance have completely been lost. – It may happen, and it has indeed happened to a considerable number of practitioners of 'introversion', that they are overcome by a very deep feeling of 'angst'; some subjects were even exposed to paroxysms of 'angst' and trembling soon after having embarked on the process of 'introversion', and after they had been screened off from the stimuli of the world outside. In the 'waking consciousness', by comparison, 'angst' is generally submerged under, or repressed by, the multifarious impressions dominating the 'waking state' – such as objects of sense perception, acts of the will or discursive thinking. But while 'introversion' is in progress, 'angst' may invade consciousness without any restraint, and it may thus gain unprecedented intensity, and may arouse agonizing and disconcerting responses, which do not only disrupt but terminate the ongoing process of 'introversion'.

It is, however, not in line with the overall conception of this study to provide a full description of the process of 'introversion'; nor does this study intend to offer instructions for the practice of 'introversion'. Therefore it is not necessary to elaborate further here on the phenomenological description of 'angst', and how to cope with 'angst' when one is confronted by it in the process of 'introversion'. It should be enough to state the fact that 'angst' can surface so forcefully during the process of 'introversion' that it will terminate its further progress, unless the practitioner succeeds in generating a

---

86   Lersch, Philipp. *Der Aufbau des Charakters*. 3rd ed. Leipzig: Barth, 1948. Quotation 57ff.

deep and stable sense of repose, so that the calmness permeating the 'sphere of the self' provides a safe haven and in this way 'angst' can be kept at the periphery of consciousness. This means that the 'sphere of the self' may be the starting point of the 'I' for removing 'angst' by means of a meditational practice focussing on the feeling of 'angst'. By applying this method of confining 'angst' in consciousness, 'angst' may be kept at bay and can be isolated at the periphery of consciousness. This stratagem allows the process of 'introversion' to proceed, and inner calm to permeate all recesses of the mind so that, finally, 'angst' is completely extinguished.

Restlessness is a phenomenon composed of several layers. Restlessness may, for instance, become clearly conscious only after the process of 'introversion' has started. Restlessness is, first and foremost, a feeling of vitality originating from a somatic sense of unrest; feeling fidgety is a rather common phenomenon shared by many individuals. The success or failure of a person's process of 'introversion' depends on whether the practitioner is able to overcome restlessness meditatively, and to replace it gradually by the state of inner calm. Restlessness is, secondly, also a widespread and a pivotal emotion in the 'waking consciousness': It is aroused by worries, anxieties, troublesome ideas, stressful activities and other stressful incidents, as well as by situations in everyday life. Restlessness, having once been aroused, tends to dwell in the mind and thus has a negative effect on the development at the incipient stage of 'introversion'. On the other hand, the restlessness originating from the 'waking consciousness' can be overcome relatively easily, and be swiftly transferred into a dormant state, by the ongoing process of 'introversion'. Restlessness – like 'angst' – can, thirdly, be aroused by or arise from the 'depths of one's existence'; the difference is, however, that restlessness – unlike 'angst' – is, metaphorically speaking, an edifice with many apartments, in which diverse emotional qualities reside without being seen, i.e. that cannot be perceived consciously. Restlessness that is deep-seated, i.e. erupting from the depths of one's existence, can only be removed by applying the mental techniques described above when dealing with 'angst'.

I am aware that the phenomenological description of 'angst' and 'restlessness' provided here is, from a scientific point of view, psychologically not quite adequate, because it relies in part on hypostatical claims, incorporates value judgements and is in part informed by concepts derived from philosophical hermeneutics.

The Second Stage of 'Introversion'

Calmness is, first of all, a feeling of the vital functions, which is rooted in the awareness of the body – which is again an essential characteristic of the process of 'introversion'. It is the perception-like character of calmness that accounts for the fact that calmness is experienced as 'arriving' in the realm of consciousness. Therefore calmness is first perceived as an object-like phenomenon. Calmness is, secondly, the pivotal component of the final state of consciousness at which 'introversion' is directed. Therefore it can be said that the calmness within determines the entire process of 'introversion'. Calmness is, thirdly, the emotional 'foundation' permeating the 'experiencing I' in the final state of 'introversion', termed 'quiet state of alertness'. The calmness within is the stable, unswerving and all-pervasive emotional condition inundating consciousness in the 'quiet state of alertness' ("Versunkenheit"); it is a kind of calmness that is enduring, immutable, and sustaining the 'quality of the whole experience'[87] in 'introversion'. But calmness also has an impact on the development of 'introversion' in that it actually controls its progress. In the 'quiet state of alertness', calmness is no longer the intended goal, but has acquired the capacity to inundate and expand all over consciousness. Calmness thus colours, assimilates and transforms any phenomenon that appears in consciousness. This latter capacity can best be illustrated by an account describing the condition of consciousness at the second stage of 'introversion'. So far we have only mentioned that the second stage of 'introversion' differs from the first stage because in it disrupting incidents have been eliminated and distracting phenomena are no longer perceived. But the second stage is not the ultimate goal of the process of 'introversion', and thus it differs from the ultimate stage, the 'quiet state of alertness', in that the ongoing

---

87 Krueger, Felix. *Das Wesen der Gefühle: Entwurf einer Systematischen Theorie.* Leipzig: Akademische Verlagsgesellschaft, 1930.

stream of events perceived in it has not yet reached complete stasis, though it is slowing down continuously. Moreover, on the second stage of 'introversion', the homogeneously structured, unperturbed space of consciousness has reached an exceptionally high degree of clarity. Disruptions of any kind are barred from entering consciousness. As a consequence, there is neither an interference by sense perceptions, nor by digressing thoughts, nor by ideas surfacing from the imagination evoked by association, nor are there any disruptions originating from remnants of the 'waking consciousness'. And there are no feelings anymore that might erupt from the current emotional condition of the 'I', or from memory.

As all potentially disruptive events have been suspended on the second stage of 'introversion', the cause for another potential response has likewise been removed: There is neither an impulse nor a stirring anymore in the 'experiencing I' to govern the progress of 'introversion'; the practitioner is no longer required to approve or disapprove of an in-coming event or an impression. The space of consciousness has reached the highest level of clarity, having been vacated from all object-related content and from any conscious activity. What remains as the last vestige of 'content' is the inclination to open up and surrender to the calmness within. What remains is, in other words, a purely receptive attitude, with the 'I' being disposed to surrender to the calmness inside. The 'experiencing I' is at this stage aware only of its current emotional condition and experiences the ongoing stream of 'introversion' only on the emotional level. The sole function of the 'I' at this stage is to grasp intuitively and with perfect clarity the state of 'inwardness', untainted by any rational reflection. But as the ultimate stage of 'introversion', i.e. the 'quiet state of alertness', has not yet been reached, inward perception and the stream of consciousness have not yet arrived at the stage of complete stasis. In this penultimate stage the ground of consciousness, though perceived with a very high degree of clarity, is still experienced as afloat and in motion. Though the stream of consciousness has considerably decelerated, ultimate stasis and, with it, the mental condition of 'empty calmness' have not yet been achieved. Diverse rare and conflicting emotions are still aroused in consciousness, which fluctuate between happiness and depression, feeling safe and secure, or lonesome. Moreover, the 'experiencing I' is overwhelmed by the longing to surrender to someone in perfect trust.

On the basis of the background knowledge provided so far, we may now deal with the most distinctive characteristic of the second stage of 'introversion': The mode of *experience has become pictorial, i.e. image-based*. This means that the stream of emotional responses becomes manifest in images (which have no symbolic import) that represent in literal or metaphoric terms features of the ongoing transformation of consciousness. A typical sequence of images appearing on the second stage of 'introversion' has the following pattern: Emotional responses, succeeded by visual representations, which have no physical characteristics, followed by structured, cognitive responses, and finally, inward experience becoming incarnate in spoken words, which are articulated more or less coherently. – Another typical sequence has the pattern: An emotional response is evoked and followed by a single word that surfaces in the mind and which recaptures the qualities of the preceding emotional response; this is in turn followed by images 'crystallising' (as it were) around the root of the word that has surfaced, with the images becoming attached to the word. These emotion-based phenomena are experienced in a state of heightened 'clarity'; the sequence by which individual impressions appear in consciousness is directed by a process of associations operating concurrently: The images that surface in consciousness are linked with each other on the basis of the given affinity with the underlying emotion. A change on the level of feelings will trigger images from memory (or other reproductive functions of consciousness), which are in part based on previous sense perceptions, and in part on images originating from the realm of fantasy. Though it is true that there are processes of association in the 'waking consciousness' as well which arise from a given emotional link with a picture from the imagination, on the whole, in 'introversion' the overall experience is governed mainly by the basic principles of association, i.e. the principle of contiguity and affinity. Though the range of feelings eliciting a chain of associations is expanded already the first stage of 'introversion', a considerable range of associations, as well as thoughts and impressions that are evoked in the process are still controlled by formal principles inherent in the patterns of association.

As 'introversion' progresses within the second stage, the image-based mode of experiencing enlarges continuously until it encompasses the entire space of consciousness. Every single image tends to dwell in the mind for quite a long time, and is observed by the function of 'inner sight' in hyper-lucid clarity. This of course does not mean that the mode of inner perception is at any moment shifted from the inward perception of images to the sensual perception of images; the experience occurs exclusively in the inner domain of consciousness: an image arising in the mind and dwelling in it for a long time is discerned and observed in 'inner sight', and it is the sole 'object' of perception.

The underlying mood of calmness can be said to unfold in a series of 'static' pictures, which can be recovered any time later (even many years later) in a process of 'introversion'. – Specific images can be exchanged by other pictures in the process. For example, the picture of a meadow observed at eventide and evoking a deep sense of hush and tranquillity may be followed by the picture of a lake spreading out beneath a starry sky, featuring as a shining mirror of the surrounding landscape. 'Static images' of this kind become more and more distinctive as 'introversion' advances. Anything that is inwardly perceived on the second stage of 'introversion' is based on pictures of this kind. A boat gliding slowly through the shining waters of a lake is an image corresponding to the underlying emotional state that is replete with the sense of silence and peace in a person who has become immersed in the advanced stage of 'introversion'.

It is important to emphasize at this point that the process of translating intuitions into emotionally consonant images during 'introversion' differs fundamentally from symbolic modes of perception, notably those occurring in the 'dream consciousness': The 'dream consciousness' is a disordered, non-directional, disintegrated state of consciousness, composed of disparate fragments of impressions and of individual phenomena that have become separated. The 'dream consciousness' is a somnolent state, and thus it is a mental condition in which the degree of clarity is significantly diminished. The images surfacing in it are, on the whole, symbolic representations of unconscious desires, strives or urges. A particular symbol is actually often a complex symbol composed of several images that are fraught with multifarious symbolic meanings. The consciousness of 'introversion', by contrast, is the most coherently structured state of consciousness we know. The images appearing in it do not emerge from the unconscious and, therefore, do not consist of clusters of isolated, incoherent images. Moreover, the images that appear during 'introversion' cannot be utilized for the purposes of psychoanalysis (unlike the images appearing in dreams). The reason is that *the images* becoming manifest in 'introversion' *have no symbolic import, but are rather the embodiments of the given emotional condition, or the expressions of responses evoked by the progress of 'introversion' itself.* These images allow us to assess the progress of 'introversion' while advancing towards the ultimate state of inner calm.

What has been stated above shall now be illustrated by a passage taken from a personal record spoken while the person was absorbed in the process of 'introversion'. It took the person about thirty minutes to articulate the recorded passage. At the beginning there is a hint at some disturbance, which demonstrates clearly that the person's 'predetermined disposition' to advance towards the state of inner calm is instantly released for the purpose of preserving the progress of 'introversion'; the recorded passage also shows that the person's 'predetermined disposition', which was encoded in the mind prior to embarking on the process of 'introversion', continues to persevere:

> "The structures sustaining the I have faded – and the connecting strings to the world are no longer felt, and seem to be asleep – the striving of the will likewise appears to be asleep.
>
> *Because of – – – a profane worry has intruded – but it has meanwhile subsided and been overcome by trust. With silent footsteps I have come to face night eternal . . .*
>
> *The stillness of eternal night embraces a mystery, like the secret behind the unceasing commotion of the sea, or like the salutary, unbroken, shining brightness of star-like existence. Thus I am wandering towards the silence that lies asleep, and in doing so, I open up to the growing stillness inside me, to the lessening of all desires and emotions, and all corporality, surrendering only to a single yearning: to be seized and caressed by the Ultimate Power.*
>
> *All tension has disappeared. I am salvaged, the boat moves on without me steering. And the waters that keep it afloat are radiant with the serene light emanating from the streams of the Ur-water that is approaching slowly . . .*
>
> *At every oar's stroke a ribbon is disbanded from the figure's shape. Each stroke of the oar causes trembling in the person waiting humbly, willing to surrender.*

> *And the barge is gliding on without a helm – makes the eye-lids close slowly and happily on the receptive soul, who is waiting in silence, filled with devotion without any desire.*
>
> *And the very last stroke of the oar, the softest one of all, renders the soul awestruck and calm.*"[88]

The descriptive analysis of the 'second stage' of 'introversion' has yielded a number of important insights:

1. The psychology of 'introversion' has discerned a process that can best be termed a process of *gathering and accumulating experiences of calmness*. 'Calmness' is indeed the key-word and the focal point at which all feelings, all images arising from the imagination, as well as all elementary cognitive processes are directed. Earlier experiences of calmness stored in memory are now recalled. New emotional experiences become manifest in images, which can later be reproduced at any time. Judgements and thoughts are related to the appropriate frame of reference within the given process of 'introversion'. The awareness of the calmness within becomes more and more intense as 'introversion' advances. In this process diverse sequences of associations are released. The experiential core includes moreover perceptions of the body, and the clear awareness that 'introversion' proceeds into a particular 'direction', i.e. the 'experiencing I' perceives that 'introversion' advances towards the intended goal, 'encoded' at the beginning, and submits willingly to the ongoing process. Therefore it is easy to understand that this complex experiential core, which continues to intensify as to become encompassing, should have a crucial impact on the present, and even more so, on the future development of the process of 'introversion'.

---

88 [Note: Italics provided. Here as elsewhere in the book, passages from the so-called "Versunkenheitsaussagen", i.e. spontaneous utterances spoken by a person while absorbed in the process of 'introversion', and therefore, transmitted without any of the rational faculties of the 'waking state' intervening, which were either simultaneously written down truthfully by a trusted bystander (either the physiotherapist or a confidant/e), or recorded on tape, have been highlighted graphically to set them off against Albrecht's explanatory comments and analytical statements. – FW.]

2. 'Awareness' ("Bewußtheit") is defined as the knowledge that something is here and now immediately present in consciousness, albeit only in a non-visual (abstract, intuitive) manner. But the *process of 'introversion' is attended by numerous kinds of 'awareness'*: For instance, I know that I am involved in a process of 'introversion', and that all active functions of the 'I' have been suspended; I am likewise aware that the course of 'introversion' is developing accordingly, unperturbed by any interference, as well as that consciousness has achieved a heightened degree of clarity, and that the flow of experience is gradually slowing down, that the fluctuations of feelings have almost entirely subsided, and that the ultimate condition of inner calmness is no longer far away. All these intuitive perceptions are varieties of what is here understood by 'awareness', because I am all the time aware of all of these components of the overall experience. In other words, 'I know without being aware that I know these things'[89]. These modes of awareness operate at the 'background' of consciousness and are thus imparted in the 'peripheral sphere' of consciousness. They function on a 'subconscious' level, i.e. they are present in the mind without being consciously recovered from memory. The different kinds of 'awareness' are parts of the stream-of-consciousness, and convey knowledge that is non-visual and non-discursive, i.e. knowledge that is not the result of reasoning or rational reflection. The diverse modes of awareness thus supply the person engaged in 'introversion' with ample intuitive information relating to his/her actual situation in space and time.

3. *The process of 'introversion' has – for methodological reasons – been subdivided into two levels, which means that this differentiation is inevitably a psychological-phenomenological construct.* In empirical reality, however, any mental state has more varied phenomenological features than those captured by the theoretical model. Even so, the stages of the consciousness of 'introversion'

---

89 Rohracher, Hubert. *Einführung in die Psychologie*. 3rd ed. Vienna: Urban & Schwarzenberg, 1948. 340.

identified phenomenologically do nonetheless serve as an important theoretical frame of reference, since each of these states provides a tangible systematic structure within the wide elusive expanse of consciousness. This classification is particularly helpful in delineating the process of 'introversion' of an individual practitioner. A similar approach has been taken in identifying the so-called 'ultimate phenomena of consciousness', notably the phenomenon of the imagination, and the impulse-like quality of the responses. The latter have likewise been split up into categories as otherwise a systematic description of these very complex and elusive experiences could not have been achieved. But again, it should be emphasized that we do not encounter such clear-cut stages of 'introversion' in empirical reality. In empirical reality 'introversion' is a single, coherent, ongoing and clearly structured process directed at a particular goal. Moreover, the various 'stages' of 'introversion' tend to overlap and are intermingled in empirical reality, and this is the reason why they cannot be sharply divided. These reservations aside, the individual 'stages' of 'introversion' still enable us to explore and elucidate systematically the distinctive psychological and phenomenological characteristics pertaining to the underlying mental processes and states of consciousness involved in the process of 'introversion'.

'The Quiet State of Alertness' ("Versunkenheit")

The 'quiet state of alertness' is a multi-layered state of consciousness. It is not possible for us here to explore all of its layers. We will thus confine our investigation for the time being to the analysis of the ultimate state that can be attained by the process of 'introversion', and this liminal state has been termed the 'quiet state of alertness' ("Versunkenheit"). This means that *our phenomenological description will at first be focused on and limited to the formal structure of the 'quiet state of alertness', whereas aspects of its content will not yet be addressed.* The various formal constituents of the 'quiet state of alertness' will be related to certain processes operating during 'introversion'. This means that each of these processes will provide a pivotal component germane to the overall mental structure of the 'quiet state of alertness'. The transformations of consciousness generated by the process of 'introversion' while advancing towards the 'quiet state of alertness' include the following: All processes governed actively by the subject are suspended and come to a standstill. The process by which consciousness becomes harmonious and unified finally results in a perfectly homogeneous state of consciousness. The process of emptying consciousness finally results in a mental condition that is entirely vacated. The slowing down of the pace in which the stream of consciousness is experienced has reached near stasis. All drives have been removed, together with any impulse for eliciting a spontaneous act of the 'I', and 'pointed feelings' have no longer an object by which they might be aroused. In the end an entirely emptied state of consciousness is achieved; it is a mental condition that is perfectly uniform, homogeneous, coherently structured and endowed with the highest possible degree of clarity.

As I have stated before, the pace of the flowing stream-of-consciousness has been slowed down and finally come to a standstill; all activities have ceased, and the process of 'introversion' itself has eventually come to a halt. There are no longer images or any other phenomena of the 'self' surfacing in consciousness, and feelings are no longer experienced as dynamic: There are no fluctuations of feelings anymore, and no emotional qualities perceived as new, and there are no changes anymore in perceiving the deep sense of inner calmness. In this ultimate state of 'introversion', the experiential quality of calmness is no longer characterized by terms such as 'cheerful', 'happy', 'saturated', 'melodious' or 'bright and lively', but as 'lucid', 'immovable' and 'empty'. These latter attributes aptly highlight the uniform and homogeneous nature of the state of inner calm permeating the 'quiet state of alertness'. Calmness no longer 'arrives', nor is experienced as absorbing anything that is discordant with the calmness within, but calmness is instantaneously experienced as the unique and prevailing quality of the overall experience.[90] The experience of inner calmness as empty and all-pervasive is also perceived as the ultimate ground in which the 'I-point' is rooted. Whereas

---

90 Cf. Krueger, Felix. *Das Wesen der Gefühle: Entwurf einer Systematischen Theorie*. Leipzig: Akademische Verlagsgesellschaft, 1930.

formerly the fluctuating feelings were clearly placed 'in front of one's (inward) eyes', the empty, motionless calmness is, by contrast, no longer experienced as an object, but intuitively grasped as the enduring, immutable and homogeneous ground of being. Thus experiencing this liminal state of calmness is no longer adequately described by the term 'feeling', but by the term 'awareness'.

In the 'quiet state of alertness', the modes of 'awareness' have likewise considerably declined in number. The 'I' knows instantaneously and without rational reflection that he/she is embedded here and now in a state of serene calmness, and knows that time has come to a standstill, and that the space of consciousness is exceptionally lucid and empty. This indicates that the 'experiencing I' has become fully absorbed in a state of heightened awareness in which he/she is reposing in calmness and in which the 'inner eye' observes the vacant space of consciousness. Thus the only active function remaining in the 'I' while absorbed in the calmness of the 'quiet state of alertness' is the function of 'inner sight'. The 'experiencing I' has thus become the medium of 'inner sight'.

'Inner Sight' ("Innenschau")

The concept of 'inner sight' (i.e. the capacity of seeing with the 'inner eye'[91]) refers to a mode of experience that is inalienably

---

91 [Note: The term "Innenschau" is a neologism coined by Albrecht; it refers to the capacity of inner perception in the widest sense. The concept corresponds to the ancient trope of the 'inward eye', which has been employed by mystics in both Western and Eastern mystical traditions. Albrecht uses the conventional term 'inner eye' only once, since he considered it imperative as a scientist to replace it with a new, clearly defined psychological concept, and one that was not charged with received meanings and connotations. The traditional topos of the 'inner eye' as used in Western (Christian) mysticism has been explored in some detail by in William Johnston in his study *The Inner Eye of Love: Mysticism and Religion*. London: Collins, 1974. – More recently, this topic has been dealt with by Richard Rohr in his study *The Naked Now: Learning to See as the Mystics See*. New York: Crossroad Publishing Company, 2009; and Samuel Sagan in *Awakening the Third Eye*. 3rd ed. Roseville, N.S.W.: Clairvision, 2007. – FW.]

linked to the 'quiet state of alertness' ("Versunkenheit"). The fact that the concept of 'inner sight' consists of two separate words requires some explanatory comment. The word 'sight' ("Schau") is supposed to be understood metaphorically as it does not primarily refer to the capacity of watching (visual) images arising in consciousness, but to the capacity of perceiving with the 'spiritual senses', i.e. inner hearing, feeling, the sense of being touched and perceiving thoughts surfacing in consciousness. The word 'inner' ("innen") has been chosen to emphasize that 'inner sight' has to be distinguished from the concept of 'turning inward' ("Innenwendung"). The notion of 'turning inward' embraces important subordinate concepts, such as 'inner perception' and 'self-observation'; the latter are, however, functions of the 'waking consciousness'. The concept of 'turning inward' is contrasted to what might be called 'turning outside towards the environment'. In the latter, the subject-object split is so clearly manifest that the 'experiencing I' perceives the space outside evidently as an object and recognizes that the 'I' as the subject is related to the surroundings by the function of sense perception, as well as by impressions arising from the imagination, and by thinking. The 'I' is moreover aware that feelings are objects of perception as well. By 'turning inward', the function of sense perception is switched off, so that any 'object' is perceived as emerging in the 'mental space within'; this may happen either when the 'I' reflects retrospectively on past or spontaneous experiences in the context of the 'waking consciousness'. *Though 'inner sight' is a function of 'turning inward', it is not a deliberate process of self-reflection occurring in the 'waking consciousness', but one that is exclusively bound to the 'quiet state of alertness'.* In order to be able to describe the phenomenon of 'inner sight', it is helpful to establish first the necessary requirements, even though these prerequisites are as such not enough for providing a clear-cut definition. Over and beyond this, it has to be admitted that the requirements stated tend to overlap: The first necessary requirement for 'inner sight' to be enabled is a state of consciousness that has achieved the highest possible degree of clarity and lucidity. That is to say that 'inner sight' can only unfold fully when consciousness has reached the ultimate state of clarity. 'Inner sight' can, moreover, not be compared to the more or less opaque condition operating when a person is 'turning inward' and becoming aware of the feelings elicited on the occasion; feelings perceived by 'inner sight' are grasped as 'objects' that are contemplated with a clear and conscious mind. The second necessary requirement is that consciousness must previously have been vacated from any 'content' of the 'waking state'. This implies that all conscious activities must have come to an end – except, obviously, the concomitant awareness of the ongoing process of 'inner sight'. The third necessary prerequisite for 'inner sight' to be enabled is that the 'stream-of-consciousness' must have decelerated (nearly) to the point of stasis. Any impression that might emerge in consciousness and is perceived as floating through the mind or appear in the vista of 'inner sight' can only be observed when it moves along very slowly. Finally, the fourth prerequisite is that the 'I' is totally passive, and has adopted a purely receptive attitude, beholding the phenomena appearing in 'inner sight' like a passive spectator. Any active effort on the part of the 'experiencing I' will instantly destroy the function of 'inner sight'. The 'I' has thus become the receptive medium of 'inner sight'. These four prerequisites must be released in the 'quiet state of alertness' for the function of 'inner sight' to be elicited. It should be emphasized that all of the four preconditions must be given simultaneously, if the function of 'inner sight' is to be released, and that this function cannot be triggered by only a single one of the four prerequisites. As stated above, in empirical reality some of the features of the four prerequisites tend to overlap and are intertwined. The distinctive features of 'inner sight' outlined here have of course been inferred from empirical data analytically on the basis of the phenomena encountered in the 'quiet state of alertness'. The résumé of these considerations may be summarized as follows: **The state of consciousness termed 'quiet state of alertness' is a sufficient requirement for 'inner sight' to be elicited. As soon as the 'quiet state of alertness' is stably established, the function of 'inner sight' will inevitably be released.**

The phenomenon of 'inner sight' is necessarily bound to an object to be observed. The particular type(s) of 'object(s)' featuring in 'inner sight' will be specified later in some detail and be termed the 'object arriving' ("das Ankommende") in consciousness. The considerations above have outlined merely the formal characteristics of 'inner sight'.

The content, i.e. the objects that can emerge and be beheld in 'inner sight', is from a phenomenological point of view at this stage of our enquiry only of secondary relevance. Therefore we will refrain from explaining the concept of 'arriving' at this point. But what must be provided at this juncture is the crucial phenomenological characteristics of 'inner sight' so that the concept can be clearly set off against received notions and concepts employed in psychological phenomenology:

1. *The concept of 'inner sight' must neither be mixed up with the concept of 'inwardness', nor with the concept of 'turning inward'.* 'Inwardness' is knowledge acquired instantly; it is knowledge that is not based on or inferred from rational reflection. It is rather knowledge that is subliminal, or, to put it more specifically, knowledge that is subconsciously available and that accompanies other processes of consciousness; hence it is knowledge residing in the 'dark, peripheral sphere' of the 'waking consciousness'. This means that 'inwardness' does not qualify as a variety of 'inner sight' when tested against the four pivotal prerequisites germane to 'inner sight': 'inwardness' is not experienced in a hyper-lucid mental condition, nor is consciousness entirely vacated from 'content', and the 'stream-of-consciousness' is not slowed down either. – But, on the other hand, 'inwardness' can be said to be an integral part of the 'quiet state of alertness', as it is a layer of consciousness that is concomitant with all altered states of consciousness; as such, 'inwardness' is the capacity that enables the 'experiencing I' to become instantaneously aware that consciousness is permeated with inner calmness and, eventually, that the 'quiet state of alertness' as the ultimate stage of the process of 'introversion' has been reached. 'Inner sight', by contrast, is not a mental state that accompanies an emotional condition, like inner calm, nor does it qualify as a mode of 'awareness' at all. In the event of 'inner sight' the subject-object division is clearly apparent: The 'I' beholds with a heightened degree of clarity an 'object' 'arriving' and dwelling in consciousness for some time. In 'inner sight' the necessary preconditions stated above (hyper-lucidity, deceleration of the flow of experience, emptiness and passive receptivity) are given, and its focus of attention is directed at an 'object' that 'arrives' in the

hyper-lucid clarity of consciousness; 'inner sight' thus differs significantly from other varieties of inward experience that occur in a state of reduced clarity, though intuitive knowledge may nevertheless be perceived in them as well.

2. *'Inner sight' is no sensory perception.* By 'inner sight' a subject does not perceive anything of his/her surroundings, nor of his/her body. Any sensory perception is mediated by the physical senses, and as such it is assumed that it conveys the object perceived in an 'objective' manner, i.e. the object is perceived in its corporality and located in external space, which is known to be objectively there. It is thus actually misleading to apply the term 'inner sense' to the phenomenon of 'inner sight', because the object of 'inner sight' is never transmitted by any of the physical senses, nor is the object perceived in 'inner sight' located in exterior space, i.e. outside the 'experiencing I'. The vista of 'inner sight' rather coincides with the subjective, inner space of consciousness of the perceiver. Over and beyond this, 'inner sight' is *no bogus or delusory perception*, because in a delusory perception – whether this is an illusion or a hallucination – the distinctive features of a sense-perception are retained, notably that it is perceived as an object located in exterior space. The 'object arriving', by contrast, appears in the subject's inner space of consciousness. This fact might give rise to the assumption that 'inner sight' is a phenomenon equivalent to an act of deliberate reflection, which derives its 'object' from impressions surfacing from the imagination, or from thoughts, or from memory. However, this supposition is flawed: *'Inner sight' does not involve any reflective thinking. It is essentially the 'beholding' of what has 'arrived' in consciousness, which is an experience that inevitably precedes any act of reflective thinking about the object currently beheld within.*[92]

---

92 [Note: The German text is semantically flawed here: "*Sie* [i.e. die Innenschau] *ist ein 'Anschauen' des Ankommenden und läuft als solches allem reflexiven Denken über das Geschaute hinaus* [sic!]" (PMB 105; italics in the original). The garbled meaning of the German sentence has been emended, stating what Albrecht appears to have intended to say. – FW.]

The Concepts of 'Introversion', 'Consciousness of 'Introversion', and the 'Quiet State of Alertness'

The following section will focus in some detail on the definitions of three key concepts: 'introversion', 'consciousness of introversion' and the 'quiet state of alertness'. These concepts have been developed from the perspective of the psychology of consciousness and are thus to be understood in strictly psychological terms only. This means that aspects transcending the confines of psychological phenomenology are not addressed and silently passed over, for instance, the fact that 'introversion' is a process depending on the notion of the 'unity of body and soul', which is an axiomatic premise that is not critically reflected on. There are, moreover, two methodological approaches by which the altered state of consciousness termed 'quiet state of alertness' can be explored, but only one of which – the psychological-phenomenological approach – is applied here and explained in some detail. The empirical approach through the natural sciences, however, is not part of our considerations. It is a scientific approach that relies on the principle of causality and on behaviourist methodologies, which focus on the external, seemingly objective somatic correlatives of the underlying experience as well as on phenomena that can be observed in a subject from outside, when he/she is absorbed in the 'quiet state of alertness'.

1. 'Introversion' is a self-induced psychological process, which develops autonomously and is determined throughout by the deliberate decision to engage in this mind-transforming process; the pivotal characteristic of 'introversion' is that it causes the 'waking consciousness' to disintegrate while generating in turn the integration of the altered state of consciousness termed 'quiet state of alertness'.

2. *The term 'consciousness of introversion' refers to the dynamic states of consciousness produced by and passed through during the process of 'introversion'; the structures of these altered states consist of both components of the 'waking consciousness' and of components of the 'quiet state of alertness'; thus the 'consciousness of 'introversion'' can, as a whole, be understood as a*

transitional state of consciousness placed between the 'waking consciousness' and the 'quiet state of alertness'. The 'consciousness of introversion" is marked by the following major distinctive features: The perception of the outside world is screened off, complex disruptions are isolated and eventually dissolved by means of a specific meditative technique, and, finally, all active 'content' still lingering in the mind as a residue of the 'waking consciousness' is transformed, harmonized and eventually eliminated or absorbed by the calmness inundating the consciousness of the 'quiet state of alertness'.

3. The 'quiet state of alertness' is a fully integrated, homogeneous, hyper-lucid and vacated state of consciousness; in it the flow of experience is markedly slowed down, its persevering underlying mood is calmness, and the only active function remaining in the otherwise entirely passive 'experiencing I' is the capacity of 'inner sight'.

Concentration and Recollecting

The definitions of 'introversion' and of the 'quiet state of alertness' imply that we have to establish not only a clear differentiation between the concepts of 'concentration' and 'recollecting' ("Sammlung"), but also to relate these concepts to other altered states of consciousness, notably the 'somnolent consciousness' and the 'hypnotic consciousness'. In empirical psychology *concentration* has been defined as focusing one's attention intentionally on a particular object and area of consciousness.[93] This definition implies that since the realm of human consciousness obviously has boundaries, the power of concentration is likewise bound to limitations. This means that the object concentration is focused on is perceived with a higher degree of clarity, while at the same time the clarity of perception of things placed at the periphery of the object of one's attention is impaired and reduced. Thus any item of perception that is not immediately

---

93 Cf. Elsenhans, Theodor. *Lehrbuch der Psychologie*. 1912. 3rd ed. Tübingen: Mohr, 1939. 445.

relevant to the given focus of attention is removed from the centre of attention and shifted to the periphery of consciousness, which is a sphere of reduced clarity. Concentration is clearly an active process controlled by the 'I', notably by the function of the will; an act of concentration can be observed from outside: it can, for instance, be inferred from the subject's countenance, or from other bodily features revealing the subject's state of tension. The focus of attention remains fastened in the mind, and is continuously controlled by the so-called 'I-point'. This means that concentration is not a free-floating psychic process. Concentration depends, moreover, on a series of pointed acts of consciousness, by which the focus of attention is again and again adjusted. The degree of 'alertness' and the degree of the mind's clarity has to be readjusted from time to time, and requires, at intervals, a deliberate decision on the part of the subject involved, as to whether the process of concentration is to be continued or terminated. These characteristics clearly indicate that concentration is an entirely different mental process than 'introversion' and that these processes do not overlap. They are rather in part diametrically opposed: 'introversion' is a relaxed, non-concentrative, self-generated, free-floating process, whereas concentration is a focussed, tense and intermittent process, depending on reiterated interventions of the 'I', in particular acts of volition. This clearly shows that *'introversion' is not a process of concentration.*

'Recollecting', on the other hand, is a process of gathering one's thoughts in view of one's future aspirations; it is as such a mental activity that is devoid of any tension and thus actually an act of relaxation. This indicates that 're-collecting' has some affinity with 'introversion', and that it differs significantly from an act of 'concentration'. Whereas 'concentration' is directed at a definitive goal, 'recollecting' is oriented at some future purpose. The act of 'recollecting' is detached from the future actions that are performed to achieve the intended purpose, both in time and in intention. 'Recollecting' is thus a special kind of 'turning inward': the person involved becomes detached in the process from the disparate, distracted or absent-minded condition of the normal 'waking consciousness', and relinquishes all activities by yielding to the emerging disposition of 'letting go'. 'Recollecting' thus generates a state of composure, for it harmonizes the psychic as well as the spiritual domains of a person, which may in turn become the basis for purposeful actions. – 'Recollecting' is, quite unlike 'concentration', a free-floating process – not a pointed or intermittent one. The functions of the 'I' are only required when the process of 'recollecting' is about to start, because some acts of self-regulation have to be initiated.

'Introversion' can be said to be a special variety of 'recollecting'. There are, however, other forms of 'recollecting' as well, albeit ones that are governed by the 'waking consciousness'. Because of this, 'recollecting' is more comprehensive in scope than 'introversion', and this is why 'recollecting' can be said to be superordinate to 'introversion'. But 'introversion' encompasses the entire field of 'recollecting', yet has several distinctive characteristics of its own. We might state the following: *'Introversion' is a form of 'recollecting', a process of consciousness that develops progressively towards the serene and homogeneous state of clarity that is the hallmark of the 'quiet state of alertness'.*

The 'Somnambulistic Consciousness'

The term 'spontaneous somnambulism' refers to the phenomenon of 'sleep-walking', which occurs spontaneously. This can be accounted for by the fact that the somnambulist is asleep only in part: though partially asleep, he/she is at the same time partially awake since he/she is able to move about in his/her surroundings and can even carry out sensible actions. But this may happen in a sane person as well while asleep, because during night-sleep not all the functions of consciousness are dormant. This indicates that a sleeping person is in part 'wakeful while sleeping', and thus able to discern unfamiliar or personally significant occurrences, and to respond to stimuli of his/her surroundings; when these stimuli are too strong, the sane person will wake up. The somnambulist, by comparison, is to a much larger extent wakeful while asleep. As Jaspers states, "somnambulism means waking up in part; yet the process of waking up is halted by certain conditions."[94] The somnambulist consciousness

---

94 Jaspers, Karl. *Allgemeine Psychopathologie. Ein Leitfaden für Studierende,*

is – though it is a state of partial wakefulness – clearly a dimmed and clouded hypnic consciousness. It is phenomenologically akin to the 'dream-consciousness'. The significant difference, however, is that in the somnambulist the dream dreamt is really physically enacted – it is *'un rêve en action'*.[95] The motoric functions are automatically set in motion by the occurrences featuring in the dream. Whatever has been learned and known in the 'waking state' is also at disposal in the 'dream consciousness'. This includes everything that has been acquired with a clear and conscious mind during an intentional educational process controlled by the 'I'. It includes furthermore all the skills that have become habitual and automated by experience, even to the extent that they can also be performed when the 'waking state' is disabled. Also any innate capacity that can be triggered automatically, and does not have to be controlled by the 'I', can be elicited in the 'somnambulist consciousness'. – When awake, however, the somnambulist usually cannot remember any of his/her actions and whereabouts during the night, though he/she may occasionally remember what the dream was about. In the somnambulist state, sense perceptions have a different level of responsiveness and are limited in range. Thus the somnambulist is usually impervious to pain and does not respond to noise or sounds (of normal intensity). The sense of smell is generally suspended, whereas the sense of touch and the sense of vision remain alive. Since the 'waking state' is never fully switched on, the few functions that are retained in the somnambulist consciousness operate without conscious (rational) control, and the actions are usually performed smoothly and without disruption. This may explain why somnambulists tend to develop enhanced proficiency in areas that are not disabled during the sleeping state.

We may distinguish between a spontaneous, natural form of somnambulism and a hypnotically induced one. The latter is evoked deliberately in a subject by a hypnotist. The hypnotic consciousness has a structure that is similar to the somnambulist state, except for the fact that the somnambulist consciousness emerges naturally and

---

Ärzte und Psychologen. 1913. 5th ed. Berlin and Heidelberg: Springer, 1948. 315. [The quotation in *PMB* is in German; English translation provided. – FW.]

95 Moser, Fanny. *Der Okkultismus.* 2 vols. Munich: Reinhardt, 1935. Vol. 2, 198.

spontaneously. Hypnotic somnambulism, by contrast, is not triggered by a dream, but by the hypnotist's suggestive 'rapport'. The psycho-physical condition evoked by the hypnotist in a person is called 'trance', if the subject develops paranormal abilities (i.e. when he/she functions as a 'medium'). In a state of 'trance' occult phenomena may appear. In a state of 'trance' a 'medium' may be transported into a state of rapture in a spiritistic séance. – In somnambulism 'fluctuating' states of consciousness tend to occur. This means that the mental state may fluctuate between the 'waking state' and the 'somnambulist state'. This kind of switching between waking and somnambulist states of consciousness may explain why a somnambulist, after having switched to the 'waking consciousness', cannot remember his/her nocturnal excursions, since his/her mind has been governed by the 'somnambulist state'. But the somnambulist is able to 'recall' the events of a previous somnambulist state in a subsequent one. This means that the somnambulist apparently is able to recall and enact the narrative of a dream in separate successive events. This is, however, a symptom of a 'split personality', and one that appears more often in the context of a somnambulist experience than in a state of hypnosis. A similar symptom of a 'split personality' has been encountered in psychopathology. The fragmented 'I' of the somnambulist, which is informed by split-off areas of the self, can become the centre of active and passive experience. (Examples will be given below.)

From these considerations we may infer the crucial difference between the 'quiet state of alertness' and the 'somnambulist consciousness': *The 'quiet state of alertness' is a highly alert and hyper-lucid state of consciousness, whereas the 'somnambulist consciousness' is a dim, blurred and hypo-lucid state of consciousness.* At this point we need to emphasize once more the distinctive features of the phenomenon of 'hyper-lucidity': Hyper-lucidity refers to a mental condition in which the power of memory is markedly enhanced both in the normal 'waking state' and the 'quiet state of alertness'; this aside, hyper-lucidity sustains and preserves the uniform state of the 'I' in both these states of consciousness. In the 'quiet state of alertness' hyper-lucidity is grounded in the fact that whatever the subject experiences, he/she is able to recall the event after having returned to the 'waking state'. The phenomenon of a 'split-consciousness', which (in theory) is believed to originate in the existence of two fluctuating 'I-points', never occurs in the 'quiet state of alertness'; in fact, a 'split-consciousness' is incompatible with the 'quiet state of alertness', because a mental state that fluctuates between two different 'I-points' can only be accounted for when the somnolent state is temporarily switched on, and when at the same time another state of consciousness is, for the time being, disabled. A state of consciousness that switches between the 'waking state' and the 'somnambulist state' is inevitably one that has a reduced degree of lucidity, hence is to be classified as a hypo-lucid or blurred mental condition. Therefore we may state: The pivotal features of hyper-lucidity are missing in the 'somnambulist consciousness'.

Other issues that have to be addressed when dealing with the difference between the 'somnambulist state' and the 'quiet state of alertness' are the question to what extent these states have been 'emptied' of all (object-related) content, and, secondly, the question to what extent the activities of the 'I' have been stalled. As we have seen earlier, the process of 'emptying' is a necessary condition for hyper-lucidity to develop in the 'quiet state of alertness'; 'emptying' is, however, not a sufficient criterion for the integration of this heightened state of consciousness. This claim is based on the fact that the dimmed somnambulist consciousness is, in a certain way, also an 'emptied' mental state. Though it is a blurred, hypo-lucid mental state, it is also one that is partially 'emptied' of certain areas of 'content'. The 'somnambulist consciousness' does contain a great variety of impressions deriving from dreams, and sense perceptions appear to function as well, albeit at a rather limited scope, and (I assume) that in the somnambulist sense perceptions operate only passively; that is to say that the sense perceptions function automatically and/or habitually, rather than by the conscious control of the 'experiencing I'. The presence of automatic responses and the absence of both any activity of the 'I' and the 'function of the waking state' indicate that the 'somnambulist consciousness' is a dimmed and hypo-lucid mental state. – A necessary, albeit not a sufficient criterion germane to the 'quiet state of alertness' is the absence of any activity of the 'I'. This means that the 'experiencing I', while reposing in calmness, has become entirely passive and purely receptive. However, passivity is alone no sufficient criterion for distinguishing the 'quiet state of alertness' from the 'somnambulist state', because the somnambulist is not caused to act by deliberate decisions of the will either, nor does he or she rely on any other of the controlling functions of the 'I'. In other words, in the somnambulist all processes of consciousness are – like in the 'quiet state of alertness' – self-induced, floating freely and autonomously. From this follows: The emptying of consciousness and the cessation of any activities of the 'I' are distinctive characteristics of the 'quiet state of alertness', but they are no sufficient criteria for distinguishing it phenomenologically from the 'somnambulist state', because similar characteristics can also be found in the 'somnambulist consciousness' (though only to a limited extent). From this follows that the only reliable criterion for distinguishing the 'quiet state of alertness' from the 'somnambulist consciousness' is the markedly enhanced degree of clarity and lucidity in the 'quiet state of alertness', whereas the degree of clarity is significantly reduced in the 'somnambulist consciousness'.

Hypnosis

The term hypnosis derives etymologically from Greek [ὕπνος] '*hypnos*' ('sleep'). However, the term is semantically misleading, as the word 'sleep' suggests that the 'hypnotic consciousness' is a sleep-like state, which is a flawed notion. A subject who has been hypnotized is not really asleep, but rather only appears to be asleep. Though it is possible that the person hypnotized may fall asleep during the state of 'hypnosis', this occurs only very rarely and is usually not an integral part of the 'hypnotic consciousness'. The crucial criterion that applies to all hypnotic states is the phenomenon of the 'rapport'. As long as the 'rapport' between the hypnotist and the person hypnotized is sustained, the state of hypnosis will continue – irrespective of the circumstances and the events that might assail the subject's consciousness in the given situation. Psychoanalysis has tried to account for the phenomenon of the 'rapport' by proposing the theory that the 'rapport' may unleash unconscious mechanisms; another theory suggests that the 'rapport' is generated by drives that are triggered subconsciously.[96] However, these theories do not appear to be persuasive to me, so I would propose that the 'rapport' is an 'ur-phenomenon of human consciousness', which as such defies rational explanation.

We speak of 'rapport' when a person's mind becomes disposed in a special way to respond willingly to the instructions of the hypnotist, and to integrate these directives into his/her own consciousness in such a way that the subject's desires, choices, acts of the will, motives and responses are elicited as if by one's own accord, and are experienced as originating from the subject's own self. Contrary to received opinion (supported by several representatives of various disciplines of science), which claims that hypnosis consists of a sequence of psychosomatic states, and especially contrary to the assertion that one of these psychosomatic states is the somnambulist state, I rather endorse the view *that the 'hypnotic consciousness' is exclusively generated by 'rapport'*, and that any of the altered states claimed to be an integral part of the 'hypnotic consciousness' are in fact interpolated subsequently. In other words, it is possible for the hypnotist to evoke in the subject absorbed in the 'hypnotic state' deliberately any other 'state of consciousness' without disrupting the ongoing state of hypnosis. The hypnotist may, for instance, induce also the 'somnambulist consciousness', and the 'state of dreaming', as well as the 'quiet state of alertness', and even the 'waking consciousness' during the ongoing state of hypnosis. The 'hypnotic consciousness' is thus a 'formal mental framework' which can be used for a psychological-phenomenological analysis. There are, however, no reliable clues for probing the 'depth' of a process of hypnosis, nor for discerning its various stages. The degree of responding to the hypnotist's suggestive power can be inferred only from the effects evoked in the subject by the 'rapport'. Even when the 'sleeping state' and the 'somnambulist state' are evoked during hypnosis, they can nonetheless clearly be identified as 'hypnotic states', which have been interpolated in the hypnotic consciousness a posteriori. In the context of hypnosis, we may consider a 'sleeping state' or a 'somnambulist consciousness' as genuine only when the 'rapport' is unexpectedly and instantaneously terminated (which

---

96 Schilder, Paul, and Otto Kauders. *Lehrbuch der Hypnose*. Vienna: Springer, 1936.

may happen at any time). As soon as the full structure of the 'hypnotic consciousness' has been established by the 'rapport' – whether this is achieved instantly, or gradually – the hypnotist always has complete control over the consciousness of the person hypnotized; thus the hypnotist can elicit any individual ability residing in the subject hypnotized. It is even possible that the abilities evoked continue to be effective for some time in the 'waking consciousness' after the state of hypnosis has ended, provided that the hypnotist's instruction to engage in a particular action does not conflict with the subject's character and/or moral values.

Hypnosis can be induced in a subject at any time and regardless of the given state of consciousness he/she finds himself/herself in, provided that the current mental state is sound and ready to be transformed, disintegrated and reintegrated. The hypnotist can apply several techniques to achieve the transformation of the mind, including the method of 'introversion'. For the purposes of this psychological enquiry into the phenomenology of 'introversion', the only relevant aspect to be considered is the deliberate decision to engage in the mind-transforming exercise termed 'introversion' (a method adapted from the practice of Autogenic Training as developed by H. I. Schultz); for example, the following practice: 'I am now going to embark on the process of 'introversion'.' Alternatively, the passive statement "*'introversion' is evoked within me*" can also be used, because in hypnosis an altered state of consciousness can be triggered by employing the following approach: First, the will of the subject who is hypnotized is substituted by the will of the hypnotist, and as soon as the 'rapport' has been established, the condition of the mind is transformed, resulting in the hypnotic consciousness. Thus in hypnosis the transformation of consciousness is caused by a 'foreign will'; in 'introversion', by contrast, the process is triggered and advanced by the subject's own volition and/or his/her 'disposition' encoded prior to embarking on the process of 'introversion'. But it is important to add that in hypnosis the 'foreign will' does (usually) not interfere in the further progress of hypnosis; thus the process of hypnosis develops autonomously. The 'rapport' is (as it were) an invisible window by which the subject is subconsciously linked to the world outside. In the process of 'introversion', however, the awareness of the 'rapport' is suspended. Secondly, the hypnotist may intervene in the process of 'introversion' at any time, if he wishes to do so; he may intervene at any time because the hypnotic 'rapport' is more effective and paramount to any of the self-generated processes occurring in 'introversion'. Such acts of intervention on the part of the hypnotist can either be supportive or be experienced as disturbing, and at times may even terminate the process of 'introversion'. An intervention is supportive when the hypnotist's directives are intended to accelerate the process of 'introversion', notably the endeavour to become detached from the outside world, or to vacate the mind from discursive thoughts and images, or to silence the mind in order to advance to the serene state of inner calmness. An intervention is inevitably experienced as disturbing when it imposes unwanted notions and instructions on the subject, such as performing actions that are incompatible with the intended goal of 'introversion'. An intervention is felt to be disruptive when the constellation of the consciousness of 'introversion' is impaired by the intrusion of the 'foreign will', and experienced as dissonant with the progress towards the serene and empty state of 'quiet alertness'.

Supportive interventions are usually accepted by the subject hypnotized, even when he/she does not recognize any more that the instructions are the suggestive influences of a 'foreign will'. A gentle touch, or reassuring words spoken by the person supervising the process of 'introversion', may facilitate the growth of inner calm, which first arises from the sphere of the body. The 'I' opens up and adopts the receptive attitude of trusting surrender and is subsequently inundated by the influx of calmness. The receptive attitude of the 'experiencing I' is the result of the subject's foregoing 'encoded predisposition' of 'letting go', and his/her endeavour to become detached from the surroundings, and of his/her willingness to renounce any act of the will. As a consequence, the subject is overwhelmed by a deep sense of trust, i.e. the desire to entrust his/her entire existence to another person. The person hypnotized has previously entrusted him-/herself to the hypnotist who initiated the process of 'introversion'. But the experiences evoked during hypnosis also encompass genuine experiences of 'introversion', notably the longing to be advanced to the ultimate goal of 'introversion', i.e. the 'quiet state of alertness'. Thus the final goal of the determination evoked by the 'rapport' thus eventually coincides with the 'encoded predetermination' known from the self-induced process of 'introversion'.

What remains to be added here is the fact that the 'quiet state of alertness' can be 'switched on' instantaneously by hypnosis, as well as the fact that the integration of the 'quiet state of alertness' may occur autonomously and instantly outside the context of hypnosis. This means that the instant interpolation of the 'quiet state of alertness' does not depend on a situation of 'rapport', but may occur outside the context of hypnosis at any time to anyone, and thus it does not depend on the process of 'introversion' as outlined above. In other words, anyone can be passively and spontaneously overwhelmed by the 'quiet state of alertness' at any time and without having initiated a process of 'introversion', either by oneself or with the support of a hypnotist.

Somatic Processes

Somnambulism and hypnosis are areas of phenomenological research that could only be explored in this enquiry, because its focus of attention was confined (for the time being) to somatic aspects. But now we have reached a crossroads, where we have to pause and recall that 'introversion', as a whole, is a psychosomatic phenomenon that can methodologically be approached in two ways. The psychological approach taken has been limited to what can be encountered in empirical reality; hence, phenomena and processes located beyond the realm of empirical psychology have not been considered. The strictly psychological approach will be the one followed in this investigation throughout. The second methodological approach we are going to embark on now will be focussed on the changes in the body and on some organic systems caused by the process of 'introversion'. The subject matter or 'content' of our enquiry is thus the objects that can be 'objectively' examined 'from outside', by methods employed by the natural sciences; this approach will require us to assess critically the causal relationship between the various 'objects'. The cause-effect relationships will be explored on the basis of both a descriptive, systematic approach, and an experimental approach, which are both approved methods in the natural sciences.

My experience of the bodily responses that tend to occur during 'introversion' is in part based on my own practice, but it is to a larger extent informed by the study *Das Autogene Training* (*Autogenic Training*) by I. H. Schultz.[97] Schultz not only offers a detailed account of the various somatic changes that are elicited by the practice of Autogenic Training, but elaborates also on the psychological impact of the experience. The reasons why I consider it necessary to summarize Schultz's psychological findings here, are the following: First, my foremost intention in this investigation is to provide a stringent, psychological-phenomenological methodology, complete with a systematic order of clearly defined concepts; secondly, for the purpose of the enquiry into the realm of mystical consciousness, I do need a very specific systematic conceptual frame of reference, which is in part supplied by Schultz. It is important to add, however, that terminologically I do not always follow Schultz; in fact, some of my key concepts, as well as my critical assessment of the 'quiet state of alertness', differ from Schultz's views. But this does in no way diminish the paramount significance of Schultz's research, and does in no way impair the significance of Schultz's novel insights into the field of the psychology of consciousness. The physical aspects of 'autogenic practice' have been outlined by Schultz so clearly and meticulously that his findings have become indispensable for future research into the nature of the process of 'introversion'.

Though the paramount significance of Schutz's research would deserve detailed consideration, it is only possible here to offer just a succinct outline of his major insights on the nature of 'Autogenic Training'. We shall confine our summary to some annotations on the somatic changes encountered during 'introversion', because this is helpful in view of the subsequent considerations relating, in particular, to the somatic changes triggered by 'introversion'. These comments on Schultz, helpful as they may be for exploring the psychosomatic dimension of 'introversion', do not yield any insights into the psychological nature of mystical consciousness, the primary concern of this study. What is relevant for us, though, in the given context is the *responses* of the body elicited while

---

97 Schultz, I. H. *Das Autogene Training. Versuch einer Klinisch-Praktischen Darstellung.* Leipzig: Thieme, 1932.

'introversion' is in progress, even though they are not rendered from the viewpoint of the experiencing subject. Yet somatic responses 'observed from outside' are conducive but not sufficient for achieving the aim of our investigation. Moreover, Schultz's speculative claims, such as the assertion that the somatic changes involved in 'introversion' are caused by mechanisms located outside the individual consciousness, are not relevant for our investigation.

But I. H. Schultz does provide a very detailed description of the varieties of corporal phenomena and somatic responses triggered by the process of 'introversion'. In the following I will summarize and paraphrase some of the key passages, supplemented by selected quotations from Schultz's book:

The state of muscular relaxation embraces the whole body, which can be examined objectively by testing muscular tension: In the advanced state of relaxation, the muscles are "soft as jelly"; another test is lifting one of the extremities cautiously – when the lifted arm, or leg, drops back unto the bed "quickly", i.e. "in a typically physical way". – The jaw "is suspended in a 'medial position'". – "The facial expression is typically relaxed and characterised by the 'casual' slackening of the facial muscles. – The rhythm of breathing changes from inhaling quickly and exhaling slowly and passively, to the almost regular rhythmical balance between inhaling and exhaling; but inhaling occurs slowly, continuously and passively – as if "being breathed through", which is "another clinical symptom to be mentioned in this context." – The rate of the heartbeat is reduced. There is neither the need, nor the wish to change one's position, which indicates that the person engaged in 'autogenic training' is perfectly relaxed and motionless, a state that in the advanced practitioner can last for several hours. The sensations of warmth and coldness in the extremities correlate with the real measurements of the body temperature. – The changes affecting the circulation of the blood become apparent in the increased volume of the arms (the circumference of the arm can be measured). – Moreover, responses to the knee-jerk can be tested to confirm the declining intensity of the knee-reflex in a subject while absorbed in an altered state of consciousness, produced by 'autogenic training'.

The practice of 'autogenic training' is described as follows: The necessary requirements are the relaxed, comfortable position of the body, and the practitioner's positive predisposition and inner willingness to engage in the mind-altering practice of 'autogenic training'. What is vital is that the practitioner is required to focus mentally on certain somatic changes that he/she wishes to be achieved; to elicit such a change he/she has to reiterate verbally a phrase addressing the intended goal of the training, and the somatic change that is to be evoked – i.e. at the beginning of the exercise, it is usually the sensation of the body's weight, later it is the increasing temperature in an arm that is focused on. The psychosomatic effect elicited in this way opens up the path to somatic transformations: The arm becomes relaxed and is subjectively felt to have become heavy, though objectively the arm shows all the symptoms of perfect relaxation. As the exercise continues, the arm is felt to become warmer, which can again be objectively verified by the increased volume (circumference) of the arm, and by the increased temperature, which can be measured. – A pivotal phenomenon is that of 'generalisation', i.e. the transfer of the initial sensation in one part of the body to all parts of the body: The feeling of heaviness of a single extremity, which was evoked in the incipient stage of the exercise, is spontaneously transferred to all extremities of the body, although there has been no foregoing decision or predisposition for this to happen. This 'generalizing' effect is caused by the fact that the tonic functions of the muscular systems are interlinked. There is empirical evidence that the myotonus of a certain group of muscles has a direct impact on the myotonus of other muscles. This is the reason why abrupt changes in the entire muscular system are possible, such as the process of relaxation elicited by the 'switching' of consciousness into an altered state (i.e. the abrupt shifting of the current, unrelaxed state of consciousness into an altered (relaxed) state).

The switching of the states of consciousness generated by 'autogenic training', which is a mind-transforming technique of relaxation, has affinities with the psychological processes involved in 'introversion'. We all know that taking a bath in warm water arouses feelings of warmth all over the body, a sensation which has a soothing, sleep-like effect; it is generally assumed that there is a functional physiological connection between the degree of muscular tension and falling asleep; similarly, we may assume that "the link between relaxation and 'introversion' originates from a deep-seated primeval response", which can be released spontaneously not only by 'autogenic training', but also by similar practices of relaxation. Seen from this perspective, the concept of 'switching' refers to both the domain of the body (i.e. changes effected in the myotonus and in blood circulation) and the domain of the psyche.

"Physiologically speaking, autogenic training can be defined as an exercise aimed at generating in oneself the 'switching' of consciousness to a more relaxed and unified state; this mind-transforming technique can be acquired by focussing the mind for some time on the realm of inner perception, while simultaneously all sense perceptions of the external world are 'screened off', leaving the practitioner in a relaxed, quiet and motionless state of repose." – The question that arises at this point, however, is if the act of 'switching' is caused exclusively by physiological processes evoked by a cluster of mental functions, or if a certain area in the central nervous system is ultimately responsible. In his statements on the autonomous nervous system I. H. Schultz relies on the empirical enquiries of A. Weinberg, whose "comprehensive research and detailed psycho-physiological measurements have resulted in the fact that a higher level of consciousness correlates with increased activity of the sympathetic nervous system, whereas lower levels of consciousness correlate with increased activity of the parasympathetic nervous system." The sympathetic nervous system enables "instantaneous success and promotes growth and encouragement", whereas the parasympathetic nervous system allows "long-term operation and inhibits, on a large-scale basis, vital functions" (Pollak).[98] Schilder[99] claims: "Functions of the myotonus are apparently linked with functions that regulate

---

98 [Albrecht does not specify the reference to 'Pollak' in *PMB*; there is neither a footnote, nor a reference in the bibliography. – Online research has identified the source: The reference is to Pollak, Franz. "Die Stellung des Vegetativen Nervensystems im Psychocerebralen Bauplan." *Zeitschrift für die Gesamte Neurologie und Psychiatrie* 137 (1931): 339-353. – The English translation of Albrecht's quotation from Pollak has been provided. – FW.]

99 Schilder quoted in Schultz, I. H. *Das Autogene Training. Versuch einer Klinisch-Praktischen Darstellung.* Leipzig: Thieme, 1932. 224.

the structure of consciousness." I. H. Schultz calls to mind that recent research has corroborated the claim that both the di-encephalon and the mes-encephalon are parts of the "control centre of the vital functions". "The intricate cooperation between subcortical, autonomous nervous arousal, and (neuro-)chemical stimuli can be considered to be vital physiological constellations involved in generating and sustaining processes of consciousness."

This concise survey of the somatic processes operating in 'autogenic training' provides persuasive data for corroborating the claim that 'introversion' is, in its entirety, a natural biological process, which can be accounted for scientifically by the principle of causality. – The concept of 'switching', however, requires some further consideration since it is the central psychological concern at this stage of our investigation. In fact, 'switching' is a key phenomenon that will prove helpful in classifying mental states and analysing the phenomena contained in them systematically. The empirical facts derived from the foregoing considerations can thus be summarized as follows:

1. *The 'quiet state of alertness' can also be 'switched on' by hypnotic 'rapport', and thus does not necessarily depend on an antecedent process of 'introversion'.*

2. *The 'quiet state of alertness' can 'switch on' autonomously in a spontaneous act, even if there has not been a conscious determination beforehand to 'switch' to this higher mental state.*

3. *The 'quiet state of alertness' can develop gradually and imperceptibly in a process originating in the 'waking consciousness'.*

The Layer Theory of the Personality

As the aim of this study is to provide a systematic psychological-phenomenological description of various altered states of consciousness, which can indeed be identified and encountered in empirical reality, and of which the 'mystical consciousness' is the ultimate concern, we will largely bypass theoretical considerations. However, this disclaimer aside, a few comments on the so-called 'layer theory' of the personality are necessary at this point of our enquiry.

The term *'disposition'* is a concept that is (strictly speaking) not a term deriving from the psychology of consciousness. It is, rather, an 'extramental' concept of "trans-phenomenal, inner-psychic origin".¹⁰⁰ A 'disposition' is thus a mental function that can be released at any time; it can become effective in consciousness when triggered by some cause. The term *'structure'* is likewise an 'extramental' concept. A 'structure' does not refer to an event, or an impression that can be experienced, but is a theoretical construct of thinking. 'Structure' is a cognitive concept that is compartmentalised, but as a whole, it also refers to a relatively closed system. The overall structure of an individual is thus the enduring "framework encompassing the entire range of a person's psychic inclinations and dispositions" (Strunz 106). A 'partial structure' is an independent framework forming a self-contained unit, which is complete, but the individual components of which are integral parts of a complex wholeness.

There is a "genetic and vertical order in the structure of dispositions. The notion of the vertical order (higher vs. lower) derives from the field of structural psychology and refers to the classification of the entire inventory of dispositions from a genetic point of view" (Strunz 120), i.e. from the perspective of their phylogenetic origin and development.

On the basis of these concise definitions we may now define the key concept of 'layer': *"Layers are tier-based structures whose constituent elements are located on the same 'level', and which form a distinct, relatively autonomous framework"*.[101]

In his study *Die Schichten der Persönlichkeit*, Erich Rothacker argues that the human individual is composed of several distinct layers. To substantiate this theoretical claim, Rothacker examined subject-matters and processes of consciousness, along with the psychic functions in a way that should enable him to attribute specific items and processes of consciousness to certain genetic layers of the personality. *The underlying schema of this theory is based on the assumption that there is a 'deep person' that determines the (so-called) 'it-mode' of life, and grounded on the 'deep person',*

---

100 Strunz, Kurt. "Über die 'Vertikale' Ordnung der Seelischen Dispositionen. Ein Beitrag zur Psychologischen Schichttheorie." *Zeitschrift für Psychologie* 154 (1943): 103-202. Quotation 107. [English translation provided. – FW.]

101 Rothacker, Erich. *Die Schichten der Persönlichkeit*. 4th ed. Bonn: Bouvier, 1948. 66 f. [All translations from Rothacker have been provided. – FW.]

there is a 'cortical person' that determines the 'I-mode' of life. Rothacker furthermore introduces several supporting concepts in which specific aspects of the 'it-mode' are contrasted to the 'I-mode'. The layer termed the 'vital-it', i.e. the basic layer of vitality in the 'deep person', is the layer of the 'animal-it', which is the layer of drives and drive-related emotions. Both of these layers are genetically the oldest ones. There is, moreover, "an emotional layer that is unique to humans, though it is located in the 'deep person' and positioned below the layer of the 'I-function'. But, on the other hand, the 'emotional layer' is placed above the biological sphere, and stands out as the most highly treasured capacity of man, since the 'emotional layer' encompasses also the spiritual dimension, including the independent power of the imagination, the domain of spiritual feelings, and last but not least, the realm of empathy and love". – "The entire range of experiences are rooted in the 'endothymic ground', as recently portrayed by Ph. Lersch, – including man's zest for life, and such qualities as cheerfulness, hilarity, sadness, dullness, self-assurance, joy, grief, expectation, hope, resignation, despair, fear, angst, different varieties of charity and compassion, all aesthetic, religious and noetic feelings, as well as man's ultimate aspirations – in other words, the entire world of feelings, is rooted in the solid ground of animalistic emotions, which can all be discerned and traced scientifically." (Rothacker 66f.).

The 'I-mode' of life is divided between the 'I-point' and the 'layer of the personality', also termed the 'personal layer'. The function of the 'waking consciousness' is assigned to the 'I-point'; the function of wakefulness is switched on whenever the free-floating experience of the 'deep person' is interrupted by controlling acts of the 'I'.

"The personal layer is the product of organisation" (Rothacker 75f.), which is formed and shaped by self-education as well as by passive educational processes; by these two educational processes the enduring moral and other individual dispositions are created.

These 'layers of the personality' are linked to cerebral areas, which can be located anatomically. The human brain can be divided into the genetically more ancient regions of the paleo-encephalon and the brainstem, and the genetically younger region of the neo-cortex, or cerebral cortex, which is thought to be an organ of control and inhibition.

In view of the varieties of experience encountered in the consciousness of 'introversion', we may summarize: Apperception, along with attentiveness, acts of the will, processes of thinking controlled by the 'I' and other activities of the 'I', such as self-reflection, the function of wakefulness and the clarity of consciousness – are all features of consciousness that can be attributed to the genetically youngest layers, and are thus related to the cortical areas of the brain. It goes without saying that the processes and phenomena referred to here are all instances of the 'waking consciousness', and are as such characterised by a high degree of conscious awareness, and which, for this reason, cannot be found in the hypnic state of consciousness of a person dreaming. Moreover, the experiences and phenomena referred to are incompatible with the consciousness of 'introversion', since they are all processes and dynamic features that are stilled and eventually eliminated from the consciousness of 'introversion'.

All the processes that proceed automatically, as well as all passive experiences, all emotional states, all spontaneous emotional responses, all perceptions of symbolic images, as well as all free-floating autonomous perceptions can be attributed to the 'it-layer' of the animated 'deep person', i.e. to the 'endothymic ground' of the individual personality.

On the basis of these theoretical considerations, it is reasonable to argue that the process of 'introversion' can be likened, by way of analogy, to the process of falling asleep: The 'switching' on/off of a mental state, it would seem, might thus be explained by the hypothesis that the function of the genetically youngest areas of the brain is temporarily disabled, and replaced by the function of the genetically older cerebral area of the 'it-layer', in which the stream of experience can flow freely and without the controlling intervention of the 'I'. However, this hypothesis turns out to be flawed and inadequate when examined from a phenomenological point of view, as it obfuscates an objective, unbiased approach to assessing the phenomena appearing in consciousness. Though we may attribute to the layer-theory some heuristic value in that it offers a plausible explanation for the way the transformation of consciousness is achieved during 'introversion', this theory is inadequate as it can neither grasp nor account for the entire range of phenomena that become manifest in 'introversion'. The mystery inherent in the very fact that there is such a phenomenon as the 'quiet state of alertness' is not addressed by the layer theory, and cannot be explained by it in any way. The latter claim can be corroborated by the following arguments:

1. The 'dream consciousness' is a dissociated and disintegrated consciousness; for this reason it is (from the perspective of the 'layer theory') classified as a 'hypo-awake', hyponoic consciousness, in which all 'content' contained in this state are seen as manifestations of the 'it-mode' of life. The 'I-mode' of life, by contrast, i.e. all conscious activities of the 'I' occurring in the 'waking state', is disabled in the 'dream consciousness'. That is to say, that the neo-encephalon is supposed to be 'asleep' when the 'dream consciousness' is switched on. – The consciousness of the 'quiet state of alertness', by contrast, is a fully integrated, coherently structured consciousness, which, however, is sustained throughout subliminally, i.e. it is alert all the time without being exposed to the conscious, active control of the 'I', and without 'switching on' the 'waking consciousness'. This is indeed a puzzling phenomenon, and one that cannot be explained by the 'layer theory'.

2. 'Hyper-clarity' is a pivotal characteristic of the 'quiet state of alertness', but in the system of the 'layer theory' there is no space where it could be located.

3. The capacity of 'inner sight' is clearly a conscious experience of the 'I', but it is a faculty of consciousness that conflicts with the proposition of the 'layer theory' claiming that the function of the 'cortical person' is totally disabled when the 'waking state' is switched off; it is moreover incompatible with the claim that the 'deep person' is in 'total control' of consciousness.

4. The various 'encoded predispositions' generated in the 'waking consciousness' in a subject before embarking on a process of 'introversion' and which are elicited during 'introversion', and in the 'quiet state of alertness', originate in different cerebral layers. Thus there are logically structured sequences of verbalized

thought, which exist side by side with sequences of pictures emerging from the imagination.

5. The fact that all drives are allayed during the 'quiet state of alertness' cannot be explained on the basis of the 'layer theory'. The absence of drives can only be hypothetically accounted for by the 'layer theory' by suggesting that the drives have been stilled temporarily, as the function of the animalistic 'it-layer' is temporarily suspended. The fact that emotional responses are predominant in the 'quiet state of alertness' is hypothetically accounted for by the assumption that the animated 'it-layer' is supposed to be increasingly effective in the ongoing process of 'introversion'.

These arguments clearly corroborate the claim that the 'quiet state of alertness' is a higher (hyper-lucid) state of consciousness for the existence and distinctive characteristics of which the 'layer theory' can provide no explanation. The 'layer theory' can neither assign the structure, nor the distinctive phenomenological characteristics of the 'quiet state of alertness' to a special layer of the individual personality. Any attempt to provide such an explanation on the basis of the 'layer theory' is bound to fail. The hypothetical assumption that during the process of 'introversion' the functions of the higher cerebral layers are diminished, or altogether suspended, and in turn replaced by functions of the lower cerebral layers, is abortive. If the concepts of 'switching' and of the 'layers of the personality' can be applied meaningfully to the consciousness of 'introversion' at all, they can only be understood in the following way: The 'quiet state of alertness' is 'switched on' in its entirety at the end of the process of 'introversion'. The ultimate mental state achieved through 'introversion' is an altered state of consciousness that is composed of elements deriving from all areas of the personality. Hence, **the 'quiet state of alertness' is a state of consciousness that is composed of various structural tiers, which are rooted in different layers of the personality.** But any enquiry into the distinctive features of the 'quiet state of alertness', as well as the question of how to classify this mental state by contrasting it to other mental states, go beyond the confines of the 'layer theory'.

Outlook

The 'quiet state of alertness' is a state of consciousness that is phenomenologically set off distinctly against any of the adjacent mental states. The 'quiet state of alertness' is a clearly structured state of consciousness, and as such, it is a perfectly sane, intrinsically human mental condition. It can be produced either by the deliberate, mind-transforming process termed 'introversion', or it can, at rare instances, also 'switch on' instantly and autonomously, i.e. without being preceded by a deliberate process of 'introversion'. The 'quiet state of alertness' is moreover the most coherently structured state of consciousness that we know: It is homogeneous, uniform, hyper-lucid and emptied of any content, except for the items that are germane to, or integral parts of, the 'quiet state of alertness'. The pace of experiencing in the 'quiet state of alertness' is slowed down to the point of near stasis, which means that all activities of the 'I' are in abeyance, and the 'I' reposes, inundated by inner calm; the 'I' is receptive only to phenomena that appear within, in the inner field of vision, i.e. in the vista of 'inner sight'. It is important to add, however, that the phenomenological characteristics of the 'quiet state of alertness' described here are a theoretical construct, though originally derived from empirical data. So we have to concede that the abstract concept cannot fully recapture the dynamic process and the entire range of phenomena becoming manifest in empirical reality. Moreover, the 'content' featuring in the 'quiet state of alertness' is inevitably also co-determined by subjective items grounded in the individual personality of the 'experiencing I'. *The 'quiet state of alertness' is thus only a formal mental framework, which embraces some 'content'.* Thus the 'quiet state of alertness' can only be understood in its entirety, if its experiential content is examined and phenomenologically described as well.

When outlining the formal framework of the 'quiet state of alertness' we have to bypass a few empirical facts, even though these items are part of the distinctive features of a subject's overall experience. For instance, we have taken for granted the proposition that the personal records quoted below provide personality-bound variables of a private empirical event, and thus every single account of an experience in the 'quiet state of alertness' is inevitably unique, and 'coloured' and shaped by the experiencer's personality.

In the following we are going to explore the 'content' of consciousness that became manifest in a subject when immersed in the 'quiet state of alertness'. In examining individual records of such experiences, we have to bypass (for the time being) the issue of implied value judgements. This means that value-related statements in these records and phenomena which are evidently informed by received moral, religious or metaphysical notions have been clipped or omitted, as they are as yet not relevant for the psychological description of the 'quiet state of alertness'. But we shall consider in some detail specific concepts relating to the psychology of values at a later stage of this investigation, when we are going to approach the mystical domain, and when we shall be better equipped methodologically for distinguishing mystical phenomena from non-mystical ones. The central concern of this study is, after all, to reveal and identify – within the confines imposed by empirical methodology – the pivotal features of man's mystical consciousness. When elaborating on the formal structure of the 'quiet state of alertness', we have identified a number of items and mental processes, which are distinctive features of the 'quiet state of alertness'. In previous research, however, several of the phenomena and processes that are to be attributed to the 'quiet state of alertness' have erroneously been ascribed to the realm of mysticism. But before we enter the domain of mystical consciousness, we have to interpolate a chapter dealing with items featuring as part of the 'content' in the 'quiet state of alertness'. By inserting this chapter here, we will be enabled to delineate the boundaries of the mystical realm more clearly, and thus we may hereafter establish criteria for distinguishing genuine mystical states and mystical phenomena from non-mystical, or pseudo-mystical ones, which may likewise surface in altered states of consciousness.

The second part of the book is thus primarily concerned with the items of 'content' that may appear in the 'quiet state of alertness'; this part of the study will also prove helpful in elucidating specific features of mystical consciousness and highlight the essence of the unique phenomena becoming manifest in it, and describe them in a manner as to allow their mystical gleam to flash up. Considering the scope of this enterprise, it goes without saying that only a limited representative selection of these phenomena and mystical experiences can be examined here. Obviously, the number of mystical phenomena appearing in the 'quiet state of alertness' is countless, which is why mystical phenomena can never be recaptured in their entirety by phenomenological research. – But before turning to the topic dealt with in part two of the book, we have to introduce and define a few more concepts. In particular, the terms 'hyper-lucidity', 'emptying' of consciousness, and the concept of 'inner sight' ("Innenschau") must be explained in some detail. Considering the importance of these concepts for the further progress of this empirical investigation, the viability and validity of these concepts have to be critically examined.

There are basically two varieties of experience that can be encountered in the 'quiet state of alertness'; they can be classified by two pivotal criteria: One is the criterion of 'enhanced proficiency'; the other concerns the presence or absence of the phenomenon of an 'object arriving' ("das Ankommende") in the vista of 'inner sight'. By 'enhanced proficiency' we understand the enhanced ability to perform psychic and psycho-somatic actions, which can be assessed 'from outside', i.e. tested, evaluated and verified scientifically by the principle of causality. A performance assessed in this way can be claimed to be objective, for the data can be measured quantitatively and assessed qualitatively. The achievement of a performance can moreover be compared with analogous results accomplished in states of consciousness outside the 'quiet state of alertness'. We speak of 'improved' or 'enhanced' 'proficiency' effected in the 'quiet state of alertness', because the exceptional quality of the achievement can objectively be verified by psychological science. Thus 'enhanced proficiency' can be proven by measurements and demonstrated by tests of memory and/or thinking. Thus the insights gained from such tests and experiments carried out when the subject was immersed in the 'quiet state of alertness' have provided ample empirical evidence that *'enhanced proficiency'* is not a spurious or irrational phenomenon, but a *real and true achievement that has been enabled by the 'quiet state of alertness', since it provides an ideal mental setting for enhanced proficiency because of its unique condition of clarity and lucidity*. Secondary processes occurring in the 'quiet state of alertness', like thinking and producing sequences of associations, also result in 'enhanced proficiency' (compared to the normal 'waking state'). Improved performance is also facilitated by the fact that the mental processes occurring in the 'quiet state of alertness' are at that time the only 'content' in the hyper-lucid, coherently structured space of consciousness. Moreover, enhanced proficiency is facilitated in the 'quiet state of alertness' because the 'experiencing I' has become engrossed in a purely receptive attitude, and because the phenomena perceived within are passing through consciousness in slow motion; i.e. the thoughts and associations 'arriving' in the vista of 'inner sight' tend to dwell in consciousness for a long time.

A few more important aspects relating to the notion of 'enhanced proficiency' have to be addressed, such as the image-bound practice of meditative relaxation (of which 'autogenic training' is a special variety). This meditative method has an impact on the function of bodily organs and the somatic system, and also affects predetermined dispositions, as well as the processes of thinking that are directed at a specific goal. 'Enhanced proficiency' can also be observed in the qualitative transformation of the verbal utterances spoken by a subject while absorbed in the 'quiet state of alertness'. Finally, 'enhanced proficiency' may also become manifest in abilities originating from the imagination. Another important feature of the experiences that may occur during the 'quiet state of alertness' concerns the phenomenon of 'arriving'. A crucial criterion for elucidating the phenomenon of the 'thing arriving' in consciousness is the subject's intuitive awareness of where the 'thing arriving' is coming from, or appears to be coming from. This means that such 'incoming phenomena' have to be tested as to whether they originate from the subject's subconscious or other recesses of his/her mind, or if they are to be identified as intruding from a sphere beyond the 'individual self'. Thus, isolated snippets and fragments of experience will be examined in the following for the purpose of ascertaining if they are or are not items 'split off' from the individual self and thus need to be identified as phenomena of a morbidly disintegrated consciousness. This critically diagnostic phenomenological analysis of recorded experience will be the focal point of part two of this book.

Additional methodological approaches will be employed to further open up the vista of 'inner sight' within the 'quiet state of alertness' so that we may finally get a glimpse of phenomena pertaining to the realm of mysticism.

PART TWO

*Experiencing the
'Quiet State of Alertness'*

The 'Quiet State of Alertness' Compared to Other States of Consciousness

Part one of this study has mainly been a phenomenological enquiry into elementary aspects of human consciousness. Most of the issues dealt with have referred to the 'waking state' and the hypolucid states of hypnosis and the 'somnambulist consciousness', in order to contrast these states of reduced clarity and alertness with the phenomena featuring in the process of 'introversion' and the heightened state of 'quiet alertness', which is the final goal of 'introversion'. The results of this comparative investigation have provided the empirical data for the definition of the process of 'introversion' and the 'quiet state of alertness'. The insights gained from this analysis have established the formal characteristics of the various states of consciousness examined. Phenomenology, however, cannot be practiced in some 'virtual space', but must be verified by empirical reality. Thus the second part of the book will explore empirical states of consciousness based on authentic records of personal experience of different mental states and the phenomena encountered, which were all spoken by individual subjects while they were immersed in the process of 'introversion' and/or absorbed in the 'quiet state of alertness'. The empirical data were thus the most authentic and immediate protocols of consciousness available to research, since they were not retrieved in retrospect from the subject's memory. In part two, we will try to verify whether the theoretical findings of part one, relating to the definitions of 'introversion' and the 'quiet state of alertness', are confirmed by the empirical data. Yet before proceeding with this task, we need to examine if, or to what extent, the structural characteristics of the 'quiet state of alertness' are grounded in the various stages that are passed through during the process of 'introversion'. In particular, the questions to be raised are the following:

1. Why is it that the second stage of the process of 'introversion' is not yet classified as the 'quiet state of alertness'? What happens in particular during the process by which the consciousness of 'introversion' is transformed into the 'quiet state of alertness'?

2. How can we identify intelligibly the structure of definite 'states' within the consciousness encompassed by 'introversion' (including the 'quiet state of alertness')?

3. Are there any states of consciousness at all that consist exclusively of the formal framework of the 'quiet state of alertness' and do not have any empirical 'content'?

As to item 1: The process of 'introversion' is triggered by the subject and his/her deliberate 'determination' to engage in a meditational exercise by which he/she may be advanced to the 'quiet state of alertness', which is the ultimate goal of this enterprise. The deliberate 'determination' to embark on this process is generated and 'encoded' in the 'waking consciousness' before the meditational practice is begun. For this reason we may expect that while 'introversion' is in progress, remnants of the 'waking consciousness' will persevere at first, but as 'introversion' progresses, more and more features of the 'quiet state of alertness' will emerge and so the structure of the 'waking consciousness' will be transformed. At the beginning of this predetermined process, the 'waking consciousness' and the consciousness of 'introversion' are thus intertwined; but in the advanced stage of 'introversion', it is the dynamic consciousness of 'introversion' and, finally, the 'quiet state of alertness' that are entwined. In the incipient stage of 'introversion', the only characteristic relating to the 'quiet state of alertness' is the 'encoded' determination to advance to the calm and serene state. As 'introversion' progresses, we may encounter ever more distinctive features of the 'quiet state of alertness': the mind is shut off from the world of sense perception, and, as a consequence, the mind has become unresponsive to sensual stimuli, and acts of the will are allayed, and so is discursive thinking; there is, moreover, a growing awareness in the 'experiencing I' that it is progressively permeated by a calmness within, emanating from the sphere of the body. These are all pivotal characteristics of 'introversion', which indicate that consciousness is about to be transformed, and the mind progressively emptied of all object-related 'content', thus becoming uniform and homogeneous in the process. However, several of the criteria necessary for an altered state of consciousness to be classified as the 'quiet state of alertness' are still missing: The mind is still responsive to disruptions and to the persevering aftereffects of occasional incidents which had happened in the 'waking consciousness'. This shows that the 'waking consciousness' has not yet been entirely been replaced by the 'quiet state of alertness', for the 'waking state' still has some detrimental influence on the ongoing process of calming and emptying the mind.

On the second stage of 'introversion' the structure of consciousness is already dominated by the pivotal characteristics of the 'quiet state of alertness'. This happens to an extent that one may wonder why the given altered state of consciousness is still considered an integral part of the consciousness of 'introversion' rather than of the 'quiet state of alertness'. The answer to this question, however, cannot yet be given and has to be deferred to the next chapter, in which some key-phenomena will be identified that are exclusively found in the 'quiet state of alertness'. At this juncture it may suffice to state that the reason why the second stage of 'introversion' is as yet claimed to differ from the 'quiet state of alertness' is the fact that the subject has at this stage still the intuitive awareness that the process of 'introversion' continues to advance and that has not yet reached the final goal. It is the lingering intuitive awareness that the growth of inner calm is still in progress and advancing towards the intended state of 'empty, motionless calmness', along with the concomitant awareness that the flow of experience has not reached complete stasis, which are all distinctive criteria for classifying the second stage of 'introversion', that corroborate the claim that the given mental condition is not identical with the 'quiet state of alertness' but rather a state preceding it.

The transformation of the consciousness of 'introversion' into the 'quiet state of alertness' is accomplished when the dynamic process of 'introversion' has ended, i.e. when the practitioner has become fully absorbed in the state of 'empty calmness' and thus become aware that he/she has reached the intended final goal of 'introversion'. It is only then that the 'encoded determination', which has so far directed the process of 'introversion', is rendered inactive. (It should be added, however, that the 'encoded determination' remains engrained in consciousness as a latent disposition, and can be activated at any time, particularly when the 'quiet state of alertness' is inadvertently exposed to some disruption, or when it is intermittently destroyed by some violent intrusion, or a traumatic event, and needs to be restored hereafter.) On the basis of these considerations we may state that *the 'quiet state of alertness' can be claimed to have become empirical reality only, if the person immersed in this altered state of consciousness has lost the awareness that he/she is still engaged in the process of 'introversion', and if any awareness that 'introversion' is controlled by the 'predetermined disposition' to aspire to the ultimate state of inner calm has disappeared in the 'experiencing I'.*

As to item 2: The definition of the 'quiet state of alertness' proposed above is exclusively founded on formal characteristics. This means that *so far the 'quiet state of alertness' has only been approached by its formal structure. But any formal structure inevitably requires some 'content'. This is why a full phenomenological description of the 'quiet state of alertness' can only be provided when features of its 'content' are considered as well.* In other words, the essence of the 'quiet state of alertness' can only be fully elucidated in phenomenological terms and with some claims to validity, when its formal framework is related to empirical items supplying its 'content'. **In empirical reality, the 'quiet state of alertness' is not only a formal mental framework, but one that is filled with experiential content that is generated by** (so-called) **secondary ('imported') dispositions, which originate from the antecedent 'waking state'.**

By 'imported dispositions' we understand dispositions that have been intentionally 'encoded' in the 'waking consciousness' for the purpose of determining the course of events both during the ongoing process of 'introversion' and after the 'quiet state of alertness' has been achieved. For example, when a person wants to restore the malfunction of a diseased bodily organ, he/she will 'programme' or 'encode' the intention of curing the malfunction into the mindset before embarking on the process of 'introversion'; this can be achieved, for instance, by applying the method of 'imaginative visualization'; the 'encoded disposition' is 'imported' and released subliminally during the *process of 'introversion'*, whereas the 'primary disposition' of aspiring to the 'quiet state of alertness' as the final goal continues to prevail. In the 'quiet state of alertness', however, the 'secondary' viz. 'imported disposition' is still active and is released and may achieve the intended purpose. (The terms 'primary disposition' and 'secondary disposition' have been introduced to facilitate understanding of the two similar, albeit different mental processes.)

When exploring individual states of consciousness, two viable systematic approaches are at one's disposal. One option is to arrange and classify systematically all the phenomena and empirical data that can be found and identified in a given state of consciousness. In such a systematic approach, there is a single category that encompasses exclusively all the phenomena that appear in, or that can be allocated to the 'quiet state of alertness', whereas the phenomena and responses that can be traced to 'secondary dispositions' are assigned to a different category. By this approach a fairly reliable and complete phenomenology of all the items appearing in the 'quiet state of alertness' can be established. In order to illustrate this approach, a practical example shall be referred to: The fleeting awareness that a phenomenon is about to 'arrive' in the vista of the 'quiet state of alertness' evokes instantly diverse 'pointed feelings' in the 'experiencing I' – but all of these feelings are phenomenologically consonant with the sensitive framework of the 'quiet state of alertness', even though these feelings are (from a formal point of view) actually responses to an in-coming 'object' that is unfamiliar and perceived as 'foreign'. Another example is the way 'thinking' operates in the 'quiet state of alertness': An inevitable prerequisite for the process of thinking to function is that the (so-called) 'cognitive apparatus' is available and 'switched on'. Yet the various modes of thinking elicited in the 'quiet state of alertness' are, phenomenologically speaking, not acts of discursive thinking at all, but cognitive processes elicited by a 'secondary' disposition' that has been 'imported' from the 'waking consciousness' and released in the 'quiet state of alertness'.

The second feasible approach is categorizing the modes of experiencing and the subject matters emerging in a given state of consciousness in the following way: All content-related issues are assigned to one category, whereas another category covers the various modes of experiencing, which will reveal that the overall experience is a complex whole. The entire complex of experiences encompasses not only all the formal characteristics of the 'quiet state of alertness', but contains also all 'secondary dispositions' and the responses triggered by them. In order to be able to recapture this empirical occurrence terminologically, we have to introduce a new concept: the term of 'the interlacing' of phenomena, i.e. phenomena originating from the 'waking consciousness' may cross over and be 'interlaced' phenomena germane to the 'quiet state of alertness'. Hence we may state: *The consciousness of the 'quiet state of alertness' is interlinked or interlaced with phenomena and modes of experience released by 'secondary dispositions', which have been transferred from the 'waking consciousness', in which they have originally been generated.*

The way in which 'interlacing' functions in empirical reality can best be illustrated by an example demonstrating how emotional states may be 'interlaced': The basic mood of 'quiet, clear, and empty calmness' can be 'interlaced' with the non-directional feeling of 'angst', particularly when the 'thing arriving' is felt to be portentous and grave, though it can as yet not be seen. Thus the underlying mood of inner calm becomes 'interlaced' with feelings that are discordant with the serene condition of the 'quiet state of alertness'. – Another example is the case of a person who reposes in a state of perfect equanimity but is suddenly overcome by feelings of defiance, when he/she is confronted with a 'thing arriving' in the vista of 'inner sight' that is experienced as something menacing. The person concerned experiences the 'interlaced' emotional response simultaneously, i.e. the sense of repose and 'trust' is instantly interlaced with feelings of fear and defiance. This indicates that the 'interlacing' of feelings, or of emotional states, occurs automatically and instantaneously, and results in a complex emotional condition. The response to disturbing feelings of this kind can only be overcome if the intrusive feeling is turned into an 'object' of meditative attention in the 'quiet state of alertness' and is dissolved by applying this stratagem. The device of obviating and dispelling unwanted feelings that might arise in the 'quiet state of alertness' or during the process of 'introversion' can be programmed (as it were) in the 'waking consciousness' thus operating as a 'secondary disposition' that can be triggered in the 'quiet state of alertness' when such an incident occurs. By applying this mental device, the state of inner calm can be preserved, while unwelcome feelings and disruptive responses are eroded.

These examples may suffice as illustrations of the phenomenon of 'interlaced feelings' that may occur in the context of 'introversion' and the 'quiet state of alertness'. It would, however, require a more in-depth analysis, if one wished to demonstrate more specifically the way in which the formal structure of the 'quiet state of alertness' and the processes elicited by 'secondary dispositions' are intertwined and 'interlaced' in empirical reality.

What has been stated so far provides ample evidence for the fact that the consciousness of a subject that is absorbed in the 'quiet state of alertness' is not really empty, but rather filled with diverse experiential 'content'. This consists (amongst many other things – as will be shown below) of intense, affect-charged emotions, pointed feelings, desires, acts of assent, a 'show of pictures', processes of meditation and even spontaneous modes of thinking, which are coherently structured even though they are not controlled by the 'I'. Irrespective of these intriguing empirical facts, which surely deserve further consideration, we need to return to the actual focus of our enquiry, which is the analysis of phenomena becoming manifest in the 'quiet state of alertness' that have mystical import. When examining a specific state of consciousness, it is indispensable to verify if the phenomena occurring in it are rooted in or originate from the 'waking consciousness', or if they are phenomena that can be encountered exclusively in the consciousness of 'introversion' and/or the 'quiet state of alertness'. In order to carry out such a discerning investigation, we first have to establish a clearly structured taxonomy of phenomena, as well as to supply tangible and reliable criteria for identifying the phenomena encountered in a given 'state of consciousness'.

The pivotal criteria for identifying the 'waking consciousness' are (as outlined above) the following: The 'waking state' is (amongst other things) generally controlled by acts of the will, replete with processes of discursive thinking governed by the 'I', as well as by deliberate acts of concentration, and marked by the continued responsiveness to external and internal stimuli. The consciousness of 'introversion', by contrast, is marked (amongst other aspects) by the presence of the subconscious 'awareness' of the 'primary disposition' to advance to a higher state of consciousness, i.e. the 'quiet state of alertness'; this 'primary disposition' is generated in the 'waking state', in which the wish to embark on the process of 'introversion' for the purpose of advancing to the 'quiet state of alertness' is instilled in a subject. The consciousness of 'introversion' can be said to be established when the subject is aware of the 'determining tendency' inside himself urging him to advance towards the desired goal of the 'quiet state of alertness'. The 'quiet state of alertness', finally, is marked in particular by its uniquely clear and hyper-lucid condition, its emptied state from which all object-related 'content' has been temporarily removed, and by the underlying mood of inner calm permeating the entire space of consciousness, and the function of 'inner sight', which is the only active function remaining in the otherwise entirely passively receptive 'self'.

But it appears necessary to add a few more explanatory comments on the characteristics of the 'quiet state of alertness' at this point. The term 'emptying' needs to be clarified to obviate misunderstandings: 'emptying' or 'vacating' the mind is a significant mental process in 'introversion'; this does not mean that all experiences and phenomena are to be eliminated from consciousness, but only that items of 'content' persevering from the 'waking consciousness' are to be vacated; this is achieved by mental processes generated by both the 'primary disposition' and by 'secondary dispositions'. 'Secondary dispositions' can usually develop freely in the 'quiet state of alertness', i.e. without being disrupted or stalled by other kinds of experience, and they can, for this reason, remain as items of the 'content' in the 'quiet state of alertness'. *From a formal point of view, the empirical condition of consciousness can be said to be 'empty' when thoughts and image-bound inner perceptions, which are triggered by secondary dispositions, and when responses to phenomena 'arriving' in consciousness occur in a state of consciousness that is otherwise entirely empty.*

This does not mean, however, that the vacated consciousness of 'quiet alertness' is entirely devoid of emotional states, and all feelings are 'laid to rest', but rather that the feelings that are elicited by 'secondary dispositions' are gradually 'stilled', and eventually absorbed by the calmness permeating the 'quiet state of alertness'. We shall see later that it is rather difficult to argue in special instances that the 'quiet state of alertness' has indeed been reached if we rely on only one criterion. It may happen, for instance, that in a person who is immersed in the 'quiet state of alertness', symptoms of emotional arousal can be observed. These symptoms, however, can be explained as originating from the changing conditions in the body during the ongoing process of 'introversion'. Such somatic responses subside, however, as soon as the 'quiet state of alertness' has fully developed. This suggests that the temporary emotional responses are stilled by the all-pervasive calmness within. The person immersed in the 'quiet state of alertness' is eventually absorbed in inner calmness and will abide in this state of repose as long as the 'quiet state of alertness' remains fully integrated.

Another concept that needs to be explained is that of 'inner sight' ("Innenschau"). This is a mental capacity and a distinctive feature of the fully developed 'quiet state of alertness'. The capacity of 'inner sight' can only evolve when all the other prerequisites necessary for establishing the 'quiet state of alertness' are given. **'Inner sight', being a function of the 'I' in the 'quiet state of alertness', inevitably requires an 'object' to be perceived – and this 'object' may either be a phenomenon surfacing from within the stream-of-consciousness, or an 'object' perceived as 'arriving' in the vista of 'inner sight' [either from within or from beyond the confines of the 'individual self'].**

A person engrossed in the 'quiet state of alertness' and aware of it will experience his/her mental state as one that is coherently structured, homogeneous and receptive to in-coming phenomena, which he/she can observe due to the capacity of 'inner sight', like a spectator reposing in calmness.

As to item 3: The intricate question as to whether there are only 'interlaced' states of consciousness in empirical reality, or if the 'quiet state of alertness' can prevail as a purely formal framework, i.e. one that is entirely devoid of empirical content, calls for a more detailed answer. We have previously stated that the 'quiet state of alertness' is not entirely without any 'content' as there is no 'inner sight' without an 'object' to be observed. Though the earlier claims are still valid, they need to be qualified further on the basis of empirical data. For this purpose we will consider the following example:

When the self-induced process of 'introversion' reaches the final goal of the 'quiet state of alertness' without any processes triggered by 'secondary dispositions' having become apparent at any stage of its progress, we are inclined to assume that the 'quiet state of alertness' attained is perfect and has been entirely untainted by other phenomena or influences. However, this is so only apparently, because once a 'secondary disposition' has been 'encoded' in consciousness before 'introversion' has started, it will remain engrained in the mind, though it does not necessarily have to be elicited in every meditational exercise or course of 'introversion'. In other words, a 'secondary disposition' may remain 'dormant' in a given process of 'introversion'. And this is the reason why the assertion that the 'quiet state of alertness' is only a formal structure without any 'content' is flawed, and has to be qualified. The 'quiet state of alertness' is an altered state of consciousness that is only seemingly empty, for it does not only contain 'secondary dispositions' as latent items of 'content', but the awareness of the clear, lucid condition of inner calm germane to the 'quiet state of alertness' is also an experience of its 'content'. In other words, the calmness, the empty and lucid condition of the 'quiet state of alertness' itself may be the 'object' of 'inner sight'. The 'primary disposition' of advancing to the 'quiet state of alertness' through the practice of 'introversion' governs the process throughout, and is not extinguished in the 'experiencing I' after it has reached the 'quiet state of alertness'. The 'primary disposition' rather tends to persevere and is inherently disposed to advance the 'experiencing I' even beyond the confines of the 'quiet state of alertness', towards the liminal realm of the 'ecstatic consciousness', in which the 'experiencing I' may become 'ecstatically' absorbed in unfathomable calmness. The stages of this liminal process can be described as follows: The calmness within is the only experiential 'content' or 'object' perceived in 'inner sight'. As long as the calmness is experienced as 'arriving' in consciousness, it is identified as an 'object' though its state-like nature continues to unfold. In the ultimate stage, calmness is no longer felt to be an 'object', but as an infinite, all-pervasive emotional condition in which the 'experiencing self' becomes gradually absorbed, until it is ultimately extinguished in it. The flow of experience slows down more and more, until any awareness of time is lost. Finally, any awareness of 'I-hood' in the perceiver is suspended, and thus the subject-object split is eroded. The 'experiencing I' becomes (as it were) extinguished and absorbed by unfathomable 'emptiness', all-encompassing 'calmness' – a liminal experience which some practitioners have metaphorically described as 'clear emptiness' and 'motionless calmness'.

It should be added, however, that none of the experiences described here will happen exactly in this way in empirical reality, because every single experience of this kind is unique and inevitably coloured by the individual personality. Over and beyond this, experiencing in the 'quiet state of alertness' depends, by definition, on the full function of 'inner sight'. This requires that the subject-object division must be maintained. During the liminal experience, however, the subject-object division is gradually reduced and ultimately disabled, when the serene state of 'quiet alertness' is transformed and replaced by elements of the 'ecstatic consciousness'. In the 'ecstatic consciousness' proper, the subject-object division is entirely suspended. For instance, when the 'experiencing self' is passively so intensely overwhelmed by unfathomable calmness that any self-awareness is eclipsed (for the time being), the function of 'inner sight' is no longer sustained. Liminal experiences of this kind are thus no longer part of the consciousness of the 'quiet state of alertness', but occur largely or exclusively in the 'ecstatic consciousness'. In the example described, the 'quiet state of alertness' has been entirely replaced by the 'ecstatic consciousness', which culminates ultimately in the state of 'no-consciousness', in which "time has come to a standstill" and "the 'I' has passed away into 'nothingness'".[102]

Some of these experiences and phenomena featuring in them can as yet not be fully understood on the basis of the insights provided so far by this investigation, as we have not yet explained some of the key concepts that are vital for enabling such understanding. This

---

102   Albrecht does not indicate the sources of these quotations. He seems to be quoting Eckhart and/or Tauler from memory.

applies in particular to the (seemingly paradoxical) *phenomenon of experiencing the condition of the 'quiet state of alertness' while immersed in this state of consciousness.* From the records examined we may infer that experiences elicited in the 'quiet state of alertness' tend to evoke subliminally the aspiration in the 'experiencing I' to probe more deeply into the "void, clear and motionless calmness" within, since this serene and tranquil mental state has become the perceiver's ultimate value. Experiencing the 'quiet state of alertness' within the 'quiet state of alertness' is a liminal event that has the pivotal hallmarks of a special (a-personal) variety of mystical experience. The distinct features of this mystical experience will be elaborated in part three of this study. At this point it may suffice to say that 'the quiet state of alertness' may be perceived within the 'quiet state of alertness' with such intensity that the awareness of a subject-object division is entirely eclipsed. It may thus be identified as a variety of mystical experience known from the records of Buddhist mystics, and (more rarely) in Western mystical tradition, for instance, from accounts of Quietist mystics.

What has been stated above has supplied a very important insight in view of the subsequent enquiries into the nature of mystical consciousness. We may thus summarize that different states of consciousness can be encountered within the overall context of the 'quiet state of alertness'; most importantly, there is the variety in which the 'quiet state of alertness' itself becomes the 'object' of perception of 'inner sight': *The consciousness encompassing the 'quiet state of alertness' may itself become the 'content' and sole 'object' of inner perception in the 'quiet state of alertness'; this, however, happens only rarely, in a phenomenological borderline-case. In empirical reality we do not encounter a 'quiet state of alertness' that is entirely devoid of 'content', because there are always items of 'content' in consciousness that are triggered by 'secondary dispositions', which have become engrained in a subject's consciousness in the 'waking consciousness' before embarking on the process of 'introversion'.*

The Focal Points of the Investigation

In the following, various states of consciousness will be explored which will collectively be referred to as experiences occurring in the 'quiet state of alertness'. The investigation will again apply primarily a phenomenological approach, though it will occasionally be necessary to supply authentic empirical data verbatim based on personal records of individual subjects. This is a methodological requirement, not least because authentic records alone can provide a sound empirical basis for the systematic scientific analysis of both the formal structure and the empirical 'content' of altered states of consciousness. To start with, it is imperative to establish the epistemological criteria and the guidelines for the subsequent enquiry:

1. *One indispensable methodological requirement is that all the empirical records examined must be specific enough to permit the formal structure of the 'state of quiet alertness' to be discerned and identified as the mental framework in which these records have been produced.* The question as to whether it has indeed been the 'quiet state of alertness' in which the events recorded have occurred, or if the recorded events refer to experiences made in different altered states of consciousness, must be clearly ascertained in each case. This stringent differentiation is necessary because it is possible that the 'quiet state of alertness' is terminated by some interference or disturbing subject matter surfacing instantly in consciousness. It may happen, for instance, that the 'quiet state of alertness' is abruptly substituted by the 'somnambulist state'; in some individuals the latter state may 'switch on' spontaneously, as it were, 'out of the blue'. Such cases must be identified and ruled out, since the aim of this study is to establish a sound phenomenology of genuine varieties of mystical experience, notably of varieties of mystical experience encountered in the 'quiet state of alertness'. Thus phenomena and experiences that surface in the 'somnambulist consciousness' have little heuristic value in the context of mysticism, though this does not mean that genuine mystical experience cannot occur in the 'somnambulist state' as well – it only eludes verification, and this is why records retrieved from the 'somnambulist state' are dealt with only in passing. Somnambulist experiences are thus considered as borderline phenomena of

consciousness, and are here used only as contrasting reference-frames for the phenomena appearing in the 'quiet state of alertness'. Phenomena that do not appear in the consciousness of the 'quiet state of alertness' are not systematically analysed in this critical enquiry, even if they could shed some light on the nature of mystical experience. *The methodology of this investigation demands, as it proceeds, that ever new criteria are supplied by which the validity of the proposed conception of the 'quiet state of alertness' is further substantiated.*

2. From amongst the great variety of experiences encountered in the 'quiet state of alertness' only those have been selected that elucidate essential features of 'mystical consciousness'. That is to say, it is not our intention to give a lively narrative of a mystical experience; we do not give a descriptive account of "how and what to experience in the quiet state of alertness"; our intention is rather to offer a representative range of phenomena that are relevant or indispensable for establishing the vital characteristics of genuine mystical experience. By applying this analytical approach it will be possible in the end to define and clarify current concepts that have mystical import, notably such traditional concepts as 'conversion' and 'preparation', by tracing the development of these notions in diverse empirical records. We are going to examine a few successive sequences of records from subsequent mystical events, in which mystical phenomena are merely flashing up, and the mystical event is described merely as an ephemeral, colourless or fleeting experience, though it is one that has a lasting after-effect. Such records thus illustrate the transformation of a subject's 'dispositions' before and after the mystical event. At the end of such recorded sequences of a subject's encounters with the mystical, a wide variety of phenomena with distinct mystical import can be identified.

3. So far the concept of 'inner sight' has not yet been sufficiently explained. Only the question referring to "the conditions required for 'inner sight' to operate" has been answered. The question, however, of what 'inner sight' actually is phenomenologically and empirically has not yet been explained. The reason for this apparent shortcoming is the fact that in order to answer this question we need to define first the crucial key-concept of 'arriving'. Defining the concept of the 'object arriving' in consciousness is thus the third focus of our

enquiry. By this we understand, more specifically, the various potential 'forms' in which an 'object' may be perceived as 'arriving' in consciousness, notably and more specifically in the vista of 'inner sight' within the 'quiet state of alertness'. We shall trace and identify a wide variety of such 'forms of arriving' and illustrate the phenomenon by representative examples.

The various experiences described in the records as occurring in the 'quiet state of alertness' have been classified by two pivotal criteria of discretion: the phenomenon of 'enhanced proficiency', which is enabled and facilitated in a subject when immersed in the 'quiet state of alertness', and the 'phenomenon arriving' witnessed in the 'quiet state of alertness'. This methodological approach has proved helpful, first, because the instances of 'enhanced proficiency' do confirm what has previously been stated on this phenomenon, and, secondly, because it offers a broad empirical basis for exploring a large number of 'phenomena arriving' in the vista of 'inner sight' in 'the quiet state of alertness'.

Enhanced Proficiency in the 'Quiet State of Alertness'

Psychosomatic Processes

Amongst the numerous varieties of 'enhanced proficiency' that may occur in empirical reality in a person engrossed in the 'quiet state of alertness', we have first chosen 'psychosomatic processes' for illustration. A psychosomatic process is pre-determined by a conscious decision and triggered in the mind (psyche), though its after-effects become manifest in the body. However, we are not concerned here with exploring the underlying mechanisms and cause-effect relationships governing psychosomatic responses, not least because these unusual processes of the psyche largely elude rational analysis. On the other hand, there is no denying that 'psychosomatic processes' do exist. This is an empirical fact that can be verified by such a commonplace situation as moving one's arm intentionally, which is a somatic response triggered by an act of the will. But the 'psychosomatic processes' addressed here are more complex and elusive; we will use only examples in which the subject has been absorbed in the 'quiet state of alertness'. Objective empirical evidence for the fact that 'enhanced proficiency' is a real phenomenon can be provided, for example, by measurements of somatic phenomena, like increased or lowered body temperature. The effect of a psychosomatic process can thus be assessed objectively by criteria derived from the natural sciences. Amongst the effects elicited by meditative practices are rather spectacular ones, like the astonishing feats of fakirs, or those of Tibetan monks, who, after long-term practice, had acquired exceptional skills in controlling the body, and which enabled them to accomplish exceptional paranormal efforts.[103] The claim that

---

103 David-Neel, Alexandra. *Heilige und Hexer. Glaube und Aberglaube im Lande d. Lamaismus / Nach eigenen Erlebnissen dargestellt von Alexandra David-Neel.* [trans. Ada Ditzen]. Leipzig: Brockhaus, 1931. – [Note: Since the 1950s when Albrecht's book was published, countless publications in the field of empirical psychology, physiology, neuroscience and neuro-theology have appeared, in which the phenomenon of 'enhanced proficiency' enabled in altered states of consciousness is examined. Several studies deal with the somatic and cognitive impact of different kinds of meditational practices and have examined the claims to objectivity of this phenomenon by the use of current scientific methodology. – A representative survey of recent empirical research in this field, notably the psychosomatic impact of Hatha Yoga, has been provided by Raub, James A. "Psychophysiologic Effects of Hatha Yoga on Musculoskeletal and Cardiopulmonary Function: A Literature Review." *Journal of Alternative and Complementary Medicine* (New York) 8 (2002): 797-812. (Raub's research report includes a representative bibliography of important studies in this field carried out during the 1980s and 1990s.) For a more recent research report on the psycho-physiological impact of the long-term practice of meditation see Dooley, Christopher. "The Impact of Meditative Practices on Physiology and Neurology: A Review of the Literature." *Scientia Discipulorum* (SUNY Plattsburgh) 4 (2009): 35-59. – The impact of Yoga, Zen and other Buddhist practices on the body and mind has been investigated on a global scale. See, for instance, Benson, H., M. S. Malhotra, et al. "Three Case Reports of the Metabolic and Electroencephalographic Changes during Advanced Buddhist Meditation Techniques." *Behavioral Medicine* 16 (1990): 90-95; see also Newberg, Andrew and Eugene D'Aquili, M.D. *Why God Won't Go Away: Brain Science and the Biology of Belief.* New York: Ballantine, 2002; and Austin, James H. *Selfless Insight: Zen and the Meditative Transformations of Consciousness.* Cambridge, MA: MIT Press, 2011. – FW.]

psychosomatic effects are an empirical fact is also evident from the practice of 'autogenic training',[104] though these accomplishments are rather trivial in comparison to the extraordinary feats of the fakirs and Buddhist monks.

The somatic impact of sensations of warmth generated by the practice of 'autogenic training', for instance, by visualizing the flow of one's blood into individual parts of the body, can be measured objectively: the increase in body temperature as well as the increase in the volume of a particular limb can be measured, thus providing verifiable empirical data. The imagined biological process, visualized in the 'quiet state of alertness', triggers the function of the vegetative nervous system, which regulates the blood vessels. In this way, the flow of blood through the capillaries, modified mentally by 'autogenic training', will remove the sensation of cold feet, or conversely, may cause a heated brow to feel cold. A Tibetan monk is able to remain seated in the snow for hours without getting any chilblains or frozen feet, even though he does not wear any clothes. The monk is even capable of causing frozen clothes, which have been put on his body, to thaw, and is, over and beyond this, even able to make these clothes dry up. Other psychosomatic events are, for instance, temporary insensitivity to pain – a phenomenon that also occurs in hypnosis. Another liminal somatic performance and instance of 'enhanced somatic proficiency' has been reported by a fakir who was able to evoke in himself a state of hibernation, in which the biological functions of the body were reduced so drastically that the fakir could even be buried alive for several hours without suffocating in the coffin. Furthermore, it is possible to cause blisters or bleeding wounds in one's body by means of imaginative visualization. There is also evidence that symptoms of diseases can either be enhanced or removed; in sports the performance can be enhanced and improved by the practice of mental training alone. These examples of psychosomatic after-effects elicited in the 'quiet state of alertness', and generated by meditational techniques, have revealed that there are three major characteristics inherent in psychosomatic processes. These

---

104 Schultz, I. H. *Das Autogene Training. Versuch einer Klinisch-Praktischen Darstellung.* Leipzig: Thieme, 1932. See particularly ch. III.

three characteristics, which are also relevant for the further progress of our investigation, are the following:

1. Image-bound meditative visualizations can be the cause and the starting point of self-generated somatic after-effects. – 2. There is evidence that certain physical features and/or the condition of a person's body can be changed by the practice of 'autogenic training'; this is positive proof that the transfer of psychic experience to the somatic sphere does occur in empirical reality. – 3. An experience occurring in the 'quiet state of alertness' can change a given disposition and will remain stored in consciousness and thus has a transforming impact on any subsequent experience in the 'waking consciousness'.

Meditative Visualization of Past Experience

The first and the third statements above will be corroborated in some detail in the following section. Meditative, image-based visualizations do not only have an impact on the progress of psychosomatic processes, but the effort to achieve what is meditatively envisioned has a persevering effect on the mental condition as a whole. Meditative visualizations may thus change the framework of an existing disposition so that, as a consequence, the response to a situation recalled from memory will hereafter be a different one. Consider, for example, the case of a shy person who is afflicted by his (apparent) disability of speaking freely in public, without stuttering, in front of an audience. He is scared and deeply upset whenever he is faced with the situation of having to deliver a speech. The task of having to speak fluently in front of a big audience triggers distressing emotions, and along with it, a 'mental inhibition', by which his potential skill and performance as a speaker are significantly impaired. The prevailing emotional condition in the given situation is extreme unease and anxiety. The feeling of unease is even more intensified by worries about his well-being, and the anticipation of the (expected) unfavourable response of the audience, and by the painful awareness of his inferiority, his deficiencies, his feelings of anxiety and self-doubt, which all result in the embarrassing desire to 'crawl away secretly'. These negative expectations and assessment of his present condition are reinforced by the memory of situations in which he likewise failed as a speaker. All these experiences accumulate, resulting in an extremely tense and agitated state of mind, in which discordant thoughts and incongruous ideas tend to persevere so that he is likely to be led astray. 'Desperate' attempts to control his concentration and line of argument impede the free-flowing course of ordered thinking even more. In the end, the speaker is no longer able to render his speech fluently and coherently, so that his pitiable state of inhibition and distress is revealed to the audience. Considering this example, the pivotal point in the speaker's mental condition (I think) is that he continues to stick to the rigid behavioural pattern of past experience, which has become deeply engrained in his mind and is triggered again whenever he is faced with such a situation. When this person is advised, however, to practice 'autogenic training', or any other meditational technique aimed at overcoming this inhibition or (supposed) disability, he is likely to succeed in changing the disruptive behavioural pattern. By applying the technique of 'imaginative visualization' in the 'quiet state of alertness', the disabled speaker is advised to imagine and focus on the situation of him delivering a speech in front of a big audience. By revolving meditatively around this mental image, a new mental image of his situation as a speaker is produced, albeit in the context of the soothing impact of the calmness of the 'quiet state of alertness'. The feelings elicited in the speaker in this new imagined situation are no longer anxiety, distress or unrest, but self-assurance and confident dedication to the task ahead. He is even able to feel empathy with the people in the audience. On the basis of these new attitudes and responses the speaker is no longer exposed to such adverse feelings as fear of failure, shyness and anxiety. The positive feelings evoked in the 'quiet state of alertness', both pointed feelings and non-directional ones, become intertwined with the image of himself featuring as a speaker, which he has previously focused on meditatively. This produces a new mental setting in which his earlier disability and inhibitions are removed. In this way a lasting positive transformation of his habitual inhibition and alleged disability is achieved. When he is required to render a speech in front of a public audience later in the 'waking consciousness', the positively modified behavioural pattern is elicited in its entirety in his consciousness. Thus the method of 'image-based meditative visualization' in the 'quiet state of alertness' has proved to be successful in this case: the seemingly disabled speaker has indeed achieved 'enhanced proficiency' after the disruptive neurotic inhibition has been overcome and removed.

Thinking in the 'Quiet State of Alertness'

Image-based meditative visualizations [perceived in the 'quiet state of alertness'] *determine a process of* [self-]*realization that provides the basis for enhanced proficiency performance; the latter is enabled when inhibiting patterns of dispositional behaviour are transformed by the use of meditative techniques; evidence of this is supplied by the changed behavioural patterns that become manifest in the 'waking consciousness', i.e. after the 'quiet state of alertness' has subsided and been substituted by the 'waking consciousness'.* In the following, we are going to consider some instances of enhanced proficiency performance; yet all the examples illustrated have been witnessed by a subject when absorbed in the 'quiet state of alertness'.

The first focus of our considerations is coherently structured processes of thinking, which may emerge in a subject while immersed in the vacated consciousness of the 'quiet state of alertness'. In this example it is free-floating thoughts that are the only 'content' of consciousness witnessed in the given situation. These free-floating thoughts are items of 'secondary content', because they are evoked by foregoing 'dispositions', 'encoded' in the subject's 'waking consciousness', subsequently incorporated in the process of 'introversion' and, finally, in the 'quiet state of alertness'. The process of 'introversion', which is commonly governed by the 'primary disposition' to aspire towards the 'quiet state of alertness', and which has been 'encoded' in the practitioner's 'waking consciousness', and will prevail until the intended goal has been reached. It is only after this goal has been achieved that the 'secondary dispositions' become effective. While absorbed in the 'quiet state of alertness,' the subject has become a passive observer, watching images and thoughts and other phenomena appear in the vacant space of consciousness. The subject can perceive in 'inner sight' how the various phenomena 'arrive' and flow evenly along in the 'stream-of-consciousness' without any disruption. If a process of thinking is elicited, the thought will prevail as long as the subject remains engrossed in the 'quiet state of alertness'. But before we can analyse such an emerging process of thinking in detail, we have to explain the difference between the way of thinking in the 'quiet state of alertness' and the way of thinking encountered in the foregoing process of 'introversion'. This clarification is called for at this juncture because the critical reader will be wondering by now why processes of thinking can at all occur in the 'quiet state of alertness', if – as stipulated earlier – all conscious activities of the 'I', and thus any structured, goal-oriented thinking, has have been removed from consciousness by the time a subject has reached the second stage of 'introversion'. The answer to this objection is that we have to distinguish between two different kinds of thinking, which must not be mixed up: There are thoughts elicited by 'secondary processes' in the 'quiet state of alertness', and thoughts that are part of the 'primary disposition' accompanying the process of 'introversion'. 'Introversion' is a pre-determined meditational process aimed at reaching the 'quiet state of alertness' as its ultimate goal; as 'introversion' advances, the structure of consciousness is continually transformed by the process of 'vacating' the mind from any 'content' deriving from the 'waking state'; thus we can distinguish between two different degrees of clarity, and emptiness as well as calmness within the entire process of 'introversion'. A conscious act of thinking will inevitably disrupt and not advance the development of 'introversion'; this is why any discursive thinking must be eliminated from the process of 'introversion'; only when discursive thinking has been removed is the subject enabled to proceed further towards the 'quiet state of alertness'. On the first stage of 'introversion', the process of emptying and of harmonizing consciousness can be accelerated by applying the method of 'meditative visualization'. On the second stage of 'introversion', the growth of inner calm can be advanced considerably if the practitioner is instructed to imagine soothing pictures and appeasing memories, which will have a calming and comforting impact. The latter kind of thinking is thus merely a meditational device, and not an act of discursive thinking. Structured sequences of discursive thinking, however, inexorably disrupt any ongoing process of 'introversion'.

In the 'quiet state of alertness' the mental processes that have governed the ongoing progress of 'introversion' are no longer required and thus have been stilled entirely. **In the empty 'quiet state of alertness', 'secondary dispositions' (generated in the 'waking consciousness') can arise without tearing apart the delicate structure of the 'quiet state of alertness'; as we shall see later, there are several kinds of psychic and spiritual experiences as well as special capacities of a subject that can be released by 'secondary dispositions', which have been mentally 'encoded' before embarking on the process of 'introversion'.** The capacity of inward perception in the 'quiet state of alertness' cannot be attributed to a particular psychic 'layer' of an individual. Though it is true that a subject who has become absorbed in the process of 'introversion' is enabled to experience a wide variety of impressions that are not accessible in the 'waking consciousness', it is in the 'quiet state of alertness' that the door of inward perception is fully open to every kind of psychic and spiritual experience, such as a slide-like 'show of images', and the entire range of phenomena that may surface or 'arrive' or in any other way become manifest in the vista of 'inner sight'. A subject engrossed in the 'quiet state of alertness' has, over and beyond this, special access to certain areas of the 'waking consciousness' as well. For instance, while absorbed in the 'quiet state of alertness', even the capacity of discursive thinking can be released, and (as we shall see later) so can the capacity to speak spontaneously without 'switching' into the 'waking state'. There are, however, also certain kinds of experience germane to the 'waking consciousness' that cannot be retrieved by a subject when immersed in the 'quiet state of alertness': These include acts of the will and any other conscious activity of the 'I'. If, however, an act of volition is triggered in a person while he/she is immersed in the 'quiet state of alertness', the fragile fabric of the 'quiet state of alertness' will immediately collapse. From these empirical facts we may conclude that a process of thinking can only surface and survive in the 'quiet state of alertness' if it is not governed by the will of the 'experiencing I', i.e. if the process of thinking is allowed to flow independently and spontaneously through consciousness without the 'experiencing I' interfering in any way.

The processes involved when a person immersed in the 'quiet state of alertness' perceives a train of thoughts arising can best be described, if we consider the various structural components of the 'quiet state of alertness' separately. First and foremost, it should be emphasized that in this mental state thoughts arise autonomously and float along independently in the emptied, hyper-lucid and homogeneous space of consciousness. The thoughts surfacing will move along being the only 'content' of consciousness. The calmness within is the sustaining ground for any of the potential occurrences emerging in the 'quiet state of alertness'. In the vacated mental state of 'quiet alertness' all object-related emotions, as well as all of the subject's drives, desires, expectations, worries and feelings of doubt, have been removed. A process of thinking may emerge and, if it does, it will progress independently, without being interlinked with another thought or perception. The empty, calm and homogeneous condition of consciousness does not admit any interference. And as the mind is screened off against any sense perceptions, there can be no response to sensory stimuli anymore. The subject's strict determination to preserve the homogeneous structure of the 'quiet state of alertness' is a safeguard against potential obstacles, such as digressing thoughts, or ideas intruding from the imagination, which could disrupt the autonomous flow of structured thinking. The chains of associations that may surface during the process are so perfectly consonant with the ongoing course of thinking that the overall result is in fact the phenomenon of 'enhanced proficiency' in thinking.

Another characteristic of the 'quiet state of alertness' is its high degree of clarity. The level of proficiency in thinking correlates with the given degree of clarity or lucidity in consciousness. Whereas in the 'waking consciousness' the degree of clarity is dependent on the level of concentration, hence on control of the 'I', in the 'quiet state of alertness' the process of thinking is not subject to the controlling function of the 'I'. This means that thinking proceeds in a perfectly clear and lucid mental condition. The exceptional clarity of this state of consciousness provides the perfect 'medium' for 'enhanced proficiency' in thinking. Thoughts are allowed to flow and are neither harnessed (as in the 'waking consciousness') by acts of concentration, nor by acts of the will. It is only 'secondary dispositions' that are involved and that tend to chaperon the ordered flow of thoughts, holding (as it were) the strings together. The person absorbed in the 'quiet state of alertness' may thus witness passively the steady flow of thoughts emerging spontaneously. This does not mean, however, that the subject is able to reflect on the ongoing process; it rather suggests that the subject is aware of structured sequences of thought streaming freely streaming through his/her mind. *When reposing in the 'quiet state of alertness', the hyper-lucid condition of consciousness affords the 'medium' in which thinking may occur autonomously and without being disrupted by other mental process. Thinking thus acquires the quality of an immaculate tool enabled to achieve the highest capacity possible, one that operates autonomously, in a self-determined manner and empowering the subject to accomplish any task within the confines imposed by his/her natural talents and abilities.*

The term 'inner sight' does not alone refer to the capacity of becoming intuitively aware of phenomena that appear in its 'vista' in the 'quiet state of alertness'. The subject immersed in the 'quiet state of alertness' is like a spectator watching individual thoughts arise, or perceiving words surfacing in his/her consciousness. The thoughts arising that are determined by the 'encoded' 'secondary dispositions' are observed in an entirely passive, receptive manner. The passive 'disposition' becomes affiliated in the process to the passive mode of thinking – a fact that may explain why thinking in the 'quiet state of alertness' can proceed without any effort.

The analysis of the process of 'meditative visualizations' and the analysis of thinking in the 'quiet state of alertness' have yielded one insight that is particularly important: **The phenomenon of 'enhanced proficiency' that is achieved in the 'quiet state of alertness' can persuasively be explained by the unique formal structure of this state of consciousness.** It is therefore abortive to maintain that 'enhanced proficiency' in thinking can only be achieved by changes in the apparatus and/or mechanisms of thinking. For it has been shown that the apparatus and mechanisms of thinking are the same in both the 'quiet state of alertness' and the 'waking consciousness'. Yet in the 'quiet state of alertness' the process of thinking is facilitated by the perfectly pure, independent and self-generated manner by which it is allowed to proceed, devoid of any constraints imposed by volition. Thinking in the 'quiet state of alertness' thus proceeds unheeded by any disruption and unimpaired by external stimuli or other external obstacles. Thus it seems to be surprising that 'enhanced proficiency' in thinking is possible in the otherwise empty 'quiet state of alertness'. But we should not so much be astonished at the fact that 'enhanced proficiency' in matters relating to mental or spiritual phenomena is enabled in this state of consciousness; we should rather be astonished at the empirical fact that such a unique, serene mental state does at all exist, and is at our disposal *ad libitum*.

It is true that in describing the 'quiet state of alertness' and, in particular, the process of thinking featuring in it, a number of audacious claims have been made, which are likely to be questioned. And it may provoke the question, in particular, if the above claims have indeed been derived from empirical research. Admittedly, the *claim that there is an autonomous process of thinking that is neither controlled by the will, nor by any activity of the 'I,' and which can moreover abide for quite a long time without interacting with other process of consciousness, and which is, over and beyond this, the only content of a state of consciousness that is otherwise entirely empty and hyper-lucid – that is to say, the claim that there is a mental process which is* (pace *these characteristics*) *coherently structured, aimed at a specific purpose and more efficient than any form of thinking encountered in the 'waking consciousness'* – is likely to arouse considerable doubt.

I must concede that I can at the present stage of our enquiry not yet offer a persuasive explanation, nor do I have as yet sufficient data to substantiate that claim. There are currently no empirical psychological studies available (or accessible to me) in which the phenomenon of autonomous thinking in a heightened state of consciousness is addressed. The empirical insights provided here are all based on records gained from a few subjects and my own long-term practice of 'introspection'. Though the findings derived from these empirical data are convincing and persuasive to me, they are certainly subjective and thus likely to be viewed with reservation or even suspicion, and may be dismissed as speculative by empirical scientists. Such critical reservations are likely to continue until veridical evidence can be supplied on the basis of objective observational research, and/or until additional empirical data from other long-term experiments with 'introspection' or the practice of 'introversion' are provided by which these allegedly unreliable claims are corroborated.

Speaking in the 'Quiet State of Alertness'

Any person who is immersed in the 'quiet state of alertness' retains his/her ability to speak. When the 'experiencing I' has become detached from all ties with the environment, which is the case when a subject is fully engrossed in the 'quiet state of alertness', the 'experiencing I' is still able to articulate aloud what he/she is experiencing at the time. These spontaneous utterances can be listened to and recorded. This is a significant empirical fact and one that will prove to be instrumental in the further progress of our investigation. There is actually no state of consciousness in which a (healthy) human being is deprived of his/her capacity to speak. Though it is true that the 'experiencing I' does not always speak when transported into altered states of consciousness, and indeed, he/she does not have to, the fact remains that the ability to speak is preserved when a subject is transferred into an altered mental state. The faculty of speech is retained in a human being, whether he/she is placed in the 'waking state', or the 'dream consciousness', the 'somnambulist state', the 'quiet state of alertness', or the 'ecstatic state'. The ability to speak is indeed an 'ur-phenomenon' and as such inalienably an integral part of human consciousness. There is ample empirical evidence that a subject can speak while absorbed in the 'quiet state of alertness', and thus this phenomenon is neither rare nor unusual. For this reason we do not consider it necessary to elaborate on the phenomenon of speaking in altered mental states any further, by referring to the numerous psychological studies in this field. Any attempt to consider this topic further here would shift the focus of the enquiry, not least because we would have to give an overview of the complex research available in the psychology of speaking, and assess the findings critically, and in particular consider the intricate issue of why speaking has to be classified as a human 'ur-phenomenon', which again has obvious philosophical implications. We just want to recall that philosophers have claimed that the structures underlying man's perception of the world are mirrored in the structure of the language, and that in the 'ur-phenomenon' of language, the dialectical 'ur-situation' of humanity is embraced in its entirety.[105] The latter claim is reflected, for instance, in the key-word 'being' ("Dasein").[106] Wilhelm von Humboldt advocates this notion explicitly in his often quoted statement: "The act by which man is 'spinning out' language from inside himself is the same as the act by which he becomes entangled in it."[107] For our purposes, however, it is enough to be informed about the psychological processes involved in the act of speaking. In particular we have to bear in mind that the 'I' that speaks when absorbed in the 'quiet state of alertness' is embedded in the realm of language, and that in the moment a person has started to speak he/she has stepped out of the primordial

---

105 [Note: These considerations are evidently based on Heidegger, and recall Heidegger's famous statement that "language is the house of Being" ("Die Sprache ist das Haus des Seins"); cf. Heidegger, Martin. *Holzwege. Gesamtausgabe*, vol. 5, Frankfurt a. M.: Klostermann, 1950, 310. – FW.]

106 Liebrucks, B. [Note: In the original text the footnote is given as quoted. – The reference could eventually be traced to a paper by the German philosopher Bruno Liebrucks (1911-1986), which he read at a congress on German philosophy in Bremen in 1950. In the 'List of Works Cited' Albrecht only supplies the information: "Vortrag auf dem dritten deutschen Kongreß für Philosophie in Bremen 1950" (*PMB* 260) without adding any further bibliographical details. – It is possible that Albrecht heard Liebrucks' lecture on the 'essence of language' at the congress and reproduced passages from his notes or from memory. But it is also possible that he had access to the published paper of Liebrucks, which appeared shortly before Albrecht submitted the manuscript of *PMB* to the publisher in 1950; in the latter case, Albrecht may not have had all the bibliographical data at his disposal. The full bibliographical data are: "Über das Wesen der Sprache. Vorbereitende Betrachtungen." *Zeitschrift für Philosophische Forschung* 5.4 (1950): 465-485. – FW.]

107 [Albrecht does not specify the source. – Albrecht appears to have taken Humboldt's quotation from Liebrucks. The exact bibliographical details in the works of Humboldt are: Humboldt, Wilhelm Freiherr von. *Über die Kawi-Sprache auf der Insel Java, Nebst einer Einleitung über die Verschiedenheit des Menschlichen Sprachbaues und Ihren Einfluss auf die Geistige Entwicklung des Menschengeschlechts*. Vol. 1. Berlin: Königliche Akademie der Wissenschaften, 1836. lxxv. – The pun on "spinnen" in German ("Durch denselben Akt, vermöge dessen der Mensch die Sprache aus sich herausspinnt, spinnt er sich in dieselbe ein") has been adopted in the translation, despite the fact that the English phrase is odd and unidiomatic. – FW.]

entanglement in language and its objects. Moreover, we need to call to mind that in spoken language every sound is based on a "threefold semantic relationship ... namely between the speaker, the recipient and the object involved."[108] But in our investigation we will focus on a very specific mode of speaking, one that is elicited during the 'quiet state of alertness', and which is understood to be a primordial mode of speaking. As we shall see later, the somnambulist, and occasionally a subject absorbed in the 'quiet state of alertness', cannot only speak but also weep and smile. This indicates that whatever is experienced in an altered state of consciousness can become spontaneously 'incarnate' in the body and in the spoken word.

Though the act of speaking may be triggered spontaneously in a concrete event, the impetus to express one's inner experience verbally is – in the given context of the practice of 'introversion' – (generally) released in the 'quiet state of alertness' by a 'secondary disposition'. But it is important to emphasize here that there is a vital difference between this kind of 'secondary disposition', by which only the willingness to speak is evoked, and other varieties of 'secondary dispositions', like the ones addressed earlier: The 'secondary disposition' aimed at uttering verbally the subject's current experience and state of mind triggers only the primeval human capacity to speak, but it has (like the other 'secondary dispositions' outlined above) no influence at all on the 'content' of the experience and/or the further development of the experience in the 'quiet state of alertness'. Thus it can be stated that *the process of speaking in the 'quiet state of alertness' does not consist of a series of impressions emerging as objects of 'inner sight'. These verbal utterances do not occur in an empty space of consciousness. Thus the process of speaking* [in the 'quiet state of alertness'] *is only the spontaneous verbal rendering of feelings and impressions 'arriving in consciousness'; that is to say that the subject's experience is conveyed spontaneously, without reflection, and thus becomes (as it were) instantaneously 'incarnate' in the spoken word.* Speaking during the process of 'introversion', and in the 'quiet state of alertness', is thus merely a potential self-expressive corollary of the subject's experience and current condition of the mind. The

---

108 Liebrucks, B. [See footnote above].

self-expressive phenomenon of 'speaking' during the 'quiet state of alertness' must be carefully distinguished from the phenomenon of 'verbalized thinking' in the 'quiet state of alertness'. Meditative visualizations, structured verbalized thoughts and sequences of associations aimed at a particular goal are all potential items featuring in the 'quiet state of alertness', which can be watched by the 'experiencing I'. Instantaneous utterances, by contrast, mirror authentically the present condition of consciousness as well as the phenomena appearing in the 'quiet state of alertness'. The verbalized expressions of mental impressions are thus never 'objects' of 'inner sight'. The subject that is immersed in the 'quiet state of alertness' is always (more or less clearly) aware that he/she is speaking. "Speaking is the expression of impressions", though "language as such is a public secret".[109] This claim is consonant with the fact that language – though it conveys mental impressions to the surface, which can thus be witnessed from outside – is an involuntary, spontaneous human phenomenon, which is as such ultimately unfathomable.

The phenomenon of speaking instantaneously in the 'quiet state of alertness' is purely expressive. Language serves as a medium for transmitting authentically an experience encountered in the 'quiet state of alertness'. Whereas an act of speech in the 'waking consciousness' is closely tied to, and governed by, the active functions of the 'I', the language of the subject immersed in the 'quiet state of alertness' is not subject to the controlling function of the 'I', and originates from a pristine ground. In the 'waking consciousness' the 'I' controls, directs and interrupts the free-flowing, autonomous process of speaking, whereas the 'I' in the 'quiet state of alertness' is no longer fettered to rational control, or to the will, but utters what is currently passing through the subject's consciousness instantaneously, without any rational reflexion or restraint. *Enhanced proficiency in speaking in the 'quiet state of alertness' is thus enabled by the fact that the act of speaking has been freed from the bondage of rational control and other active (impeding) functions of the 'I'.* The language emitted spontaneously in the 'quiet state of alertness' has been liberated from the controlling functions of the 'I', and may thus evolve freely,

---

109 Liebrucks, B. [See footnote above.]

becomes pliable and assumes an ever changing 'body', in which the flow of inner experience is mirrored and becomes 'incarnate' in the spoken word.

The central phenomenon dealt with in this section has been that of language as a mode of expressing impressions that become manifest in the 'quiet state of alertness'. By way of conclusion, we want to consider a few general theoretical aspects of language and of the act of speaking, which are also relevant to psychology. Words are the kernels of concepts and symbols, around which the domain of feelings and the sphere of the imagination are placed. Words are the crystallizing 'core', which are encircled by a 'conceptual halo';[110] the latter may, in the course of a lifetime, develop structural and semantic patterns broadening its meaning. Words are the embodiment of some content; they are 'content' that has become 'incarnate' in language. This notion of language is a perennial facticity – language is an 'ultimate phenomenon' by which we can explain why individual words can at all emerge in the individual consciousness – in other words, why individual words may 'arrive' in the individual consciousness. Though the process of speaking itself cannot be observed by the 'experiencing I' when immersed in the 'quiet state of alertness', it is nonetheless a proven fact that a single word can 'arrive' in the vista of 'inner sight' in the empty space of consciousness, thus becoming the object of inner perception. Amongst the various 'forms' in which in-coming phenomena may 'arrive' in consciousness (which we will examine in detail below) and identified in this enquiry, one is that of a single word appearing in the vista of 'inner sight' that is comprehended and intuitively grasped to be the herald of what, for the time being, must remain shrouded in mystery.

---

110 [Note: For an explanation of the terms 'conceptual core' and 'conceptual halo' see footnote 42 above – FW.]

Associating in the 'Quiet State of Alertness'

We have considered so far 'meditative visualizations', 'autonomous processes of structured thinking' and the phenomenon of 'autonomous speaking in the 'quiet state of alertness', which are all examples of the complex phenomenon termed 'enhanced proficiency' enabled by the 'quiet state of alertness'. One requirement that must be given if performances of 'enhanced proficiency' are to happen is that they are embedded in a free-floating stream of associations. We are now going to focus on the phenomenon of freely floating associations in the 'quiet state of alertness'. We shall see that the sequences of associations that surface in the 'quiet state of alertness' are particularly helpful for explaining how 'enhanced proficiency' is achieved in consciousness.

Researches into the condition of the hypnotic and the somnambulist consciousness,[111] and studies exploring the impact of 'autogenic training',[112] have persuasively shown that enhanced memory performance can be achieved by a person when immersed in any of the above mentioned altered states of consciousness. The results of empirical research in this field have been so astonishing that some scientists have assumed that different reproductive mechanisms are at work in these altered states of consciousness than those operating in the 'waking consciousness'. For instance, in the 'waking state' the commonplace situation that may often happen is that the name of a

---

111 Trömner, Ernst. "Steigerung der Leistungsfähigkeit im Hypnotischen Zustand." *Journal f. Psychologie und Neurologie* 20.2 (1913): 181-184. – [Note: The bibliographical data have been supplemented; the data given in Albrecht's "List of Works Quoted" are flawed; they are given as: "Trömner Arch. Psychol., 1913, zit. b. Schultz, I. H. [*Das Autogene Training*, Leipzig: Thieme, 1932], S. 96". Albrecht appears to have taken the reference to Trömner's article from Schultz; but Schultz gives neither the page references, nor the title. This aside, Schultz's data are apparently incorrect, as the only printed source of Trömner's article that could be traced is not "Arch. Psychol." (i.e. *Archiv für Psychiatrie und Nervenkrankheiten*), but the *Journal für Psychologie und Neurologie*, volume 20.2 of 1913. – FW.]
112 Cf. Schultz, I. H. *Das Autogene Training. Versuch einer Klinisch-Praktischen Darstellung*. Leipzig: Thieme, 1932.

familiar person cannot be remembered at a given moment, though the name can be recalled a short time later. But when a person's name has definitely been forgotten, it cannot be recovered from memory any more in the 'waking state'. However, if the same person is transferred into the 'quiet state of alertness' the seemingly forgotten name can be recovered. Enhanced power of memory is also demonstrated by the following example. A person who can no longer fully remember the lyrics of a song learned in childhood when immersed in the 'waking consciousness' is able to recover the entire text of the song as soon he/she has become immersed in the 'quiet state of alertness'. – Similarly, a person who in the 'waking consciousness' can only remember a few hazy fragments of the day when he had an important exam is able to remember even every single detail of the examination after having been transported into the 'quiet state of alertness'. Even trifling details such as the weather conditions on the day of the exam, or the food he had for breakfast, and the conflicting feelings aroused on his way to the place of the exam – all these relatively unimportant features of the actual event have emerged from memory after the person had entered the 'quiet state of alertness'.

The phenomenon of achieving enhanced proficiency in memory performance can persuasively be explained by the unique structure of the 'quiet state of alertness'. It is a serene and lucid state of consciousness that permits the stream of associations to move freely, without any intervention by the 'I', and is (largely) impervious to disrupting influences from outside. The only content in consciousness in the examples quoted is the memory of the initial situation of the seemingly forgotten items, in which the 'experiencing I' becomes absorbed. The initial memory sparks off a train of free-floating associations. Thus, referring to the example of the forgotten lyrics above, the person can 'see' in the vista of 'inner sight' with acute clarity the visual image of the text of the first stanza of the song, and this mental picture continues to 'stay, stand still and repose' in the lucid space of consciousness. There is no external incident that might dispel or blur the person's inner perception of the visual image. As a consequence, the image contemplated evokes a series of associations, which are triggered by interlaced feelings and ideas emerging from the imagination. All these phenomena are perceived inwardly in a heightened state of clarity, which eventually supplies also the forgotten passages of the text. On the basis of such evidence, we may refute the claim that improved memory performance is achieved by a change in the mechanisms of the 'reproductive functions' (i.e. memory), since this capacity can more persuasively and exhaustively explained by the function and unique structure of the 'quiet state of alertness'. *The [unique] structure of the 'quiet state of alertness' alone offers a sufficient explanation for the phenomenon of 'enhanced proficiency' [in memory performance]; enhanced proficiency means that something that has been inaccessible to memory before is made accessible later [in a person absorbed in the 'quiet state of alertness'], and will remain accessible in the given person ever after.*

These considerations on the issue of 'enhanced proficiency' should suffice for the purpose of our investigation. But there are of course numerous examples of 'enhanced proficiency performance' from other areas of human experience. It is, however, not our intention to write a book on the striking favourable after-effects of the 'quiet state of alertness', but our aim is to provide a comprehensive phenomenological analysis of mystical consciousness. By way of conclusion, we may summarize the findings of this foregoing chapter as follows:

1. *What has been inaccessible to memory in the 'waking consciousness' may become accessible in the 'quiet state of alertness', and will remain accessible to consciousness ever after.*

2. **In the 'quiet state of alertness', the structure of 'dispositions' can be modified and new 'dispositions' generated, so that the response to stimuli of the environment is changed permanently, and this transformation continues to be effective after the 'quiet state of alertness' has ended. This empirical fact is the basis for the phenomenon of 'transformation' to evolve, which is an integral part of the process of 'introversion'** (which will be an important issue in the subsequent enquiries).

3. When exploring 'enhanced proficiency performance' in the context of the process of associations, we for the first time have encountered a phenomenon that 'arrives' in the vista of inner

perception of a person absorbed in the 'quiet state of alertness'; an object 'arriving' is thus an empirical event that does not occur in the 'waking consciousness'. The phenomenon of an 'object arriving' in the vista of 'inner sight' is crucial to different altered states of consciousness, and its phenomenological characteristics need to be explored in detail, particularly in view of our enquiry into the nature of mystical consciousness.

'The Object Arriving' ("Das Ankommende")

Any attempt at establishing a phenomenology of the 'object arriving' in the vista of 'inner sight' in the 'quiet state of alertness' must start from a definition of the term. Psychology has introduced the term 'stream-of-consciousness',[113] a metaphor referring to the continuous flow of thoughts, feelings and perceptions in consciousness. The term thus denotes the empirical fact that there is an ongoing flow of fluctuating phenomena appearing as 'objects' in consciousness, which can be perceived when the function of 'inner sight' is effective in the 'quiet state of alertness'. Any phenomenon 'arriving' in consciousness is perceived as something real and something new, since the 'object' observed is recognized as something alien, not known from previous experience, and as something that disappears again after some time from conscious awareness. A phenomenon 'arriving' usually resides in the space of consciousness only for a short time, thus the conscious awareness of the presence of the 'object' that has 'arrived' is generally rather limited in all states of consciousness, except for the 'quiet state of alertness'. An object that appears in

---

113 [Note: The term 'stream-of-consciousness' was coined by the American psychologist William James (1842-1910), and first defined by James in his *Principles of Psychology*. New York: Holt, 1890. 296-307. – The concept has become widely adopted in Europe, and it was well established in European psychology by the time Albrecht wrote *PMB*. From the 1950s onward, 'stream-of-consciousness' became also a technical term in literary studies, notably in narratology. – Cf. Goodman, Russell. "William James", *The Stanford Encyclopedia of Philosophy* (Winter 2013 Edition), Edward N. Zalta, ed. = http://plato.stanford.edu/archives/win2013/entries/james/ – FW.]

consciousness can be considered from the perspective of how it has become manifest in consciousness. Most of the 'objects' surfacing in the mind obviously just enter consciousness instantaneously, and are perceived as abiding there for some time. There is a clear awareness in the 'experiencing I' that the objects and phenomena 'arriving' are really present in consciousness, but the 'experiencing I' is unable to recognize *how* these in-coming phenomena enter consciousness, nor can the pathway of their 'arrival' be traced in retrospect by rational analysis. Thus we can only state that the phenomenon of an 'object arriving' in consciousness does exist and is a proven empirical fact; but the question of where an 'object' that has 'arrived' has actually come from, or originates, ultimately eludes rational explanation. We are faced with a borderline phenomenon, crossing the boundaries between individual consciousness and the realm of extra-mental reality. Empirical psychology cannot supply a scientific, rational answer as to how these 'objects arrive' in consciousness, and where they are coming from.

The term 'arriving' has been chosen as a technical term, because the verb 'to arrive' suggests a dynamic process. Here it refers to the process of 'becoming inwardly aware of an object' in the vista of 'inner sight'. This means that the concept of the 'object arriving' applies exclusively to a phenomenon 'arriving' in consciousness that is marked by distinct empirical characteristics: Only an 'object' or phenomenon 'arriving' which is intuitively grasped to be part of a complex whole, and which itself eludes comprehension by the 'experiencing I', qualifies as an 'object arriving'. In other words, the 'object arriving' is perceived intuitively as coming from beyond the confines of the individual consciousness, which is an integral part of an extra-mental wholeness. This extra-mental wholeness, however, can gradually reveal its 'essence' successively, and may thus be more and more clearly discerned with any consecutive perception of the 'object arriving'. We may illustrate this experiential process by way of analogy using an example of a sense perception in the 'waking consciousness': When looking at an object in a poorly lit room, which merely allows only to discern vaguely the rough outlines of an object, the perceiver will try to identify the object hypothetically, anticipating its real features. This hypothesis can be verified later, when the given object is finally revealed in the room after the light has been switched on. Or to refer to an example from another area of human experience: A feeling that is evoked in consciousness may instantaneously be linked with a sense of foreboding, or elicit the intuitive awareness that it is heralding an unknown sphere within consciousness, one that will be revealed in the future. Experiences of this kind are spontaneous, and enter consciousness unexpectedly at an instant. This is another distinctive feature by which spontaneous experiences differ from deliberate acts of cognition, in which the presence of an object that is located outside the realm of individual consciousness can always be accounted for rationally. This means that the concept of the 'object arriving' denotes a very special sequence of experience: a series of inner perceptions in which a wholeness gradually unfolds itself. At the beginning, parts of the whole are comprehended, but these parts hint ambiguously at something that exists outside the realm of the individual consciousness. At the end of such a sequence of events, the complex whole (as illustrated by the example above) can be recognized in its entirety, and this is why the word 'arriving' is particularly appropriate for designating this elusive phenomenon. Yet, we have to concede that the concept of 'arriving' is, strictly speaking, not a term derived from the psychology of consciousness, as it refers to an empirical phenomenon that does not belong to the realm of the individual consciousness, but to one transgressing its boundaries. **By the concept of the 'object arriving' we designate a wholeness that is thought to be situated outside the realm of the individual consciousness and that reveals itself increasingly to the 'experiencing self' in a series of consecutive events.**

This proposition defines, in the widest sense, what is understood by the term 'arriving'. For the purpose of our investigation, however, we have to specify this broad conception further, and define the concept more stringently, notably in two respects:

1. In this investigation the concept of the 'object arriving' is used exclusively as a term referring to experiences encountered in the 'quiet state of alertness'. This means that experiences of a similar kind, which might as well occur, for instance, in the 'waking consciousness' and/or the 'dream consciousness', have been eliminated and not classified as instances of 'arriving'. From this follows that the

'quiet state of alertness' is indispensable as the relevant mental frame of reference for the use of the concept of the 'object arriving'. This also means that the *"object arriving' is a concept supplementary to that of 'inner sight"*. Thus whenever a wholeness that is known to be located outside the confines of the individual consciousness reveals itself in a series of events featuring an 'object arriving' in the vista of 'inner sight', it is thus perceived by the 'experiencing I' in a hyper-lucid, clear and alert mental state that is inundated by calmness and otherwise completely empty.

By connecting the concept of 'arriving' strictly and conditionally to the 'quiet state of alertness', the wide range of phenomena that usually emerge in the 'waking consciousness' are ignored and excluded, though some of these phenomena are likewise marked by the feature of 'arriving' and may hint at a wholeness that becomes progressively manifest in consciousness in a sequence of events. Here I would like to call to mind the experiments on human perception undertaken by Eilks,[114] in which small figurines were put up in a darkened room, with the lights being dimmed so that the shapes of the figurines could no longer be clearly discerned. At the beginning of the experiment, the observer can merely discern the rough outlines of a figurine and thus perceives the figurine merely as an unstructured object, i.e. as a 'preliminary gestalt'. After the initial impression, the observer, adapting to the darkness, is gradually able to discern a structured shape, and eventually, when the conditions of lightning are improved, he can see the full image of the figurine. The process the perceiver passes through in this experiment has been termed 'actual genesis' ("Aktualgenese") in the Berlin School of 'gestalt psychology'. This phenomenon has been dealt with in detail by the representatives of this school of empirical psychology. Eilks's experiment has established as an empirical fact that visual perceptions are linked with both feelings and acts of thinking. But from this we may establish a close analogy between the 'actual genesis' described in the example above and the experience of a person

---

114   Eilks, Hans. "Das Vorgestalterlebnis unter Typologischem Gesichtspunkt." *Zeitschrift für Psychologie* 143 (1938): 19-79. – [Note: Page references, the full title of the periodical and the year of publication have been supplied. – FW.]

who – while absorbed in the 'quiet state of alertness' – observes phenomena 'arriving' in the vista of 'inner sight'.

The enquiries into the ways and psychological mechanisms underlying the perception of a 'gestalt' as outlined above were focussed on, and confined to, an event occurring in the 'waking consciousness'. In these experiments a physical object is placed in external space and has been the perceiver's only focus of attention. The object has clearly been the centre of attention of the perceiver, and hence been the focus of his will, as well as of his powers of concentration and conscious perception, which are all activities controlled by the 'I'. This indicates that all impressions experienced during the experiment were transmitted by sense perceptions (photoreceptors) – hence the object has definitely been seen with the physical eyes alone, and not perceived by the function of 'inner sight'.

2. The second condition stipulates that any sense perception, and any experience involving active responses, do not qualify as 'objects arriving' even when they are not linked to the 'waking consciousness' and appear in the 'quiet state of alertness'. In order to be able to understand this claim, we have to turn to an empirical phenomenon for illustration, which will reveal that the structure of altered states of consciousness is rather intricate. As stated previously, one crucial prerequisite for the 'quiet state of alertness' to develop is that the practitioner is strictly screened off against sensual stimuli and thus to ensure that all sense perceptions are shut out. It is possible, however, that the 'shutting out' of sense perceptions is achieved only partially, which means that individual sense perceptions can still be switched on even when the subject has been transferred into the 'quiet state of alertness'. This may happen when an (experienced) practitioner has previously 'encoded' in his 'waking consciousness' the 'secondary disposition' to respond to sensual stimuli before embarking on the process of 'introversion'. In this case, the 'secondary disposition' can be released without disrupting the 'quiet state of alertness', and the intended effect can be elicited. The practitioner may listen, for instance, to a musical performance with his physical senses, while the other functions of his self are dormant while he is immersed in the 'quiet state of alertness'. In such an instance, the 'waking consciousness' is not switched on by the sound of the music, because the other

necessary requirements for sustaining the 'quiet state of alertness' are preserved throughout. This may happen, for instance, in a concert with a person listening to the music while he/she is absorbed in the 'quiet state of alertness' and thus is enabled to remain engrossed in the homogeneous, calm, hyper-lucid and emptied state of consciousness. The 'I' reposing in calmness is only passively 'open' and receptive to phenomena 'arriving' from outside. In this example, the phenomenon of 'arriving' appears in the 'gestalt' of music. Individual sounds are perceived as integral parts of an extra-mental wholeness, which 'arrives' successively in the sequence of tunes resulting in the harmony of the melody. The tunes of the music are 'trickling' (as it were) into the space of consciousness, which is otherwise devoid of thoughts, reflections and acts of volition. Though the 'experiencing I' attending the concert is intuitively aware that the tunes ('objects arriving') come from an area outside the individual consciousness, it is an awareness that does not result from conscious reflection; there is no indication at all that the listener immersed in the 'quiet state of alertness' has any awareness that something is transmitted to him from outside through the sense of hearing: The sounds are rather perceived as if surfacing from within the depths of his consciousness. The sounds are perceived with heightened clarity and experienced as if they were 'figures of sound and shining light'. This means that what is experienced is no longer attributed to the auricular 'receptors' transmitting external stimuli, but as a holistic mode of inner perception. This mode of experiencing can explain why synesthetic perceptions are much more often encountered in a person when absorbed in the 'quiet state of alertness' than in a person abiding in the 'waking consciousness'.

The example of a complex sequence of auricular perceptions in the 'quiet state of alertness' described above is also useful for addressing a few more aspects of the complex process of 'introversion', and of the intricate structure of human consciousness. We want to illustrate this by an example of an 'inverted' process of 'introversion' triggered by music. It is not unusual for a person who listens intently to music to be transported into the 'quiet state of alertness' in the process. This shifting into a different mental state may either be triggered intentionally (by an encoded 'primary disposition'), or it may occur autonomously. The latter may happen, for instance, when a person listening to a musical performance in the 'waking consciousness' with rapt attention is instantaneously transferred into the 'quiet state of alertness', without having passed the path of 'introversion', and without an encoded 'primary disposition' having been released. This suggests that the full passive surrender to an object of perception – the unrestrained, receptive 'openness' to music – may likewise trigger a transformation in consciousness, and thus effect the shifting into the 'quiet state of alertness'. In everyday speech the phenomenon of becoming absorbed in an altered mental state is mirrored in the phrase: "This person has become 'absorbed' ("versunken") in the contemplation of an Alpine landscape in front of him." Experiences of this kind suggest that the 'quiet state of alertness' do not depend on a process of 'introversion' but can also be elicited autonomously and be an integral part of mundane experience. This insight opens up a particularly interesting field of empirical research, which can, however, not be explored in this investigation, let alone in this chapter, which is supposed to offer a detailed phenomenology of experiences encountered in the 'quiet state of alertness'.

The second limitation imposed on the definition of the 'object arriving' is the requirement that it does not include any 'objects' that can be traced to the external world of sense perception. Considering the experiences and phenomena just described, we need to qualify this defining criterion, conceding that an experience transmitted by auricular receptors and perceived in the 'quiet state of alertness' may, in rare instances, assume the quality of a phenomenon 'arriving' in the space of consciousness.

We have thus explained what is understood by the proviso that all experiences related to sense perceptions do not qualify as phenomena classified as 'objects arriving'. However, the question that remains to be answered is how to deal with telepathic experience. Empirical research conducted by Bender[115] has shown that there are

---

115 Bender, Hans. "Zum Problem der Außersinnlichen Wahrnehmung. Ein Beitrag zur Untersuchung des 'räumlichen Hellsehens' mit Laboratoriumsmethoden." *Zeitschrift für Psychologie* 135 (1935): 20-130. – [Note: Full title, year of publication and page references have been added. – FW.]

several varieties of telepathic experience. Some telepathic experiences can be shown to have analogies and affinities with sense perceptions. Insights derived from recent research, notably from 'gestalt psychology' and the experiments with 'emerging figurines' recorded above, appear to corroborate this claim. Von Winterstein, for instance, has reported a telepathic experience in a recent study,[116] which was methodologically based on spontaneous utterances, spoken aloud by a subject while transferred into a telepathic-somnambulist state, and/or temporarily into a telepathic state proper, which became interpolated in the 'quiet state of alertness'. The accounts of these experiences can be taken as reliable empirical testimonies, and thus enable us to assess the phenomenon of the 'object arriving' critically in the context of a telepathic experience. We are going to quote the entire document recording the spontaneous verbal utterance spoken while the subject was transferred into a telepathic state. This record is particularly helpful for our enquiry, because it addresses a wide range of characteristics that are germane to the phenomenon of 'arriving', and is thus relevant for our subsequent considerations. The telepathic utterance is quoted verbatim:

> *"For a long time, everything black. Now a spotlight, how dazzling – my eyes are nearly blinded by it. The spot of light is moving, coming closer and closer. Now darkness, W's head. Wearing something on his head. It looks as if he is sitting on something, I have to look upwards to see his face. The background around him is rather dark, only his face is lit somehow. Now again the bright spot of light coming nearer. High above the light, W's face. Almost uncanny. He must be standing on something, or sitting elevated on something. I have the feeling that I have to look up to see him."*[117]

---

116 Winterstein, Alfred Freiherr von. *Telepathie und Hellsehen im Lichte der Modernen Forschung und Wissenschaftlichen Kritik.* Leipzig: Leo, 1937. Cf. 99.

117 [Note: Italics provided. In the original German text, the passage quoted is not printed in italics and not indented. In the translation italics are used to indicate that this text is an empirical document and not part of the text of Albrecht's scientific analysis, which is printed in regular font throughout. The same principle applies to all the other quotations from empirical documents in this translation. – FW.]

After having consulted W's. [i.e. Winterstein's][118] notes describing this event, it becomes clear that Winterstein was riding a bike on a country road when the experiment was in progress. The bike was lit by a lamp fuelled by hydrocarbon gas. The report illustrates quite clearly that the impressions perceived as 'arriving' in the telepathic consciousness emerge in a series of successive perceptions; thus the experiment shows "the gradual emergence and piecemeal growth of most of the impressions conveyed by telepathy". The report also demonstrates that the 'telepathic vision' is entirely sensory. The cognitive aspect, i.e. the subject's ability and/or endeavour to recognize what the impressions actually signify, is of secondary significance. However, we have to concede that there are telepathic experiences in which other forms of 'arriving' than the visual one illustrated here become manifest. For instance, the 'messages' communicated in near-death experiences show great diversity as regards the form in which they are revealed. "The messages of dying persons show the entire scale of emotional responses that an individual has at his/her disposal, ranging from a diffuse feeling of fear, which is frankly articulated, through a state of unease and disquiet . . . to a fully developed stage of hallucinations, elicited either by a singular sense, or by all the sense organs, in which a delusory 'apparition of a ghost or of a spirit' may be evoked, or a dramatic scene may appear, in which some action takes place, which can be watched from a distance, and which is presented (more or less realistically) like on a reel. However, a scene like this can also have symbolic import."[119] Typical symbols featuring in hallucinations of dying people include, for instance, a shroud, a sympathy card, written on the occasion of the death of a beloved person, or a black cross – to name only a few.

From these enquiries we may establish four of the so-called 'forms of arriving', which typically occur in the telepathic consciousness:

1. The 'object arriving' is revealed progressively, little by little, and is grasped in a quasi-perceptual manner.

---

118 [Note: The abbreviation "W." obviously refers to Winterstein though Albrecht does not explicitly say so. – FW.]

119 Moser, Fanny. *Der Okkultismus*. 2 vols. Munich: Reinhardt, 1935. Vol. 2, 359.

2. The 'object arriving' is accompanied by intense feelings and emotions affecting and transforming the emotional condition of the 'experiencing I'.

3. The 'object arriving' consists (mainly) of pictorial images that appear as fragments of a whole that is known to exist outside the individual consciousness.

4. The 'object arriving' appears in the form of a symbol representing the extra-mental whole.

The 'object arriving' in the subject's telepathic consciousness has several characteristics by which it can (more or less unequivocally) be identified as a telepathic phenomenon. As stated in the testimony quoted, the distinctive features of the 'object arriving' in the state of telepathy are its uniqueness and its overwhelming impact. The 'object' perceived can, however, be clearly identified as a hallucinatory one, which has symbolic import, and one that triggers intense emotional responses. Finally, the telepathic 'object arriving' emerges instantaneously, but the phenomenon remains isolated and the overall experience is incoherent, because the chain of associations operating in the telepathic consciousness is rambling rather than clearly structured. But considering the data from subjective records supplied by telepathic experiments, we have to admit that the documentary materials collected are too few, too sparse and too unsystematic as regards their 'content' to allow a reliable scientific evaluation. They are not sufficient for establishing a representative analysis, let alone exhaustive phenomenology of telepathic consciousness. There is as yet no systematic phenomenology of telepathic consciousness available, and therefore we have decided not to include the few data of telepathic research that are available for the purposes of our psychological investigation. In the accounts examined, it is not even possible to discern clearly if the given telepathic experience has occurred in the 'telepathic state of consciousness' or in the 'waking consciousness', or else in the 'quiet state of alertness' or in the 'somnambulist state'. The second reason for excluding telepathic phenomena from our strict concept of the phenomenon 'arriving' is that we do not yet know anything about the extra-mental entity that is involved in the mechanisms underlying the perception of telepathic phenomena. Though there are numerous hypotheses and metaphysical hypostases, the fact remains that we do not know anything about the elusive, mysterious mechanisms that are at work when impressions and pieces of information are transmitted mentally across time and space at a long distance. For this reason it is more expedient for the purposes of our investigation to rely exclusively on dependable data, which can alone supply a reliable empirical basis for a phenomenology of consciousness that has claims to scientific validity. But still, this above excursion into the realm of telepathic experience has provided some valuable insights, notably into the so-called 'forms of arriving', i.e. the various ways in which phenomena 'arriving' in consciousness can be perceived. By way of summary we may state: **The phenomenon of an 'object arriving' in consciousness consists, in the narrow sense, of a trans-sensate sequence of experiences that is witnessed by the function of 'inner sight' in the 'quiet state of alertness'; this means that the 'quiet state of alertness' is a necessary condition for perceiving an 'object arriving'.** The 'object' 'arrives' in the vista of 'inner sight', either instantaneously displaying its entire 'gestalt', or appearing gradually, in fragments that are part of a whole, which, however, remains concealed for the time being. The manifestation of the entire whole of the 'object arriving' is a liminal experience, ultimately happening instantaneously. Hence the ultimate experience of the 'object arriving' is not a dynamic event anymore, but an instantaneous eruption. It is a forceful event that will be explored in the subsequent stages of this investigation.

The classification of the 'forms of arriving' discerned here is based on, and related to, the specific response elicited in consciousness by the given 'object arriving' – for any event in which an object perceived as 'arriving' in the vista of 'inner sight' in the 'quiet state of alertness' becomes an empirical fact only if it evokes a distinct response in the 'experiencing I'. **The 'forms of arriving' are thus identical with the 'forms of inner sight'.** It is important in our enquiry to be constantly aware of this identity between the 'forms of arriving' and the 'forms of inner sight'. But we shall nonetheless henceforth refer to 'forms of arriving' rather than to the 'forms of inner sight' if we explore the phenomenon from the perspective of the 'object' perceived; conversely, we will refer to 'forms of inner sight' when the perspective is shifted to that of the 'experiencing I'. Amongst the many 'forms of arriving' encountered in empirical reality, we will distinguish between those in which a person experiences the 'arrival' of intimations of a pointed feeling, and those in which a series of pictorial images are perceived and understood to be fragmented items of a wholeness that is about to 'arrive'. We will furthermore discern 'forms of arriving' in which a symbol appears that is intuitively grasped to be a harbinger of the wholeness, though the latter itself remains as yet undisclosed. The number of potential 'forms of arriving' is bigger than the few varieties as yet considered. So we need to explore a few more. *Any response to an 'object arriving' embraces always some immediate cognitive awareness relating to its provenance – i.e. some intuitive knowledge as to 'where' the 'object arriving' has come from or appears to be coming from.* An 'object arriving' is not only perceived on the levels of the emotions, the imagination and the symbol, nor is it alone grasped intuitively to be fragmented manifestations of a distant wholeness, but it is also experienced as coming from a specific 'direction'. Hence the 'experiencing I' has always some awareness of the direction where an incoming phenomenon is 'arriving' from. Though this awareness is not always a clear cognitive component of the experience, and may be impaired by some flicker of a doubt, we may still maintain the following claim to be empirically valid: When experiencing an 'object arriving' in the vista of 'inner sight', a particular 'space' is [intuitively] assigned to it, from which it is felt to be coming from, or seems to be coming from. Within the consciousness of the 'quiet state of alertness', the act of discerning the provenance of the 'object arriving' is spontaneous and intuitive, and thus never involves any rational reflection. The sense of direction evoked by the 'object arriving' is rather instilled by intuition, which accompanies and sustains the process of perception; this is also reflected in the emotional and imaginative responses evoked in the 'experiencing I' in the event.

Split-Off Items from the Unconscious ("Das Abgespaltene") (The First Five 'Forms of Arriving')

If we wish to break some new ground in exploring the phenomena of 'arriving' in consciousness, it is necessary to continue where we have left off the enquiry into the 'sequences of associations' occurring in the 'quiet state of alertness'. We have referred above to the example of a person who was able to recall the forgotten name of a friend only after having become immersed in the 'quiet state of alertness', and the example of the lyrics of a song learned in childhood that could not be fully remembered in adulthood, but which became accessible again to the person after having been transferred into the 'quiet state of alertness'. We have moreover considered the examples of the forgotten details of events from the remote past, which could eventually be recovered from memory after the person had been immersed in the 'quiet state of alertness'. These are all persuasive examples that provide positive proof that improved memory performance can be achieved in the 'quiet state of alertness'. In all these cases something that had been forgotten or unavailable to memory in the 'waking consciousness' could be recovered when the subject concerned was transferred into the 'quiet state of alertness'. In one of these examples the forgotten memory comes back at an instant, in a flash of insight. In another example, the memory is retrieved only gradually in a series of fragmented memories, like the recovery of the full text of a partly forgotten lyric. In such a process of recollecting by shifting to the 'quiet state of alertness', the initial response was emotional, followed by a sequence of visual images, before finally the whole text could be remembered. But these are not merely examples demonstrating the phenomenon of improved memory performance, but also instances in which we can discern different varieties of experiencing an 'object arriving'. For this reason it has been useful to elaborate on the way associations operate in the 'quiet state of alertness' in some detail. Some of the characteristics of the process of association are akin to, and have served as an initial pointer at, the phenomenon of 'arriving'. The process of retrieving forgotten memories is also relevant in this context, albeit for yet another reason. Although the recovery of forgotten memories in the 'quiet state of alertness' has some affinities with the experience of an 'object arriving' in the vista of 'inner sight', it differs significantly from the latter in one crucial aspect: the 'experiencing I' knows that the memories recollected come from within his/her own consciousness; it is recognized as something that has merely slipped from one's mind, and thus has the same 'quality of the I' as the things that are constantly on one's consciousness. Whatever a person thinks to have forgotten remains nonetheless stored in the mind and an integral part of the personality; that is to say that (seemingly) forgotten memories are – unlike the extra-mental phenomena perceived as 'arriving' in the 'quiet state of alertness' – not experienced as 'arriving' from a 'space' beyond, but rather from within, the realm of the individual consciousness. Or if we apply the 'layer-theory' we may state: *Whatever has just been forgotten does not have the quality of an 'it'*.[120]

An 'object' that 'arrives' and can be identified as an item of [the subject's personality] *that has been 'split off' from his/her consciousness* [and stored in the domain of the sub- or the unconscious] *is the first phenomenon in our enquiry that fully reveals all the pivotal characteristics of the 'object arriving' – (i.e. it is the first phenomenon revealing all the vital features of the 'object arriving', except for the phenomena occurring in the telepathic consciousness, which have, however, been excluded from the category of 'objects arriving' for the reasons stated above).*

When exploring items that have been 'split off' from the individual psyche and transferred into the realm of the unconscious, one inevitably enters the area of psychopathology. At first sight, dealing with phenomena encountered in the consciousness of individuals

---

120 [Annotation: This is a rather truncated statement which calls for an explanatory comment: What Albrecht wants to convey here is that the act of recalling a piece of memory in the 'quiet state of alertness' is not accompanied by any intuitive awareness that the item remembered comes from a foreign, unknown sphere, beyond the confines of the individual consciousness, but that individual memories are rather attended by the cognitive awareness that they have surfaced from within the realm of the individual consciousness. Hence the recovery of a forgotten memory is clearly not an experience of a 'foreign object', which is why the experience of recalling a personal memory does not have the experiential quality of an "it". – FW.]

suffering from psychic disabilities, or even explicitly from a psychopathological disease, might seem to be an approach that cannot yield tangible results. Dealing with psychopathological cases in the given context may thus appear to be a detour or cul-de-sac in our empirical investigation. However, the subsequent analysis will demonstrate that this objection is unfounded. We may supply the following arguments in favour of this approach:

1. Psychotherapy can offer numerous empirical materials, in which we may encounter numerous varieties of an 'object arriving' in consciousness. As regards the phenomenon of mysticism, some psychologists and scholars have claimed that mysticism is merely a magnificent psychological experiment. Yet, contrary to this view, it is also possible to argue by way of analogy that, in psychotherapy, altered states of consciousness are deliberately generated which can offer a wide variety of valuable empirical materials for scientific analysis.

2. Mysticism is a normal phenomenon of human consciousness. Yet mysticism can only be elucidated unambiguously and established as a sound and genuine phenomenon of human existence if it is contrasted to, and critically differentiated from, psychopathological phenomena.

The term 'split-off' item of consciousness is not a concept introduced by the psychology of consciousness. It was rather coined by Jaspers, who first defined the phenomenon in his study on psychopathology,[121] claiming that the 'splitting off' refers to an abnormal, extra-mental ("außerbewußt") mechanism. "What 'splitting off' actually means has not yet been explained – neither methodologically, nor systematically." Attributing the origin of the process of 'splitting off' to some intelligible event does not provide us with any insights into the hypothetical mechanisms involved. The mental processes subsumed under the umbrella terms of 'defence', 'brushing aside' and 'repression' do not 'explain' the sub-conscious causes by which a complex of experiences becomes 'split off' from consciousness permanently. The fact that a complex of experience becomes forever inaccessible and unavailable to consciousness, even though

---

121 Jaspers, Karl. *Allgemeine Psychopathologie. Ein Leitfaden für Studierende, Ärzte und Psychologen*. 1913. 5th ed. Berlin and Heidelberg: Springer, 1948. 317f.

it continues to have an impact on the mind after having been 'split off', shows that we are dealing with a pathological phenomenon, because sane and natural phenomena of the psyche are all tied to the personality. "The split-off phenomena encountered in normal psychic conditions are always related to, or experienced as belonging to, the whole. This means that it may happen that in an event a part of the personality is on the verge of being 'split off', but the 'split-off' item is quickly reconnected with the personality when the psyche is healthy and well-balanced. The mechanisms operating in a morbid psychic condition, by contrast, do not re-connect the 'split-off' item; thus what is 'split off' will remain to be 'split off' forever, and what becomes isolated from the whole, will not become an integral part of the whole anymore." "There are different categories of 'split-off' phenomena, and the ways in which they are perceived, and become manifest in consciousness are rather diverse": Thus a 'split-off' item may be recognized by the symptom of compulsive behaviour, which may become manifest in neurotic delusions, or in compulsive actions; but 'split-off' items may also be the cause of disrupted, incoherent psychic processes, or of the disintegration of the personality, like in a schizophrenic, or in the experience of a 'double I'; other symptoms are obsessive gestures, or some peculiar idiosyncratic behaviour – for instance, the case of war veterans suffering from shell-shock, which becomes apparent in the uncontrolled shaking of a veteran's body, or the repressed experiences of neurotic persons who notoriously feel the urge to destroy established standards of order.

Binswanger[122] states: "It is a fundamental principle of the phenomenological method to limit the analysis to what can really be found in consciousness; or to put it differently, to what is immanent in consciousness." On the basis of these premises we may now postulate that *the 'split-off' complex is a theoretical borderline concept of the psychology of consciousness. It points towards the fact that there is (amongst other things) an extra-mental empirical ground by which it is possible to explain why forgotten past events may still have an impact on a person's present and future experience.*

---

122   Binswanger, Ludwig. *Ausgewählte Vorträge und Aufsätze.* 2 vols. Bern: Francke, 1947. Vol. I, 25.

For the purpose of maintaining the clear-cut systematic order of our phenomenological investigation we will not enter upon enquiries concerning the essence and potential causes of the processes and phenomena triggered by 'split-off' items. We shall therefore focus only on the analysis of the phenomena encountered in the empirical records. For the same reason we will have to refrain later from asking similar questions concerning the essence of mysticism. The field of the psychological phenomenology of consciousness is after all not an explanatory science, but a descriptive discipline. But as such it must not be dismissed condescendingly as mystical metaphysics; and it has to be acknowledged that psychological phenomenology is something entirely different from psychotherapy.

Psychotherapy, however, can only be practiced – when it is seriously practiced (i.e. conceived as an art of healing that requires charismatic commitment on the part of the therapist) – if it is open to include metaphysical hypostases in therapy as well. For, after all, such concepts as 'the soul', 'the unconscious', the 'id-experience', 'deep-person', 'archetype', 'demon' or 'angel' are also key-concepts used in psychotherapeutic treatments. From the perspective of psychotherapy, a purely psycho-phenomenological approach like the one undertaken here, and the use of strictly scientific concepts by the psychology of consciousness, must appear to be deficient, since they are inadequate for establishing an 'existential communication' between patient and phenomenological psychotherapist. This objection is surely justified, since psychological phenomenology as a scientific discipline must bypass the metaphysical dimensions of human consciousness. It is indeed the methodological constraints and the particular aims of this study that require us to adhere strictly to the principles of empirical science and to avoid transgressing into the realm of metaphysics. This is the reason why the results of psychotherapeutic research and the expert knowledge in this field have not been included in the subsequent considerations. The realm of mystical experience will therefore exclusively be explored from the perspective of the phenomenological psychology of consciousness – not least because nearly all the studies on mysticism (published to date)[123] are to some extent

---

123 [Note: This refers to studies on mysticism published in, and prior to, 1950, i.e.

impaired, biased and obscured by the fact that they view mysticism generally as an experience in the 'twilight zone' of ideas and concepts derived from psychology, philosophy, metaphysics and theology. Our endeavour, by contrast, is not to conflate psychological phenomenology with any of the notions and concepts of the disciplines referred to above. It seemed necessary to add this clarifying remark here, to obviate potential misunderstanding of the subsequent critical considerations on 'the unconscious'.

'The unconscious' is a term with many connotations and diverse meanings. In common usage, the meaning of the term has changed over the past few decades, both in scope and semantic content. The term 'the unconscious' has been used to refer to anything that is not consciously recognized or perceived. However, the word has also been used to denote the realm outside an individual's conscious awareness. The two notions are obviously incompatible as both notions are based on different empirical foundations, for which the same term has been applied. This means that a new term was coined in each case, but one that had different meanings. It is also possible to conceive of 'the unconscious' as an organic substratum, i.e. the central nervous system, which causes physiological responses. The term can moreover be understood to refer to the metaphysical assumption that there is a psychic reality of which a human being is not conscious. The latter was termed by Ach[124] the "psychonomic sphere". Yet another meaning of 'the unconscious' is suggested in recent empirical psychology, in which the word is related to the notion of the 'deep-person', and the 'layer theory' of the personality; here 'the unconscious' is assigned either to the animalistic 'id-life', or to the emotional 'id-life' of the psyche. The term 'the unconscious' has furthermore been used metaphorically to designate the ultimate ground from which all creative activity originates, and it has been used as a metaphor in which 'the unconscious' is conceived as a receptive vessel for perceiving what is ultimately unfathomable and all-comprising. But whatever the meaning attached to the term of 'the unconscious', the fact remains that

---

the year in which Albrecht submitted *PMB* to the publisher. – FW.]
124   Ach, Narziss. "Über den Begriff des Unbewußten in der Psychologie der Gegenwart." *Zeitschrift für Psychologie* 129 (1933): 223-245.

'the unconscious' is an empirical reality which has unquestionably some value for our existence, and in particular, for the meaning of our existence, not least because it functions as a moral instance that inevitably has an impact on human behaviour.

The diverse notions attached to the concept of 'the unconscious' indicate that the meaning of the term as used in everyday speech is multifarious, fuzzy and elusive. But it is likewise an ambivalent and controversial technical term as used in psychotherapy, and this is why it is not possible to provide an unequivocal definition. Analysing the concept more closely, we will recognize that the term 'the unconscious' has rather the characteristics of a symbol than those of a scientific concept. Many colourful and often changing nuances are attached to the word, and this is why 'the unconscious' cannot be rationally grasped. Anyone who tries to recapture the concept intelligibly will inevitably be confronted with something that is irrational. There are always new answers, new options for relations, always new points of departure for the interpretation and understanding of 'the unconscious'. But all these endeavours have turned out to be merely a more or less 'visible' representation of what ultimately is concealed and incomprehensible. However, despite all these deficiencies, the term 'the unconscious' is nonetheless valuable and cannot be dispensed with, and it is particularly helpful for advancing self-understanding and empathy. Any psychological approach that involves empathy is doomed to fail and will be 'sterile' unless it is related to 'the unconscious'. The concept has indeed become indispensable to any 'existential communication' in psychotherapy. On the other hand, it can be argued that the fact that the term has great practical value in psychotherapy does not qualify it as a scientific concept. The word has moreover so many different colourful meanings and has great significance also as a source of meaning, notably as the source of inspiration for the artist, the therapist, the lover or even the believer. Seen in this general context the term is vital as a universal umbrella term, but as such does not qualify as a scientific concept, and must therefore be replaced by scientific concepts, which are unambiguously defined.

We will proceed with our investigation and are going to explore the process in which items are 'split off' from consciousness and transferred into the realm of the 'unconscious'. We will especially consider the impact that 'splitting off' items may have on an individual. We will illustrate special instances of 'split-off' items on the basis of authentic empirical records. In particular, we are going to ask what a subject afflicted by the memory of a 'split-off' item is actually aware of, many years after the event had occurred, and we will also trace the impact that a 'split-off' item has on the person concerned in cases when the 'split-off' item, and the event that has caused it, remains entirely concealed.

There are different degrees by which a person may become aware that he/she is exposed to experiences elicited by a 'split-off' item from his/her consciousness. The different degrees of intensity in which these processes are experienced correlate with the intensity in which the incidents were experienced which caused the 'splitting off' of an item in a person's consciousness. The following degrees of awareness in experiencing encounters with a 'split-off' item can be distinguished:

1. The subconscious of the subject is fully aware of the entire complex that has been 'split off' earlier. The repressed complex is known to have been suppressed, though the entire complex of events continues to linger perseveringly in the subconscious. This means that, for example, an upcoming exam or an embarrassing event can be isolated in the peripheral sphere of consciousness; this mechanism enables us to 'sidestep' mentally (as it were) a stressful situation of the past.

2. The subconscious is only aware of a part of the 'split-off' complex; this part is, however, not accessible any more to the 'waking consciousness', as it has been removed from conscious memory; because of this, the individual's chance of coming to terms with the situation in a process of self-reflection and rational analysis is forestalled. The subconscious, however, is still aware of the distinctive features of the item 'split off'; in most cases, the immediate awareness that the item that has been 'split off' is 'still there', is retained (albeit to a limited degree), though the 'split-off' item is experienced as something distressing, which is mysteriously concealed and threatens to surface again in consciousness. What

can be cognitively grasped in the subconscious is only the emotionally charged response to the traumatic experience of the past – i.e. repression, resistance, withdrawal into oneself, and refusal to deal with the 'split-off' phenomenon rationally. Furthermore, the person concerned is subconsciously aware that the behaviour generated by the haunting memory of the 'split-off' events is abnormal.

In the case histories quoted below, there is one record of a young woman for whom the act of 'drinking milk', or even the thought of 'drinking milk', arouses intense nauseating feelings. The thought of 'drinking milk' is part of a 'split-off' complex, in which this situation evokes intense embarrassing emotions and feelings of distress in the young woman. The impact on her behaviour is extreme revulsion: whenever she is required to drink milk, or faced with such a situation, she is seized by fits of vomiting; these symptoms are recognized by her (at least on a subconscious level) to be abnormal; she is aware that this anomalous behaviour is caused by some taboo zone, which must, however, be silently passed over, because it is apparently full of embarrassing and painful memories, the details of which are now suppressed and (in part) forgotten. The young woman is thus clearly aware of the 'direction' from which the fragmented intimations of past experience arise; she is also aware that these are pathological symptoms, and aware at which 'direction' the ominous symbol that has surfaced from the unconscious is pointing. This means that she knows a great deal about the nature of the 'split-off' phenomenon, and of its violent impact on her behaviour, though she refuses to reflect on these phenomena and intuitive insights. She tries, rather on the contrary, to suppress any critical thoughts and bars any impulse at engaging in a process of self-understanding.

3. The case of a person who is totally unaware of the existence of a 'split-off' item – that is to say, the 'split-off' item hardly surfaces in the person's consciousness anymore. Though there appears to be some awareness of the symptoms of mental disintegration when the person ponders these symptoms in self-observation, and although a few symptoms of a 'split-off' item may be observed

by the therapist, otherwise there is no awareness of what the substance or cause of the 'split-off' item actually is. Complex phobias and fixations that have become 'split off' so completely are usually not accessible anymore, or can at best be retrieved from consciousness by psychotherapy; but it is also possible that they become manifest spontaneously in the guise of a 'partial I' in a somnambulist state.

4. The item 'split off' can no longer be traced in consciousness. This means that the 'split-off' item is not accessible by any methodological approach, and does not have any impact on the person's consciousness anymore. This fact explains why it does not produce any symptoms. The integration of the personality is in no way impaired by the 'split-off' phenomenon, as there is no awareness at all that it had earlier been a 'split-off' item in consciousness.

The first of the three degrees of experiencing a 'split-off' item described above will be dealt with later. In the 'waking consciousness', a person has always some 'knowledge' (as we have seen) that a particular part of his/her consciousness has become 'split off', when this has happened. This knowledge is often merely a vague subconscious awareness, but this knowledge may also result from rational reflection. The same applies to the experience of a 'split-off' item in the 'quiet state of alertness': the 'experiencing I' is generally aware of, and able to discern if, a phenomenon 'arriving' in consciousness has the characteristics of a complex of fixations that have become 'split off', or if the 'object arriving' has characteristics that cannot be traced to the 'individual self'. But even when a 'split-off' phenomenon is experienced in the 'quiet state of alertness' as an 'object' that has the quality of an 'it' when 'arriving', the 'experiencing I' is nonetheless aware that the 'it' that 'arrives' had previously been a part of the 'I'. The 'it-complex' is thus a complex of repressed memories. The dynamism of the 'it' therefore corresponds to the dynamism of the person's 'split-off' complex. Even when the 'it' is purely perceived as an 'it', there still remains an immediate awareness in the 'experiencing I' that the 'it' was previously a part of the 'I', and that it will acquire the former quality again, when it has 'arrived' in consciousness as a whole.

However, the claim that any 'split-off' item perceived as 'arriving' has all the hallmarks of an 'it' is not valid for all states of consciousness. It does not apply, for instance, to the 'somnambulist consciousness', because in this state we encounter sometimes sudden irruptions of the 'split-off' phenomenon in its entirety. The 'it' appears instantaneously in the full shape it actually is – namely, as a 'part of the 'I', or in the guise of a 'former I'. The entire whole of the 'I' is split apart. The part that is 'split off' from the 'I' transgresses the given domain of consciousness and takes over functions that normally operate only in the 'waking consciousness' and/or other non-somnambulist states: Thus the 'I' is still capable of feeling pain, taking action and speaking while the 'somnambulist state' prevails. As long as the 'waking part' of the 'I' is in part alert in the given mental condition, the 'partial I' is able to watch its own activities; if this happens, the 'split-off' complex can be overcome, as the parts of the 'double I' are 'fused', resulting in a single coherent 'I'. But when the capacity of the entire 'I' of experiencing on its own remains disabled, the 'split-off' complex is preserved, since it is a prerequisite for the process of self-recognition to become effective that the 'experiencing I' must have some conscious awareness that an intrusion of this kind has actually occurred. The external observer can witness this phenomenon, since he/she can discern the subject shifting from the 'waking state' to the 'somnambulist state'.

Our description has by now entered the field of psychotherapy, hence the area of treating the mentally diseased. Thus we have arrived at the area of 'existential communication', i.e. the domain of self-realization ('individuation') that is achieved by self-knowledge ('introspection'). But we are going to proceed along this path of psychopathology only as long as the study of 'split-off' phenomena can help us to elucidate important features of the 'quiet state of alertness', both as regards content and form. We should add that the reason why the 'split-off' phenomenon has at all been considered an instance of 'arriving' is the fact that plenty of invaluable empirical data have previously been collected from my long-term practice as a psychotherapist. And these authentic empirical records enable us to specify further the various 'forms of arriving'. It should be added at this point that *all 'forms of arriving' are the same in any state of consciousness, that is to say, the 'forms of arriving' are phenomenologically alike, irrespective of the nature of the 'object' that 'arrives' in consciousness, and regardless of whether the given 'object' can be traced as being neurotic, telepathic or mystical in origin.*

In the course of my practice as a psychotherapist I have gathered numerous empirical records from patients, which were spoken spontaneously while they were immersed in altered states of consciousness, and these accounts are used as precious documentary materials for the purpose of this investigation. The personal records of individual patients will here be quoted (either selectively, or occasionally in full) for illustration, though of course without disclosing the patient's identity; hence the reference to individual patients is indicated by tags like "Mrs. B." or "Mr. F.", etc.). Methodologically, the empirical records have been acquired from spontaneous utterances spoken while the patient was absorbed in the 'quiet state of alertness' (or intermittently, in other altered states of consciousness, notably the 'somnambulist state'). That is to say that a patient's psycho-cathartic verbal utterances were recorded verbatim (either on tape or written down), after he/she had reached the 'quiet state of alertness'. These spontaneous utterances reveal authentically what the subject has experienced while immersed in the 'quiet state of alertness', and thus they reflect reliably the phenomena perceived as 'arriving' during the event. The experience thus has become, as it were, 'incarnate' in the words articulated by the subject aloud. *Patients speaking in the 'quiet state of alertness' can furnish us with objective, clearly defined documentary materials, which are in turn accessible to rational assessment.*

Our focus will be on the empirical records gained from situations in which the subject was immersed in the 'quiet state of alertness'. Because of this, however, we cannot explore 'split-off' phenomena individually any further, to trace them to their potential origins. Only occasionally will we consider phenomena reported as occurring outside the 'quiet state of alertness', notably in events when the 'quiet state of alertness' is temporarily torn apart by a 'secondary experience'. In the following I am going to present some selected excerpts from the often rather long utterances of patients. In the few instances when the mental framework was not that of the 'quiet state of alertness', but supplanted by the 'somnambulist consciousness' (which usually did not last long), the original utterances have been kept in the quotation, because they offer useful information about the psychic mechanisms at work when the mind 'switches' from the 'quiet state of alertness' into the 'somnambulist state' and back again. These data are, as we shall see, particularly relevant at a later stage of this investigation. It should also be added that the record that follows has been abridged in that passages revealing some intimate details of the patient's privacy have been eliminated. However, the passages omitted are not really as epistemologically relevant in this phenomenological study as they would be if our study had been in the field of psychopathology. (It should be noted that permission to publish the excerpts from the recordings made during the sessions of psychotherapy has been given by each of the patients concerned.)

Any 'split-off' item that 'arrives' in the vista of 'inner sight' and is cognitively grasped in the process inevitably causes a response in the 'experiencing I'. As a consequence, the 'quiet state of alertness' is transformed by an upsurge of emotions, which are elicited by the 'split-off' items perceived as 'arriving'. The response elicited may also consist of a sense of oppression, of feeling scared, awe-struck or filled with fear and trembling. These negative responses may become so intense that the mental framework of the 'quiet state of alertness' is about to be torn apart. But what is even more striking than this affect-laden impact on the 'quiet state of alertness' is that it is possible for an observer to witness from outside that the 'quiet state of alertness' is afflicted by emotional upheavals, before this serene mental state is torn to pieces. When the 'quiet state of alertness' is wrecked by some experience, it is, however, not completely replaced by the 'somnambulist state': some structural components of the 'quiet state of alertness' are still preserved, and along with it, the 'experiencing I' retains the capacity (albeit in considerably reduced fashion) to function as an observer of its own experience. The fragmented and disrupted state of consciousness resulting from this does of course not qualify as a 'quiet state of alertness' proper, so that the instant intrusion of the 'somnambulist state' in the 'quiet state of alertness' will result in a hybrid form of consciousness, composed of elements of both mental states. Moreover, the 'quiet state of alertness' is the mental environment to which the 'experiencing I' aspires to return. During the time the patient is absorbed in the 'quiet state of alertness', he/she is overwhelmed by powerful impressions and emotions, and this response is reflected in the patient's physiognomy and other somatic responses, thus providing objective evidence of the ongoing mental process. The agonizing fear and anguish by which the patient is afflicted in the given event becomes manifest in paroxysms of trembling and shaking, as well as in tears and deeply emotional utterances, while the patient's eyes remain shut and the body continues to lie still on the bedstead, enabling him/her to return again smoothly to the state of inner calm and composure after the turmoil of emotions has subsided.

The first example presents a sequence of events encountered in the 'quiet state of alertness', in which **the 'object arriving' is (mainly) perceived like a series of images appearing in a 'newsreel' or on a 'filmstrip'**. In this mode of 'arriving', a series of consecutive pictures are evoked from memory, linked by associations; in these pictorial memories the patient appears to be passing through past events. When observing the 'filmstrip', the 'core image' of the 'split-off' complex comes more and more closely into focus, albeit without being fully disclosed, for the time being. In the incipient stage, the patient's emotional response is not tinged by feelings of distress and agitation. The basic mood of calmness continues to persevere. However, as soon as the distressing core images begin to surface in the 'quiet state of alertness', this mental state is destroyed by the storm of emotions evoked by them. In this experience, the 'split-off' complex is to a large degree separated from the 'experiencing I', and the 'partial I' intrudes, featuring as an 'experiencing agent'. The 'partial I' in this example is that of the patient at the age of ten, which was the time when the complex of childhood memories were 'split off'; it is the 'I' of the ten-year-old child that becomes the agent in the scenes revealed in the 'somnambulist state', which is intermittently switched. The 'somnambulist state' terminates when the entire sequence of events ('filmstrip'), emerging from memory, has come to an end. However, this 'somnambulist state' is embedded in the structure of the 'quiet state of alertness', and elements of the latter can clearly be inferred from the fact that the patient, after returning to the 'waking state', is able to remember (albeit only in a blurred manner) what had happened when she was transported into an 'altered state of consciousness'. This also shows that the 'partial I' was again merged with the person's entire 'I'. The events that had for a long time been 'split off' from consciousness and previously been inaccessible to memory have now become accessible again. As a consequence, the patient is greatly relieved because the domain of the 'I', in which she felt safe to move, is considerably widened in scope.

When the female patient concerned ("Mrs. A.") was a child, she lived mainly in overseas countries, where she was evidently exposed to child abuse by a housemaid (with whom she was often left alone, without parental supervision). The most striking symptom of the woman's neurosis could thus be traced back to the years of her childhood abroad. It was impossible for her to drink milk. The very notion of having to drink milk instantly caused feelings of nausea, revulsion, fear and dismay. Whenever she had drunk milk, the immediate reaction was vomiting. The following passage describes a scene in which she was abused in childhood and provides the reason why 'drinking milk' became a traumatic experience, one that is morbidly associated with feelings of nausea, oppressive fear and a deep sense of guilt and shame. As a consequence, she even became terrified of herself. After this complex cluster of negative experiences had become 'split off' and suppressed, the pattern of haunting emotions that were associated with the act of 'drinking milk' was subsequently released at any time, in any similar situation. In the first paragraph, a sequence of events is described that surfaced while the patient was absorbed in the 'quiet state of alertness'; from the second through the fourth paragraphs, actions and verbal responses of the 'partial I' are reported which were triggered when the 'somnambulist state' had been interpolated. The third paragraph records the course of events that caused the session with the psychiatrist to be disrupted. Already on the first evening after the first psycho-cathartic treatment the patient reported that anything she had eaten even hours after the treatment tasted like milk; however, when she deliberately decided afterwards to drink milk against all odds, she was able to drink two glasses in succession without being afflicted by feelings of revulsion:

Mrs. A.: *"A tram – much laundry – the curtains are long – small brown shoes were standing there – there are knots in the shoe laces.*

No, I am not going to wear them – I did not get them dirty. No – (groaning) – I want to have white ones – thank you, many thanks. – Erna – – Erna! I do not want to ask! – I would so much like to see once more where the milk is coming from – This evening? – No, I won't be asleep – No I will stay awake – but don't tell Daddy – Erna, it should be soft again – milk does not always flow from it – .

I don't want any milk, no, the milk is so thick – don't like it (she is shaking her head) – don't want to drink milk – it comes out of a bladder – no milk – please no milk – I am going to pour it out, aunt Else – I don't want to drink any milk – no, it is so warm – no – it does not come from a cow at all – no – no – this is not true – it comes from that thick bladder – I do know that! – (She is moaning, tossing and turning) – thank you – I want to eat a morsel – but no milk.

Erna, may I touch? May I undress further, Erna, may I, please, please. – Please, I don't hurt at all – I want to press it – look when the milk is coming – but don't tell anybody, don't tell anybody – Please, dear Erna – I have not done this – but this surely is blood – no this is blood – no, this is not true – You must not say this – this surely is blood, I have not done this – this is certainly blood – Erna don't show this to me again!"

The second example conveys a 'split-off' complex that 'arrives' in the vista of 'inner sight', but one that is less distinctly isolated from a part of the self than the one described in the previous example. For this reason the following example is more easily accessible. The record was again recovered when the patient was initially transported into a 'somnambulist state', which switches over into the 'quiet state of alertness', and in which the 'partial I' is perceived as an intrusive agent. In the passage quoted, only the initial sequence of the incidents is given, in which the 'partial I' is involved. For this reason the overall context cannot be inferred, and it is not possible to infer the specific subject matter the 'split-off' complex is concerned with. We can discern, however, that the way in which the 'split-off' item 'arrives' differs significantly in this example from the one considered above. The 'I' that is immersed in the 'quiet state of alertness' perceiving the 'object arriving' is aware of the changes effected in consciousness. The 'objects arriving' in 'inner sight' are observed with a heightened degree of clarity. This suggests that in this experience **it is the emotional response that is instantaneously evoked in the 'quiet state of**

alertness', and which can thus be identified as the 'form' in which the 'object arriving' first becomes manifest. In the current example, it is the image of a familiar countenance that appears initially and which is charged with strong emotions; in fact, the emotional impact is so intense that the 'quiet state of alertness' is rent apart and replaced by the 'somnambulist consciousness':

> Ms. B.: "It tosses – I am so low – fully bound – everything is moving back – it is only me who is so heavy – what is circulating around me is dark – it is circulating. I cannot find a beginning. I also must circulate. – This fear, there is a deep sense of fear – dark – I am so heavy – I cannot lift myself up – it is chasing me, I cannot recognize it – it is chasing me, it is tearing me – tearing inside, there is a narrow room – oh me, this enormous, heavy darkness is coming – approaching towards me – fear – it is so great – it crushes me – oh – I am disgusted . . . I cannot recognize anything – only the nausea – I cannot recognize its countenance – I cannot get through to it – I will try the path through these agonies of nausea – it confuses me – it is surrounding me – I cannot see the lights – yes – no – oh no – I have only been afraid – no, I did not want it – I did not want it at all – oh what trickery – not anymore – I have not truly – cheating – I cannot trust.
>
> It is always you who turns up! Always – your face is close to me – I must face it – always your face – oh – oh – that face – oh – your beloved face – oh – why? – Go away! – God, I am afraid, what shall I do? – are you coming? – oh, I am afraid of you . . ."

The third form in which a 'split-off' item can 'arrive' in consciousness is that of the symbol. We consider the concept of the symbol in some detail later. At this point it is enough to give just two examples in which a symbol arises as the 'object arriving' in the 'quiet state of alertness'. In the first example, a female patient decided, before embarking on the process of 'introversion', to 'encode' the 'secondary disposition' into the process, that she must not flinch from the sight of the hideous 'object' that tends to surface in the mind as soon as the capacity of 'inner sight' has fully unfolded. The person was thus clearly determined to face the repellent 'object arriving' without restraint or reservation. This stratagem was meant to enable her to face and endure the sight of whatever shape the 'objects arriving' would appear in, even though she expected them to be rather terrifying, haunting and even potentially harmful. She opted for this stratagem despite the hazards involved, because by taking this approach it was hoped to get closer to the core of the 'split-off' item by enabling the patient to face the 'object arriving' for a longer period and just for a fleeting moment after its 'arrival'. The latter had happened in all of the previous sessions with this patient, which all ended prematurely. It turned out, however, that with this patient applying this methodological approach came too early. For it so happened that at the very first moment, when the 'split-off' complex became apparent, the 'quiet state of alertness' was instantly and completely torn apart; the patient was shattered and abruptly removed into the 'waking state', in which she was exposed to a most distressful emotional turmoil. It should be added, however, that in this example the recorded experience was not rendered during the 'quiet state of alertness', but supplied in retrospect by the psychotherapist after the patient had returned to the 'waking consciousness'. Yet despite this proviso, this patient's testimony shows quite clearly that the 'split-off' 'object' which 'arrived' appeared in the shape of a symbol – more specifically, in the shape of a grotesque, uncanny, contorted grimace of a hideous, dangerous animal. This symbol was generated by a 'split-off' complex of agonizing memories and can thus be seen as the symbolic manifestation of deeply oppressive, agonizing emotions originating in a traumatic past event, which had become 'split off', isolated, suppressed and stored in the subconscious.

> Mrs. C. speaking while immersed in the 'quiet state of alertness': "... *something is sitting there that does not belong here, and I will never get rid of it again – nor do I know exactly where it is sitting – I think it has been placed there by mistake – oh, I don't like it –* " At this point, the patient is able, for a short time, to cope with the scowling grimace appearing in 'inner sight', but she can do so only because of the supporting impact of the 'secondary disposition' which she had 'programmed' in her mind before embarking on the process of 'introversion'; however, when she is confronted with the sight of the hideous beast, the calmness of the 'quiet state of alertness' is destroyed by both the outburst of emotions triggered by the vision, and by the psychosomatic response evoked by the event: All of a sudden, she starts screaming terribly, and her face becomes distorted. Horror, disgust, nausea and fear afflict the patient and give evidence of her extreme state of agony and despair, which is so intense that the 'waking consciousness' is instantly switched on. During this emotional turmoil the patient starts crying uncontrollably: *"It is like a hideous face staring at you*

– that is not true at all! – you are not to have it – inside over there – this is a beast – it can bite also – I cannot do it again – it is still aching so much!"

Another example in which a 'split-off' complex becomes manifest in the form of a 'symbol' in the 'quiet state of alertness' appears in the report of the woman referred to above who suffered from lactophobia. In this personal account she describes another traumatic experience which generated an even more distressing 'split-off' complex, one that had an even more grievous and harmful impact on her life than the neurotic nausea evoked when drinking milk. In the recorded experience the patient perceives a sequence of pictures in 'inner sight' in the 'quiet state of alertness'. When absorbed in the 'quiet state of alertness', however, she is suddenly transferred into the 'somnambulist state' whenever she is faced with events in which a doll named Joanna appears. In the 'somnambulist state' the patient takes part in the events revealed in 'inner sight' with her 'partial I', acting in the scene in the way in which she appears to have acted in the disturbing events that had happened in her childhood. Unlike in the previous example, the doll named Joanna is not a symbol referring to a disturbing 'split-off' complex, because the doll had featured as a symbol already in the events recorded earlier, which had deeply affected the patient. In the given instance it is rather a series of scenes in which the symbolic doll appears in the 'somnambulist consciousness' and in which scenes the 'partial I' participates. She performs actions and speaks aloud as long as the 'somnambulist state' lasts. Thus it is not yet the real core of the 'split-off' complex that becomes manifest here, but a symbolic scene disguising (as it were) the real event. That is to say that the scene displayed in the 'somnambulist state' foreshadows the 'arrival' of the 'split-off' complex proper, and which can be expected to be revealed in subsequent therapeutic sessions. The fact that the actual 'split-off' complex and the real situation with all its painful truth is not revealed instantly, but delayed and in a series of successive events, can be explained as a protective mechanism, by which the 'experiencing I' is gradually prepared to be able to cope with the uncanny and humiliating situation; the full impact of the agonizing complex of 'split-off' memories is concealed for some time and revealed piece by piece rather than by a single event, which would be a devastating and potentially harmful blow with long-term after-effects. (It is not relevant for the progress of this investigation to disclose details of the private context and the disturbing traumatic incident by which these distressing memories had been 'split off'; this aside, it goes without saying that respecting a patient's privacy and complying with the principle of medical confidentiality are imperative in this study.)

> Mrs. A.: *"A cat – slippery – do the children walk about on stilts? – Albert is dancing on stilts – I am always falling down – John as well, he is holding me fast – Charles is up there at the window – he is waving – I want to get up to him – a horse's leash – Charles is playing with the horse – Charles's wardrobe of toys is open – Aunt Berta is approaching – she offers something to Charles – "I have nothing" – Charles puts it away – Charles is tight-fisted – I also want to see it – Charles is moving over to my wardrobe of toys – you must not play havoc with my things again – this is my game of lotto – you must not mess up things all the time –"* (The somnambulist state is now about to set in – she is shouting at Charles:) *"What have you got, Charles, leave Joanna alone – give Joanna to me – dare you harm Joanna once more! – Hand Joanna to me right now! – Oh, you are entering it with your finger – mind, you are killing Joanna! No killing – no killing!! – don't kill!! – You have killed Joanna, I want to have Joanna back – Aunt Berta, Charles has damaged Joanna – and I have loved Joanna so much! – I want to have Joanna back – I will tell Daddy – I want to have my former Joanna back – Joanna back – have Joanna back again!"*

The fourth 'form' of an 'object arriving' in consciousness has extraordinary characteristics. This is why this 'form' is relatively rare and is usually encountered only in liminal events in the 'quiet state of alertness'. In this case, the 'object' that 'arrives' in consciousness does not appear in the shape of a visual image, nor in the form of an emotional response, nor as a symbol, but in the form of an 'intense somatic seizure'. Strictly speaking, the 'object arriving' in this case does not appear as an object of 'inner sight', but is rather **the sudden eruption of a 'symptomatic somatic seizure', or spasmodic contortions of the body, by which the 'experiencing I' is overwhelmed while abiding in a purely receptive state filled by the calmness and clarity of the 'quiet state of alertness'.** In other words, the person concerned is afflicted by symptoms of 'possession'. It is a fit-like spasm which is triggered spontaneously and has affinities with an epileptic seizure, albeit with the significant difference that the 'experiencing I' exposed to a 'symptomatic somatic seizure' is immediately returned to the 'quiet state of alertness' after the spasmodic fit has ended – which means that the function of 'inner sight' and the hyper-lucid condition of consciousness are instantly restored after the 'seizure' so that the subject is enabled to observe the impact and corollaries of the after-math of the 'seizure'. Considering that this is a rare, liminal experience, I do not have a scientific answer explaining the potential cause(s) of such 'somatic seizures', nor can I identify the psychological and physiological elements of which this exceptional state of consciousness consists at the time when the outburst is triggered. What can be stated for sure, however, is that in the actual case recorded, the patient was definitely absorbed in the 'quiet state of alertness' both before and after the somatic seizure. It can also be confirmed and stated as an established fact that during the seizure neither the 'waking state' nor the 'dreaming consciousness' were switched on. I would suggest that the 'somatic seizure' appears to have occurred in a hybrid mental state, which – for some unknown reason – became instantly blurred and diffuse for some time. I cannot offer a more specific phenomenological explanation of this spasmodic phenomenon on the basis of the testimonial available, which was recorded during a therapeutic session:

> Mrs. C.: (After having reposed silently for some time in the calmness of the 'quiet state of alertness', Mrs. C. became increasingly restless, and soon after the 'somatic seizure' erupted): *"I don't know – What is happening to me?"* – (The patient's face becomes distorted by pain, her head tossing to and fro, her hands are shaking and convulsed, the seizure grows in intensity, she is violently banging her hands at the ground; she does this so vehemently that her bones are about to break) *"Just let me go! Just let me go!"* (she is wailing and beating around with her arms) – *"Does it have to?"* (she is screaming, beating with her hands and threatening) – (shortly afterwards, completely exhausted, she calms down and is restored to the composure and calmness of the 'quiet state of alertness'; in this state she instantly is alert and intent on perceiving memories experienced as approaching and about to 'arrive'): *"Now I have been able to make it dead, now all is well, really well. – But how come? – Something is present here inside that I do not recognize at all, otherwise it would not do such a thing,*

would not behave like that. What is it? – I think there is no harm done, I just do not know yet that no harm has been done by it. – It only must be willing to believe – How bad all this was earlier! It had to get out, otherwise I would have been choked by it. And yet it was good somehow. It had both of it – until it became so bad, but then the other thing came to help, so that I could kill it . . ."

(A few days later, another seizure occurred) "This is terrible – does it always have to be like this? – Is there no end to it? (crying) I don't think that I can ever end this – I must be able to manage – I have not got enough strength to do so – no I have not! (sobbing) – But I have to – yet I cannot get through! (shedding tears profusely) – I don't know how to do it – it still is so far away – does it really have to be? – I am not ready yet – I am right in between – between the two – I can as yet neither do the one thing, nor the other – I am indeed not as good as I sometimes think I am – I am not really good – I am not really good at all – There are so many things that are pulling me down – I must be left in peace – nobody can stand this – I have to find her – and she must not be false anymore – she must be entirely honest – and this is so difficult."

(Three days later, a similar incident occurred; this is another example illustrating that the 'quiet state of alertness' is instantly destroyed by the sudden intrusion of a 'symptomatic seizure' originating from a 'split-off' complex. The patient's utterances continue after a severe spasm has been overcome): "Oh, – again and again – all this makes me feel better somehow – how strange – something is falling off that has formerly held on so fast – something has been liberated – something that is rooted so fast and so deep – which cannot be released in any other way – nor do I want to have it in any other way – Has every human being such a devil dwelling within? – No! This cannot be! – It cannot be – I have buried it" (growing increasingly restless when observing the 'arrival' of the 'split-off' complex) "No" (another seizure) – "Again and again – it is entrapped there – come! – no – no – no! –" (This final vision perceived in 'inner sight' triggers the third somatic seizure, which is so intense that the 'waking consciousness' is switched on.)

The fifth form of 'arriving' is linked closely to some of the key-phenomena of the 'quiet state of alertness'. We will try to supply a representative description without claiming that this is to be seen as a definition of the concept. The 'I' of the 'quiet state of alertness' is predisposed to 'watch' the 'arrival' of a set of phenomenological 'objects' which have as yet been concealed, and/or previously been inaccessible and thus unfamiliar to the 'experiencing I'. This unfamiliar, 'dark' and 'expansive' domain of past experience has a core (like any 'split-off' complex) that is fraught with affect-laden, or even dangerous and potentially harmful emotions. This emotionally charged core is, however, not aroused at the very beginning of 'inner sight'. At the beginning, the phenomena that appear in the vista of 'inner sight' are phenomena located at the periphery of consciousness, but which are somehow linked or associated with the core. In this 'form of arriving', these peripheral phenomena may open up a new path to self-understanding. Thus **the 'object arriving' consists of a structured sequence of memories, which provide a visual mode for advancing self-understanding.** This variant 'form of arriving' enables a subject to attain spontaneous insight into his/her past experience, past events and their causal coherence, and enables the 'experiencing I' to relate to and understand these past experiences in the wider context of his/her life. This 'form of arriving' thus elicits a subject's intuitive awareness of the condition of his/her 'self', and to recover from memory (seemingly) forgotten thoughts, responses and value judgements. An outside observer is likely and mistakenly to consider that these 'insights' are derived from reflective thinking. However, though it is true that these thoughts are 'reflective' in the literal sense, i.e. in the sense of 'mirroring' past experience, they do not derive from rational, discursive thinking. It is, in other words, an autonomous mode of thinking that is passive and non-discursive, and not one that is initiated by an act of the will, and controlled by the rational faculties of the 'I'. The 'objects' 'arriving' in the vista of 'inner sight' are events retrieved from memory and conveyed by a sequence of thoughts, which appear spontaneously. This mode of 'arriving' thus opens up a unique path towards self-understanding, one that is authentic, truthful, not subject to delusion or potentially bogus like notions evoked by the imagination. The sincerity and truthfulness that are revealed in the spontaneous utterances of the subjects' testimonials are extraordinary and astonishing to an observer. Yet the inherent aspiration for absolute sincerity and candour is not a quality springing from the subject's moral character in the first place, but is something rooted in the 'object' that has arrived; it can be seen as an authentic reflection of what has actually revealed itself in the hyper-lucid and vacant space of consciousness. The perception of one's 'self-understanding' is elicited spontaneously in the 'quiet state of alertness' and imposes on the 'experiencing I' the wish to articulate what has revealed itself truthfully and authentically. We will address *this special form of 'inner sight', by which this particularly pure and authentic form of self-understanding is initiated and facilitated,* repeatedly in the subsequent chapters. The foregoing explications of this special 'form of arriving' can be further substantiated by the following authentic testimony, spoken by a subject while absorbed in the 'quiet state of alertness'.

Mrs. C., the patient who had also supplied the record of a 'split-off' complex, in which the 'quiet state of alertness' was torn apart by a 'symptomatic somatic seizure', was also bestowed with intimations of 'self-understanding' in several sessions of her therapy. In the following only a few excerpts from the recorded testimony are given (the full record contains some intimate private matters that must not be disclosed here). The 'split-off' complex 'arrives' in the form of insights that are evidently conducive to self-understanding. The 'I', immersed in the 'quiet state of alertness', is bestowed with a sequence of memories that she intuitively recognizes to be not random phenomena, but ones related to her. She recognizes that they are fraught with meaning and intelligible. At first memories relating to the peripheral sphere of the 'split-off' complex become apparent, whereas memories relating to the core of the 'split-off' complex become manifest only later. The sequence of events retrieved from memory in the 'quiet state of alertness' thus corresponds to the sequence of memories initially experienced merely as approaching. At the beginning the process of self-understanding elicited consists mainly of real events from the patient's life, but soon the ideas and thoughts that 'arrive' in 'inner sight' become more and more intimate, personal and eventually result in a sincere confession. The final passage quoted below, though incomplete, can undoubtedly be termed a genuine confession, albeit one uttered spontaneously and unrestrainedly, since all controlling, volitional and inhibiting functions of the 'experiencing I' are dormant in the 'quiet state of alertness'. In this state the subject concerned observes the flow of memories as they 'arrive' in the vista of 'inner sight' and articulates truthfully what she is experiencing.

We should add that the 'quiet state of alertness' has never been suspended or replaced by the 'waking state' or any other mental condition; we likewise have to bear in mind that the person concerned has surrendered (as it were) to the autonomous process of inner vision. However intense and diverse the emotions aroused by the 'objects arriving' are on this occasion, they are all passive responses, the subject 'suffers' them to occur. Hence the responses recorded are consonant with and truly expressive of the way the 'objects' are 'arriving' in 'inner sight' – or, metaphorically speaking, the 'objects arriving' are conveyed in the way they are perceived while passing through the receptive 'vessel' of 'inner sight':

> [Mrs. C.:] "... I had no need for many things. – Only a person who could have restored goodness in me. Then I might have been cheerful again, and would have believed everything he told me. – But, in the end, I was left alone, and became more and more lonely, the more I have surrendered to be changed [for the worse]. When it finally became overpowering ... it got out and urged me on, and was my master. I had changed. I was lost – and could not be found – I was at some location where there were no other human beings – and then I remained as I was. – In this way everything was kept by me, I have not lost anything. I only was lost to all the others. It secretly continued to stay with me, and no one ever has seen it, for it got a new face – an entirely new one, utterly stern and repulsive, and totally merciless, and loveless and hard. And whatever had been good before, what had been so loving, so rich, has hereafter become so hard, and stood sentinel over me, and it has never, never again left off, and stayed with me as my sentinel against everything that had formerly been so plentiful ..."

A few weeks later, the core of the 'split-off' complex in Mrs. C. revealed itself in her 'inner sight' in the 'quiet state of alertness'. I am going to quote only a few selected passages, which describe the further development of her encounter with the 'split-off' complex. The dots refer to omissions in the original testimony, in which real private events are described. Despite these omissions, it is possible to discern clearly, and without having to read the full report, that the 'object arriving' has revealed itself consecutively, becoming more and more distinct in the process. Eventually it became manifest in 'inner sight' in its real and inalienable shape:

"*I am afraid of looking – as if I will be struck with blindness if I opened my eyes – I must not look at it – there it is – oh – oh – oh! – . . . How could I have done that? How should I . . . – I didn't know anything of it – I think like this only now* – It reveals itself quite clearly [this phrase is printed in italics for emphasis in the original] – *but this was not* me ["me" in italics in the original] *– this was someone else – but perhaps I wanted it – but did not do it – Have I done it? – really done it – really done – have I done* this? [italics in original] – It was no one else! [italics in original] – *It cannot be – this is impossible – this is not possible at all! – I did not know at all . . . – Can it be otherwise? . . . No, it cannot be – it just cannot be!* (She is moaning heavily) . . . *Has that happened at all? – I am only thinking of it, now – I do not want to believe it. I only want to tell how it appeared to me:* [italics in original] . . ."

In the following passage Mrs. C. tells what she has 'seen' in 'inner sight'. She is able to face the 'split-off' complex, which in this way could be integrated again into the overall structure of her personality.

So far the enquiry into the 'split-off' complex that emerges in consciousness as the 'object arriving' has not yielded any additional phenomena that might prove helpful for the further progress of this investigation into the diverse 'forms of arriving' in the 'quiet state of alertness'. But as we shall see later, it is possible to identify a few more than the five 'forms of arriving' considered so far. Before we continue with this enquiry, however, we have to turn briefly to other issues. One of these concerns the notion of the 'self' and its manifestations in the 'quiet state of alertness'. To begin with, we have to interpolate a section on various key concepts, including the 'self', 'self-understanding' and the 'symbol', which are all important concepts that have to be defined in view of the further progress of our investigation.

The Self, the Symbol and Self-Understanding

Before proceeding with our psychological enquiries, we have to address a philosophical concept (for the first time in this study). This philosophical concept is best denoted by the term "*basic knowledge*", which was coined by Karl Jaspers. Jaspers states:[125] "Basic

---

125 Jaspers, Karl. *Allgemeine Psychopathologie. Ein Leitfaden für Studierende, Ärzte und Psychologen*. 1913. 5th ed. Berlin and Heidelberg: Springer, 1948. 295 and 275.

knowledge is knowledge that establishes the very foundation for what is encompassed by any other knowledge." – "The scope of basic knowledge shows how man views himself and the world." – "Basic knowledge is also termed the *apriori*: We may distinguish between the general *apriori* of consciousness, which encompasses the categories of reason, the *apriori* of the spirit revealed in ideas, and the *apriori* of being as manifested in drives and forms of responses . . . basic knowledge is part of all major types of perception, the modes of seeing and thinking about ur-phenomena and empirical facts, it includes the ways of being human, and the conception of the world . . . as well as the prevailing value judgements and tendencies. Within the area of basic knowledge symbols have a universal and all-pervasive significance."

We must not bypass the concept of ideas. Ideas are, psychologically speaking, thoughts. Within the realm of consciousness encompassed by the 'quiet state of alertness', ideas are very rarely encountered as objects of 'inner sight'; the peripheral sphere, however, which covers the subconscious and various modes of awareness, does contain ideas, which can be recalled at any time from the given store of knowledge. Moreover, a person immersed in the 'quiet state of alertness' retains a subliminal awareness of himself/herself, which enables him/her to understand himself/herself spontaneously, and to 'reflect' on himself/herself. One item of knowledge that is part of man's store of knowledge, and which is intuitively and spontaneously conveyed, is the awareness that man is subject to time and thus to change. Although one is sure that the identity of the 'I' has been preserved throughout one's past, and is preserved in the present and will be so in the future, man is clearly conscious of the future directedness of the process of living and being, hence man knows that he/she has been created in view of the future. Without the category of becoming, man would neither be able to conceptualize nor to understand himself/herself.

The 'self' is strictly speaking not a scientific, nor a philosophical concept. The 'self' cannot be grasped by merely attributing facts of consciousness cumulatively to it. *The self is an idea, and as such the self has many different regulative functions in every single individual consciousness*. The notion of the 'self' transcends not only the concept of personality, but also that of the character. If we define 'character' as the epitome of all potential reactions that can be generated by a person's individual talent, the notion of the 'self' extends beyond that of 'character' in that it includes the notion of a predetermined design, that is, the scheme of evolution. The 'self' is – like Goethe's notion of the primordial plant – the idea of the wholeness of the individual, accomplished by the faculties that are elicited in the course of the individual process of individuation. The concept of personality, by contrast, refers to the current manifestation of the 'self', and thus it mirrors only a part of the 'self', while the remaining (latent) potential and faculties have not (yet) evolved. If a conscious mind tries to conceive of him/herself within the context of the idea of the 'self', he/she will increase the qualities referred to above by appropriate value judgements. *The 'self' is not only the idea of a wholeness that becomes – to a greater or lesser extent – manifest individually in the course of life, but the 'self' is also the ideational focal point at which the consciousness of one's personality is going to develop.* The 'I' considers the 'self' to be a future being, towards whom the growth of the individual personality should be directed. The desire for the 'self' and the will to accomplish one's [true] 'self' are the empirical features of this aspiration, which accompany the process of personal growth. *Moreover, the words self-elucidation, self-understanding and self-reflexion denote processes of thinking that are subsumed already under the categories of being and the idea of the 'self'.*

We do need the concept of the 'self' as we have to attribute to it those empirical phenomena of consciousness that – in the widest sense – have retained some quality of the 'I'. It has been stated above that a 'split-off' complex that 'arrives' in the vista of 'inner sight' has the experiential quality of an 'it'. Despite this fact, the 'split-off' item 'arriving' does belong to the sphere of the 'self', because otherwise it would be impossible that the awareness that a 'split-off' complex is related to the 'I' can be temporarily lost, but recovered again, when the 'split-off' complex 'arrives' in consciousness and is eventually integrated again into the overall structure of the personality. (But this is only a remark in parenthesis, since we are no longer concerned here with considerations of the 'split-off' complex featuring as an 'object arriving'.)

We are now going to focus briefly on phenomena that are unmistakably perceived as 'arriving' from 'within the sphere of the self'. These phenomena are items of 'the self', but ones that have never become 'split off' from consciousness. These are phenomena that appear as a 'wholeness' in the space of consciousness.

We have stated above that the 'object arriving' can assume the shape of a symbol. Compared to the other 'forms of arriving' mentioned so far, the symbolic form is particularly fraught with meaning. It is therefore a special variety, because the hallmark of a symbol[126] is that it signifies a wholeness, which as such remains (for the time being) concealed. Whereas symbols are only rarely encountered in the 'waking consciousness', they are abundant in the 'dream consciousness'. The 'quiet state of alertness', by contrast, is a highly alert and lucid mental condition, but one which is, like the hypo-lucid and blurred 'dream state', highly receptive to the perception of symbolic pictures. The flow phenomena with symbolic import in consciousness is facilitated in the 'quiet state of alertness', because all the controlling functions of the 'I' are suspended. Whenever the 'quiet state of alertness' is fully established, and when all self-generated processes of autonomous thinking released by 'secondary dispositions' have been stilled, it is usually a symbol or a metaphor that tends to surface as the 'object' that 'arrives' in 'inner sight'. For the purpose of our investigation we have to clearly define, first of all, the terms 'symbol' and 'metaphor': *A symbol is a visual representation in the shape of an image that hints at something unknown and unknowable.* What cannot be recognized cognitively appears visually as a symbol; this means that a symbol cannot be grasped as a specific rational 'object'. *A metaphor, by contrast, is an image that refers to a known object, a known fact or to a real item by way of substitution.* A metaphoric experience is therefore an illuminating experience. A symbolic image contains real facets of the psyche, which can be grasped intuitively, or divined, longed for, loved or dreaded, but a symbol can never

---

126 Jaspers, Karl. *Allgemeine Psychopathologie. Ein Leitfaden für Studierende, Ärzte und Psychologen.* 1913. 5th ed. Berlin and Heidelberg: Springer, 1948. 276ff. – Jung, C. G. *Psychologische Typen.* Zurich: Rascher, 1925. 674f.

be understood rationally like a concept or an idea. There are, however, objects in empirical reality that have become symbols in personal or communal history; for instance, a formidable personality may become a symbol of a dark, unknown realm that is about to reveal itself. In the given context, however, we are not concerned with symbols that refer to the external realm of empirical reality. Our focus is exclusively on symbols that appear in the inner space of the individual consciousness. Symbols of the latter type arrive in 'inner sight' in a person when immersed in the 'quiet state of alertness'. A symbol of this kind has (if it is indeed a genuine symbol) a grave and portentous meaning as well as a lasting after-effect. A symbol that becomes manifest in consciousness must be examined as regards its significance, i.e. its symbolic import, what it is referring to or hinting at. We have encountered the experience of such a symbol when we analysed 'split-off' phenomena, notably the case in which a dangerous, hideous animal appears, which is a genuine symbol that hints at a concealed, frightening, portentous, unknown entity. However, a symbol does not just appear in the form of a concrete shape or image, it can also appear in diverse other forms of manifestation, suggested by the specific qualities that adhere to the 'object arriving' when it is experienced.

In order to be able to elucidate such opaque symbols in some detail, we have to refer back to what we have said about the 'self'. The 'self' is an idea of a wholeness represented in the individual consciousness. From amongst the plethora of items that may surface in consciousness, several can be identified as relating to, or originating from the individual 'sphere of the self'. Any attempt at providing a structured understanding of the 'sphere of the self' depends on both the conception of the 'self', and correspondingly, on a clear understanding of the categories of becoming. *When talking about the areas of the self that 'arrive' as entire entities in consciousness, we need to know that some varieties of these entities arrive in the form of a metaphor, others in the form of a symbol, and that these entities are manifestations of ideas, or antecedents of ideas* that belong to the 'sphere of the self'. This means that we must be aware that 'behind' these symbolic or metaphorical manifestations there are empirical entities that cannot be causally explained.

Self-understanding is inexorably a capacity of the 'I'. Every individual organizes the inventory of his/her own consciousness by criteria informed by rational understanding. Self-observation and self-understanding are concepts that denote processes of consciousness that are part of, and accompany, every experience. Though the degree of self-understanding may differ considerably between individuals, there is no human consciousness that can dispense with self-understanding for long. The notion of the unity of the 'self', and the different ideas that are contained in the 'self', are the focal points of 'self-understanding'. One speaks of different 'aspects' of a personality, and of areas of a personality that have been impeded in their development. Self-understanding enables us to overcome setbacks and to direct our lives at new future aims; it furthermore allows us to situate our memories in the proper context, and to recognize their causal coherence as well as their impact on the 'self', regardless of whether this impact is a positive or a negative one. Self-understanding finally helps us to discern, and cope with, some shared guilt or error. All these partial areas of the (so-called) 'sphere of the self' ("Selbstsphäre") must be tied to our personality, and continuously integrated into the process of personal growth – all this is achieved by self-understanding. But when this process of integration fails, or is disrupted, for instance, by an act of rejection, or by suppression, or by 'forgetting', these isolated experiences and suppressed, subconscious components of the 'self' tend to emerge in consciousness in the shape of some 'object' that 'arrives' in the vista of 'inner sight'. This object is initially usually obscure, mysterious and incomprehensible. It is therefore easy to understand that ideas of such an elusive wholeness will become manifest, first and foremost, in the shape of a symbol. It is one of the achievements of C. G. Jung[127] to have analysed the import of symbols, which appear in dreams and in the 'somnambulist consciousness'. They are understood to be personified ideas originating from areas of the self, or else conceived as prototypical representations foreshadowing a person's plans and

---

127 Cf. Jung, C. G. *Wandlungen und Symbole der Libido*. 3rd ed. Leipzig and Vienna: Deuticke, 1938. – Jung, C. G. *Über die Psychologie des Unbewußten*. 6th ed. Zurich: Rascher, 1948.

intentions for the future. It was the achievement of Jung's lifetime research to have established a comprehensive systematic scheme for interpreting symbols, in which the symbols that surface in dreams and in spontaneous paintings and drawings, as well as the symbols that emerge in 'somnambulist states', were related to the universal domain of symbols featuring in the myths, folk-legends and fairy tales of all peoples.

It is not possible in this context, nor is it necessary, to consider the metaphysical implications of the findings of C. G. Jung. His claim that there is such a thing as the 'collective unconscious', which is the homestead of primordial images, is indeed a metaphysical idea that we do not require, if we merely want to acknowledge the fact that symbolic experience is an "ur-phenomenon" of humanity, which is corroborated globally by man's cultural heritage. It is a proven fact that mankind has produced similar, or even identical images across time, space and cultures. The question as to whether these primeval images, or the archetypes on which they are based, are to be taken as an *apriori*, or whether these symbols and images have been imparted in a secondary creative act into the individual consciousness by the collective Spirit, does not have to be considered here; nor is it necessary here to consider the question of where archetypes are located, i.e. in which sphere outside the individual consciousness they are supposed to dwell, if they are claimed to be a facticity given *apriori*.

It is sufficient here to consider two examples for illustration. The term 'anima' is such an idea of a wholeness that surpasses all intelligible contexts, and which, being a part of the self, may not be effective, or apparent in a male person who leads a conspicuously virile life. 'Anima' is the complementary part of the psyche, i.e. the female part of a male. The 'anima' aspect appears, for instance, in the 'dream consciousness' in the symbol of Cinderella, who is forced to live in the storage rooms of a cellar, and who comes across the landlord of the castle only rarely, and when this happens, he is rather perturbed and embarrassed by the chance encounter. Cinderella, the cursed daughter of the king, and the victim of a magic spell, appears to him as a woman who is uncanny, haunting, intimidating, alluring and quizzical.[128] – In the second example, a person's plans for the future are symbolically foreshadowed.[129] The path is a primeval image with symbolic import, which can be found in countless varieties in pictorial (and literary) representations: The boundaries of the pathway (when read in physiognomic terms) indicate the dawning of self-understanding, which is burdened by conflicting drives and motives; the signpost foreshadows symbolically that the individual is about to redirect the course of his/her future life; getting lost on the way signifies that the person's self-understanding is still vulnerable and as yet in the incipient stage, hampered by discouraging memories. These are all examples in which a symbol 'arrives' in consciousness which is portentous and opaque, but which has a great impact on the individual and his/her future development. *This means that individual parts of the self can appear as a unified whole in the process of 'arriving'.*

However, from what has been stated above, we must not infer that the symbol is the only form in which a part of the self can reveal itself in the process of an 'object arriving'. It rather seems to me that in the 'quiet state of alertness' the symbol is certainly not the predominant 'form of arriving'. Symbolic experiences are rather more important and abundant in the 'dream consciousness' and the 'somnambulist state', and in dreamlike states within the 'waking consciousness'. The reason for the relatively sparse appearance of symbols in the 'quiet state of alertness' compared to other states of consciousness is the fact that in the 'quiet state of alertness' the capacity of perceiving a wide variety of in-coming phenomena in 'inner sight' is in no way confined, whereas certain limitations are imposed by the specific structures of the 'state of dreaming', 'the somnambulist state' and the 'waking state'. So far we have distinguished five 'forms of arriving', but only in one of these 'forms' are symbols the main (or only) 'content'. In the 'quiet state of alertness' a practitioner can, as we have repeatedly shown, incorporate a 'secondary

---

128 Cf. Heyer, Gustav R. *Der Organismus der Seele: Eine Einführung in die Analytische Seelenheilkunde*. Munich: Lehmanns, 1932. Ch. 11.

129 Cf. Meinertz, Josef. *Moderne Seinsprobleme in Ihrer Bedeutung für die Psychologie*. Heidelberg: Schneider, 1948. 28ff.

disposition' into the process of 'introversion', and in doing so he/she may 'encode' in his mind the propensity to be especially alert to symbols as 'objects arriving' in the 'quiet state of alertness'. When applying this approach of focussed inner perception, it is possible to discern in 'inner sight' a wide variety of symbols originating from myths and fairy-tales, which may all surface as 'objects arriving'. But overall, we can still support the claim that the experience of symbols is less frequent in the 'quiet state of alertness' than in any of the other states of consciousness. And there is a persuasive reason for this distinctive phenomenon: Any genuine, fully developed symbol is a pictorial representation of something unknown, and as such every symbol inevitably calls for an interpretation. An act of interpretation, however, necessarily requires the function of discursive thinking, and thus the switching into the 'waking consciousness'. Interpreting the implied and potential meaning(s) of a symbol can thus be achieved only when the rational faculties are switched on, thus when the mind is able to engage in a process of logically coherent thinking, which is clearly directed at a specific aim. The latter is applied and achieved, for instance, in psychotherapy, in the joint enterprise between patient and therapist. *When a symbol that appears as an 'object arriving' in the 'quiet state of alertness' is perceived by a person in a situation not related to psychotherapy, the process of perceiving can only be fleeting and transitory, regardless of how deeply emotionally charged and semantically loaded the symbol may be.* This means that a symbol that surfaces in the 'quiet state of alertness' cannot abide in the mind and tends to fade out quickly as it will be replaced by other 'forms of arriving', i.e. 'forms of arriving' that have no symbolic import.

In the 'quiet state of alertness', *the 'object arriving' appears more frequently in the form of a metaphor than in the form of a symbol.* Here we should add that when we have stated above that in the 'quiet state of alertness' image-based experiences tend to prevail over ideational experiences, we had the metaphoric type and not the symbolic 'form of arriving' in mind.

A Fragment of the Self Featuring as an 'Object Arriving' (The Sixth, Seventh and Eighth 'Forms of Arriving')

The 'metaphorical form' is the sixth 'form' in which an 'object' can 'arrive' in consciousness in the vista of 'inner sight'. When a metaphoric image appears in the realm of 'inner sight', it is less opaque than a symbol, and its meaning is less ambivalent. The reason why metaphoric images can be comprehended more easily and are more immediately intelligible is not only grounded in the fact that metaphoric representations are more distinct and transparent, but also in the fact that they are 'parts of a whole' that allow us to discern some vestiges of the entire 'whole' that is about to 'arrive'. Metaphoric images foreshadow, as it were, the 'whole' that is as yet concealed though it is intuitively felt to be hovering at the threshold of 'arriving'. When an 'emotional response' is the 'object' that first 'arrives' in consciousness, it tends to evoke images, and these images are an intermediate stage before it is moulded into a particular concept. Images surface and present themselves as objects of 'inner sight'; for the most part, however, such emerging images are items that arise from the stream of feelings that is floating through consciousness. This means that in empirical reality the 'metaphoric form' and the 'emotional form of arriving' are usually (though not always) intertwined. The *phenomenon that the 'emotional' and the 'metaphoric form of arriving' are intertwined, resulting in a single experience,* is, however, not unique but occurs with other 'forms of arriving' as well: **Feelings may be intertwined with symbolic and metaphoric experiences as well as with the 'form of reflective self-understanding' and 'intuitive knowledge'** (which will be considered below), **resulting in a composite 'overall form' of experiencing an 'object arriving' in 'inner sight', which is multi-layered and yet homogeneous.**

We have now clearly defined the terms of symbol and metaphor. In our analysis we must henceforth clearly differentiate whether any image 'arriving' in the 'quiet state of awareness' has to be classified as a symbol or as a metaphor. The difficulty is, however, that there are no such clear-cut borderlines between metaphor and symbol in empirical reality as stipulated in the definitions of the concepts, as there is a broad transitional zone between the two in actual experience. This means that we have to decide in the analysis of recorded experience in each case which of the two concepts applies or is more appropriate in the given context.

Moreover, the 'metaphoric form of arriving' must be distinguished not only from the 'symbolic form', but also from the 'form of arriving' termed 'news-reel-like series of images'. As outlined above, the latter 'form of arriving' consists of a sequence of pictorial memories which emerge in 'inner sight' and pass through consciousness like on a newsreel or a filmstrip. These visual memories have no symbolic or metaphoric import, and are thus neither portentous, nor predictive, i.e. they do not foreshadow anything relating to the future life of the 'experiencing I'.

The analysis of the following accounts of experiences witnessed in the 'quiet state of alertness' will focus on 'objects' that 'arrive' from within the 'sphere of the self'. At this point, I should call to mind that we have decided to postpone questions relating to the realm of mystical experience, even though some phenomena are addressed in the reports quoted below that have (as we shall see later) the hallmarks of mystical experience. However, the following records also describe phenomena that have only the semblance of being 'mystical', and which can be shown to be actually phenomena originating from within the 'sphere of the self', and thus do not qualify as 'mystical phenomena'. By critically assessing the phenomena recorded in the subsequent testimonies, we can discern several formal characteristics featuring in all of them. (The following records derive from spontaneous utterances of three persons, spoken when they were absorbed in the 'quiet state of alertness' and recorded during several sessions.) The common features identified in all of these records are the following:

1. *'Inner sight' enables a person to perceive inwardly with clarity the whole condition of his/her soul ("Seele"), revealing it as it truly is in the given situation.* Though it is certainly true that a person is also able to report something about his/her present psychological condition in the normal 'waking state', the kind of self-knowledge attained in the 'waking consciousness' is to a considerable

extent subject to, and hence tinged by, self-delusion. In the normal 'waking state' it is usually unlikely to achieve an unbiased, balanced self-assessment, but rather one that is biased and impaired by numerous factors, including fluctuations in the focus of attention, controlling (and manipulating) acts of the will and by rational reflection (to name only a few); in other words, the process of self-knowledge is (in part) tainted by the person's 'waking consciousness' and its rootedness in worldly bondage. This refers in particular to the function of drives, which are inevitably involved in the process of self-knowledge, and because drives are emotionally charged, they are conducive to self-deception. A person immersed in the 'quiet state of alertness', by contrast, is entirely passively faced with the condition of his/her psyche, perceiving it in the emptied, hyper-lucid state of consciousness, and thus, the 'experiencing self' may grasp the condition of the soul as it truly is. He/she is able to comprehend intuitively the current condition of the soul, and is aware of the future direction at which his/her self is going to develop (though during the event he/she may not be clearly conscious of this). Thus he/she is able to comprehend the 'design' of the process of self-realization in which he/she is currently immersed. When a person who is restless and depressed in the 'waking consciousness' engages in 'introversion' in order to attain the calmness of the 'quiet state of alertness', he/she will become immediately aware of the radical change of his/her state of mind achieved by 'introversion', as he/she is now permeated by inner calm, has become composed and at ease. This indicates that a person who suffers in the 'waking consciousness' from the awareness of the (apparent) stagnation in the growth of his/her personality will recognize instantly, when transported into the 'quiet state of alertness', that his/her process of self-realization has after all made some significant progress.

2. The term 'design' can be defined as the deliberate plan for the orientation of one's life at a particular aim. The plan to advance the growth of one's personality, when conceived and carried out in the 'waking consciousness', always depends on volition, hence the intended aim is consciously determined by the will. *In*

the 'quiet state of alertness', by contrast, we do not find a plan for personal growth, but we rather encounter *antecedents of a plan relating to the self*, which becomes manifest in encounters and insights perceived passively in 'inner sight', i.e. in an experience in which the self is exposed to a power acting upon him/her. Such antecedents of a plan or design of personal growth may consist, for instance, of intricate stirrings, feelings, drives and thoughts. Though the following records are rather diverse, not least because they have been derived from different personalities of different gender and age, the three speakers shared a similarly advanced level of self-realization and were unanimous in their avowal that they have only now 'embarked on the way' towards their 'true self'. They were all filled with a deep sense of longing and with anticipation, and shared the sincere desire to surrender to the sphere of 'light' that has opened up in them. These are all clear indications that each of the three persons was aware that a crucial transformation has occurred within his/her self, and that the capacity for 'inner sight' has deepened and continued to 'advance', whereas the 'shadows' and the 'darkness', the 'fear' and anything that was not 'authentic', or consonant with their personality, had been left behind. Each of the three subjects was adamant that in his/her life "a new morning had broken", and "a fertile nest had been bestowed". These expressions are metaphorical ways of describing their mental condition, which in the given records were at times interspersed with symbols. In the last record quoted below, we may also identify the 'form of self-understanding' as an integral part of an intertwined, composite experience of 'objects arriving' in the 'quiet state of alertness'.

3. *In empirical reality the particular direction at which feelings, ideas, drives and thinking are oriented, is always an integral part of the system of values shared by the individual subject.* This aspect has to be addressed at this juncture, although we will deal with the function of values in the context of 'introversion' in some detail later. This passing reference is required as it would be difficult otherwise to understand the nature of the emotions that are released during the process of personal growth, if we were

not aware that self-realization is a highly esteemed achievement, and perhaps even the highest ranking value of all in the life of an individual, because it is the ultimate goal at which all hopes, desires and aspirations of a human being are directed. The idea of the 'self' is regarded as a 'primordial value' ("Urwert"), as the 'ultimate, pristine state of being'; the 'self' is the 'being of the soul in its primal condition', or whatever other the metaphorical expressions may be used to describe the pristine nature of the 'self'.

4. *Experiences of this kind encountered in the 'quiet state of alertness' will trigger, as an after-effect, a process of transformation in the area of dispositions* after the 'quiet state of alertness' has subsided. This, in turn, effects a *change in the person's reactions and patterns of behaviour* in the 'waking consciousness'. The causes of this change in the 'self' are clearly perceived by the individual concerned when absorbed in the 'quiet state of alertness', and the awareness of the person's progress in the process of self-realization is so clearly conveyed that these insights are stored in consciousness and continue to dwell consciously in the 'waking consciousness'. These insights are conferred in the 'quiet state of alertness' and have a lasting impact on the person's motives for engaging in future actions. Another after-effect is the awareness that feelings, the function of the imagination and acts of thinking are interrelated.

5. Some of the metaphoric images featuring in the records below appear to be pointing even beyond the 'sphere of the self'. The *very name* by which the 'object arriving' is addressed seems to indicate or point at something that is transpersonal, transcendent and all-comprising. But we must be clear that the mere fact that the 'object arriving' is addressed in transcendental terms is something entirely different from actually experiencing that the 'object arriving' has the quality of an entity that is 'all-encompassing'. *In the three records quoted below, the 'object arriving' is in each case one that emerges from within the 'sphere of the self', even when it is individually hypostasized in a person's subjective*

experience in metaphysical terms, even to the extent that the 'object arriving' seems to be referring to a realm beyond the individual 'sphere of the self'.

6. These three particular records have been chosen because they recapture various 'forms of arriving', which can be juxtaposed and analysed; together they provide valuable data for our phenomenological analysis. The first record is an example in which responding feelings are the main 'form of arriving'. The emotional form of responding to the 'object arriving' is in this case intertwined with the 'metaphoric form of arriving'. For this reason this particular record appears somewhat obscure and difficult to comprehend. But I can confirm that the speaker ("Ms. B") of this record was fully absorbed in the 'quiet state of alertness' when she conveyed these impressions, and her mental condition was perfectly clear throughout the event. The second record ("Mr. D.") is more lucid and less impenetrable to the reader than the previous one. It describes mainly the metaphoric mode of 'arriving', which is intertwined in a few passages with the symbolic mode. The third example ("Mrs. C.") is fairly clear and straightforward in its statement; it can easily be understood by an empathetic reader, not least because it renders the experience in which 'intuitive self-understanding' is instilled in the receptive mind.

Ms. B.: "*It is hovering – it is* a path ['path' set in italics for emphasis in the original text] *– it is rushing – I am entirely immersed in rushing* [sound] *– it is tearing – it is ballooning – it is pulling – it is something dark, big, an infinitude that is like a tree – the rushing sound is all around me – it is rather like a dome, or a vault arched over me like silence – struck with awe I have even more inklings of what it is* [italics in original] *– like a mist or haze – the haze is heavy – now there is nothing any more – the haze has turned into silence – in the deep a growing* shadow [italics in original] *is cast – the shadow is growing become more intense like a boundary – the shadow evokes fear – I can see the shadows – they are touching me – I have a foreboding of* grief [italics in original] *– grief is pouring in – it is received – tears are pouring in – a veil is still ballooning – something more profound is trying to approach* [italics in original] *– I am able to receive – I am allowed to wait – now it is ascending – it is a field – it is permeated – I am breathing in the clarity of what passes by flowing – around me, space* is expanding like a pristine morning [italics in original] – *my steps are insecure – I am feeling my way into it – its borders are bruising me – I am ascending as if coming out of a bowl – the bowl of longing is enfolding me – desire is breathing within me – it is like water swelling in me – it [desire] is abating [while I wander] from room to room – I do not see anything yet that is bright – only deep down within me I have a foreboding of words – they are like beams – this darkness has boundaries. – Earth is weighing [me] down like a heavy body – I must separate it* [italics in original] – *This is like a cutting edge, but unrest continues – it protects me – also the tears protect me – I can believe – I can look into the streams like into a promise – around me everything is declining – falling like the cataracts of a gigantic lake – like a gale in the evening – it is pushing into me – digging into me – it is groaning – it is falling – falling – and everything is floating into an even greater abyss. – Horror is liberating itself – I can encompass it – I can watch it – also unrest is heard rushing in a distance – I look through it with confidence – I am becoming more truthful – I am moving out of myself* [italics in original] – *it is disclosing itself."*

Mr. D.: *"The sword is cutting through the room above me, right in the middle. Its cutting edge spiked in the middle of my body, as if demanding a decision. – O what a miraculous slash right into the storage chamber of awakening! – The fertile nest full of seeds shall be removed from the darkness, and located in the brightness facing the light. – The body is open like the fresh furrow of a field. But the seeds have been placed in it before, watched with my eyes like living beings on a merry-go-round, like unborn infants. The breed is waiting, as if asleep, for the cool breath of morning, exhaled by the darkness as the first sign of dawn. – The midnight of eternity is hovering over the site, covering it with its protective warmth. – The seeds are the twinkling planets of the soul. – The slash has released the blood, which has poured down to form a sacred lake in the middle of my body. And on this purple lake the seeds are blossoming like budding flowers. – Silent and breathless with suspense, the holy shrine opens to receive the kiss of God."*

Mrs. C.: *"It doesn't get through, everything is opposed to it – so staunchly opposed to it – it cannot get through it. Somehow it steps in between and says no – I am not able to do it, I don't want it – there is so much that stands in between, which I cannot change, as if I had touched something final, touched a big part – that is so rotten. – . . .*

Inside me is like hell, but a hell that has never been fully unleashed before, but it is so now; it has somehow been freed from its fetters, and now it must see the light of day. And all the longing that the other should come, is now futile . . . I just am, what I am – like this hell here, how life is down there, thus life is to me; for if you think badly, you are bad - this is what you really are – it doesn't help, if you struggle against it, for then pretence and hypocrisy will return, distorting what is best. –

It is no use glossing over what is bad – somehow you have to live with it. But how is it possible to live with it? It must be possible somehow to mingle it with the very big thing. I must not be overwhelmed by a singular power. It must be governed by a supreme power – it must be possible, perhaps once – once perhaps. But not in the state I am in now, being split in two, and certainly not as long as I am possessed by evil. – It shall not be like this, it shall be different somehow."

The concept of 'intuition'[130] is here exclusively defined in psychological terms. Intuition is a sudden and spontaneous insight into real and ideational facts, which are subjectively understood to be evident. A moment of intuition cannot be intentionally generated, but occurs always instantaneously. During the event, the 'I' experiences that some 'content' has all of a sudden been 'infused' in the mind. This may be an incident in which some judgement is instantly instilled, for example, a judgement that is not derived from logical reasoning, but has appeared spontaneously 'out of the blue', and which is immediately known to be true and valid. Intuitive knowledge is knowledge that becomes a fact in one's consciousness without being preceded or inaugurated by an empirical process – whether emotional, imaginative or cognitive. For the purposes of our enquiry it is not necessary to consider the question as to whether a somatic, or a psychonomic process (or both), is involved in an intuitive event, even though the answer to this question might provide an explanation as to why the experience of 'intuition' is marked by a definitive sense of 'closure'. That is to say, the conviction inherent in any act of 'intuition' that the insight 'infused' is something final, true, valid, and evident. There is no need in this psychological study to consider any of the complex philosophical questions relating to the cognitive value of insights

---

130   Cf. Jung, C. G. *Psychologische Typen*. Zurich: Rascher, 1925. 641ff. – Gruhle, H. W. *Verstehende Psychologie (Erlebnislehre). Ein Lehrbuch*. Stuttgart: Thieme, 1948. 130ff.

attained by intuition, nor do we intend to elaborate on the potential metaphysical significance of intuition, since this is likewise an area pertaining to philosophy. In passing, we just refer to the epistemological considerations of Nicolai Hartmann,[131] who has proposed the notion of the "stigmatic" nature of intuition and considered 'intuition' as an ideal mode of knowledge. Henri Bergson[132] should also be mentioned in this context. He has suggested that 'intuition' is a unique experience in which the individual touches immediately upon the 'élan vital', i.e. the creative energy of life accessible to 'heroic individuals' who are capable of empathy.

Instances of 'intuition' can be witnessed in several areas of human experience: A painter may have a clear intuitive vision of a painting before actually starting to paint the picture; a scientist may be bestowed with the solution of a long-sought problem in the flash of a moment – confident that the solution imparted by 'intuition' is right and final, and this insight is immediately evident. There is, moreover, the phenomenon of intuitive eidetic vision of an essence (as conceived by philosophical phenomenology), in which a single entity of an essence is isolated from the entire complex of essences and perceived individually so that it "is no longer viewed from the perspective of reason, but is stigmatically contemplated." Empathetic psychology depends inalienably on the capacity of intuitive perception for establishing a coherent and intelligible system of concepts. Immediacy and the subjective awareness of evident truth, which go with any intuitive judgement, are thus distinctive features of 'intuition'. They tend to spark off a process of discursive thinking; thus 'intuition' is never the result of rational reflection but, on the contrary, it initiates a process of discursive thinking. In the context of this stringently scientific phenomenological investigation, we have to abstain from proposing a speculative hypothesis concerning the potential origin of 'intuition', or the potential causes by which it might be triggered, and thus must refrain not only from proposing a metaphysical interpretation, but

---

131 Cf. Hartmann, Nicolai. *Grundzüge einer Metaphysik der Erkenntnis*. 2nd ed. Berlin: de Gruyter, 1925. Chs. 67 and 68.
132 Cf. Bergson, Henri. *Denken und Schöpferisches Werden*. Meisenheim am Glan: Westkulturverlag, 1948.

also from assessing this phenomenon in terms of its existential value. Because of the strictures imposed by science, we do not define the philosophical concept of 'intuitive vision'. However, we have to clarify here that *'inner sight', conceived as a function of the 'I' in the 'quiet state of alertness', must not be equated with intuitive experience, or what is subsumed by the concept of 'intuitive vision'.* We have shown that the 'object arriving' in the vista of 'inner sight' may appear in a wide variety of different 'forms': In the form of a dynamic sequence of images ('newsreel'), as a symbol, a metaphor, a symptomatic somatic seizure, or as a word surfacing in consciousness during the process of 'introversion' in the 'quiet state of alertness'. Sometimes, however, the 'object arriving' is experienced in a 'flash of intuition'. In the latter instance, the 'content' of the 'object arriving' may remain partly concealed, but some items of its 'content', or in certain events even the entire whole of the 'object', can be grasped instantly, and this 'intuitive' moment elicits immediately a deep sense of certainty, even when the 'content' revealed is entirely unrelated to the subject's previous experience, or to anything by which the immediate sense of certainty evoked in the 'experiencing I' by the intuitive experience could be rationally explained. We have stated above that the 'forms of arriving' are usually intertwined in various ways. Therefore it is not surprising that flashes of intuition are likewise often intertwined with metaphoric and other forms of 'arriving', notably the 'form of self-understanding', in which 'intuitions' often provide instantaneous value judgements. In the preceding section we have merely tried to corroborate the claim that **'intuition' is another distinct 'form of arriving', thus the seventh 'form' in our taxonomy.**

The eighth 'form of arriving' is that of 'language'. In this variety, a word, or a sequence of words, 'arrive(s)' as the 'object(s)' of 'inner sight'. At the beginning of this form of perceiving an 'object arriving', a word emerges either visually or audibly perceived by 'inner hearing'; the word perceived is usually unfamiliar, unknown, and appears to be coming from afar. The word surfaces all of a sudden, unexpectedly, without having been called for, and is often incomprehensible to the 'experiencing I'. Like other 'objects arriving', the word appearing in 'inner sight' tends to linger for some time in consciousness. One of its distinctive features is that it hints at some otherness as yet unknown and incomprehensible, something that has not yet revealed itself as a whole. *This 'form of arriving' in which something becomes manifest in a single word, or in a sequence of words, that is as yet unrecognizable, is a process that is phenomenologically clearly to be distinguished from the expressive phenomenon of spontaneous 'speech' accompanying the process of 'introversion' or the 'quiet state of alertness'.* Verbal utterances articulated spontaneously during the 'quiet state of alertness' are merely a mode of expressing subjective impressions currently experienced in the ongoing process of 'introversion' and/or while absorbed in the 'quiet state of alertness'. Language is thus only a corollary of the 'quiet state of alertness' and not a spontaneous utterance of a 'word' perceived as an 'object arriving' in 'inner sight'. There are different modes in which a word that 'arrives' in consciousness while the 'experiencing I' is absorbed in the 'quiet state of alertness' can become apparent. Sometimes the word 'arriving' is a symbol or a metaphor, and may appear without a given context and without being related to any other event. But more often the word, or sequence of words emerging, turns out to be the concrete embodiment, or a crystallization of what is currently passing through the stream of feelings in consciousness. It occurs quite often that the words appearing in 'inner sight' are spontaneously and truthfully articulated aloud by the person immersed in the 'quiet state of alertness' in the order in which they have surfaced. When this happens the 'experiencing I' is (usually) unaware of the meaning of the individual word, or of the sequence of words. This means that the subject can verify only after the 'quiet state of alertness' has ended *that he has expressed words, sentences and rhythms, and that these words describe adequately the verbal 'object(s)' that has (have) 'arrived' in the vista of 'inner sight'.* Though the meaning of the word revealed can be grasped by the 'experiencing I' while 'inner sight' is in progress, the meaning of the complete sequence of words revealed during the event is not comprehended by the subject during the ongoing experience, but he/she is able to provide an explication after the event in the 'waking consciousness'.

The experience of a word 'arriving' in the 'quiet state of alertness' does not, however, happen always in the way described above. More often than not the word that surfaces from the depths of consciousness is felt to be not perfectly equivalent, or adequate for rendering the perception of an unknown 'object arriving' along with it. The 'I' knows something of the qualities encompassed by the alien 'object arriving'. The 'I' has some intimations of its essence, it is emotionally aware of the nature of the incoming 'object', and has some awareness of the direction from which it seems to be coming. The word that surfaces in the mind jointly with the invisible 'object' as yet hovering at the threshold of consciousness becomes manifest like an 'object' in 'inner sight'. The 'experiencing I' can either 'accept' or 'reject' the word 'arriving' on such an occasion (which is a feature that also applies to the perception of a metaphor, a symbol, and other incoming phenomena in the 'quiet state of alertness'). Acceptance or rejection depends on whether the emerging word is or is not considered a perfectly adequate or appropriate 'embodiment' or 'linguistic shape' of the true essence of the hidden 'object' that is about to 'arrive' in consciousness. The word that has emerged will dwell in the space of consciousness for some time, and evoke an emotional response correlating to the experiential quality of the encounter with the unknown, i.e. which can be either appreciative or dismissive. If the word is accepted, feelings of concord, harmony and reassurance will be articulated; but when feelings of unease, fear, disgust or doubt are evoked, the word is rejected and not articulated. That is to say that only the word that is approved is uttered aloud, whereas the word that is rejected is suppressed, and, as a consequence, fades away and disappears from consciousness. All these processes occur spontaneously and entirely passively, i.e. without any active (volitional and rational) involvement of the 'experiencing I'.

So far we have distinguished and outlined eight 'forms of arriving': 1) the sequence of reel-like images, 2) responding feelings, 3) the metaphoric 'form of arriving', 4) the symbolic 'form of arriving', 5) a somatic seizure as a 'form of arriving', 6) self-knowledge as a 'form of arriving', 7) intuition and 8) language. In empirical reality these eight 'forms of arriving' are variously intertwined. Yet irrespective of the interlaced nature of these 'forms of arriving', it is also a proven fact that **every single human being has an intimately personal, thus a unique, 'overall form' of experiencing 'objects arriving' in the 'quiet state of alertness'** [because any 'overall form' is inevitably also

shaped and 'coloured' by the individual personality]. Having examined a representative corpus of recorded utterances spoken by subjects when absorbed in the 'quiet state of alertness', we are provided with sufficient empirical data to support the claim that every single individual perceives the 'object arriving' in a unique and personal way, i.e. in a manner co-determined by, and consonant with his/her distinctive personality. We have encountered a number of 'composite forms of arriving', in which – depending on the type of personality – either feelings predominate in the response evoked, or else the metaphoric form, or the cognitive form of self-understanding. The postulate that every individual has a distinctly personal 'form' of experiencing an 'object arriving' has been substantiated independently by the studies of Jaensch and his disciples.[133] One of them, Hans Eilks,[134] examined the so-called "Vorgestalterlebnis" [i.e. the 'conjectural perception of 'gestalt' *a priori*] from a typological perspective. Such a conjectural experience occurs, for instance, when a person is required to focus his/her attention strictly on figurines that are placed in a darkened room (the experiment was described above). Here we are primarily interested in Eilks's comments on the differences in the modes of perception witnessed by subjects belonging to one of the three (so-called) "I-types", and those belonging to the S_1-type: "In the I_1-type, the 'I' is considered to be like an open, empty room, or like a vacant bowl into which the impressions of the outside world are poured, where they create an image of the world that is related to reality. Whereas the S_1-type directs his/her feelings at objects, the I_1-type brings an open-minded attitude to the objects of the external world. – In the I_2-type, i.e. the conditionally integrated person, this attitude has become largely reduced, because he/she is only interested in objects of the external world which are beneficial to his/her own interests and well-being. In the I_3-type the willingness to observe the figurines (external reality) is missing altogether. This

---

133 Jaensch, Erich R. Über den Aufbau der Wahrnehmungswelt. Leipzig: Barth, 1923. – Jaensch, Erich R., and H. Ruppert. Über den Aufbau des Bewußtseins. Leipzig: Barth, 1930/31.

134 Eilks, Hans. "Das Vorgestalterlebnis unter Typologischem Gesichtspunkt." *Zeitschrift für Psychologie* 143 (1938): 19-79.

latter type is dominated by the will to act, and this is why a character with such a personality profile does not depend on the sensual perception of a given situation. For him/her the experiment with the figurines is neither an emotional experience nor a special test of his/her sense perception, but considered merely as a task imposed by the experiment. – A typical feature of the S_1-type is that the emotions aroused in the event subside and are eventually *dissolved* in the course of the experiment. With other participants, however, the process of visual perception is impaired by lingering affective responses to the environment, which usually include oppressive and frightening notions."

In the S_1- and I_1/S_1-types in particular, we may witness a process of perception in which the emotional response enhances the subject's attention directed at the object: "Disruptions in the entire constellation of the assumed shape of the figurine are equivalent to disruptions on the level of emotional attention."

In the reports supplied by subjects when immersed in the 'quiet state of alertness', we may discern (it seems to me) composite forms of 'inner sight', which are shaped by features of the individual personality, which in turn can be particularly related to the S_1, S_1/I_1 and the I_1/I_2 types. But this is only a parenthetical remark suggesting *that the type of personality does have an impact on a person's way and ability of perceiving an 'object arriving', not least because every individual faced with such an experiential event will respond in the manner he/she is capable of responding.* This means that it appears to be more likely for an individual of the S_1, S_1/I_1 and the I_1/I_2 types to experience an 'object arriving' in the 'quiet state of alertness' than in individuals of other types of personality.[135]

---

135 [Note: In the translation, the German text, which is apparently flawed and semantically ambivalent here, has been emended, as Albrecht does not endorse an elitist or discriminatory view of mystical experience, which might be inferred from the German wording as it stands: "Es darf aus dieser Bemerkung nicht mehr herausgelesen werden als der Hinweis, ... daß die Möglichkeit in der Versunkenheit ein Ankommendes zu erleben, nicht grundsätzlich für jeden Menschen vorhanden, sondern nur auf gewisse Typen beschränkt ist" (191-2). This might be misread as a statement suggesting that the experience of an 'object arriving' is not a universal and

Jaspers[136] repeatedly and poignantly has emphasized the claim: "Ideal constructions of types are no real categories of characters. They may help us to understand certain relationships. They refer to aspects of understanding but not to substances of being."

In the empirical records quoted below, some idiosyncrasies of

---

perennial capacity of the human soul since this experience is not accessible to certain "types of personality". Such a view is evidently at variance with the teachings of the mystics of both Eastern and Western tradition, and a view certainly not shared by Albrecht. The ambiguity derives from Albrecht's incorrect use of "Möglichkeit" ('possibility'), which in the given context is equivalent to 'capacity', whereas the appropriate noun would have been 'probability', i.e. the noun "Wahrscheinlichkeit" should have been used instead of "Möglichkeit". Hence the German phrasing is inadvertently flawed, which is why the meaning and phrasing of this sentence have been emended in the English translation. – To justify this emendation further, it should be added that Albrecht emphasizes throughout his writings that 'receiving' 'mystical phenomena' and responding to them is not a prerogative of certain 'types of personality', but a 'natural capacity' of man, irrespective of race, gender, religion, type of personality and cultural heritage. In *PMB*, for instance, he states explicitly (see above 238) that "mysticism is a normal phenomenon of human consciousness", which clearly implies that the capacity of experiencing mystical phenomena is innate to the human psyche and valid universally and perennially. The same view is reiterated emphatically in other writings. In a letter (dated 12 June 1964) to the philosopher Hans-A. Fischer-Barnicol, for instance, Albrecht summarizes the most important insight gained in the decades of empirical research into the nature of 'mystical consciousness', in a single aphoristic sentence: *"The soul of man has been chosen to be the passageway for the entrance of the Mystery into the world."* ("Die Seele des Menschen ist erwählt, Durchgangsraum zu sein für den Eintritt des Geheimnisses in die Welt." – This letter was published by Fischer-Barnicol in *Das Mystische Wort*, 190.) Albrecht thus advocated the view throughout his life – which to him was an inalienable empirical fact – that every human being is endowed with the capacity of receiving and responding to mystical phenomena, and that the Sacred Mystery may become manifest in the "heart" of every single individual in rare moments of revelation. – Albrecht, it is true, is most explicit on this issue when he speaks in the personal voice of the mystic rather than the voice of the scientist. – FW.]

136 Jaspers, Karl. *Allgemeine Psychopathologie. Ein Leitfaden für Studierende, Ärzte und Psychologen*. 1913. 5th ed. Berlin and Heidelberg: Springer, 1948. 362.

the individual personalities become apparent, which we have not yet encountered in the records analysed so far. Thus it is open to interpretation if the personal experiences recorded in these testimonies when the practitioners were immersed in the 'quiet state of alertness' can already be seen as instances of mystical experience. For it seems that the 'object arriving' described resonates with qualities pointing at a realm beyond the 'sphere of the self', though the overall experience was entirely rooted in the individual 'self'. Silence is a pivotal manifestation of the condition of the 'self' in the 'quiet state of alertness', and a significant stage in the process of self-realization. The experience of silence within causes moreover the detachment from all habitual ties to the world, which results in a so-called "creative caesura", i.e. a state filled with the yearning to surrender entirely to the special kind of silence, which is creative. By becoming detached from all familiar ties to the world, while reposing in the peace and silence within, enables new potentials for personal growth. However, it must not go unheeded that the silence that appears as the 'object arriving' in the 'quiet state of alertness' has clearly and foremost features of an 'it', of which the 'experiencing I' is unaware. This means that the 'experiencing I' does not recognize during the event that the silence has previously had qualities of the 'I', which disappear as soon as the 'object' has 'arrived', nor is the 'experiencing I' aware that he/she will get these qualities back after the event. Thus the silence that 'arrives' is, on the one hand, experienced as something alien and overpowering, but has, on the other hand, also characteristics familiar from and known to be an integral part of 'the sphere of the self'. In this twilight-zone between the 'self' and the [transpersonal][137] realm of mysticism, I would argue that the experience of silence as recorded here is a liminal experience, albeit one that is more deeply rooted in 'sphere of the self' than in the realm of mysticism. We will consider the psychological concept of revelation (which is implied in the statement above) later. At this point, only a concise explanatory remark is to be supplied on this issue: In the subsequent testimonies provided by several subjects, we will encounter several features that are typical

---

137 [Note: The qualifying epithet "transpersonal" has been added for clarification. – FW.]

and distinctive of an event of 'revelation', even though these personal records are, by and large, essentially still spontaneous accounts of occurrences perceived within 'the sphere of the self', rather than verbalized testimonies of an encounter with the mystical. I have decided to include these reports at this point of our investigation, as they show quite clearly how the two 'forms of arriving' referred to, i.e. 'arriving' in the form of 'intuition' and 'arriving' in the form of 'language', are intertwined with the other 'forms of arriving' (outlined earlier). The features of the 'it', when perceived as 'object arriving', are rather diverse in the individual accounts: The 'it' is, for one, described metaphorically as 'silence', or referred to as 'nothingness', or 'the Ur', or else, as 'blackness', as a 'rock' and as 'emptiness'. The 'it' is moreover described as an 'object' that affects and deeply moves the recipient emotionally at the moment of its 'arrival', eliciting intense feelings and emotional states in him/her, notably fear, awe, but also a deep sense of devotion and yearning for surrender. It is thus the 'form of responding feelings' that is a vital integral part in these records, though the 'metaphoric form of arriving' is the "primary" mode in which the 'object' becomes manifest in 'inner sight'. This becomes clearly apparent in such expressions as "towering rocks piled up one upon the other", "the flowing brook", "the black water of the moor" and "the cloak of reposing stone". These metaphors recapture in visual images the primary form in which the 'object' 'arrives' in the given event. These records also demonstrate that genuine 'intuitions' are also involved in the underlying experience, i.e. moments yielding immediate insight into truths of existence and creation, insights which surface suddenly in consciousness, experienced with a deep sense of certainty: "the primary beginning is here" – "origins are opening up" – "in the middle of the heart, the most intimate gift will be born". All the statements are informed by intuitive insights instilled spontaneously, and which refer to processes involved in the subject's path of individuation. These records provide, moreover, evidence that the 'form of language' is likewise an integral part of the composite experience of perceiving 'objects arriving' in 'inner sight': Several words in the spontaneous utterances recorded are charged with portentous meaning; these words appear to have 'arrived' in the subject's consciousness acoustically rather than visually; the very sound of these words is fraught with meaning so that these words became the 'garment', as it were, for the 'object arriving'. Though the person absorbed in the 'quiet state of alertness' is able to confirm in retrospect (i.e. after having returned to the 'waking state') that the four 'forms of arriving' discerned here have indeed been constituent elements of his/her experience, he/she is unable to say how these four 'forms of arriving' were actually intertwined during the event. From this we may infer again that what is perceived by a subject when absorbed in the 'quiet state of alertness' cannot be fully grasped by the 'experiencing I', because there is no process of 'self-observation' possible that might operate on a subliminal level simultaneously with the passive function of observing the events in 'inner sight'. However, the various states of awareness concomitant with the 'quiet state of alertness' can be retrieved from memory in the 'waking consciousness' only fragmentarily. In empirical reality, 'inner sight' is exclusively focussed on a single 'object arriving' in the otherwise vacated state of consciousness; this 'single object' may, however, consist of a 'composite form', in which several 'forms of arriving' (in the case described below, altogether four 'forms') are intertwined.

> Mr. E. has supplied the following testimony; it consists of several spontaneous utterances, spoken in several subsequent sessions while he was absorbed in the 'quiet state of alertness': *"Nothingness is the essence permeating primordial space. Tenebrous darkness enshrines the rough primeval block. – The flowing brook has surrendered. The black unfathomable water of the moor has reclaimed it. All the movements afloat have subsided and soaked up by the death of time. Anything in creation, and anything that has been part of becoming has been wrapped up in the cloak of reposing stone ... Whatever has been given birth, has returned and recovered – the primordial beginning is here. The circle reposing is aware of itself being a mystery ..."*
>
> *"Power is piling up. The rocks are shaking. Beginnings are opening up ... Everything alive shivering with loneliness. Every living being is rejoicing at his/her capabilities."*
>
> *"Silence is the rock in the middle. The middle reposes in itself. It is the heart of all things. The room is arched like a bowl. From it, the bright and warming light is emanating ... Reverent awe addresses the silence. A little bird is singing a song in a low voice: From the middle of the heart, the most intimate present will be born."*

These utterances have been clipped from the overall context and taken from recordings spoken during consecutive sessions for the purpose of psychological analysis. By doing so, the special atmosphere conveyed in the complete and original testimonials has obviously been lost. For this reason the scattered utterances quoted here must not be assessed critically in view of their syntactic coherence and meaning, or as regards their aesthetic value. The same proviso applies to the passages from records of mystical experiences, which will be quoted later in this study.

The 'Ecstatic Consciousness'

In psychology the term 'subject-object split' refers to the phenomenon in which the consciousness of the 'experiencing I' is confronted with objects towards which his/her feelings, sense perceptions, imagination and thinking are oriented. The degree in which this contraposition between subject and object is experienced in a given event (which can be more or less pronounced) provides the gauge for measuring the clarity of consciousness. If the boundaries between subject and object become blurred, we are concerned with a state of consciousness with a reduced degree of clarity. The 'quiet state of alertness' is a particularly lucid consciousness, in fact, it is the mental state with the highest degree of clarity. Since we have inferred our data from the 'quiet state of alertness', we have been able to demonstrate that there is a clear contraposition, or a 'split' or 'division', between the 'subject' ('experiencing I') and the 'object' perceived. The concept of the 'object arriving' has been claimed to be one of the necessary conditions for establishing the concept of 'inner sight'. When we considered the 'object arriving' that is a 'split-off item' of the unconscious, we have seen that the hyper-lucid 'quiet state of alertness' can instantly be torn to pieces when the 'experiencing I' is confronted with the overwhelming impact of the 'object arriving'. As soon as the 'partial I' had become the centre of action, the 'quiet state of alertness' disintegrated, and was substituted by the 'somnambulist consciousness'. This means that the 'quiet state of alertness' must be superseded by an alternative state of consciousness as soon as the 'subject-object split' is no longer clearly discerned – whatever the reason may be for the declining awareness of the existence of such a 'split'. The range of degrees in perceiving the 'split' between 'subject' and 'object' covers anything between a distinct, clear-cut awareness, down to zero awareness, i.e. a liminal stage in which the 'I', though still capable of experiencing, is no longer able to discern any division between subject and object. The state of consciousness, however, in which the distinction between subject and object is almost entirely suspended can no longer be classified as a 'quiet state of alertness', but must properly be termed 'ecstatic consciousness'. Psychologically speaking, the 'ecstatic consciousness' is a borderline state of consciousness situated beyond the 'quiet state of alertness': The latter ends, phenomenologically, when the subject-object split has approached the degree of near-zero; the 'ecstatic consciousness', in turn, can be said to be fully developed when the awareness of a subject-object split has been extinguished. There are, however, three aspects that have to be considered when analysing the degrees of reduced awareness in experiencing the subject-object split:

1. The 'I' of the 'quiet state of alertness', who (as we know) has become entirely detached from the active functions of the 'waking state', is the medium of 'inner sight'; as such it is still the focal point to which all experiences are related. This means that in a subject who has a clear awareness of what is being perceived, the subject-object split is retained throughout. The clear awareness in the 'experiencing I' of being the focal point of an experience as well as the medium that is juxtaposed to the 'object arriving' can gradually be lost, however, notably when the ecstatic experience reaches its climax, which may culminate, in the end, in the total loss of self-awareness. Such a liminal peak experience, however, transgresses the confines of the 'ecstatic consciousness' proper, and is classified as a trans-ecstatic state of consciousness. This means that the experience in which any awareness of 'I-hood' is dissolved occurs in a mental condition beyond the state of ecstasy, hence in a trans-ecstatic state, or rather a state of no-consciousness. For when the 'perceiving I' is no longer able to sustain even the minimal function of an observer, since any self-awareness has been lost, the mental state is one of 'no-consciousness' [in the German

text, literally 'unconsciousness', "Bewußtlosigkeit"].[138] Therefore

---

138   [Note: The German term "Bewußtlosigkeit" is, like the English equivalent "unconsciousness", a vague and ambivalent umbrella term, as it refers to collectively to any mental condition involving the loss of consciousness. But there are significant differences in the manner and the degrees in which the apparent loss of consciousness can be experienced. The loss of consciousness can be short-lived, and be caused, for instance, by a stressful situation, or by exhaustion; in that case it usually lasts for only a few minutes. The loss of consciousness can, however, also refer to a long-term pathological state, which may be caused, for instance, by an accident, by an epileptic seizure, an indeterminate state of coma, or a mental state in which the conscious awareness of the 'experiencing I' is temporarily suspended for whatever reason, though the subliminal function of the brain and the power of memory are retained, thus allowing the person to recall some features of the event that happened while he/she had "passed out". Modern neurological research employing EEG and computer tomography can display the different degrees and varieties of states of 'unconsciousness' graphically. – In the given context, Albrecht has a state of consciousness in mind in which the 'experiencing I' does not drop into a state of coma, but is rather transferred into a mental condition beyond ecstasy, in which the subject has lost any awareness of a difference between himself/herself and an object; thus the subject has no longer any concomitant awareness of being the participant in an empirical event, though this state does not – like the pathological state of coma – erode the function of memory. Thus the subject is able to remember that he/she has been transported into a state of 'no-consciousness', when returning to the 'waking consciousness'. In Hindu and Buddhist mystographical records we find numerous descriptions of this ultimate, trans-ecstatic state, labelled 'state of no-consciousness' in English translation, rather than 'state of unconsciousness'. (Cf. for instance, Mahesh, Mehta. "Ineffability Reconsidered." Ed. Coward, Harold. *'Language' in Indian Philosophy and Religion.* Calgary: Calgary UP, 1976. 63-82.) This is why the term 'state of no-consciousness' is phenomenologically more appropriate for denoting the trans-ecstatic state of consciousness. This term is also the one more consistent with what Albrecht means by the word "Bewußtlosigkeit" and this is why the term "state of no-consciousness" has been adopted in this translation as the standard term for this mental condition. – Recent and current research in assessing the varieties of trans-ecstatic states as states of no-consciousness has reached proportions that go beyond the capacity of a single scholar to trace. Only one explanatory comment from a study describing the state of no-consciousness, in which the

the 'ecstatic consciousness' can be said to be an intermediate state between the 'quiet state of alertness' and the trans-ecstatic condition termed 'state of unconsciousness' [more accurately: the 'state of no-consciousness'].

2. The second variety of experiencing the annihilation of the subject-object split is elicited when the perceiver is overpowered violently by the 'object arriving'; in such an event the sense of being overwhelmed, inundated or annihilated by the 'object arriving' is instantaneously aroused in the subject. Whereas in the first variety a growing desire to abandon oneself to the 'object arriving' is evoked, in the second variety the 'I' is no longer the (seemingly active) centre of the experience, but a passive recipient, who is overpowered by the violent intrusion of the 'object arriving'. As long as the 'ecstatic consciousness' is sustained, some residue of some consciousness of 'self' must remain, in which the 'experiencing I' has a faint awareness of being a passive observer of what is going on in consciousness.

3. In the third variety, the distinction between the 'I' and the 'object' is extinguished altogether. The total loss of self-awareness is caused by intense states of emotion, or emotional responses to the 'object arriving'. In such an event, the entire space of consciousness is filled with emotions – which are the pivotal characteristic

---

subject-object split is (temporarily) dissolved, shall be quoted here: "Our innermost consciousness is identical to the absolute and ultimate reality of the universe. At this level we identify with the Universe and our consciousness becomes space-less and timeless, and therefore, eternal and infinite. This is the state of *nirvana, samadhi, satori, and enlightenment*, the state of completely liberated consciousness and peaceful mind. There is no more distinction between subject and object, self and not self, seer and seen. There is no more sending and receiving of information – man is what there is and all there is. This is the state where a homogeneous dielectic medium, our 'Genie,' *completely dissolves*. Paradoxically, it can also enable the inflow of *all* information into *One* universal consciousness." Vitaliano, Gordana. "New Integrative Model for States of Consciousness." *NLP World* 7 (2000): 41-82. Quotation 81f.) – FW.]

of this mental condition. It is a state teeming with exuberant emotions of great intensity and diversity, such as a deep sense of bliss, 'the delight in oneness', becoming overwhelmed by agonizing sorrow, or feeling inundated by eternal peace and tranquillity. These are only a few examples of the intense emotional states aroused in this ecstatic experience. There is, however, one feature that these diverse ecstatic experiences have in common, and this is a space of consciousness permeated by persevering, homogeneous feelings, in which any awareness of a difference between the 'experiencing I' and the 'object' perceived has subsided, and ultimately dissolved, hence subject and object are experienced as an undifferentiated oneness.

It goes without saying, however, that the three aspects of ecstatic experience outlined here are merely theoretical descriptions of what in empirical reality is one coherent, uniform process of consciousness. But these descriptions enable us nonetheless to recapture the elusive mental state in phenomenological terms. Yet it is a proven empirical fact that the 'quiet state of alertness' tends to change over into the 'ecstatic consciousness' (either gradually or abruptly). But it is also true that components of ecstatic experience can also be encountered in the 'waking consciousness' as well as in the 'quiet state of alertness', and these components can be regarded as 'antecedents' of phenomena encountered in the 'ecstatic state of consciousness'. Therefore we can find several 'antecedents' of ecstatic experience in the subsequent records, which were all spoken during the 'quiet state of alertness'. It would, however, be erroneous to infer from this that the 'I' has a special inclination, or predisposition, to pass into the 'ecstatic consciousness' when immersed in the 'quiet state of alertness'. It is common knowledge that we may encounter numerous experiences in everyday life in the normal 'waking consciousness', in which the subject-object split is likewise suspended almost entirely: whether this is enthusiastic devotion, or moments in which one is oblivious of one's own self, or the entire range of zealous feelings by which one is transported into states of ecstatic rapture. Jaspers[139] has termed the

---

139 Jaspers, Karl. *Psychologie der Weltanschauungen.* [1919]. 3rd ed. Berlin:

inherent inclination of the individual to overcome the subject-object split a "mystical disposition". However, in doing so, the word "mysticism" is used to refer to a phenomenon that may also occur as a 'formal opportunity' in any empirical reality in any context, irrespective of the state of consciousness the subject is currently situated in, and irrespective of the 'content' of the experience. *Therefore, I would argue that the word 'mystical' should not be used to refer to the phenomenon of 'ecstatic disposition'. Though it is true that mystical ecstasy is a proven phenomenon, there are also ecstatic experiences outside the realm of mysticism, which can be identified as primordial phenomena of human experience.* [Italics in original.] Examining the records quoted below (which were all transmitted while the subject was absorbed in the 'quiet state of alertness') we will see that the 'object arriving' which emerged from within the 'sphere of the self' sparks off genuine ecstatic experience. This is reflected in the linguistic features of the utterances, recorded while the subject was transported into a state of ecstasy: The language becomes truncated, consisting of seemingly incoherent snippets, elliptical utterances, expressive stammering, and truncated exclamations. These truncated utterances are typical of the 'ecstatic state' of consciousness, because coherent words and syntactic and semantic structures that are intelligible to bystanders can only be spoken when the 'experiencing I' is immersed in the 'quiet state of alertness'.

The following records have been selected because they illustrate quite perceptibly varieties of a burgeoning ecstatic experience, as well as instances describing the "union" between the 'experiencing I' and the 'object arriving'. Moreover, these accounts clearly show that the incipient ecstatic experience is rooted quite clearly in the fully integrated 'quiet state of alertness', and that the phenomena 'arriving' in the vista of 'inner sight' can all be traced to the realm within the 'sphere of the self'. Thus all the experiences reported can be traced to

---

Springer, 1925. [Note: In the 'List of Works Quoted' in *PMB* ("Literatur-verzeichnis", 259) the reference is to the 2nd edition – "2. Aufl., Berlin, 1925". But this seems to be an error as the 2nd edition of Jaspers's study was published in 1922; it was the third edition that appeared in 1925. Thus either Albrecht's reference to the edition or the year of publication is incorrect. – FW.]

the realm of the 'self', hence can be identified as phenomena originating within the 'sphere of the self' and do not qualify as "mystical" in the sense "mysticism" is defined later in this study.

> Mr. E. [supplied this oral testimony of experiences encountered in subsequent sessions in the 'quiet state of alertness']: "... the 'quiet state of alertness' gives birth to happiness in a soul that has discovered the ultimate value within itself, a soul that has torn to pieces the garment it has been draped in, and beholding its sublime essence. – The feelings by which the soul is inundated originate from the realm of bliss ... In its ultimate state of being alone, the soul is gratified with the bliss of knowing this one thing: That it is aware of its own being, conscious of its primeval birth, its pristine fullness and primordial bond."
>
> "... The eye, bathed in water, is granted a glimpse of the [primal] Ground. And the soul is preparing to embark on the path of silence, the path of becoming still. Removing all garments, which tarnish it with colours, releasing the I, and relinquishing all conscious acts of thinking. – And the final thought, the ultimate knowledge, is to comprehend that some streaming, floating and undulating is taking place, that a boundary has been cast off..."
>
> "... Words cannot express what is happening when the I dives into it, when it is inundated, and smiling, dissolves, when it is transformed, and when tremors reverberate through duality, when the big circle encompasses both, when holy peace has become the colour of unearthly splendour and lightness, when primordial murmur resonates from the sacred round of perennial space, when there is neither thou, nor I, only It [italics in original for emphasis] *being the sole Reality*..."
>
> "When being is permeated entirely like a cheerful sound amidst thunder, at the time, when all doors and windows have opened, all walls been removed, all curtains dropped, all openness has turned to me and become receptive, and when overwhelmed and inundated in the big event – then the soul has drowned alive in itself..." "When the I removes its ties, the soul is set free, removed from its encasement and then it is transformed into pure vitality, and inundated and saturated by feelings ineffable..."

In these personal records, spoken spontaneously when the subject was engrossed in the 'quiet state of alertness', the four 'forms of arriving' [addressed above] can clearly be discerned. The preferred 'object' of 'inner sight' is the image of a preconceived self, hypostatized as something of great value, at which the antecedent notions of ecstasy in the subject's process of individuation are oriented.

Intuitions have a considerable share in the inward perception of the ongoing process of individuation.

The experiences documented so far as instances of spontaneous utterances elicited in the 'quiet state of alertness' reveal quite clearly that the 'object arriving' is located within the domain of the self, surfacing in the vista of 'inner sight'. Many similar examples could be provided from the records compiled – examples that would be particularly helpful for elucidating further aspects of the rather complex and elusive nature of the 'self'. I think, however, that the empirical records supplied and analysed so far should be informative enough for the purpose of illustration. They provide, after all, a reliable empirical reference frame that will enable us to identify phenomena 'arriving' from 'within the sphere of the self', and to differentiate those from the phenomena experienced as coming from beyond the confines of the individual 'self', and which can ultimately be attributed to the realm of mysticism.

Value Judgements ("Die Wertung")

Before turning from the area of the 'self' to the discussion of 'mystical consciousness', we wish to consider the concept of the 'self' from the perspective of its relation to 'values'. So far we have been able to do without concepts derived from the psychology of values. Mystical consciousness, however, cannot adequately be explored without including value judgements and other issues concerned with human values. The structure of, and adherence to, the system of values upheld by a person who engages in the process of self-realization through the practice of 'introversion' [or other mind-transforming practices] can be said to be analogous to the hierarchy of values sustained by the mystic. Individuation,[140] i.e. self-realization, can be said to correspond to the mystical processes of purification and preparation. For this reason it seems to be appropriate to begin with a concise survey of the psychology of values. In doing so, we will have the opportunity to assess from a different perspective the states of consciousness passed through by the process of 'introversion', including the 'quiet state of alertness'.

---

140   Jung, C. G. *Psychologische Typen*. Zurich: Rascher, 1925. 637.

Scholarly research in the field of the psychology of values has not yet been very comprehensive.[141] Values and the way they are conceived and experienced have for a long time been a neglected topic in psychology. Therefore it does not come as a surprise that in the early days of psychological studies values were not recognized as 'ultimate phenomena of consciousness' ("Bewußtseinsletztheiten"). In 1898 Krueger[142] could still maintain: "The notion of what is valuable is still conceived in rather general terms today, since it may on one occasion refer to what is pleasant and sensually gratifying and, on another occasion, it may refer to a desired object, or an aim to be aspired to." Krueger claimed that the process of evaluation is linked in some way to the area of desires: "Something is valuable for me only when I desire a thing relatively *constantly*, and when my aspirations are consistently directed at a particular thing in certain psychological situations, i.e. when the special features [of the object desired] are present." Fifty years later, in 1948, Rohracher[143] still claimed: "For a human individual anything is considered 'valuable' that complies with his/her drives, desires and interests." – It was Haering[144] who realized that the 'value' of something is an independent phenomenon: "Evaluating means assessing something as valuable that has previously been acknowledged as such, or which is related to a set of experiences that has been approved as valuable." – "According to Haering, the experience of an approved value is an event that occurs

---

141 Cf. Krueger, Felix. *Der Begriff des Absolut Wertvollen.* Leipzig: Teubner, 1898; Haering, Theodor. *Untersuchungen zur Psychologie der Wertung (auf Experimenteller Grundlage) mit Besonderer Berücksichtigung der Methodologischen Fragen.* Leipzig: Engelmann, 1920; Messer, August. "Zur Wertpsychologie." *Archiv für die Gesamte Psychologie* 34 (1915): 157-188; Stern, Erich. "Beiträge zur Psychologie der Wertungen." Diss. Strassburg, 1917; Gruehn, Werner. *Das Werterlebnis*, Leipzig: Hirzel, 1924.

142 Krueger, Felix. *Der Begriff des Absolut Wertvollen.* Leipzig: Teubner, 1898.

143 Rohracher, Hubert. *Einführung in die Psychologie.* 3rd ed. Vienna: Urban & Schwarzenberg, 1948. 478.

144 Haering, Theodor. *Untersuchungen zur Psychologie der Wertung (auf Experimenteller Grundlage) mit besonderer Berücksichtig-ung der Methodologischen Fragen.* Leipzig: Engelmann, 1920. 311.

within the context of a given (intended) sphere of values; if an event does not belong to the acknowledged sphere of values, it will result in a negative experience of values."[145] The experience of values is based on a subsumption: "But not every subsumption-based experience is an evaluation. A value judgement only occurs when a sphere of values exists, in which a value-judgement is subsumed. The awareness of a given sphere of values does not have to be specific – it is enough when there is some consciousness of its scope or range, as Haering has aptly put it."[146] [Haering's term is "Umfangsbewußtsein"]. "Any psychological-phenomenological analysis of values must be traced to pre-established values. – We come across evaluations everywhere, but we do not encounter newly established values everywhere."[147] We may distinguish four types of human beings as regards the manner in which they conceive of, and respond to values: 1. The type that evaluates spontaneously on the basis of responding feelings; 2. the type that arrives at his/her value judgements on the basis of both feelings and critical reflection; 3. the type whose value judgement is instantaneous and entirely intellectual; 4. the type whose evaluation is not instantaneous but based on careful rational consideration. "When classifying a type we do not only have to consider as to whether feelings and/or intellectual processes are involved, but we have to assess whether it is the emotions or the intellect that are decisive in making a value judgement. As for the first type, the crucial issue is if a given value or lack of value triggers feelings of pleasure or displeasure in the individual. The intellectual type arrives at his/her value judgement exclusively by way of intellectual reflection, without any

---

145 Stern, Erich. "Beiträge zur Psychologie der Wertungen." Diss. Strassburg, 1917. [Note: Page references to Stern's doctoral thesis not given by Albrecht. – FW.]
146 Stern, Erich. "Beiträge zur Psychologie der Wertungen." Diss. Strassburg, 1917. [Note: No page number of this passage from Stern's doctoral thesis given by Albrecht. – FW.]
147 Haering, Theodor. *Untersuchungen zur Psychologie der Wertung (auf Experimenteller Grundlage) mit besonderer Berücksicht-ung der Methodologischen Fragen*. Leipzig: Engelmann, 1920. 311.

involvement of feelings of pleasure, or displeasure."[148] Gruehn,[149] referring to Giergensohn's[150] empirical enquiries in the field of the psychology of religion, aptly pointed out that Haering's scheme of subsumption is inadequate, for it cannot reasonably explain the process of evaluating. It is true, however, that the experience of belonging to a particular sphere of values plays a crucial role in the value judgements of an individual, because a thing or item is evaluated in view of its place in a given system of values. Such an experience, however, cannot be considered to be the only decisive factor in establishing a new value, or for arriving at a re-evaluation of a thing or a person. In order to achieve the latter there must be a current, living relationship between the I and the object concerned. On the basis of detailed empirical research Gruehn claimed that the genuine source of values is rooted in two basic processes, which he termed "act of adoption" and "act of rejection". The process of 'adopting' an object as valuable occurs gradually and consecutively, and is sustained by a number of intense, I-related experiences, which have a crucial impact on the act of evaluating. When an object has been adopted as valuable by the 'experiencing I', the object will remain related to the 'I'; this becomes apparent in the memories that are analogous to the current situation, in which a value is to be assessed; the object that is to be assessed can alternatively, be related to current desires, wishes, feelings and ideas of the 'experiencing I'. Such a living I-relationship is also felt spontaneously in a series of actions, albeit in a slightly modified manner, so that a conflict may arise in the 'experiencing I' as to whether a given experience shall be 'accepted' or 'rejected'. The actual value judgement ensues as soon as the value of an object or an experience has been approved intuitively, without any critical reflection. It is an intense experience in which a value is related to the 'experiencing I'. I do not refute the claim that 'acts of acceptance'

---

148   Cf. Haering, Theodor. *Untersuchungen zur Psychologie der Wertung (auf Experimenteller Grundlage) mit besonderer Berück-sichtigung der Methodologischen Fragen.* Leipzig: Engelmann, 1920.

149   Gruehn, Werner. *Das Werterlebnis,* Leipzig: Hirzel, 1924.

150   Girgensohn, Karl. *Der Seelische Aufbau des Religiösen Lebens: Eine Religionspsychologische Untersuchung auf Experimenteller Grundlage.* Leipzig: Hirzel, 1921.

and 'acts of rejection' play a role in establishing values, and may be relevant for transforming a received system of values; but I would object that the experimental conditions in which these insights were gained might have resulted in a biased reading of the results. For it is a proven fact that we may encounter new value judgements in empirical reality which are entirely spontaneous, and which do not involve any act of reflection.

For assessing the value of the experiences encountered in the 'quiet state of alertness', we need to consider the following basic facts: *Value-related experiences are part of any human experience; they have a crucial impact on all events and processes in the life of a human being, and thus influence also the future course of a person's development.* The system of values that a person brings to the experience when immersed in the 'quiet state of alertness' is rooted in the person's given disposition(s). This means that certain 'spheres of values' are provided to which the experience of values is related. *Evaluations established in the 'quiet state of alertness' are nearly always geared to experiences of belonging, or not belonging to a particular 'sphere of values'*; this does not mean, however, *that there no spontaneous instances of evaluation, or that there are no evaluations that are generated by reflective thinking. Evaluations, it is true, often originate from the immediate knowledge of belonging, or of not belonging* [to a particular 'sphere of values']. *More frequently, however, we are concerned with instantaneous acts of evaluation which are triggered by feelings.*

The given system and order of values can hardly be overrated as regards its significance for our understanding of both the process of 'introversion' and of the phenomena surfacing in the 'quiet state of alertness'. Anyone who endeavours to discover his/her 'true self' in the 'quiet state of alertness' is clearly aware that the 'idea of the self' is a 'primordial value' ("Urwert") in his/her life, and that the encounter with this 'primeval image' ("Urbild") of the 'self' in the 'quiet state of alertness' is a most valuable, high-ranking experience. Because of this distinct awareness, the 'quiet state of alertness', and along with it, the process of 'introversion', are both attributed a very special value, to which all other mental processes are compared and evaluated. To obviate some misunderstanding, we have to modify a statement made earlier: It has been said that in the 'quiet state of alertness' all active functions of the 'I' are suspended, and that the only 'function' the 'I' is still capable of performing in the 'quiet state of alertness' is the function of passive inward perception, i.e. the function of 'inner sight'. This statement must now be qualified as the 'experiencing I' in the 'quiet state of alertness' is also able to assess values, not least because evaluations are part of any experience at any time, and this inevitably applies to any experience witnessed in 'inner sight'. Because of the emptied and hyper-lucid condition of the 'quiet state of alertness', and the extended time-span in which the 'object' 'arriving' is perceived by the 'experiencing I', the process of evaluation is elicited independently, and instantaneously, and occurs without any disruption. An external observer is likely to classify the entire sequence of events occurring in the various stages of the 'quiet state of alertness' in terms of 'perceiving', or 'seeing', and 'evaluating'. The observer will be inclined to consider these stages as conducive to advancing the process of individuation, and/or analogously, endorsing the growth of the mystical path of preparation. In other words, we are provided here with a composite mode of perception, which might be termed ***value-related 'inward perception', or 'intuitive evaluation'***. As stated above, there is no human experience that is not imbued with value judgements. But the process of 'introversion' is endowed with some implicit value, which motivated a subject to engage in the process at all. The subject knows that the process of 'introversion' may enable him/her to achieve enhanced proficiency and improved performance in any area, and thus ascribes to the process a priori some 'value'. However, the ultimate aspiration is that the subject is enabled to advance through the practice of 'introversion' to the highest-ranking values, values relating to the ultimate meaning of human existence. When this aspiration is elicited, 'introversion' has become a stage in the subject's path of individuation, viz. path of mystical preparation. Therefore we have to modify our definition of 'introversion' proposed earlier in this study. It has been stated that 'introversion' is a self-generated psychic process, albeit one that is co-determined and initially triggered by a foregoing act of the will. In empirical reality, however, both the intended aim and the impact of the pre-determination imparted on the progress of 'individuation' are accompanied throughout by spontaneous acts of evaluation as well. This means that the process of the disintegration of the 'waking consciousness' required to elicit the process of 'introversion' is, as regards evaluation, negatively connoted, whereas the integration of the 'quiet state of alertness' is fostered by positive value judgements. Experiences that occur in the 'waking state' are consequently assessed to be "not authentic" or "genuine", because in the everyday world there is "a bondage to what is not authentic", that is, a bondage to what is "not wholesome". Hence becoming detached from one's environment is seen as the "liberation from entrapments". The negative response in the incipient state of the process of 'introversion' is thus first and foremost directed against any kind of disturbance; thus anxieties, feelings of oppression, worries burdening the 'waking consciousness', and which continue to persevere and impair the smooth progress of 'introversion', are compared to "shuddering goblins, laughing and sneering"; fear and disquiet that tend to surface from the depths of consciousness are portrayed as "hostile powers, menacing forces, entanglements and stains worn on the path like a heavy burden of this world". Reflective thinking is considered as "an evil form of seeing"; "impatient, reckless desire is censored as foolishness". It is instantaneous evaluations of this kind by which the value of the environment is recognized as inferior, and, as a consequence, any activity of the 'I' is disparaged that encompasses stirrings of the will and of desire, and any response conflicting with repose and tranquillity. Unlike negative evaluations of this kind, there are a number of positive values and affirmative value judgements involved as well. A supreme value is a state of consciousness imbued with calmness. "*Calmness* is deeply rooted in the soul, and the encounter with calmness [heralds] the approach of the pristine waters springing from primordial Being. – The influx of calmness instils into the soul the reassurance that the ultimate essence of Being is about to be restored to freedom."[151]

In the personal records analysed, feelings of joy, cheerfulness and delight are described as "infants of light, helping friends on the journey of the soul". When a practitioner advances towards the clearly

---

151 [Note: The source of this quotation is not given by Albrecht. The same applies to several other quotations in this chapter. – The most likely (albeit speculative) assumption is that these lyrical and philosophical avowals of subjective experience derive from Albrecht's own recordings of spontaneous locutions spoken by him while absorbed in the 'quiet state of alertness'. – FW.]

structured 'quiet state of alertness' he/she is not merely aware of "becoming calmer and calmer", but also of "becoming increasingly sane and whole". The distinctive features of the 'quiet state of alertness' as such are likewise assessed in positive terms. "*The soul is endowed with a* clear and lucid eye, *a blissful eye of faith . . . The gaze of the soul dispels any bogus phantom. – The transparent,* stable and static *clarity is going to catch and absorb all discord and divides. – The soul is gathering its entire wholeness, storing all its properties, displaying its entire fullness and wholeness.*" Authentic descriptions of this kind recapture the ongoing and unadulterated 'flow' of experience in the 'quiet state of alertness' and mirrors the true and unbounded life of the soul; the adversary of the 'soul' is the controlling and disrupting function of the 'I'. This is why the process in which all active functions of the 'I' are dormant and removed to a latent stage is termed 'purification' and 'preparation' [in Jungian psychology]. The 'form of self-understanding' as a mode of perception in the vista of 'inner sight' permits insights into the way past and present situations of life are truly interconnected. When the first signs of this mode of self-understanding begin to surface and finally take shape in the ongoing process of 'introversion', they are intuitively known to be a pathway leading to truthfulness.

These considerations demonstrate that the 'quiet state of alertness' is ranked very highly on a person's scale of values, because it is a mental state that can open up pathways to a variety of experiences not accessible in other states of consciousness, and which remain, in particular, disclosed to the 'waking consciousness'. The 'quiet state of alertness' is thus the mental ambience in which the soul can alone "perceive the splendour of its profundity", and "find its radiant primeval value", in which (from the mystical point of view) man is vouchsafed to encounter directly "God in action". "*When the soul has become one, it is prepared to receive what is poured into it – the heart is open, and so are the intimacy and the liberated self and the state of inwardness, which has been removed from any fear and stretches out towards the primeval light.*" [Italics provided to indicate – as throughout in this translation – that the quotation is from an unnamed subject's personal testimony.]

Summary of the Findings of Part One and Part Two

Before we proceed to explore the domain of mystical experience, it is helpful to summarize the pivotal results of the foregoing empirical investigation.

1. In part one of the book the structure of the state of consciousness termed 'quiet state of alertness' has been explored phenomenologically in great detail resulting in the following definition: *The 'quiet state of alertness' is a coherently structured, hyper-lucid and homogeneous state of consciousness, whose mental space is vacated and permeated throughout by calmness.*

2. The term *'quiet state of alertness' refers to the formal framework of a very special, altered state of consciousness; as a formal concept it inevitably requires a complementary phenomenological notion, i.e. the items or phenomena constituting its 'content'.* In empirical reality, however, the hyper-lucid, vacated state of consciousness is never entirely empty, and thus never a merely formal structure alone, since there are always secondary pre-dispositions imparted in it a priori – i.e. certain dispositions or attitudes and experiences are 'encoded' in it deriving from the 'waking consciousness' – and which are released in the 'quiet state of alertness' when the process of 'introversion' has reached its goal [i.e. the full integration of the 'quiet state of alertness'].

3. *Any state of consciousness may incorporate the pure, unadulterated structure of the 'quiet state of alertness', and be subservient to a mental framework* in which 'secondary processes' are stored. *The 'quiet state of alertness' can thus be interlaced with other states of consciousness, even to the extent* that it is difficult to assess if the given features of the 'quiet state of alertness' are indeed sufficient to classify the overall structure of the mental state in terms of the 'quiet state of alertness'. *Finally, we have provided evidence for the empirical fact that the structure of the 'quiet state of alertness' can be torn apart* [in certain circumstances] *by secondary experiences.* That is to say, the structure of the 'quiet

state of alertness' can be replaced, more or less abruptly, by the intrusion of the 'somnambulist consciousness', or the 'ecstatic consciousness', or the 'waking state'.

4. It can be taken for granted that the full structure of the 'quiet state of alertness' is given, when the following distinctive features can be identified in it: hyper-lucidity, a coherent, homogeneous structure, and the basic mood of calmness permeating the entire space of consciousness. *Seen from the perspective of evaluation, it can be claimed that the 'quiet state of alertness' is the highest state of consciousness that we know.*

5. *The 'quiet state of alertness' is a necessary condition for eliciting the function of 'inner sight'. The first part of the book has delineated the formal requirements necessary for 'inner sight' to function; the second part of the book has explored the distinctive features of 'inner sight'. But the concept of 'inner sight' inevitably requires a complementary concept relating to its 'content', hence an 'object' that appears or 'arrives' in its vista and that is perceived by it.*

6. The process triggered by a 'secondary disposition' may either develop autonomously and as such its 'flow' can be beheld in 'inner sight', featuring as its 'object'; alternatively, the object perceived in 'inner sight' in the 'quiet state of alertness' can be experienced as an 'object arriving' in consciousness. *But the full function of 'inner sight' can phenomenologically be identified only when there is an 'object arriving' that appears in the vacated space of consciousness and is observed in 'inner sight' by the 'experiencing self'.*

7. The 'object arriving' is a wholeness intruding from outside the realm of the individual consciousness; it is discerned as an incoming phenomenon by the distinct responses evoked by it; it tends to become manifest progressively in the space of consciousness in successive events. *Altogether we have (so far) been able to identify eight 'forms of arriving', each distinct 'form of arriving' can*

be linked with any other, and be intertwined, resulting in a single 'composite form'.

8. *The 'object arriving' has distinctive characteristics which indicate where it is coming from.* The 'object arriving' can thus be a component that has previously been split off from consciousness and stored in the subconscious, or it can be an integral part of 'the self'. In case of the former, it has been possible to identify and classify the phenomenon 'arriving' more clearly than in case of the latter, because the notion of the item 'split off' and surfacing from the subconscious could be more clearly grasped and defined than the concept of 'the self'. Moreover, the claim that a genuine 'object arriving' originates from an extra-mental wholeness could more clearly and more persuasively be substantiated when it was compared to 'split-off' items from consciousness, as they are composed of a rather stable and solidified set of memories, and thus are distinctly perceived as concrete objects, more distinctly than an 'object' emerging that is part of 'the self' could ever be. *For this reason 'split-off' phenomena featuring as 'objects arriving' proved to be more helpful for establishing a phenomenology of 'objects arriving'; whereas the phenomena identified as 'arriving' from within the 'sphere of the self' proved to be more reliable and conclusive for gauging the boundaries between 'the self' and the realm of mysticism.*

9. *The 'quiet state of alertness' is a hyper-lucid state of consciousness, and as such it is inevitably exposed to the experience of the subject-object split. A mystical object that arrives in the 'quiet state of alertness' will always be perceived as something that is clearly juxtaposed to the 'experiencing self' and its function of 'inner sight'. This means that the typical pattern in experiencing a 'mystical object' in the 'quiet state of alertness' is that of an encounter. The subject-object split can be suspended or dissolved only when the state of consciousness has been transformed into an 'ecstatic state of consciousness'. In the 'ecstatic consciousness', however, the pattern of experiencing a 'mystical object' is that of 'union'.* The 'quiet state of alertness' can be transferred

and superseded by the 'ecstatic consciousness'. However, the 'ecstatic consciousness' is, phenomenologically speaking, beyond the domain in which 'secondary dispositions' can be elicited.

The 'quiet state of alertness' and the 'ecstatic consciousness' are the two states of consciousness in which [varieties of] *mystical experience can be encountered.* In order to be able to establish a clearly and consistently defined concept of mysticism, we have to resort to the results of our phenomenological enquiries into the nature of the 'quiet state of alertness'. *This special state of consciousness is the first pillar (out of three) on which the concept of mysticism is founded.* The stones forming this pillar have been placed one upon the other, and beside each other, so that they should have (it seems to me) sufficient stability to resist any normal natural 'strain'. *The second pillar of the edifice is the concept of the 'object arriving'* ("das Ankommende"). This pillar had to be built equally carefully, and this is why the phenomenology of the 'object arriving' has been developed and compiled as meticulously as possible. The arch connecting the two pillars is indispensable for establishing the concept of mysticism, and this connecting link will be supplied and specified in part three of this book. This third concept is crucial and inalienable for defining the concept of mysticism convincingly and unambiguously. *This concept is that of 'the All-encompassing'* ("das Umfassende"). *When the 'object arriving' in the 'quiet state of alertness' is experienced as something marked distinctly by the quality of being 'All-encompassing', we are justified to call such a mental state a 'mystical state of consciousness'.*

PART THREE

The Mystical Consciousness

The 'All-encompassing'

The analysis of the empirical nature of individual states of consciousness has yielded illuminating insights. It could be shown not only that a sick person can speak in the 'quiet state of alertness' spontaneously and without any reflexion, and utter the impressions elicited by a 'split-off' item appearing in his/her consciousness, but also that a sane person and mystic has likewise the capacity of verbalising spontaneously what he/she is experiencing [when transported into the 'quiet state of alertness' and/or the 'ecstatic state of consciousness']. In the next stage of our investigation we will include and explore in detail authentic recordings of experiences spoken by persons when absorbed in the 'quiet state of alertness'. These personal testimonies were recorded by a witness of the event. It can justly be claimed that the phenomenon of speaking in the 'quiet state of alertness' is not simply a corollary of the experience, i.e. an accidental utterance issued by a person while immersed in the 'quiet state of alertness', but an occurrence in which the act of speaking itself has a modifying impact on the nature of the ongoing experience. "By the very act in which the individual is spinning forth language from inside himself/herself, he/she is spinning himself/herself into it."[152] Several of the eight 'forms of arriving' are evidently susceptible to be modified by the impact of language: A response that is purely emotional can only be verbalized when it is tinged with some metaphoric experience. The form in which the 'object' 'arrives' in the shape of a word, or a sequence of words, is inevitably the one most easily affiliated with acts of speaking. That is to say, we have to concede that it is possible that an experience can be modified by language during the ongoing event. However, the significance or extent of such an

---

152 [Quotation from Humboldt. See annotation footnote 107. – FW.]

influence of language is often overestimated, not least because there are also 'silent' [i.e. non-verbalized] experiences which often contain sub-verbal forms of language as well.

In our attempt to elucidate the realm of mystical consciousness, we can take recourse in plenty of authentic empirical materials, i.e. recorded verbal utterances spoken by subjects while absorbed in the 'quiet state of alertness'; these records cannot be dispensed with, since they are spontaneous locutions that enable us also to get unique insights into mystical occurrences in *'statu nascendi'*. Records of mystical experience reported from memory after the 'quiet state of alertness' has ended are often prone to self-delusion and fictional transformation, because the actual event is usually modified in retrospect by subjective notions and secondary acts of reflection. Verbal utterances, however, that are spoken instantly during an ongoing mystical event, with the subject being immersed in the 'quiet state of alertness', will convey authentically and as veridically as possible the stream of experience as it happened during the event. That is to say that the stream of impressions passing through consciousness during a mystical experience becomes incarnate [as it were] in the words spoken by the 'experiencing self' while absorbed in the 'quiet state of alertness'. These verbal testimonials can thus be claimed to render truthfully and with greatest possible immediacy the subject's actual experience and state of mind. Automatic writing, by comparison, is no adequate alternative for a recorded utterance recovered from a spontaneous speech act, because it is a phenomenon more closely linked to the 'somnambulist consciousness' and/or the 'ecstatic state' rather than the 'quiet state of alertness'; in fact, 'automatic writing' has hardly ever been witnessed as occurring in the serene and 'quiet state of alertness'. But even if such an event occurred, it would be subject to the corrupting and transforming influence of language, of the kind addressed above.

In this final part of the book we will also define the concept of 'the All-encompassing'. For this purpose, testimonies spoken by subjects while immersed in the 'quiet state of alertness' will be quoted and analysed. In each case we shall begin with a subject's recorded experience, in which the 'arrival' of a phenomenon perceived as 'all-encompassing' is encountered for the very first time.

PSYCHOLOGY OF MYSTICAL CONSCIOUSNESS   311

Mrs. C. had, for many years, been harassed by experiences in which 'split-off' items from the subconscious 'arrived' as 'objects' in the vista of 'inner sight'. (Passages of her report relating this occurrence have already been quoted above.) The realm of 'split-off' items arising from the subconscious became accessible to her in a self-revelatory act of confession. In this event her mind was opened up to perceive an 'object arriving', which had an entirely new, as yet unknown, quality:

Mrs. C. "*There is something – on the threshold of approaching – – there is something approaching towards me. It is a smooth, huge movement towards me. It touches me from time to time, though only very softly, in a manner that I hardly notice it, and yet I can feel it somehow, – later, when it is gone, when it is not there anymore, I long for it, though at the same time I am afraid of it, and frightened that I will be no longer the person I am now, that I will give up something hereafter, that something will change significantly, and that I will not be asked any more, that I can no longer decide myself. – Then, when the time comes indeed that this gigantic closeness affects me deeply, it will be decided over me, and I will be faced by that and I am going to – I don't know what – then something is going to happen that I can neither express, nor know, only that I am frightened by this closeness and by its drawing nearer and nearer so that, deep inside, I rather wish to evade it and hide from it, for it is something that* (Mrs. C. becoming agitated) *I cannot fathom at all, something that cannot be known. – I don't know how, and I don't know what for. I don't know how I can stand it – if I am be able to endure it* (Mrs. C. moaning). *I don't know, if I can really cope with it, for it is something really vast – something very special, which will take hold of me fully – and cover me entirely – entirely – no – cov . . .* [sic!] *completely, overwhelm me – entirely – it is so hard to say – it is the Absolute [the Unconditional] – this is what I am do scared of – and yet what I so much desire – what I don't know – and what I do not want to know – and yet it is something that I am yearning for somehow.*

And it is approaching – it has – I don't know how – but it has been summoned (weeping). *It has been called on by me, or by a voice in me, which I have not known either, invited to come, and now it is approaching, evoking fear in me, for it is advancing [imbued with] unknown, unintelligible and unfathomable powers and forces, which I can no longer control, which I can no longer grasp, which I can no longer – which I cannot cope with, for they are more [powerful] than – me. They are closer somehow. They are also painful, because they are so much beyond my pale. They are not of the kind that might lift me up – lifting me up in great love, but they are even more [overwhelming].*

> *They are something unconditional and uncanny, and they come from – a realm to which I have no access, which I cannot penetrate on my own. – [These powers] come from the vast, unknown realm of which I only know that (no, I do not know, I only feel) that it is something – no – I cannot say what it is. But I do know that it does not belong to the realm in which I have lived till now. Nor has it actually been a realm but rather a world [cosmic domain].*
>
> *It is something that exists, independent of me, something that just is there, though I have neither asked nor pleaded for it to alight. This is something that simply is there, and that goes beyond what I wish, or desire, or do. It is something – vast. It is much bigger, and it is as if – it is so difficult to express in words, for it is as yet ineffable. Because everything that is spoken about it now, might turn out to be false, though it could just be so, as if this vast realm – I don't know if it is true when I say – is going to send – a harbinger, who is fully backed by it – who is fully supported – by this [vast] demesne. And this harbinger is approaching towards me. Yet I do not know, if it is right when I put it this way, for it might be different, though there is no doubt that something is indeed advancing, but there is as yet a big distance, a big abyss between what is about to approach and myself. There is also the fear in me – something within me is not yet ready, and still clinging to the world that I have been."*

This detailed testimony of Mrs. C., spoken while she was immersed in the 'quiet state of alertness', has been chosen (from amongst several other similar records available) to begin with, because it addresses in particularly lucid and explicit terms the pivotal characteristics of 'the All-encompassing'. Mrs. C. had, in a series of previous sessions, perceived merely 'objects' that 'arrived' from within the sphere of the 'self' and could be identified as 'split-off items' of her unconscious; in the record quoted, however, she is for the first time faced with an 'object arriving' that is experienced as 'alien' and appears to be coming from afar, beyond the 'sphere of the self', and thus has clearly the crucial characteristics of 'the All-encompassing'. The record furthermore gives evidence that the 'arrival' of an 'All-encompassing' in a person immersed in the 'quiet state of alertness' is an event that happens entirely unexpectedly.

In order to delineate some of the new qualities of the 'object arriving', we will consider the phenomenological characteristics addressed in detail. The 'object' that 'arrives' in the space of consciousness is – unlike the 'objects' described in any of the previous records – perceived as something 'entirely different', thus as an 'otherness' that is utterly foreign. The 'object' approaches quite clearly from a domain that is entirely *unknown* to the perceiver; it is thus a realm that is neither part of the 'self', nor does it derive from a realm of experience passed through previously, nor is it something located in, originating from this world. This means that the 'object arriving' described in this testimony has no 'I-quality' at all: It does not relate to any of the past and present experiences of the 'experiencing self', and thus does not contain anything previously known and stored in memory, nor does it refer to a realm that one might have at one's disposal in the future. It does not emerge from a domain of the self that has as yet remained unknown and has now become manifest symbolically, nor does the 'object' appear in a person-like manner; it is rather an 'object' *experienced as if it were something completely foreign, a total 'otherness'*. But this 'object' is not only perceived as something entirely foreign, it is also something that is *immeasurably vast and overwhelming*, something that "surpasses" the confines of not only the individual self, but the confines of "everything else". "It is something that goes beyond what I wish, or desire, or do." It exists for itself and is not dependent on anything that the 'experiencing self' has ever known – it is an 'ultimate vastness' and as such numinous and 'uncanny' – the source of powers that are perceived as threatening and uncanny. The 'object arriving' has thus clearly *the distinctive characteristics of the 'numinous'* – to borrow a term coined by Rudolf Otto.[153] The woman concerned experiences the 'object' intruding upon her in the 'quiet state of alertness' simultaneously as a *mysterium tremdendum* and a *mysterium fascinosum*. "It is the Unconditional – that of which I am terrified – that for which I am burning with desire." "I want to avoid it and hide from it, but [at the same time] I want to be able to endure it somehow."

The 'object arriving' is, thirdly, not just something unknown from any prior experience, but *is experienced as if it was something totally unknowable, something that never becomes visible entirely in consciousness, but as something that makes its gradual approach known*

---

153 Otto, Rudolf. *Das Heilige. Über das Irrationale in der Idee des Göttlichen und sein Verhältnis zum Rationalen*. 1917. 5th ed. Breslau: Trewendt & Graniers, 1921.

through 'harbingers'. An 'object' that can be identified as a 'split-off' item from an individual's consciousness (which appeared in an earlier record of Mrs. C.), becomes successively manifest here, revealing its ineffable vastness. This aside, an 'object' that 'arrives' from within the 'sphere of the self' has the tendency to remain entirely tied to the personality of the 'experiencing self'. *'The All-encompassing', by contrast, is marked by the distinctive features of its inscrutability and unknowability.*

Fourthly, the very first intimations of 'the All-encompassing' arriving in the 'quiet state of alertness' (as described here) are particularly useful for our attempt to define the concept of 'the All-encompassing', because the 'experiencing I' can communicate only a few of its sparse and general characteristics, but it cannot specify whether 'the All-encompassing' has any features of a persona, or if it is entirely a-personal.

Before we proceed with the definition of 'the All-encompassing' on the basis of the record quoted, it is necessary to call to mind once more very clearly the distinct boundaries between the disciplines of philosophy and psychology. *The new quality of the 'object arriving'*, which we have termed 'the All-encompassing', *refers to a special quality of the experience and, therefore, is, epistemologically speaking, something entirely different from the philosophical concept of 'the All-comprising'*. It could be objected that in introducing the empirical, psychological concept, a different term than 'the All-encompassing' should be used, i.e. a term that is less likely to be confused with the established philosophical concept of 'the All-comprising' as introduced and defined by Karl Jaspers. However, several of the empirical records we are going to analyse suggest that the 'object arriving' is evidently and patently experienced *as if* it was an entity perceived as 'all-encompassing', or 'overarching', 'enveloping' and 'all-enclosing'. Karl Jaspers,[154] in his later works, preferred to use the term "*das Umgreifende*" [rendered here by 'the All-embracing'][155] over that of "*das Umfassende*", i.e. 'the

---

154 Jaspers, Karl. *Allgemeine Psychopathologie. Ein Leitfaden für Studierende, Ärzte und Psychologen*. 1913. 5th ed. Berlin and Heidelberg: Springer, 1948. – Jaspers, Karl. *Vernunft und Existenz*. Bremen: Storm, 1947.

155 [Note: In the English translation of Jaspers's works, the translators have

All-encompassing' (which Jaspers occasionally uses interchangeably in his earlier writings), I considered it pertinent to adopt the latter term for the exclusive purpose of psychology.

There are, however, other reasons why the term 'All-encompassing' has been considered the best option, despite its affinity to, and irrespective of the potential danger of being mixed up with the philosophical concept of 'the All-embracing': Psychologically speaking, there is no experience that is not tinged by 'philosophical' reflections, in the widest sense. Being human inevitably means being bestowed with what has been termed 'basic knowledge' ["Grundwissen"]. "Basic knowledge is the universal *a priori* of consciousness, as given, in particular, in the categories of reason, and the *a priori* of the spirit [revealed] in ideas . . . Basic knowledge is furthermore reflected in prevailing value judgements and attitudes."[156] This means that every empirical subject matter is comprehended, assessed and interpreted instantaneously within the context of a person's 'basic knowledge'.

---

rendered the German term "das Umgreifende" as "the Encompassing", and this term has become standard usage in philosophical studies on Jaspers in academe in English-speaking countries. Cf. Schilpp, Paul Arthur. *The Philosophy of Karl Jaspers*. New York: Tudor, 1957. 144. – The English word, however, does not exactly recapture semantically the meanings connoted by the German verb "umgreifen": "umgreifen" derives etymologically from "greifen", i.e. "to gripe", "grip", "clasp", "clutch", and thus it is more closely related semantically to the English verb 'to embrace' than to the verb 'to encompass'; therefore the appropriate English translation of Jaspers's term would have been 'the Embracing' (alternatively 'All-embracing'), and this is why 'all-embracing' is the term used in this study in the translations of Albrecht's quotations from Jaspers's German works. – Albrecht's term "das Umfassende", by contrast, has none of the anthropomorphous connotations of Jaspers's term; this is why "the encompassing" has been opted for as the English term that is most closely equivalent to Albrecht's concept of "das Umfassende". However, in order to avoid confusion with the term 'the encompassing', as used in the standard English translation of Jaspers's works, and hence in current anglophone philosophical discourse, Albrecht's concept has eventually been translated as "the All-encompassing". – FW.]

156 Jaspers, Karl. *Allgemeine Psychopathologie. Ein Leitfaden für Studierende, Ärzte und Psychologen*. 1913. 5th ed. Berlin and Heidelberg: Springer, 1948. 275.

A subject who experiences, when engrossed in the 'quiet state of alertness', an 'object arriving' that is 'all-encompassing' is able to discern this very special quality on the basis of the 'basic knowledge' about the being instilled in him/her. He/she can only grasp 'the All-encompassing' if he/she conceives of it on the basis of his conception of "absolute unity". He/she will finally "assess" the relationship between this "absolute unity" and the multiplicity of the 'items' contained in consciousness, on the basis of such categories as "becoming or progress, substantiality and determination".[157] For this reason a subject that is absorbed in the 'quiet state of alertness' will resort to expressions such as "Ur-being", "Ur-union", "the Ultimate", the "Ur-ground", i.e. relating to the origin and essence of Being, or the Creator. These metaphoric expressions are, however, not the result of rational reflection in the 'waking consciousness', but originate from the 'basic knowledge' which is inherent – though only on a peripheral scale – in any human experience, and is always readily available.

But we do not wish to separate the discipline of psychology radically from that of systematic philosophy, since they tend to overlap in the area of mysticism. However, we have to emphasize that our psychological considerations are exclusively based on empirical research, i.e. from what has actually been experienced and spontaneously recorded by subjects when transported into the 'quiet state of alertness'. This means that, strictly speaking, an 'object arriving' is subjectively experienced *as if* the 'object' is marked by characteristics that are most adequately described by the term 'all-encompassing'. The question, however, as to whether the 'object arriving' that is subjectively experienced as 'all-encompassing' is indeed 'all-encompassing' in ontological terms is a philosophical question which inevitably transcends the boundaries of science, and thus the intentions of this book. The aim of this study is only to provide, on the basis of empirical data, a psychological [and not an ontological or a theological] assessment and classification of mystical phenomena that become apparent in certain states of consciousness.

---

157 Hartmann, Nicolai. *Philosophie der Natur: Abriss der Speziellen Kategorienlehre.* Berlin: de Gruyter, 1950. 251f.

The philosophical concept of "das Umgreifende" ['the All-embracing'] is not an empirical concept, but a liminal cognitive term. "As we can only recognize appearances, and not 'being' as it is, we encounter and acknowledge these limitations by concepts of liminality." – Such liminal concepts are, for instance, nature, the world, transcendence, 'being', consciousness *per se*, spirit, reason or existence. Thus 'the All-embracing' is a "multifarious concept". "Liminal concepts of this kind do not refer to an object, but to something by which I am embraced and sustained, and which includes all objects. – As 'the All-embracing' tends to reveal itself continuously and ever more fully and multifariously as [human] knowledge continues to grow, it paradoxically becomes more elusive, withdrawing itself in the process, remaining entirely immaterial. – Though the ways in which 'the All-embracing' operates are unfathomable, they can nonetheless be expounded and elucidated.[158] 'The All-embracing' is encountered in two diametrically opposed ways: It is both present to us and evanescent – either as 'being' itself, which is everything in which, and through which, we are; or as 'the All-embracing' by which we become our [true] self ... In both these instances 'the All-embracing' is identical with the wholeness that is the ultimate and self-sustaining ground of 'being', whether this is 'being' for us, i.e. what we call 'being in this world', consciousness *per se*, spirit, reason and existence.[159] – Turning 'the All-embracing' into an object, and considering it as something intelligible, is a paradoxical reversal of our way of thinking. Thinking is capable of affecting us emotionally and of enabling us to recall things rather than of turning thinking itself into an object of cognition.[160] – The original notion of 'the All-embracing' is inevitably forfeited, if it is conceived in abstract terms, or regarded as an isolated, established and fixed concept. That is to say, when 'the

---

158 Cf. Jaspers, Karl. *Allgemeine Psychopathologie. Ein Leitfaden für Studierende, Ärzte und Psychologen*. 1913. 5th ed. Berlin and Heidelberg: Springer, 1948. 632.

159 Cf. Jaspers, Karl. *Vernunft und Existenz: Five Lectures*. Bremen: Storm, 1947. 2nd lecture.

160 Jaspers, Karl. *Allgemeine Psychopathologie. Ein Leitfaden für Studierende, Ärzte und Psychologen*. 1913. 5th ed. Berlin and Heidelberg: Springer, 1948. 632.

All-embracing' is objectified, the notion no longer signifies what 'the All-embracing' truly is."[161]

These are selected statements by Jaspers which show quite clearly that "das Umgreifende" ('the All-embracing') is a liminal concept of cognition. *The psychological concept of 'the All-encompassing'*, by contrast, is an empirical concept, derived from empirical data, i.e. authentic experiences recorded instantaneously by individual subjects. Etymologically, the verb 'to encompass' signifies metaphorically that something is 'enfolded', 'enclosed', 'comprised' and 'embraced'. Though the verb 'to encompass' connotes, like the verb 'to embrace', some active quality, in this connotation it is less explicit in the latter verb. The word 'to encompass' evokes, unlike 'embrace', the sense of 'upholding something permanently', or of 'sustaining something'. Its meaning might be compared, for instance, to the 'setting' of a piece of jewellery, which 'encompasses' the gemstone: The gemstone is enfolded, enclosed, encompassed and sustained by the golden or metallic setting. The prefix 'en-' emphasizes the notion that something is securely and safely 'enfolded' and 'encompassed' by something 'surrounding' and 'encompassing' it. Thus the word 'to encompass' is an apt metaphor for conveying the notion that a special realm of human existence is enfolded, surrounded and upheld by another realm of 'being'. The semantic range of the verb 'to encompass' is broad enough to comply with the considerable diversity of active and passive experiential features adhering to any encounter with 'the All-encompassing'.

We have decided to use the term 'the All-encompassing', as it is a fitting innovative term that hints in particular at the new experiential quality of the 'object arriving'. In the record of Mrs. C. quoted above, we can discern quite explicitly two of the seminal characteristics of an encounter with 'the All-encompassing' in the 'quiet state of alertness': 1) the hallmark of a given sense of direction, i.e. the 'experiencing self' has a clear awareness that the 'All-encompassing' approaches and/or arrives from an unknown, 'foreign' domain [from beyond the individual consciousness], and 2) the hallmark that 'the All-encompassing' is something supreme and ultimate; hence 'the All-encompassing' is experienced

---

161 Jaspers, Karl. *Vernunft und Existenz: Five Lectures.* Bremen: Storm, 1947. 2nd lecture.

as the absolute ground to which human consciousness, and anything contained in it, is inexorably related in some way or other.

The awareness of the direction from which 'the All-encompassing' appears to be 'arriving' is a unique distinctive feature, and thus a necessary condition for defining the concept of 'the All-encompassing'. This single distinctive feature is, however, not enough for 'the All-encompassing' to be verified as such, because the awareness of something coming from a 'foreign' sphere is an integral part of other experiences as well. Any object experienced by sense perception is known to be located in a real, objective space outside the observer's 'sphere of the self', and to be the external source of sensual stimuli. Telepathic events (when recognized by the subject to be such) have likewise the experiential quality of coming from outside the individual self; in a telepathic experience the so-called "source points"[162] are clearly located "somewhere else", i.e. beyond the individual consciousness. For this reason, an additional criterion is required if we wish to establish that an 'object arriving' is indeed 'all-encompassing' in essence. This additional criterion is the awareness elicited in the 'experiencing I' that the 'object arriving' originates in a "primeval" realm of existence, i.e. a primordial domain in which the "source points" of all experiences of man are supposed to be found.

We may thus offer the following proposition: **An 'object' perceived as 'arriving' [in the vista of 'inner sight'] is termed 'all-encompassing', when it is experienced by a person absorbed in the 'quiet state of alertness', as if it was something 'arriving' from a foreign sphere, and as if it was an ultimate and unknown entity at whose total oneness all past, present and future experiences are linked in some inexplicable manner.**

In view of the progress of our [phenomenological] enquiry into the nature of 'the All-encompassing', it is indispensable to distinguish between 'the All-encompassing' 'as-it-is-itself', i.e. [ontologically] conceived as an unfathomable essence, and the tangible manifestation of 'the All-encompassing' in a subject's consciousness. This means that 'the All-encompassing' *per se* is not a finite 'object'

---

162 Walther, Gerda. *Zur Phänomenologie der Mystik*. Halle a. S.: Niemeyer, 1923. [No page reference given in *PMB* – FW.]

appearing in 'inner sight', but the actual 'object' is the dynamic process of 'the All-encompassing' perceived as 'arriving' in the 'quiet state of alertness'. That is to say that the 'experiencing I' does observes some 'object arriving' in the vista of 'inner sight', which has a distinct 'countenance' or 'appearance'. When referring to the distinctive qualities of 'the All-encompassing' and the modes of its 'arrival' in consciousness, we do not refer to the inscrutable 'object' of 'the All-encompassing' *per se* [i.e. what it truly is in ontological terms], but to the various 'forms' in which 'the All-encompassing' may reveal itself, and in the 'shape' of which it is experienced by a subject. As a person perceiving the 'arrival' of 'the All-encompassing' while immersed in the 'quiet state of alertness' is (more or less) aware that something of the true essence of 'the All-encompassing' remains concealed and is unfathomable, the experience is thus actually an encounter with an effigy, or a cypher, a symbol, a proxy, a harbinger, a gift or a token of 'the All-encompassing'.

This means that 'the All-encompassing' is as such ultimately incomprehensible and inscrutable, even when it becomes manifest in distinct 'forms of arrival', and is intuitively grasped by the 'experiencing self' as something infinite, supreme and 'all-encompassing'. It is the special feature of being ultimately inscrutable and incomprehensible that distinguishes the true encounter with 'the All-encompassing' from an encounter with any other 'object arriving', in particular an item 'split off' from the subconscious and surfacing in the vista of 'inner sight', and any phenomenon emerging from within the 'sphere of the individual self'. As long as the 'quiet state of alertness' is the given mental environment in which in-coming phenomena are perceived, and as long as the subject-object split is sustained when the 'object arriving' is perceived, 'the All-encompassing' is inevitably discerned as something elusive and incomprehensible. However, when the experience becomes so overwhelming that the 'quiet state of alertness' is replaced by the 'ecstatic state of consciousness', in which the dividing line between the perceiver and the 'object perceived' becomes indistinct and is ultimately dissolved, the 'experiencing self' may get some fleeting glimpse of 'the All-encompassing'; in the ultimate 'ecstatic state of consciousness' the awareness of the total incomprehensibility of 'the All-encompassing' appears to be eroded.

At this point we have to introduce another novel concept: *The psychological concept of 'revelation'*. The conventional definition of 'revelation' is that it refers to the self-manifestation of an existing entity. In theology, the concept is confined to the self-revelation of God. In this psychological study, however, the term is understood strictly in psychological terms and thus hinges on two classifying criteria: First, the psychological concept of 'revelation' is strictly limited to phenomena occurring in the 'quiet state of alertness', and, secondly, the concept only applies when the 'object arriving' is experienced as 'all-encompassing'. The psychological definition of 'revelation' is thus restricted to the 'cognitive experience of the 'All-encompassing' in the 'quiet state of alertness'.

We have stated earlier that the 'forms of inner sight' correspond to the 'forms of arriving'. Some of the 'forms' identified so far have provided us with some insight into the essence of 'the All-encompassing', notably the awareness of its approach and 'arrival' in consciousness. Whereas 'split-off' items surfacing from the sub- or unconscious, as well as items emerging from the 'sphere of the self', are usually experienced as 'arriving' like in a 'newsreel', i.e. in the 'form' of a series of reel-like pictures, or else, in the form of symbols and in the form of self-understanding, 'the All-encompassing' reveals itself predominantly in some metaphorical form, as well as in the form of a word emerging in consciousness, and in the form of an intuition. The manifestation of 'the All-encompassing' in these particular 'forms of arriving' cannot be understood in any other way than as an act of self-revelation. This claim can be substantiated by the fact that when an 'object' 'arrives' that can be traced to be a 'split-off' item of the subconscious, there is no sense of 'revelation' elicited at all. The same applies to an item emerging from the individual self and becomes manifest in 'inner sight' in the 'form of a symbol'. The symbol is not inscrutable and open to interpretation, but does not yield any sense of revelation. Thus the [psychological] concept of 'revelation' is inextricably linked with the encounter with 'the All-encompassing'. This implies that 'the All-encompassing' is inalienably experienced as an 'it', as something that remains ultimately concealed and exists-for-itself; it is experienced as something 'foreign', and thus as a 'total Otherness' dwelling beyond the 'sphere of the individual self'.

Any 'split-off' item becomes gradually intelligible to understanding, whereas 'the All-encompassing' reveals itself by 'modes of arriving' [in 'inner sight' in 'the quiet state of alertness' and/or 'ecstatic states of consciousness'].

In the following section the several specific qualities of 'the All-encompassing' will be explored and illustrated on the basis of the testimonies spoken by several subjects when they were immersed in the 'quiet state of alertness'. The relevance of these personal records in view of providing an authentic description of an encounter with 'the All-encompassing' must, however, be critically tested against the following criteria, which are couched in terms of key-questions which must all be answered accordingly, if the experience is to be assessed as a genuine encounter with 'the All-encompassing':

1) Is the given state of consciousness truly the clear and unadulterated 'quiet state of alertness'?
2) Can the phenomenon of 'arriving' be unmistakably identified, and what are the given 'forms of arriving'?
3) Is the 'object arriving' marked by all the essential characteristics of 'the All-encompassing', or is it possible to trace these features to the subject's 'sphere of the self'? Does the 'object arriving' impart a 'sense of revelation'?
4) How is the 'experiencing self' affected emotionally by the 'object arriving'? Is the 'All-encompassing' experienced as something numinous?
5) Is the 'All-encompassing' experienced as something that is entirely a-personal, or else as 'a harbinger' of the Personal, or is it experienced as a Persona?
6) Is there some concomitant awareness that the 'All-encompassing' is ultimately unfathomable and unknowable?
7) What are the incipient forms of ecstatic experience aroused in the 'quiet state of alertness' when 'the All-encompassing' becomes manifest?

These questions call for some explanatory comment: **The 'all-encompassing Oneness' may reveal itself as an entity that is entirely a-personal, or as a Being that intrudes, and is experienced like a person**

acting [within and/or upon the 'experiencing self']. All the other potential forms in which 'the All-encompassing' may reveal itself are located between the two poles of 'personal vs. a-personal'. Experiences like, for instance, 'all-encompassing Calmness', or 'all-encompassing Nothingness', and/or 'the Void' are (almost) entirely a-personal. At the opposite pole, we may discern vestiges of a[n invisible] Persona shrouded in 'the All-encompassing', or an experience that foreshadows what has been termed 'the presence of Him'. In between the two poles we may distinguish other distinct qualities, which have variously been described [in the records quoted] by such terms as "the Ur", "all-comprising Life", "Ur-Heart", "Ur-Love", "Ur-Light", or "Ur-Beauty". These are terms referring to qualities of the essence of 'the All-encompassing' identifying it as the 'ground of Being'; in other testimonies specific person-like qualities of the Oneness are described, which suggest the self-revelation of the 'All-encompassing' in the 'form' of the [invisible] presence of a Persona that remains ultimately unknowable.

The numinous quality of the 'All-encompassing' when experienced in the 'quiet state of alertness' can be more or less overt and intense in a given event, depending on the subject's individual response. Encounters with "Nothingness" and "the Ur", for instance, tend to arouse profuse feelings of the *tremendum*, whereas feelings of the *fascinosum* are evoked when 'the All-encompassing' becomes manifest, for instance, as "[all-encompassing] Love", or "Light". The qualities of the *fascinosum* are thus obviously more intense and more pronounced in the person-related event of experiencing "all-encompassing Love" than in the entirely a-personal experience of "Nothingness".

It is true, however, that several of the entities addressed (like Love, Calmness, Nothingness) can emerge in the context of our normal emotional states, and thus do not depend on an encounter with 'the All-encompassing'. Therefore a careful process of critical discernment is indispensable; every single experience of calmness, silence, emptiness, vitality or love (to name only a few) must be subjected to careful scrutiny before we can decide whether a given numinous experience is the outcome of a normal event in everyday life, or whether the numinous feelings are indeed a genuine, spontaneous response to the 'arrival' of 'the All-encompassing' in consciousness. The latter can only be confirmed if the 'object arriving' is experienced as something unknown, alien, unfathomable, coming from afar, and as a primeval, all-encompassing, infinite Being.

'All-encompassing Calmness'

We are going to examine several qualities adhering to 'the All-encompassing' when experienced in the 'quiet state of alertness'. The varieties in experiencing 'the All-encompassing' include, for instance, a deep sense of calmness, bliss, emptiness, nothingness, the encounter with the "Ur", or "Ur-love", and the awareness of the presence of an 'all-encompassing Persona' [controversially termed "He" ("Er") by Albrecht].[163] The first part of this chapter provides

---

163 [Albrecht's choice of the male personal pronoun ("He", "Him") for referring to the personal quality in experiencing 'the All-encompassing' in the 'form' of the non-visual presence of an 'all-encompassing Persona', is obviously controversial and provokes criticism: First, because "Er" is no psychological concept, but one clearly imbued with religious meaning in this context. It is surprising that Albrecht should have opted for this word, not least because this choice conflicts not only with the principle of scientific objectivity, but also with Albrecht's practice of sticking strictly to scientific terminology throughout, by drawing a clear line between the science of psychology and the disciplines of theology. However, by deciding for the use of "Er", spelt with a capital letter, as a metaphor for the personal variety of experiencing 'the All-encompassing', Albrecht exposes himself to the charge of having projected his own belief in the personal God of Christianity on to the notion of 'the All-encompassing' experienced as a non-visual Persona. Over and beyond this, the use of "Er" corroborates the traditional notion of the masculinity of God, which has meanwhile – since the time this book was first published – become a highly contentious issue in current theological debate. Albrecht could have chosen a much less contentious term, for instance, like Martin Buber, the archaic personal pronoun "Thou", to refer to the direct encounter with God perceived as a Persona, or he might have paraphrased the person-related variety of mystical experience by using a paraphrase like 'the All-encompassing experienced as a Persona'. – We can only speculate why Albrecht, a most conscientious and meticulous scientist, opted nonetheless for the divisive and religiously charged "Er". A potential answer to this conundrum is that

a phenomenological analysis of the experience of '[all-encompassing] Calmness', the experience of Emptiness and/or Nothingness. The enquiry into the nature of the experience of 'all-encompassing Calmness' in this section of the book will show that we have to deal with a borderline case in experiencing 'the All-encompassing'. At this juncture I would like to call to mind the considerations on the growth of inner calmness during the process of 'introversion' addressed in part one of this book, as well as the pivotal characteristics of the 'quiet state of alertness' outlined above, and the considerations relating to the ultimate state to which the 'quiet state of alertness' may be advanced. Dealing with 'Calmness' as an entity perceived as 'all-encompassing', we need to remember that inner calmness develops in consciousness already during the process of *'introversion'*, and has a positive impact on the progress of 'introversion'. We also need to remember that inner calmness is an integral and pivotal part of the *'quiet state of alertness'*, and it is so in a twofold manner: Calmness is both a part of the 'content' of consciousness and an element of the formal structure of the 'quiet state of alertness'. This means that there are two approaches for exploring the complex phenomenon of inner calmness. These approaches rely on two important

---

the use of "Er", in lieu of a neutral concept like "Thou", is most likely grounded in his own mystical experiences: There are several statements in his letters and other documents (some of them published in *Das Mystische Wort*, 1974), as well as in the insights he gained when writing his second book, *Das Mystische Erkennen* (1958), notably in the chapters on the "Blick Gottes" ("The Glance of God", 188ff.) and on "die personale Struktur des Umfassenden" ("the personal structure of the 'All-encompassing, 236ff.), which suggest that he was "burdened with responsibility" and summoned by "Him" to write truthfully about his deeply intimate mystical encounters with "Him". It appears that he felt morally and religiously obliged, both as a mystic and as a scientist, to render faithfully what had been revealed to him. Having been bestowed with the "mystical glance of Him", it would indeed have been an act of betrayal not to address the "mystical presence of God" in the way "He" has revealed "Himself" to Albrecht. Violating the divine summons imposed on Albrecht in an act of special grace would indeed have been a profanation of a sacred mystery. And this might explain why he adopted the idiom of the Christian mystic in using "He/Him", rather than the neutral stance and jargon of the scientist. – FW.]

empirical conditions: 1. In the final stage of the process of 'introversion', the structure of the consciousness of 'introversion' and that of the 'quiet state of alertness' are intertwined. This merging of the two varieties of calmness can explain why during the ongoing progress of 'introversion' calmness is both the intended goal of 'introversion' and the pivotal feature of the formal structure of consciousness. 2. "The consciousness encompassing the 'quiet state of alertness' can – in a phenomenological borderline case – become itself the content [i.e. 'object'] of perception." This is a rare, exceptional experience, in which the 'quiet state of alertness' itself is turned into the 'object' observed in 'inner sight'; this results in a rare liminal experience, in which the calmness within expands and assumes an all-encompassing quality, and is ultimately perceived as a supreme essence.

The first item addressed above requires some further explication: At the beginning, the pre-determined goal of the *process of 'introversion'* is to attain a serene state of inner calm. As 'introversion' progresses, however, the calmness within acquires the quality of 'arriving' and expanding in consciousness: "Calmness is growing within the 'I'. It arises from the sphere of the body, and inundates all areas and recesses of consciousness, overwhelming, and finally displacing anything that might interfere with the growth of calmness. Calmness thus allays and harmonizes the emotional state and pulls the 'I' (as it were) into the process of 'introversion', keeping it stable when a disturbing or repulsive object emerges." – "During the process of 'introversion' the object-like character of calmness is gradually transformed and assumes a state-like quality. Towards the end of 'introversion', calmness has completely inundated consciousness and become its only 'content'; at the end of 'introversion', the mental state has become uniform, homogeneous, emptied and calm. Calmness is thus a pivotal hallmark of the 'quiet state of alertness'."

Initially, the focus of the 'experiencing I' is on the process of 'introversion': Achieving inner calmness is the goal of the pre-meditated exercise; inner calmness continues to grow as the framework of the 'quiet state of alertness' is developing. On the first stage of 'introversion', calmness emerges featuring as an 'object' that 'arrives' in consciousness: The perception of calmness 'arriving' and spreading gradually all over consciousness is a concrete experience; calmness is felt to be arising from a domain beyond the individual consciousness; at close analysis, however, in this initial stage calmness is merely the result of a physiological process originating from the sphere of the body; it is, in other words, the somatic awareness of tranquillity growing within. But the calmness that arises during the process of 'introversion' differs significantly from the somatic awareness of calmness emerging. The latter has none of the essential characteristics of the calmness that 'arrives' and is perceived as an 'object' of 'inner sight'. The phenomenon of 'arriving' is inevitably linked to the 'quiet state of alertness', and thus the calmness 'arriving' in this state is intuitively grasped to be an unknown, extra-mental wholeness, becoming manifest in the process of 'arriving'. This means that the calmness that merely emerges from the body does not qualify as an 'object arriving'. This may explain why we cannot identify different 'forms' of calmness 'arriving' in the incipient stage of 'introversion'. Moreover, this may also account for the fact that the quality of 'arriving' and the object-like nature of the calmness can no more be discerned after some time during the process of 'introversion'. Therefore we may claim, by way of summary, that the calmness that is perceived as emerging from the somatic sphere during the process of 'introversion' has none of the pivotal characteristics of the calmness experienced as 'arriving' and 'all-encompassing' in the 'quiet state of alertness'.

Concerning the second point addressed above, calmness is, basically, the enduring and underlying emotional condition of the *'quiet state of alertness'*; it is thus a vital component of the 'quiet state of alertness'. It may happen, however, that the 'quiet state of alertness' is transformed into a self-contained mental condition, i.e. an autonomous mental state, which becomes itself "the only object of perception" [in 'inner sight']. The empty state of calmness permeating consciousness thus becomes the object of 'inner sight', which means that calmness is no longer merely the underlying foundation of experience, but perceived as an unfathomable primordial essence, or primeval ground of Being, and as a wholeness to which all things are related. This vast and immeasurable calmness within is intuitively grasped to be the subject's "highest Good", to which all his/her aspirations and experiences are related and directed. The 'quiet state of alertness' is, phenomenologically speaking, a concept that refers merely to a formal mental structure. In empirical reality, however, the emptied space of consciousness in the 'quiet state of alertness' is not really entirely empty, but filled with singular items of content, such as the pre-determined disposition to achieve inner peace by advancing to the 'quiet state of alertness'. The 'quiet state of alertness' may, in turn, be regarded as a desired mental state, which has as yet remained beyond the reach of an individual. But when a person has achieved this goal and abides in the 'quiet state of alertness' and the emptiness facing him/her for a long time, the calmness and emptiness of the 'quiet state of alertness' may themselves assume the characteristics of the 'All-encompassing'. That is to say that when the 'quiet state of alertness' becomes the object of 'inner sight', it may be experienced as an all-encompassing Oneness; the distinctive features of this experience are absolute emptiness, absolute tranquillity and total loss of any sense of time. The 'experiencing self' is, however, no longer capable at this liminal stage of distinguishing between these qualities of the 'All-encompassing', and this is why the same experience is often variously described in retrospect as an experience of 'all-encompassing Calmness', or an experience of complete 'Emptiness', or of 'the Void', or 'Eternity', or 'Nothingness'. We may therefore infer the following important insight from this phenomenological analysis: *When the 'quiet state of alertness' becomes an autonomous, self-contained mental state, we have to acknowledge that the calmness germane to the 'quiet state of alertness' and perceived as the sole 'content' of 'inner sight' has the seminal characteristics of the 'All-encompassing'.*

What remains to be explained is the question as to whether the 'all-encompassing Calmness' experienced in the 'quiet state of alertness' is marked by the characteristic of 'arriving' as well. On this issue we may clearly state: *Calmness is an all-encompassing ultimate state of consciousness, and though calmness can be observed in 'inner sight', it is entirely motionless – it thus neither intrudes, nor 'arrives'* [in the vista of 'inner sight']. As an object of 'inner sight' it is continually present in the 'quiet state of alertness'. Calmness is an ultimate entity towards which a person immersed in the 'quiet state of alertness' advances. Thus the progress towards the ultimate state of calmness does not depend on the experience of calmness 'arriving', but this goal is achieved when the few active functions remaining in the 'experiencing I' have become dormant or extinguished. The experience of 'all-encompassing Calmness' is generally intertwined with the awareness of timelessness, emptiness and absolute nothingness; this evidently indicates that the experience of 'all-encompassing Calmness' is entirely a-personal. In Buddhism such an experience is exclusively understood as an a-personal experience, and conceived theologically, is termed *nirvana*. In a Christian mystic, however, the experience of the 'I' dissolving in the empty, lucid and timeless and infinite Calmness is rather rare; but if it occurs it is esteemed by the Christian mystics as a state of *sancta indifferentia*, in which the will of the contemplative has become entirely assimilated to the Will of God.[164] Yet the experience of 'all-encompassing Calmness' has also been described by Western mystics in terms of "a soundless desert in which nobody is at home",[165] or as "the vast expanse that has neither image, form nor quiddity",[166] and which is, at the same time, the desert of the Godhead.

We have pointed out that the experience of 'all-encompassing Calmness' differs significantly from other experiences of 'the All-encompassing' in that it is a unique liminal occurrence: When experiencing it, not only the phenomenon of 'arriving' is missing, but also the awareness that it is ultimately unknowable or inscrutable – which awareness accompanies all the other experiences of an 'All-encompassing'. A subject who experiences 'all-encompassing Calmness' does not encounter something that is unfamiliar, since calmness

---

164   As represented, for instance, by the Quietists, and by Madame Guyon in particular. Cf. Heiler, Friedrich. *Die Buddhistische Versenkung*. Munich: Reinhardt, 1922. 53ff.

165   Eckhart, Meister. *Schriften und Predigten*. Ed. H. Büttner. 2 vols. Jens: Diederichs, 1921. [Albrecht does not indicate the exact source of this quotation from Eckhart. – The quotation as given by Albrecht is an abridged version of a passage from Eckhart's *Sermon 48*. – FW.]

166   Tauler, Johannes. *Predigten*. Transl. and Introd. Leopold Naumann. Leipzig: Insel, 1923. [Note: The phrase is from Tauler's *Sermon LXXI* on the Feast of the Nativity of St. John the Baptist (*"Hic venit in testimonium, ut testimonium perhiberet de lumine."* John I.v.7) – Albrecht does not give the exact data of the source. – FW.]

is a well-known, comforting feeling and an integral part of the process of 'introversion' and the 'quiet state of alertness'. The feeling of calmness emanating from the body is not only a 'soothing' corollary of the process of 'introversion', but is, now and again, also an integral part of the normal 'waking consciousness'. Hence calmness as such is not something alien or inscrutable, nor a feeling experienced as 'arriving' in the 'quiet state of alertness', or intruding from beyond the realm of the individual consciousness. However, irrespective of the given phenomenological characteristics, which would seem to be incompatible with our conception of 'the All-encompassing', we still uphold the claim that this special variety of Calmness does qualify as an experience of 'the All-encompassing'. From the data available, we may state by way of summary, that the experience of 'all-encompassing Calmness' is a rare, liminal occurrence, in fact, it is, phenomenologically, a borderline-case, as the calmness within is experienced as being 'all-encompassing', though it does not have – like any other experience of an 'All-encompassing' – the characteristics of being 'foreign', 'unknowable', nor does it 'arrive', or elicit a sense of 'revelation'.

The exceptional phenomenological structure of the experience of 'all-encompassing Calmness' explains why the subject's emotional response differs so strikingly from any of the responses evoked by encounters with other varieties of 'the All-encompassing'. From this we may infer that, when experiencing 'all-encompassing Calmness', the range of potential emotional responses triggered by the 'numinous' nature of the 'All-encompassing' (as conceived by Otto) is drastically reduced or seem to elude the 'experiencing self'. The reason for the sparsity of responding feelings in this context is the fact that the experience of 'all-encompassing Calmness' can only arise and abide in a mind that has been radically vacated from any emotional arousal; in other words, all feelings and emotional states have to be removed or stilled in consciousness before calmness can fully inundate consciousness and thus be perceived as 'all-encompassing'. To the Buddhist, the experience of *nirvana* is the ultimate goal, the "*summum bonum*" [of his mystical path]; to achieve this goal, it does not suffice to achieve merely the 'quiet state of alertness' [through long-term spiritual exercise], but the Buddhist's mystical path affects his entire life and existence. Thus it may happen that at the beginning of the path of purification, the initial intimations in perceiving 'all-encompassing Calmness' may elicit some fleeting numinous feelings, but the Calmness perceived as 'all-encompassing' never arouses feelings of a *mysterium tremendum,* and only very rarely (if at all) fleeting feelings of a *mysterium fascinosum.* When a Buddhist becomes absorbed in the 'quiet state of alertness', there is no emotional response at all to the 'all-encompassing Calmness' in which he becomes immersed. To the Buddhist, the serene experience of 'all-encompassing Calmness' is the ultimate goal of his spiritual path; it is an experience that culminates in the state of *nirvana,* which is, phenomenologically speaking, a state of 'no-consciousness'. This ultimate experience tends to coalesce with the awareness of [unfathomable] silence, emptiness and nothingness.

It is true, however, that the encounter with 'all-encompassing Calmness' can evoke an 'ecstatic response', which demonstrates again that this is a unique and exceptional experience. Phenomenologically speaking, ecstasy is, when fully developed, a state of consciousness inundated by diverse feelings of ultimate intensity. The state of ecstasy, as a liminal peak experience, is however generally incompatible with the experience of calmness. Amongst the three types of experiencing ecstasy, in which the subject-object split becomes suspended, there is only one in which the experience of calmness is sustained even when the 'experiencing self' is transported into the 'ecstatic consciousness'. The variety in which the subject is gradually overwhelmed by the 'object arriving' is obviously ruled out since calmness does not 'arrive'; the variety in which the 'experiencing self' is annihilated when it is abruptly transported into states of rapture is likewise ruled out; thus the only variety of 'ecstatic experience' remaining is the one in which the 'subject-object split' is felt to be slowly declining, ending finally in the loss of any self-awareness. The gradual dissolution of any awareness of self is a phenomenon that can be encountered in a rare and unique variety of 'ecstatic experience'.

In order to illustrate the unique mode of experiencing 'all-encompassing Calmness', we have to turn to examples and empirical records from the tradition of Buddhist mysticism. In the Buddhist practice of 'meditation', the specific stages of the growth of inner calmness, and of the gradual loss of self that goes with it, are described in great detail.[167] The Buddhist scheme of *"jhâna"*,[168] for example, consists of four successive stages. We have to examine, first, if the four stages of *"jhâna"* correspond indeed to the stages and states of consciousness that we have identified as part of the process of 'introversion'. We have to establish, in other words, if the stages of *"jhâna"* are different or similar levels of consciousness compared with the levels of 'introversion' and the 'quiet state of alertness'. This rather intricate question can only be decided on the basis of a detailed comparative phenomenological analysis. Answering this question is particularly difficult because of the dual nature of calmness, as outlined above. In the process of 'introversion', the premeditated goal is to achieve a state of perfect inner calm. In the 'quiet state of alertness', the calmness within is, however, the essential underlying emotional condition and part of the formal framework of this state of consciousness. On the other hand, calmness is also the intended goal of 'introversion', and for the Buddhist, it is the ultimate state towards which he is determined to 'advance'. We therefore need to find criteria that enable us to decide if the first stage of *"jhâna"* corresponds to the first stage in the process of 'introversion', or if it is already a stage of consciousness that corresponds to the incipient stage of the 'quiet state of alertness'. [If we apply the criteria established earlier concerning the phenomenology of 'introversion' versus the phenomena germane to 'the quiet state of alertness', and relate them to the phenomena featuring in the first stage of *"jhâna"*, we may state the following:]

1. All sense perceptions have been switched off, the mind has become unreceptive to distractions [or distractions have no impact on the mental condition of the practitioner anymore]. This shows that the initial level of 'introversion' has clearly been surpassed.

---

167 Cf. Heiler, Friedrich. *Die Buddhistische Versenkung*. 1918. Munich: Reinhardt, 1922. – Hauer, Jakob W. *Der Joga als Heilsweg. Nach Indischen Quellen Dargestellt*. Stuttgart: Kholhammer, 1932.

168 [Note: Albrecht uses the Pali term *jhâna,* corresponding in Sanskrit to *dhyâna;* both terms denote the "means for transcending the impact of sensory stimuli and our normal response to it." (Conze, Edward. *Buddhism*. New York: Harper, 1959. 100.) – FW.]

2. Several structural elements constituting the 'quiet state of alertness' can clearly be discerned: the calmness within, emptiness and hyper-lucid clarity are essential components of this mental state; this aside, the emptied space of consciousness allows meditative processes to unfold freely.

3. We may take for granted that the practitioner has no longer any awareness of the ongoing progress of 'introversion'. This indicates that we are no longer concerned with the incipient stage of 'introversion', in which the structure of the 'waking consciousness' is gradually dissolved, and in which the transformation of consciousness into the direction of the 'quiet state of alertness' has begun, but we are here concerned with a different process – the process of 'purification' – in which the practitioner's 'self' undergoes a change.

The meditative processes involved at the first stage of "*jhâna*" are no longer aimed at eroding distractions and other hindrances, or at advancing the ascent towards the desired goal, but the meditation rather revolves around the "noble truths" of Buddhism. This stage inevitably requires the Buddhist practitioner to become fully absorbed in what corresponds to our conception of the 'quiet state of alertness'.

For these reasons I am convinced that the four stages of "*jhâna*" are actually successive stages of consciousness that correspond to the mental framework encompassed by the 'quiet state of alertness'. The path through the four "*jhânas*" is, after all, conceived as a mental process of "un-becoming", i.e. a process in which the 'I' of the practitioner is increasingly eroded and ultimately extinguished. By advancing along this path, the practitioner is enabled to perceive with the 'inner eye' the ultimate, uniform essence of being; the perfect practitioner finally reaches the stage culminating in the total (temporary) extinction of the 'self' while immersed in 'all-encompassing Calmness'. The four stages of "*jhâna*" can therefore be identified in our conceptual framework as four distinct states of consciousness falling inside the domain of the 'quiet state of alertness'.

The first state of "jhâna" is a mental condition in which meditational processes are still active [and transform] the structure of consciousness. The "noble truths" the practitioner is required to revolve around meditatively are "the brevity and vanity of life", "the nothingness and insubstantiality of existence" and "universal suffering".[169] The "Bhikkhu" [Buddhist monk] is deeply moved by his "reflexions and intellectual ruminations" on these truths, and as a consequence, is shattered and filled with dismay and nausea at his own dismal state; after this agony, however, he endeavours to achieve complete detachment [from worldly things], and, having successfully done so, he is filled with an enduring sense of peace and happiness. Hence he is inundated by 'happy calmness', which is the prevailing mood at this stage. The phrase used to describe this state in Buddhist teaching is: "Becoming detached from sensual desires – becoming detached from all impure conditions – attaining – aided by consideration and reflexion – and born from detachment – the joyful and delightful first stage of "*jhâna*" – thus [the practitioner] is abiding."

On *the second stage of "jhâna"* all active meditative processes have ceased. The person absorbed in the 'quiet state of alertness' is permeated by "ocean-like tranquillity"; the practitioner's mind is filled with 'cheerful calmness'; the mind has been vacated from all 'content' except for the deep sense of calmness. He contemplates 'all-encompassing Calmness' in a state of hyper-lucid clarity, and feels the calmness flooding his mind like "cool water".[170] The practitioner responds to the calmness within with silent cheerfulness. The Buddhist instruction to the seeker aspiring for the second "*jhâna*" is: "And now the Bhikkhu becomes – after his reflexions and ruminations have been stilled – immersed deeply in peace and mindfulness – and one in spirit – detached from all thoughtfulness and reflexion – attaining the second, joyful and exuberant level of *jhâna* – born from recollection – thus [the Bikkhu] is abiding."

The Buddhist description of *the third state of jhâna* emphasizes even more strongly the clear, lucid and empty condition of consciousness. On this level, calmness is no longer tinged with such feelings

---

169 Heiler, Friedrich. *Die Buddhistische Versenkung*. 1918. Munich: Reinhardt, 1922. 13. (English translation provided.)

170 Heiler, Friedrich. *Die Buddhistische Versenkung*. 1918. Munich: Reinhardt, 1922. 20. (English translation provided.)

as cheerfulness and bliss, but the practitioner is immersed in an ever expanding state of even-mindedness. The zest-like quality of the prevailing mood fades away, as the practitioner is deprived of the sense of happiness and rapture; he is now subjected to a process of purification and annihilation of the self, which in turn results in a state of serene 'mindfulness' and silent bliss. On this stage, the flow of all experience is slowed down, while the sense of equanimity, ease and harmony continues to intensify. Visionary experiences originating from the imagination are now rare, since all image-based meditative processes have ended on the second stage of *jhâna*. Emotions have largely subsided, though we may still discern a few residues of emotional response, but these consist essentially in the awareness of abiding silently in bliss. The Buddhist formula of this state is: "When the Bhikkhu – after fading out of zest – abides in balanced equanimity – mindful and fully aware – experiences joy and bliss permeating his body – the very condition the sages have in mind when they say: 'The person abiding in equanimity and composure is the one who dwells in happiness' – thus he abides attaining the third *jhâna*."

The fourth state of jhâna is the stage of "icy cold indifference".[171] All emotional responses have subsided. The 'experiencing I' still has some awareness of himself, albeit a rather faint one, but this indicates that the subject-object split has been considerably reduced, though not yet entirely extinguished. The 'I', absorbed in silent repose, is mindful only of the calmness within. The Buddhist formula is: "And then again the Bhikkhu – after having left happiness behind – after having left pain behind – and freed from the feelings of zestful pleasure and displeasure of the earlier level – purified by equanimity and composure – he enters the fourth *jhâna*, which is devoid of joy and devoid of pain – and thus he abides."

The fourth state of *jhâna* is the mental state preceding *nirvana*. "Nirvana is nothing but the culmination of the prolonged path of 'un-becoming', which begins with the process of becoming detached from this world, and continues throughout the process of

---

171 Heiler, Friedrich. *Die Buddhistische Versenkung*. 1918. Munich: Reinhardt, 1922. 21. (English translation provided.)

'introversion' (and the 'quiet state of alertness')."[172] *Nirvana* is thus the 'ecstatic' culmination of the 'quiet state of alertness', in which the subject-object split is entirely extinguished. "The one who has reached perfection has trailed off into pure being, which is nothing but himself."[173] "The vast ocean is deep, unfathomable, inscrutable ... and so is the one who has reached perfection, he is deep, unfathomable, inscrutable." *Nirvana* is absolute calmness, absolute nothingness, perfect cessation, "a state of having become divested entirely from one's own being".[174] The one who has reached perfection is the one whose self has become eclipsed. The 'ecstatic union' with empty calmness does not arouse ecstatic feelings of rapture, nor the sense of being overwhelmed [by feelings of ecstatic joy], but evokes a deep and ineffable sense of oneness, peace and indifference. *Nirvana* culminates in a condition in which all self-awareness has been eclipsed; it can thus be seen as a state of 'no-consciousness'. This is a liminal experience at the threshold of consciousness, which is preceded by the dim awareness that one is near losing consciousness, and followed by the awareness of arising from this experience as a person transformed.

'The Ur' [The Primeval Ground of Being]

We have explored the Buddhist states of *jhâna* in detail because we wanted to demonstrate the distinctive features of a purely a-personal mode of experiencing the 'All-encompassing'. The experience of 'all-encompassing Calmness' is entirely a-personal, and thus it is juxtaposed to encounters in which the 'All-encompassing' is experienced as a persona [we will come back to this topic later]. We should add that the empirical records at hand did not provide sufficient data for illustrating the radically a-personal variety of 'the All-encompassing', which is why we have turned to texts from the Buddhist

---

172 Heiler, Friedrich. *Die Buddhistische Versenkung*. 1918. Munich: Reinhardt, 1922. 36. (English translation provided.)

173 Heiler, Friedrich. *Die Buddhistische Versenkung*. 1918. Munich: Reinhardt, 1922. 38. (English translation provided.)

174 Heiler, Friedrich. *Die Buddhistische Versenkung*. 1918. Munich: Reinhardt, 1922. 37. (English translation provided.)

mystical tradition. The relative sparsity of radically a-personal experiences of 'the All-encompassing' in the West might be explained by differences in cultural heritage and differences between Eastern and Western meditational practices. In any case, I have been unable to gather enough data from the empirical records recovered from the Western practitioners available to evolve a comprehensive phenomenology of the a-personal experience of 'all-encompassing Calmness', whereas I have collected numerous records yielding insights into other varieties of a-personal and personal experiences of 'the All-encompassing'. The authentic documents collected have all been recovered from spontaneous utterances by subjects, which were spoken when they were absorbed in the 'quiet state of alertness'. These testimonies naturally provide livelier and more immediate descriptions of encounters with the 'All-encompassing' [than the Buddhist texts of spiritual guidance can do].

We shall now turn to another a-personal variety of 'the All-encompassing', termed encounter with 'the Ur' [i.e. the Primordial, or abysmal Ground of Being]. To begin with, we are going to consider varieties that can phenomenologically be located between the experience of 'all-encompassing Calmness' and the experience of 'the Ur'. In dealing with 'the Ur' we encounter qualities [of the 'All-encompassing'] we have met in part when analysing 'all-encompassing Calmness', and when dealing with items 'arriving' from within the 'sphere of the self'. Nothingness, experienced as [eloquent] silence, has been identified, first, as a hypostasis of a certain area of the 'sphere of the self'; Nothingness, perceived as the Void, has, secondly, been discerned as a phenomenon contiguous with the experience of 'all-encompassing Calmness'. Nothingness has now, for the third time, become the focus of our enquiry, even though it has (in the given instance) a quality that differs markedly from the one in which it appears to be a hypostasis of the 'sphere of the self'. It also differs from the variety discerned when Nothingness was intertwined with the experience of 'all-encompassing Calmness'. If we wish to render the formal characteristics of mystical experience intelligible, we need to split up the homogeneous experiential core and isolate a single component for the purpose of our investigation. It is, however, not our intention to examine a complete sequence of testimonials recorded in successive sessions. We will rather limit our analysis to representative excerpts from several recordings, in which pivotal characteristics of 'the All-encompassing' and the major 'forms of arriving' are addressed. Although some of these records also contain items in which the 'object arriving' can be identified as surfacing from the 'sphere of the self', they are not relevant to our enquiry and will therefore be bypassed in the analysis. We have already referred to the fact that there is a "twilight-zone" between the domains of mystical and non-mystical experiences, i.e. the liminal area in which an individual experience extends into the realm of mysticism. We have pointed out that the 'object' that 'arrives' in this liminal "twilight-zone" is best described as [abysmal] 'Silence' or as 'Nothingness', and that these phenomena seem to have the pivotal characteristics of 'the All-encompassing'. However, the qualities inherent in these seemingly 'all-encompassing' phenomena can be shown to be secondary and/or subservient to the qualities of the primary phenomena surfacing from within the 'sphere of the self'. It is thus not surprising that we will come across records, which were spoken during consecutive sessions in 'the quiet state of alertness', in which the 'object arriving' does not surface from the 'sphere of the self' but can be identified as 'arriving' from beyond the 'sphere of the self', and thus has all the essential characteristics of the 'All-encompassing', including the sense of 'revelation'. The following passages from these personal testimonies demonstrate that the distinctive characteristics of the 'All-encompassing' clearly prevail over concurrently perceived qualities of phenomena surfacing from within the 'sphere of the self'.

Calmness and inner peace are experiential phenomena that are likely to appear in the "twilight-zone" between phenomena surfacing from the 'sphere of the self' and phenomena perceived to be 'all-encompassing'. [In the accounts reported] calmness is described as 'emerging' in the course of the process of 'introversion' from the 'sphere of the self', more specifically, from the sphere of the body. It is only after the process of 'introversion' has ended and been replaced by the serene and 'quiet state of alertness' that Calmness is experienced as 'all-encompassing'. When the 'object arriving' is perceived as 'silence' rather than as calmness, the "twilight zone" has a different empirical nuance. On the one hand, the encounter with the 'silence within' brings to the fore the 'sphere of the self' particularly forcefully, which might be seen as an intuitive response by which the mind is to be advanced to the serene state in which 'silence' is perceived as 'all-encompassing', thus resulting in the mystical experience of 'Silence'. However, 'Silence' can also be experienced as 'arriving' exclusively from beyond the 'sphere of the individual self'; when this happens, the experience of 'silence' is more often tinged by a sense of 'Nothingness', or a sense of 'Emptiness', and, therefore, the overall experience is usually described in these terms in the testimonials quoted. The word 'Nothingness' evokes quite persuasively the notion of the boundless and formless essence of 'the All-encompassing':

> Mr. E., record spoken during the session of 20 September, 1942: *"Emptiness has filled all the space around. – Nothingness is Being becoming effective. – Nothingness is ruling with its omnipotence. – Silence belongs to it, being its blood. – What has been separated, has again been redeemed. The clock-hand is pointing at zero.*
> *Nothingness, complete and vacant, has been from the beginning of time. – From the primeval beginning, to primeval beginning* (sic!). *– Nothingness has devoured the world. All that is, has collapsed into Nothingness. Nothingness does not speak. It cannot be addressed. – There is no counterpart. – There is nothing, but Nothingness. – If there were an I, wandering about aimlessly in search of its soul, it would expire before finding it. – No brightness – no darkness – no warmth – no coldness – no day – no night – no heaven – no earth. – Nothing, but the 'Ur'."*

The quality of 'the All-encompassing' experienced as Calmness, and the quality of 'the All-encompassing' perceived as 'Nothingness', are obviously rather different experiences. In the records, the quality of translucent emptiness when describing 'Nothingness' (envisaged more and more distinctly in the successive accounts), appears to be waning, whereas this was the prevailing hallmark of the experience of 'all-encompassing Calmness'. 'Nothingness' rather appears to emanate from the realm of 'iron-like Silence'. 'Nothingness' thus appears to have changed its initial quality in the course of successive events, even to the extent that a new word has to be used, to refer to it adequately: 'Nothingness' has metamorphosed into the 'Ur'. After the session recorded on 20 September, several other records were documented, in which the prevailing experience is characterised as 'silence' – an ambivalent word which may refer either to the silence within, emerging from the 'sphere of the self', or to the 'Silence' 'arriving' in the vista of 'inner sight' and perceived as 'all-encompassing'. After a fleeting interval, however, the full impact of the 'Ur' 'arriving' is experienced, which has all the essential qualities of 'the All-encompassing':

> 19 October 1942: *"The 'Ur' has inhaled the room. – All things have wilfully surrendered to the whirling Power, and have plunged into all-devouring Silence. – The Void tumbles into Silence. – Nothingness congeals at the violent impact of the rocks. – Selfhood and resistance have drowned in the Void. –*
>
> *The 'Ur' had stopped breathing. The frontier had erupted menacingly from the mystery, the frontier, the 'Ur-point', in which movement and being, in which the end and the beginning, in which only a single breath lies between death and being cast out to freedom."* (At this point the 'quiet state of alertness' was instantly replaced by the 'ecstatic consciousness'; the shift is indicated in print by the three dashes.)
>
> 30 October 1942: *"Assailed by the overwhelming power of the rock, the black rocks have been aligned to form a wall. This secret – roomless, furrowless, tenebrous – is the veiled countenance of the 'Ur'. The blackness conceals the holy primeval colour. The formless plainness seals the 'Urgestalt'* [primeval shape]. *The brazen, timeless repose keeps the acts of silence in store . . ."*
>
> 16 November 1942:
> *"There is a tranquillity that is brazen and powerful, like the force of rocks,*
> *There is a tranquillity in which the heart is immersed in the sound of primeval thunder,*
> *There is a tranquillity that is Finality itself.*
> *This is the tranquillity that gives birth to Silence that is absolutely final.*
>
> *A gale that has wafted timidity all over the land.*
> *The last breath of the 'Ur' permeates all being.*
> *The heart is redeemed from sorrow.*
> *It offers itself up to death.*
> *And its final beat is fading away*
> *In the breath emanating from the 'Ur'.*
>
> *The Ultimate Potentiality has been reclaimed from time,*
> *restoring timeless Tranquillity."*

When reading these accounts (spoken by Mr. E. in consecutive sessions in about one month) one may recognize quite easily that they recapture qualities of 'the All-encompassing' that are quite different from the specific features while experiencing 'all-encompassing Calmness'. If we apply the seven criteria (formulated above) to the passages quoted, we can establish some striking differences between the experience of 'all-encompassing Calmness' and the experience of the 'Ur':

1. It can be taken for granted that the subject was immersed in the 'quiet state of alertness' at the time and that this was the mental state while the events described were in progress; this fact is even more clearly established than in the texts from the practice of Buddhist meditation quoted above, for the simple reason that I myself was the eyewitness and present at all sessions when these records were spoken. I can thus confirm that the 'quiet state of alertness' was fully developed, and served as the sustaining fundament throughout the recorded experience. This aside, there is indirect evidence in that the attentive reader will surely be able to recognize the exceptional clarity of vision becoming manifest in these testimonies.

2. The 'object arriving' described is quite unmistakably experienced as a totality from beyond the confines of the individual consciousness; the 'object arriving' reveals itself more and more clearly to the 'experiencing I' in the successive sessions. From amongst the eight 'forms of arriving' that we have identified so far, we can discern four that apply here, albeit they are intertwined, establishing a 'composite form', in which the experience of an extra-mental totality is grasped to be something real and unique. These four 'forms of arriving' are: the 'metaphoric form', 'intuition', 'the form of language' and the 'form of responding feelings'. The predominant 'form' is that of language, i.e. the appearance of individual words in consciousness.

3. The object that 'arrives' is experienced as 'all-encompassing' in nature; it is addressed by a particular name: the "Ur"; this word has evidently been suggested by the concomitant awareness of the special experiential quality adhering to the "Ur". The "Ur" is

an entirely unknown, foreign entity, experienced as coming from beyond the 'sphere of the self'. There are no phenomena that might surface from within the individual self that could be denoted by such a word. Moreover, the word "Ur" indicates not only its foreignness, but also its essence as something primordial and ultimate. The "Ur" is perceived as an 'all-encompassing Oneness', from which everything that exists originates. It is, moreover, recognized as the source of all creative acts, and though as yet unknown, is an entity about to reveal itself. "The ur-potentiality has been restored from the temporal and returned to primeval Silence." The "Ur" is pregnant and ready to give birth to something new. The "Ur" is the final primordial Ultimate, the primeval ground of Being, and the ground for whatever is going to happen in the future. Amongst the many different varieties in which the 'All-encompassing' may manifest itself, there is hardly any other that is so clearly marked by the pivotal features of the 'All-encompassing'.

4. Unlike the experience of 'all-encompassing Calmness', in which the person absorbed in the 'quiet state of alertness' is (as it were) ushered into an ever deepening state of Calmness, the "Ur" elicits a different movement. The 'experiencing I' is overpowered by the forceful intrusion of the "Ur" in consciousness; the "Ur" is perceived as ineffably powerful, vast and intimidating. The "Ur" is, in other words, clearly perceived as a *mysterium tremendum*, which arouses an intense [negative] emotional response, notably fear, awe, feeling shaken and scared. This demonstrates that the numinous response evoked by the "Ur" is much more pronounced and powerful than the numinous response elicited by the experience of 'all-encompassing Calmness'. Moreover, when experiencing the "Ur", the characteristics of the *tremendum* are clearly predominant, whereas features of a *mysterium fascinosum* hardly adhere to it.

5. The experience of the "Ur" is, like that of 'all-encompassing Calmness', almost exclusively a-personal. In our phenomenological analysis, we have only pointed out that the experience of the "Ur" is accompanied by the intuitive awareness that it is the

primeval origin and hidden ground and cause of all future developments, but we did not consider the aspect whether the experience has or has not got any person-like quality. Although the "Ur" is felt to be extraordinarily powerful, striking the 'experiencing I' dumb with its awesome force, and although it is experienced as a forceful, dynamic entity, it does not have any characteristics associated with a persona. The "Ur" has rather predominantly cosmic characteristics, because the 'forms' in which it reveals itself are rather impersonal and multifarious. To illustrate this issue, we would like to refer to the example of Jacob Böhme[175]. He was bestowed with a wide variety of visionary and non-visual mystical experiences, which endowed him with penetrating insights and resulted in a complex vision of the 'cosmic drama'. Böhme, like any other person gratified with an encounter with the "Ur", does not respond to the "Ur" as if it was endowed with the characteristics of a Persona. It is possible, however, that a subject may reflect on the "Ur" retrospectively in the 'waking consciousness', and hereafter attribute to the "Ur" person-like qualities. If this happens, the experience of the "Ur" might evoke the sense of being sent by some originator; or a subject might sometime later in life be gratified with the insight that the experience of the "Ur" has been the harbinger [or forerunner] of an experience in which the 'All-encompassing' has revealed itself as an 'all-encompassing Persona' ["He"[176] in the German text].

6. The passages quoted demonstrate persuasively that while the inward experience is in progress, the 'experiencing I' is continuously aware that it is currently confronted, or surrounded by a realm that is ultimately incomprehensible and unfathomable, and which is 'hidden' behind the "Ur".

7. If we consider the question what kind of 'ecstatic response' is evoked by the experience of the "Ur" (if any), we can infer from the texts that the "Ur" arouses feelings of the 'incipient stage of

---

175 Böhme, Jakob. *Schriften*. Leipzig: Insel-Verlag, 1923.
176 [Note: see footnote 163. – FW.]

ecstasy' albeit in a manner that is quite different from the one evoked by the experience of 'all-encompassing Calmness'. In our records, the "Ur" is not perceived as an entity towards which the 'experiencing I' advances, and in which it desires to become dissolved, or united with. The "Ur" rather imposes itself forcefully on the 'I', it is experienced as something threatening, towering up and overpowering the 'experiencing I'. In other words, what we are concerned here with is the second type of ecstatic experience: 'becoming forcefully overpowered' by the 'the All-encompassing'.

'Ur-Love' [Primeval Love]

After having answered the basic critical questions required for identifying the typical features of the experience of the "Ur", as well as for corroborating the claim that the "Ur" is a variant form of manifestation of the 'All-encompassing', we may now focus on a new quality of the 'All-encompassing'. The phenomenological analysis of this new quality can be facilitated if we study several records together (all of them were spoken in the 'quiet state of alertness' in subsequent sessions, albeit with different temporal intervals in between). A subject who practices 'introversion' for a longer period will notice that the events occurring in the 'quiet state of alertness' in subsequent sessions differ from each other, and that 'the All-encompassing' that 'arrives' tends to appear in different forms of manifestation in different events. To illustrate this point we are going to analyse the record just quoted above; choosing this document again has the advantage that there is no need to answer once more the critical questions required for assessing the experience. At close analysis, we may discern in the experience of the "Ur" described above some visual quality. The "Ur" is referred to as the 'Ground of Being', from which new, i.e. as yet unknown, entities emerge. For this reason the 'Ground of Being' has been described as "pregnant with a new birth". A distinctive feature of the "Ur" is that it undergoes a metamorphosis while the experience progresses, and this change is caused by the "Ur" itself. This dynamic aspect of cognition is implied in the phrase "the cloak has been inverted, and when it was opened, the other side can be recognized." The "Ur" gives birth to entities revealed in a process of creation and known to have cosmic dimension. These new-born entities are labelled "Ur-Heart" and "Ur-Love". They refer to the special qualities by which the 'All-encompassing' becomes manifest in the given event. When the "Ur" has become a visible manifestation of 'the All-encompassing', 'all-encompassing Love' emanates from inside it. For this reason there is no need to suspect that the feeling of love has merely surfaced from within the 'sphere of the self'. The feeling of love elicited is described in the subsequent accounts as "Love absorbing" and thus genuinely experienced as Love that is 'all-encompassing', not as an emotion surfacing from 'within the self':

20 November 1942: "*Silence is pensive and profuse with fundamental darkness. Black is the silence reposing in the Ur . . .*"

25 November 1942: "*Ur-calmness has ended its motionless state. Ur-calmness is about to end its spacelessness. The black abyss has enfolded the place that has been released from sunkenness. – The soul remains rooted in the past. And the 'Ur' alone is reality. But the formless Being readjusts itself within itself. It is as if invisible, threadlike beams are piling up the primeval shape of the rocks, and as if the net of rays, all entangled, signposted the place at which the eye of foreboding is directed. – The Ur wishes to terminate its peace . . .*"

8 January 1943: "*. . . the black rock is bursting apart. And the blinding, dazzling blaze is gushing from the gaping abyss across the silent, white countryside. There is a powerful maelstrom inhaling and melting down everything, vanishing in the crimson blood of the blazing sun. Reverted to [contemplate] the flowing rush of glistening light, transformed by tears of happiness, transported into jubilation . . .*"

29 January 1943: "*The pitch-black cloak of silence has concealed the inner room of the Ur, which was abiding in the powerful domain of empty nothingness. – The clock-hand is fixed at zero. But the cloak has been turned inside out, when it was opened. – A golden-red blaze, the blossoming blood of the sun, a rushing stream of colour, jubilant, sets ablaze the inner lining of the black garment. – The other side has been recognized . . .*"

"*In the middle of the ground, on the site where the innermost intimacy of the sea of light lives, blazing and radiant, this is where the primeval Heart [Ur-Heart] reposes. Devotion and adoration, the freedom renounced by a soul redeemed by silence, is transformed by the dazzling force of revelation, and rent apart, into the exultant, inebriating bliss of death. And [the soul] dwells in primeval silence, lost in the holiness of the Heart.*"

Although only a few selected passages from the entire sequence of records have been cited here, it is not difficult to recognize that the speaker is describing encounters with 'objects' evidently experienced as 'arriving' in the vista of 'inner sight'. The 'object' perceived is, moreover, explicitly identified as a dynamic power, "moving on its own", a feature that has also been encountered in the experience of the "Ur". In the events described above, the 'experiencing I' is instantly overwhelmed by the rash intrusion of 'the All-encompassing'. The primeval "Heart", identified as the opposite side of the "Ur", dashes (as it were) into the vista of 'inner sight'. Yet the setup of the joint 'forms of arriving' has changed in the perception of the "Ur-Love", compared to that of the "Ur". The 'emotional response' has become the predominant 'form' in which the 'All-encompassing' 'arrives'. Whereas in the encounter with the "Ur" the emotional state of the 'experiencing I' remains remarkably even and stable, the experience of primordial Love triggers a rich array of directed feelings. This is a clear indication that the nature of 'the All-encompassing' has changed in the given event. The encounter with the "Ur" has only a slight effect on the emotional condition of the 'experiencing I'; in fact, it arouses only marginal emotional responses, perceived in terms of differing nuances of Silence. When the 'experiencing I' is touched by the "Ur-Heart", or "Ur-Love", by contrast, he/she is deeply affected emotionally and almost instantly transported into near-ecstatic states; the latter is verbally reflected in the testimonies in such expressions as inebriation, happiness, exultation, rapture, and by references to somatic responses such as tears, as well as in words like intimacy, devotion and adoration. All these emotional expressions indicate that the 'experiencing I' desires to overcome the subject-object split. Though it is not possible here to specify further the impact these emotional responses have on the consciousness of the subject, and how the responses evoked develop during the empirical event, we suggest that the numerous metaphorical expressions have been evoked by the encounter with 'all-encompassing Love' rather than by novel images or pictures appearing as 'objects' of 'inner sight'. We may thus infer from these accounts a new quality in experiencing 'the All-encompassing': its numinous nature. Though features of the *mysterium tremendum* can be discerned in some places, it is clearly the qualities of the *fascinosum* that prevail and increase considerably in number in successive experiences. Love, experienced as 'all-encompassing', is (unlike the "Ur") a highly intense *fascinosum*, which has an enduring transforming impact on the subject. Love has the tendency to arouse feelings of love in response. In this way the ground is prepared for ecstatic feelings to erupt in such an event. As long as the subject-object split perseveres in such an experience, the desire to overcome this division will increase, culminating in the longing to surrender wholeheartedly to 'all-encompassing Love'. This development in experiencing 'the All-encompassing' does not always go smoothly. There are two potential hazards for the 'quiet state of alertness' to be rent apart by an intense emotional experience of this kind: First, we know from the reports about the 'arrival' of 'split-off' items [surfacing from the unconscious] that extreme states of arousal tend to destroy the 'quiet state of alertness'. Secondly, the 'quiet state of alertness' tends to be displaced by the 'ecstatic consciousness' [in situations of intense emotional arousal]. From the three varieties in which the 'quiet state of alertness' may be replaced by the 'ecstatic consciousness', it is the third variety that applies here: The subject is overwhelmed by a single exuberant emotion, which is aroused with such a great intensity that the subject-object split is blurred and eventually eroded. The fact that the subject-object division is (temporarily) suspended can be inferred from the record quoted below. It must be added, however, that this testimony was not retrieved from spontaneous utterances spoken while the subject was transported into the state of ecstasy, but was recorded retrospectively after the ecstatic event, i.e. when the subject had returned to the 'quiet state of alertness'. This is the reason why the speaker switches in the record quoted into the past tense, when referring to the foregoing ecstatic experience, while the impressions perceived in the ongoing 'quiet state of alertness' are rendered in present tense:

> 30 March 1943: "*Entering through the portal of bliss, the heart is stunned by paroxysms of joy, confident of being redeemed by the Mystery. – Filled with thirst unquenchable, the soul, dissolving, drank the clear devouring fire, inundated by the flow of splendour, and voided by it; rent apart by the primeval power of Light, and soaked with tears, awestruck by the gentle intimacy of absorbing Love. – The soul has now chimed in with*

the unfathomable Mystery. Silence has become transfigured, and primeval clarity metamorphosed into Light."

The word "Light" addresses a phenomenon that we have not yet considered. Light and fire are expressions referring to 'objects' affiliated with the experience of primordial Love, as well as with qualities of 'the All-encompassing' perceived as a Persona. Fire in this context is usually a metaphor for intense feelings. The expression suggests the notion of being inflamed emotionally, and denotes the awareness that the "soul" is about to be consumed by fire in ecstasy. All these connotations and metaphors are evoked by a corresponding experience of 'the All-encompassing'. "Light" refers generally to a visual perception, i.e. either an act of 'seeing' inwardly, or to an 'object' appearing in the 'shape' of "light". The latter experience may also be a manifestation of 'the All-encompassing' in the 'metaphoric form'; this phenomenon raises the question, if we are not faced here with a different 'form of arriving' in 'inner sight' than the 'metaphoric form' of perceiving Light. We cannot answer this question as yet, and have to defer the answer to a later stage of this investigation. To round up our analysis of the experience of 'all-encompassing Love', we will finally examine a record, retrieved from the 'ecstatic consciousness'. That is to say that this account was not recovered from a spontaneous verbal utterance spoken in an 'ecstatic state', but from 'automatic writing', taken down by a subject while transported (in part) into the incipient stage of ecstasy. For illustration a section of this document is printed below; the idiosyncratic graphic style indicates the subject's state of agitation while transported into the 'ecstatic state'. The passage does not, however, deal with the given ecstatic experience per se, but with items of pre-ecstatic experience; the passage referring to the 'ecstatic experience' was written by pencil, yet the handwriting was too faint to be used for photographic reproduction [by the technical standards of the early 1950s]; the passage illustrated is thus merely a snippet from the part of the document written by pen:

[*Illustration:* Passage from a document of 'automatic writing', written when the subject was about to be transported into the incipient stage of the 'ecstatic consciousness' – FW.]

The subject who produced this document of 'automatic writing' started out in the 'waking consciousness', which is reflected in the relatively controlled handwriting at the beginning; the abrupt[177] rift and declining line after the first paragraph indicates that the writer was in that moment transported into a state between the 'quiet state of alertness' and the 'ecstatic consciousness'. This shift is indicated graphically by the striking, fading line and the irregular shaky hand. In the experience recorded, 'the All-encompassing' becomes manifest in a 'form' we have not yet dealt with in our investigation: It is the elusive experience of 'pristine Beauty':[178]

---

177 This is mirrored in the sudden shift to a new line at a lower place, and the declining control in the handwriting, as well as in the different size and outline of the letters, which suggests that a deeper dispositional layer has been switched on.

178 [The passage in German reads: "Übermächtig, ahnungstief tönt die Stille in mir. Eine zögernde Angst, ein scheues Glück fallen in die Stille. Ich horche in die

350   CARL ALBRECHT

> 2 August 1945: "*Overpowering and portentous is the silence reverberating within me. Hesitant fear and shy happiness are descending unto the silence. I harken into the silence, and fear dissolves in the single redemptive pose of surrender to the Mystery, from which* . . . (after being transferred into an altered state of consciousness) [annotation by Albrecht – FW.] *A holy murmur is reverberating through silence – the aureate blessing of the Light is flowing into the soul, and reigning supreme as Truth – inundated by Love, the soul is inhaling the glory of Eternal Beauty – in the stillness of being whole, the Light is bowing towards the temple* . . ."

The author of this document was a woman who, at the time when she had psychotherapeutic treatments, experienced 'split-off' items from the unconscious, featuring as 'objects arriving' in the 'quiet state of alertness'. During these therapeutic treatments, the 'quiet state of alertness' was almost always destroyed when the 'split-off' item 'arrived' as an 'object' of 'inner sight', and was instantly replaced by the 'somnambulist consciousness' (something that also happened with many other patients in such a situation). After the woman had been healed, the shift from the 'waking consciousness' through the consciousness of 'introversion', and, at times, to the 'ecstatic consciousness', occurred always rather abruptly. Such an instant switching into a different mental state usually happens when the 'quiet state of alertness' is not fully developed. The initial passage quoted below was written when the woman had for a short time been immersed in the 'quiet state of alertness', whereas the other parts of the recorded experience occurred outside the 'quiet state of alertness'. The subsequent ejaculations and snippets render what she experienced while transported into the incipient stage of the 'ecstatic consciousness':

Stille und die Angst verströmt in der einen erlösten Hingabe an das Geheimnis, aus dem (nach Umschaltung) Ein heiliges Raunen zieht durch die Stille – der goldene Segen des Lichtes fließt in die Seele und waltet als Wahrheit – liebeerfüllt atmet die Seele die Herrlichkeit des ewigen Schönen – in der Stille des All*seins wölbt sich das Licht zum Tempel* . . . ". (PMB 239f.) – This illustration is printed on a separate (unnumbered) page in *PMB*, facing page 240. – FW.]

" ... I am opening myself up and I can see and hear and feel that there is something that knows me, that connects with me without asking who I am and what I am doing. I feel to be a part of what is giving itself as a bequest. Every sound is transformed into silence, I am only listening to silence, silence (after an abrupt shift to an altered state has occurred): *The circle has been broken – Light shimmering around me – stooping towards me and offering itself to me – a luminescent libation – I am drinking the Light – God bursts open the shell of Love – Beauty – oh Beauty – can I fathom thee entirely – shaken by awe I behold a mystery – death and life – – – Love is overflowing – –"*

The critical analysis of ecstatic utterances of this kind is inevitably faced with the problem of verification: Though the distinctive features of the 'All-encompassing' described are likely to be encountered in empirical reality, such a claim cannot be verified scientifically. I would argue, however, that the 'object arriving' described here has the genuine hallmarks of 'the All-encompassing', though I would leave it undecided, if, or to what extent, latent components of the self still have a share in shaping the experience. This objection aside, I consider it helpful to have included this example, as it is an authentic document yielding reliable and immediate insights into the nature of 'ecstatic experience' (e.g. the words "Love is overflowing" were written in the margin, set deliberately aside from the main text, which mirrors the person's state of exuberance at the time of writing). The second reason why I consider this document particularly relevant is that the experience of Love described as 'arriving' suggests the deep sense of a living personal relationship between the 'experiencing I' and the 'object experienced'. "Primeval Love", perceived as a different variety of experiencing the 'All-encompassing', is primarily experienced as something entirely a-personal. In a visionary experience of Love in the 'ecstatic consciousness', by contrast, Love is, however, perceived expressly as a gift by [a transcendental Being referred to as] "Him",[179] but also "He" is "Himself" recognized as the ultimate source and originator of "Love", and this is evidently a new quality of experiencing 'the All-encompassing'. This means that "Love" can be experienced as an entity that is 'all-encompassing' *per se*, albeit in

---

179 [Note: See the annotation in footnote 163. – FW.]

different qualitative varieties: Love can be experienced as something entirely a-personal; but Love can also be perceived as the gift or as a harbinger [of a loving transcendental Being], and Love can, finally, be perceived as the self-revelation of the essence of "Him" [i.e. the Divine experienced as a Persona]. The analysis of the phenomenon of "Love" has thus taken us to the threshold of an alternative [mystical] experience, in which the 'All-encompassing' becomes manifest as a Persona. Having reached the frontiers of psychological enquiry, we only wish to add a final clarifying remark: Choosing "Calmness", the "Ur" and "Love" for illustrating variant forms of experiencing 'the All-encompassing' has been more or less arbitrary, and motivated only by the attempt to portray different a-personal varieties in experiencing 'the All-encompassing'. It goes without saying that there are several other a-personal varieties in which 'the All-encompassing' may become manifest in the 'quiet state of alertness', for instance, in the 'all-encompassing Essence of Life' ("Alleben"), or '[Sublime] Beauty'.[180] But as we have accomplished our task to establish criteria for elucidating 'the All-encompassing' featuring as an 'object arriving' in the 'quiet state of alertness' and the incipient stage of the 'ecstatic consciousness', there is no need to elaborate further on other a-personal varieties of experiencing 'the All-encompassing'.

---

180   Cf. Plotinus, *Enneads*. [Note: The German edition of Plotinus's works used by Albrecht and referred to in the "Works Quoted" is *Die Enneaden des Plotin*. Trans. Hermann F. Müller. Berlin: Weidmannsche Buchhandlung, 1878. – Plotinus deals with the topic 'On Beauty' in Book I.6. Here Plotinus, "following Plato in *Symposium*, ... traces a hierarchy of beautiful objects above the physical, culminating in the Forms themselves. And their source, the Good, is also the source of their beauty (I. 6.7). The beauty of the Good consists in the virtual unity of all the Forms. As it is the ultimate cause of the complexity of intelligible reality, it is the cause of the delight we experience in form (see V. 5.12)." (Gerson, Lloyd. "Plotinus". *The Stanford Encyclopedia of Philosophy*, Summer 2014 Edition, Edward N. Zalta, ed., http://plato.stanford.edu/archives/sum2014/entries/plotinus/) – FW.]

The 'All-encompassing' as a Persona
["Das Umfassende als Person"]

The reason why we have decided to distinguish in our phenomenological taxonomy between personal and a-personal modes of manifestation of 'the All-encompassing' has not been inspired by any philosophical or theological considerations. It has not even been important for our investigation to consider, if a person who has encountered 'the All-encompassing' in the 'quiet state of alertness' in purely a-personal terms confirms later in retrospect after having returned into the normal 'waking consciousness' that the encounter was entirely a-personal, or if he/she attributes to an experience like 'all-encompassing Love', or 'the Ur', or 'Primeval Beauty' retrospectively a personal nature, or an event that has established a personal relationship between the 'experiencing I' and 'the All-encompassing'. That is to say that the differentiation between personal and a-personal varieties in experiencing 'the All-encompassing' is purely based on psychological criteria. And conceived as a purely psychological analysis, this empirical enquiry can be carried out in a fairly clear, detailed and persuasive manner: First, because the experiential qualities adhering to 'the All-encompassing' are always experienced by the subject with supreme clarity and an unflagging sense of certainty, and, secondly, because any encounter with 'the All-encompassing' has such a unique and lasting after-effect on the 'experiencing I' that the emotional response elicited differs significantly between individuals as well as between individual events. Thus, the encounter with 'the All-encompassing' 'arriving' in consciousness perceived as a Persona is an encounter with a 'Thou' – and this 'Thou' is not merely a Power that has an impact on the 'experiencing I', but is perceived as an acting being that operates within, and acts upon the 'experiencing I'. Thus the 'I' is not only [emotionally, cognitively and/or somatically] affected [by the 'Thou'], but also addressed, summoned, laden with responsibility, judged and loved. This shows that any experience of 'the All-encompassing' that has person-like qualities affects the 'experiencing I' existentially, transforming the subject since the event has an enduring impact on all the layers of his/her personality. It would be helpful for the further progress of our investigation to corroborate and illustrate these important facts and findings on the basis of authentic records in which encounters with 'the All-encompassing' perceived as a Persona are described. Several testimonials of this kind have been entrusted to me, in which individual subjects give intimate accounts of very personal experiences of 'the All-encompassing' experienced as a Persona, referred to by "Him", 'arriving' [in the vista of 'inner sight'] in the 'quiet state of alertness'. All of these records are described with remarkable clarity, but as they are deeply private and intimate confessions of personal religious and mystical experiences, I have refrained from quoting them in full for reasons of decency and in order to protect them against potential misuse. As I do not wish these confessions to be subjected to undue profanation, I decided to publish only a few excerpts, which do not disclose personal data or intimate details of the private religious and mystical experiences, but which may still offer invaluable insights for the purposes of this study. (The full records are preserved; anyone who wishes to study these testimonies confidentially is welcome to contact me in person to be given access.)[181]

The 'All-encompassing' experienced as an actively intervening Persona [in German literally "He"] *is the originator of whatever occurs in the 'quiet state of alertness'*. There is no single aspect in the entire experience that is not related to the all-encompassing Originator. This means that none of the forms of manifestation of 'the All-encompassing' considered so far are self-sufficient, i.e. independent, or produced *sui generis*: The experiences of 'all-encompassing Void', 'all-encompassing Nothingness' and 'all-encompassing Love' are all perceived either as a gift by the Ultimate Originator, or as 'harbingers' of the Originator, or else as a special mode of self-revelation of the Originator, or as a cypher [veiled token] of the Originator. The Void and Nothingness are "the most quiet and softest ways by which the impact of His closeness can be felt".[182] The "circles of Love projecting into the realm of the infinite",

---

181 [Note: A considerable number of the original empirical records compiled by Albrecht during the many years of his empirical research have been preserved; many of them are still available in the private archives of the Albrecht family in Germany. – FW.]

182 [Note: Albrecht does not give the source of this quotation; the same applies to several other short quotations in this chapter. It can be assumed, however, that Albrecht is quoting from the undisclosed private testimonials of religious mystical

experienced as a mode of 'arriving' have, by comparison, a much more urgent and animating impact on the 'experiencing I' [than the experience of the Void and/or of Nothingness]. The sense of being related to a Persona ['arriving' from beyond the realm of the individual self, and perceived as 'all-encompassing'] is immediately evident to the perceiver, and the same characteristic adheres to the experience of the Void, or of Nothingness, and/or Love.

Whenever an image surfaces in consciousness that has symbolic import, it is accompanied by the clear awareness that it is a [veiled] image of the One who is ultimately unknowable. "The seam of His aura", "the purple curtain, which is a piece of the inside wall of His heart", the image of the "dark Thou", are all expressions referring to symbols which have been "bestowed" [i.e. imparted into the mind], and which can actually be seen in the vista of 'inner sight'. These images, moreover, elicit the awareness that they really represent aspects of the personal nature of 'the All-encompassing', who "Himself", however, remains ultimately unknowable. The person-like manifestation of 'the All-encompassing' is not only intuitively grasped to be the Originator of the various 'objects' or images 'arriving' in the perceiver's consciousness, but also, and above all, as the Originator of all the changes effected within the perceiver him-/herself and of the long-term after-effects on his/her 'self'. When the person immersed in the 'quiet state of alertness' becomes aware of "Him" 'arriving', he/she will perceive with clarity the present state of his/her own 'self', albeit in a manner previously unknown to him/her. The condition he/she finds himself/herself in in the given event is recognized to have been effected by the Originator. This knowledge is immediately evident to the perceiver, and this fact is reflected in the metaphorical expressions evoked. The person immersed in the 'quiet state of alertness' perceives the current condition of his body and mind as if it was "living glass, transparent and susceptible to being breathed through"; the perceiver thus compares himself/herself to "a column of glass, ablaze amidst the boundless Void", and to "a bow taut tight, with the bow-string fully drawn", or to "a child clasped by unknown hands".

These phenomena have to be distinguished from the impact that the personal 'All-encompassing' has on the perceiver during the event,

---

experience gathered from several subjects. – FW.]

as well as from the various after-effects it has on him/her. These effects are intuitively perceived as springing from a cause-effect relationship that is established temporarily between the perceiver and 'the All-encompassing'. The awareness of this causal relationship becomes manifest linguistically in metaphorical expressions such as "the wind is blowing painfully [through me]".[183] The sense of 'the All-encompassing' working within and upon the perceiver inevitably arouses diverse unique and intense emotional responses, which are thus part of the rarest, most refined and most spiritual feelings man is capable of experiencing. Because of the unique quality of these feelings, the perceiver recognizes intuitively that 'the All-encompassing' is, in essence, a rare and unique Being that deeply affects the moral nature of the perceiver, and summons him/her to respond accordingly.

The 'arrival' of 'the All-encompassing' as a Persona thus establishes an 'I-Thou relationship' of a special kind. The empirical nature of such a relationship comes to the fore impressively in the value judgements evoked by it in the perceiver. The 'object arriving' in the vista of 'inner sight' is instantly acknowledged to be of supreme value. Consequently, a sphere of ultimate values evolves around it. Contrasted to it is a sphere deficient of values, to which the current existential condition of the perceiver's self is assigned. In the perceiver's hierarchical system of values, the experience of the 'Thou' that 'arrives' is reigning supreme, whereas the perceiver is aware that his 'self' is separated by an "abyss" from the supreme 'Thou'. The awareness of the insuperable gulf between the domain of values and the sphere deficient of values dominates all experiences of the subject on his/her path [of personal growth]. Any feelings aroused on this stage in the subject's spiritual development, and any idea, and any thought arising are instantly related to the given scale of

---

183 [Note: Albrecht outlines a few more features of this rare somatic experience below. – Accounts of sensate experiences, like "the body being blown through" by a spiritual energy rendered metaphorically as "wind", can be found in several mystical writings of Christian saints, visionaries and mystics. In these mystographical records the painful experience of being "blown through" is identified by the Christian recipient in the context of his/her religious faith as the self-revelation of the Divine *Pneuma*, or "Holy Spirit", vouchsafed individually in an act of special grace. – FW.]

values, and assigned either to the sphere of approved values or to the sphere deficient of values. These instantaneous evaluations are, in most instances, based on feelings, though these feelings may occasionally be linked with a fleeting awareness that one has assessed an experience as valuable or as worthless. The 'experiencing I' responds to the 'Thou' with diverse emotional reactions, of which many are unfamiliar to the perceiver and considered inadequate [in view of the ultimate value of 'the All-encompassing']. In particular, the subject feels that his/her responsive love, when overwhelmed by 'the All-encompassing' 'Thou', is wholly inadequate: Such responses as 'languishing love', 'devotion', 'ardent love', combined with 'joy' and 'bliss', are all variant forms of loving devotion aroused by the 'Thou'. However, none of these loving responses are considered sufficient, and are therefore instantaneously judged as inferior. From amongst the great diversity of feelings, thoughts and imaginative ideas that appear in the subject's vista of 'inner sight', only a few are approved and become part of the [ultimate] sphere of values. The values that are accepted become forever engrained in the subject's consciousness, and thus inevitably also a part of the 'waking consciousness'. In this way a conscious store of approved values is compiled.

In the rather complex process of 'mystical purification' value judgements of this kind are instrumental in advancing spiritual growth. "Facing the 'Thou' acting inside, the soul is exposed to the furnace of purgation until it has achieved in her the capacity of loving that is commensurable to the value of the 'Thou'."

If we consider the issue of the types of 'ecstatic experience' that are evoked and can be identified when the 'experiencing I' encounters 'the All-encompassing' perceived as 'Thou', we will see that they are of a very special kind. In fact, all the three types of ecstatic experience distinguished above are involved, when the subject-object split between the 'experiencing I' and 'the all-encompassing perceived as Thou' is suspended. The 'I' "disappears – is immersed – and expires" in the zeal of devotion and surrender; 'the All-encompassing' intrudes upon, inundates and overwhelms the 'experiencing I'. The emotions unleashed in the 'experiencing I' when the 'Thou' [literally "He"] 'arrives' in the vista of 'inner sight' permeate the entire consciousness, thus eroding any content, and culminating in a singular unified emotional state [which is ultimately ineffable]. This overwhelming emotional state is neither composed of 'all-encompassing Calmness', nor 'ineffable bliss' – but a rare state of ardent Love, which is best expressed in the liturgical prayer of the [Roman Catholic] church: "*Accendat in nobis Dominus ignem sui amoris et flammam aeternae caritatis.*" ["Let the Lord kindle in us the fire of His love, and the flame of eternal charity."][184] – (This mystical testimony speaks for itself and requires no further comment.)

The Ninth, Tenth and Eleventh 'Forms of Arriving'

The foregoing analysis of the encounter with 'the All-encompassing perceived as a Persona' and of the long-term impact it has on the perceiver, is indispensable for establishing distinct criteria and tangible features for distinguishing phenomenologically between personal and a-personal varieties of experiencing 'the All-encompassing'. What still has to be examined, however, is the question as to what the prevailing 'forms of arriving' are in such a context, and/or if we have perhaps come across here other 'forms of arriving' as yet unidentified, and yet specifically associated with the experience of 'the All-encompassing as a Persona'. The records quoted above have evidently shown that responding feelings are the most prevalent components in any encounter with 'the All-encompassing'. We have also shown that both the metaphoric and the symbolic 'form of arriving' are often involved in the experience of 'the All-encompassing as a Persona', and thus they are important constituent elements. 'Intuition', by contrast, is a 'form of arriving' that does not feature prominently in this context in the records quoted, and if so, it appears to be rather accidental: The testimonials do not endorse a reading that the personal nature of 'the All-encompassing' is in any way grasped on the basis of some 'intuitive experience'. What can be inferred from these testimonies, however, is that whenever the 'sense of revelation' is evoked by 'the All-encompassing' 'arriving', 'intuition' is involved

---

184 [Cf. Foley, Edward, gen. ed. *A Commentary on the Order of Mass of The Roman Missal.* Collegeville, MN: Liturgical Press, 2011. Ch. "*In spiritu humilitatis*". No page numbers provided. – FW.]

as the predominant 'form of arriving'. On the whole, however, the 'forms of arriving' distinguished so far do not recapture all the varieties of experiencing 'the All-encompassing as a Persona' featuring in the records, and thus in empirical reality. Therefore our investigation has to proceed further, if we wish to identify and describe phenomenologically additional 'forms of arriving'.

To begin with, we may infer from the evidence of the empirical records that a perceiver may be bestowed with a non-visual, non-imaginative and immediate knowledge about the presence of a Persona grasped to be 'all-encompassing'. The awareness of the presence of the ['all-encompassing'] 'Thou', however, occurs hardly ever in a single, separate experience, i.e. an experience that is not intertwined with other 'forms of arriving'. In fact, such an event is not only always accompanied by responding feelings, but also by the simultaneous appearance of symbols in the vista of 'inner sight'. Yet even though there is no supporting evidence in the records examined that there is such a phenomenon, I have no doubts that 'the non-visual awareness of the presence of the All-encompassing perceived as a Persona' does occur in empirical reality and that this experience is also the empirical basis of the metaphoric 'forms of arriving'.

One characteristic feature of the instantaneous awareness of 'the all-encompassing perceived as a Persona' is the 'sense of presence' elicited by it; i.e. the 'experiencing I' has a distinct intuitive awareness of the non-visual presence of a Persona, who is felt to be "there" at a given place and its surroundings, both within and outside the individual consciousness. Thus the Persona [in German the term used is "der Urheber", i.e. 'the Originator'] is felt to dwell in the "room of the heart" without being 'seen'; or alternatively, the 'Originator's' invisible presence is perceived (as described in a record) as if "walking along with me on the right side". In experiences of this kind the non-visual awareness of the presence of the 'All-encompassing' perceived as a Persona is affiliated with a clear sense of location. By this spatial quality the function of 'inner sight' is emphasized even more. This kind of 'seeing inside', i.e. 'seeing' without visual representation, was termed "intellectual vision" by Madame Guyon.[185] However,

---

185 [Note: Albrecht does not give a bibliographical reference, neither here, nor

the "intellectual vision" has to be distinguished terminologically and phenomenologically from both the metaphorical 'form of arriving' perceived by 'inner sight' and the perception of hallucinatory apparitions believed to occur in external space, and which are perceived by the physical eyes. **The non-visual [intellectual] awareness of the presence of the All-encompassing as a Persona is the ninth 'form of arriving'.** This is a special 'form of arriving', and one that is never found when the 'object arriving' is a 'split-off-item' from the unconscious, nor does it occur when the 'object arriving' is a part of the 'self'. A-personal varieties of 'the All-encompassing' never 'arrive' in this particular 'form'. **We have thus been able to verify the existence of a 'form of inner sight' that is exclusively affiliated with the 'arrival' of 'the All-encompassing as a Persona'.**

The tenth 'form of arriving' is the 'auditory form'. Here the 'object' that 'arrives' in consciousness becomes manifest in the form of 'inner hearing'. When this occurs, ideas or words surface acoustically (rather than visually) in consciousness at an instant, seemingly arising 'out of the blue'. It may happen, for instance, that a sequence of harmonious tunes appears suddenly in the realm of inward perception, or that a single verbalized thought 'arrives' in an auditory manner in consciousness. The latter phenomenon has been termed

---

in the 'List of Works Cited'. – This aside, Albrecht erroneously attributes the term "intellectual vision" to Madame Guyon (1648-1717): It was not the French Quietist mystic who coined the term; Madame Guyon merely adopted the concept, following a long-standing Christian tradition, which can be traced to St. Augustine. It was Augustine who, in *De genesi ad literam XII.7*, introduced the concept *visio intellectualis* as part of his tripartite scheme of mystical visions; the other two types of visionary experience in his scheme are the *visio imaginaria* (or *spiritualis*) (i.e. a vision perceived by the 'inward eye'), and the *visio corporalis* (i.e. a vision in corporal likeness seen with the physical eyes; hence an apparition perceived in external space). By *visio intellectualis* Augustine understands the experimental knowledge of God that is entirely non-visual. Augustine's tripartite scheme became a standard model in the history of Christian mysticism. – Cf. Brusati, Celeste, Karl A. Enenkel and Walter S. Melion, eds. *The Authority of the Word. Reflecting on Image and Text in Northern Europe, 1400-1700*. Leiden and Boston: Brill, 2012. 650ff. – FW.]

'interior locutions'[186] ["Einsprachen"] in mystical tradition. Words, or sequences of words, revealed in auditory form [in consciousness], are perceived as an 'inner voice' imparted by 'the All-encompassing'; syntactically these inner 'locutions' are often couched in terms of an imperative, i.e. an express order, or an explicit summons addressed individually to the perceiver.

However, 'interior locutions' are not necessarily linked to the experience 'the All-encompassing as a Persona'; it is possible that the phenomenon of 'inner hearing' is elicited by the unconscious, notably by 'split-off items' of the 'self' that become 'articulate' in a given situation. Yet it is possible to distinguish phenomenologically between 'genuine locutions' originating from beyond the realm of the individual consciousness and bogus auditory experiences elicited by the unconscious. The former can be identified as an acoustic variety of 'inner sight', classified as 'listening to a voice within', which may occur in the hyper-lucid 'quiet state of alertness'; in this mental state the 'experiencing I' is alone fully and unconditionally open to 'receive', thus fully alert to what is about to 'arrive' in the vista of 'inner sight' in an auditory manner; the spoken words are experienced as 'arriving' from an unknown and 'alien' sphere, infused by 'the All-encompassing', and imbued with a sense of revelation.

The eleventh 'form of arriving' is the 'somatic response to the All-encompassing'. When exploring the experiences elicited during the process of 'introversion', we have seen that sensations related to the vital functions are gradually harmonized and finally stilled,

---

186 [Note: The term 'interior locution', corresponding to 'Einsprache' in German, has become a standard concept in Christian spirituality and mystical theology. Anselm Stolz, O.S.B., elaborates on this phenomenon, referring to St. Thomas Aquinas's *De veritate*, q.18 a.3.: "... there is 'an exterior speech by which God addresses us through preachers, and an interior locution in which he speaks to us by interior inspiration ... [However] by His interior inspiration God does not exhibit His essence to be contemplated, but some sign of His essence, namely a spiritual likeness of His wisdom.' To illustrate this point, St. Thomas refers to Psalm 84:4: 'I will hear what the Lord God will speak in me.'" Cf. Stolz, Anselm, O.S.B. *The Doctrine of Spiritual Perfection*. Trans. Aidan Williams, O.S.B. Eugene, OR: Wipf and Stock, 2013. 100. – FW.]

becoming absorbed in the basic mood of inner calm. The psychosomatic abilities of fakirs provide empirical evidence that premeditated dispositions can later be released [in altered states of consciousness], and thus modify significantly the capacities and functions of the body, even to the extent that certain parts of the body acquire object-like characteristics. The fourth 'form of arriving' (considered above) termed 'somatic seizure' triggered by an 'object arriving', corroborates the claim that diverse, paranormal somatic responses can be generated [in the 'experiencing I' while immersed in altered states of consciousness]. The eleventh 'form of arriving' proposed here is in some way related to the 'form of the somatic seizure'. It is, however, a special type of somatic experience, which differs significantly from the 'somatic seizure', in that it is not an isolated, 'split-off' part of the body that is observed as if from outside, but a new 'form of arriving' in which preternatural changes in the body, or in parts of the body, are effected that cannot rationally be explained in any other way than as instant responses to the 'arrival' of 'the All-encompassing'. For example, the recorded experience of a subject, in which he was overwhelmed at an instant by the awareness of a mysterious "wind" 'arriving' in consciousness, and blowing (as it were) right through his body, painfully piercing every cell. Other somatic responses to the 'arrival' of 'the All-encompassing' documented in the records analysed are, for instance, the experience in which the person is suddenly struck by the awareness of being forcefully grabbed by the arm by 'the all-encompassing Persona' [literally 'the Originator'], or the event in which a subject feels to be touched by his feet, or the event in which a person is physically branded by a mysterious seal 'arriving' invisibly and inexplicably [the scar caused on the person's forehead remained to be seen after the event]. These are all instances of preternatural somatic experiences, which caused real somatic changes in the recipient's body, which cannot be attributed to natural causes, and thus cannot but be classified as the impact of an active intervention of 'the all-encompassing Persona', and hence as experiences to be classified phenomenologically by a different category, i.e. the eleventh 'form of arriving'.

Having provided this analysis of eleven 'forms of arriving', we do not claim that this classification is complete or exhaustive. But it has not been our intention here to establish a full taxonomy of the potential 'forms of arriving'; our intention has merely been to demonstrate that it is possible to infer from selected empirical testimonies phenomenological characteristics of several distinct as well as 'composite' 'forms', in which 'the All-encompassing' may become manifest in empirical reality in concrete events witnessed in 'the quiet state of alertness'. It has been our express purpose to elucidate the phenomenon of 'arriving' by identifying distinct categories of 'forms of arriving'. We have to concede, however, that we had to exclude from our analysis the 'forms of arriving' encountered in the context of hallucinatory experiences, even in cases when hallucinatory phenomena appeared in the 'quiet state of alertness'. It is true that apparitions perceived in external space, and the phenomenon of hearing voices within the mind, are sensations that may occur as integral parts of mystical events as well, even when the subject is immersed in the 'quiet state of alertness'. But these are paranormal phenomena which have to be assigned to a borderline zone of human experience, i.e. to the "twilight-zone" between sane and bogus or pathological experience. A mystical state of consciousness, i.e. more accurately, mystical experiences witnessed in the 'quiet state of alertness', by contrast, is a healthy and normal phenomenon of life. Experiences, however, that cannot be unambiguously distinguished from pathological phenomena have, as a matter of principle, been excluded from this psycho-phenomenological investigation.

We may now summarize the findings relating to the 'forms of arriving': The 'arriving' of 'the All-encompassing perceived as a Persona' differs phenomenologically markedly from the experience of 'arriving' of any other variety in which an extra-mental Wholeness becomes manifest. The 'overall form' of 'inner sight' is composed of several individual 'forms', which in empirical reality are usually intertwined. There is, however, one very special 'form of arriving' in which the 'All-encompassing' reveals itself as an [invisible] Persona: This special variety is the 'non-visual awareness of the Presence of "Him"'. – This special 'form' may be experienced individually, but it can also be an integral part of a 'composite' experience of 'the All-encompassing'.

The Path of Preparation and Conversion

The portrayal of a mystic must not be reduced to the description of his/her path towards a higher state of consciousness (notably the 'quiet state of alertness'), nor to the analysis of the experiences he/she has been gratified with. A mystic must rather be assessed in the wider context of the development of his/her entire life. The hierarchy of values is a vital criterion in assessing the stage of a mystic's existence, and this assessment is not measured against the state of consciousness to which he/she has advanced. In general we may state that a mystic is always conscious of the system of values endorsed by him, and this knowledge is in part instilled in him by the (so-called) "basic knowledge" that is generally at the disposal of every human being at any time without having to reflect on it. The system of values is an ordered structure, in which the 'All-encompassing' is esteemed as the supreme value. It is possible that the event of 'conversion', or 'awakening'[187] (either of which may indicate the beginning of the mystical journey), in which 'the All-encompassing' is experienced in a concrete encounter and instantly grasped to be the highest value, does not suffice as an initial impetus by which a complete reassessment of one's hierarchy of values is achieved. However, as the mystic progresses on his/her path, the system of values and the criteria for ranking them become more stable.

The mystic's hierarchy of values and the [moral, religious, social and spiritual] dispositions acquired on his/her way are closely related. Any change in the hierarchy of values has inevitably an impact on the acquired dispositions, which in turn respond to stimuli from the environment. When a mystic is gratified with the event of 'awakening', a new focal point is instilled in him/her for arranging the hierarchy

---

187 Starbuck, Edwin D. *Religionspsychologie. Empirische Entwicklungsstudie Religiösen Bewußtseins*. Trans. Friedrich Beta. 2 vols. Leipzig: Klinkhardt, 1909. [Note: Starbuck's study was first published in the United States in 1899, entitled *The Psychology of Religion. An Empirical Study of the Growth of Religious Consiousness*. London: Scott, and New York: Scribner, 1899. – Starbuck uses the term "awakening", rendered by Albrecht as "Erweckungserlebnis", and the term "conversion", which is equivalent to Albrecht's concept of "Wandlung". – FW.]

of values. And this event inevitably has repercussions on the mystic's general attitude to the world, in particular on the way he/she responds to creation, but also on his/her ability to cope with existence. In other words, the moment of 'awakening' affects the mystic's outlook on life and reality fundamentally. As a result, a radically new orientation in his/her life has occurred, which has long-term after-effects on his/her future, in that he/she is willing to subject his/her life to a long and arduous process of 'un-becoming'[188] ("Entwerdung"). The path of preparation, which is part of this process of 'un-becoming', does not only affect all areas of life determined by the 'waking consciousness', but also areas encompassed by the 'quiet state of alertness'. The path of preparation is, psychologically speaking, a process of restructuring consciousness, which includes the dispositions fostered by the individual at the time. The progress of this process of restructuring the mind depends on the values and their hierarchy sustained by the subject. It is not necessary here to give a detailed account of the many ways in which the path of preparation may be experienced and change the life of a mystic or a seeker who

---

188   [Note: There is no verb in English that exactly corresponds to the German verb "entwerden", and respectively, to the noun "Entwerdung". These terms have been variously translated into English. – In this study the word 'un-becoming' is used for "Entwerdung", which was first employed by Karl Zimmer in his English translation of the works of Rudolf Steiner. Cf., Steiner, Rudolf. "Meister Eckhart." *Mysticism at the Dawn of the Modern Age*. Trans. Karl E. Zimmer. Englewood, N.J.: Rudolf Steiner Publications, 1960. – It should be added that the terms "entwerden", viz. "Entwerdung", were originally coined by the 14th-c. German mystic Meister Eckhart, who follows the teaching and terminology of Pseudo-Dionysius, and thus the tradition of 'negative theology' established by Pseudo-Dionysius. 'Negative theology' advocates the mystagogical teaching that anyone embarking on the contemplative quest must divest him-/herself from all sensual desires and self-will, since the path to perfection requires an arduous process of 'un-becoming', i.e. of annihilating the ego, and the perfect conformity between the will of God and the will of the contemplative. Only when ego and self-will have been entirely extinguished, the seeker has attained the ultimate condition of the spiritual quest: 'perfection', a stage in which he is gratified with the ultimate experience of the Divine in the *unio mystica*. – FW.]

has embarked on the mystical quest, because many of the actions and experiences involved in the path of preparation are familiar and commonly known, e.g. opting for a life of ascetic renunciation, or deciding to lead a virtuous, religious, social life, or entering a life of prayer, or a life dedicated to acts of charity. These are all practical forms of life and ways of living that are not bound to the 'quiet state of alertness', which must be identified when assessing a mystic's spiritual growth, if we wish to distinguish these aspects from the impact an empirical encounter with 'the All-encompassing' in the 'quiet state of alertness' has on the transformation of a mystic's existence.

When we examined the various experiences occurring in the 'quiet state of alertness', we have also tried to refer to distinctive features linked with and indicative of a seeker's path of 'conversion'. When we examined the perception of images that were retrieved meditatively from memory in the 'quiet state of alertness', we came to the conclusion that the 'quiet state of alertness' may cause changes in a subject's behavioural patterns and initiate new developments in his/her life, which become manifest at a later stage, or after the 'quiet state of alertness' has subsided. The changes effected in a person's dispositional attitudes are lasting and often striking. The imaginative ideas, feelings and thoughts that emerge in the vacated, hyper-lucid space of consciousness dwell in it for some time, and thus combine with and result in a new set of experiences. The preceding enquiries into items 'arriving' in consciousness that have been 'split off' from the unconscious have shown that formerly rigid patterns of associations can be changed and rearranged, and have also provided evidence that seemingly forgotten memories and (seemingly) lost abilities of the self can be restored in the 'quiet state of alertness'. Intelligible occurrences that happened earlier in life can be recovered in the vista of 'inner sight' in the lucid 'quiet state of alertness' and perceived precisely in the way they had occurred in the past. The current condition of the self as well as the intuitive anticipation of the future development of the self (which is not accessible to the 'waking consciousness'), become apparent in 'the quiet state of alertness' and remain available hereafter. Value judgements and value-related experiences that have occurred during the 'quiet state of alertness' have a lasting impact on the 'experiencing I', and tend to become more and more influential. Amongst the responses to the 'arrival' of the 'All-encompassing' we have encountered emotions that had unique and highly differentiated qualities, none of which had ever been encountered in the 'waking consciousness'. Pictures and symbols that have vividly been present in the mind have a powerful impact on the subject's future. The analysis of the corpus of rather miscellaneous, albeit authentic testimonials, spoken during the 'quiet state of alertness', has provided a broad and ample empirical foundation for our understanding of the mystically induced process of 'conversion'. The mystic highly esteems this process of 'conversion', because he/she is 're-form-ed' by it spiritually and somatically when he/she is immersed in the state of inner calmness, which is the preferred mental condition for advancing the processes of 'purification'. The mystic insists that he/she is exempt from self-will and self-delusion, and purged from any impulse of lying to him-herself, when absorbed in the 'quiet state of alertness'. In this serene mental state the person concerned is confronted with the mirror of truth, and thus exposed to purgatorial pains. For this reason the impressions and responses evoked by the process of 'purification' cannot be dismissed as delusory, or fabrications of the mystic's fantasy, but need to be acknowledged as real empirical phenomena. During the series of sessions in which the subject concerned was immersed in the 'quiet state of alertness', he had been detached from anything that was 'deficient of value', and had been wholly receptive to the dawning relationship with the ultimate Good. From this account we may infer that everything that appears in consciousness is instantly assessed, and whatever is perceived and assessed as inappropriate is instantly dismissed; on the other hand, whatever is judged to be conducive to personal growth, and able to prepare the perceiver for the 'arrival' of "Him", is instantly approved. Whenever the 'quiet state of alertness' is fully developed, mystical events may occur and be perceived with clarity, because the given condition of consciousness is the clearest and most homogeneous state of consciousness accessible to man. The very special encounter with the 'Thou' [i.e. 'the All-encompassing perceived as a loving Persona that is invisibly present'] elicits a most intense and unique emotional response, which has long-term after-effects on the recipient: It instils in him/

her the persevering and unflagging desire to open up his/her heart and mind in loving compassion to his/her fellow men.

The experiences encountered in the 'quiet state of alertness' are all imbued with high moral and spiritual value and become an integral part of the processes of 'preparation' and 'conversion'. This evidently applies even more to the ultimate mystical experience, in which the subject is overwhelmed by 'the All-encompassing' and transported into the state of ecstasy.[189] The experience of 'conversion' results in the re-arrangement of the hierarchy of values previously held. The ultimate value becomes the focal point of all other experiences. The events evoked during the 'quiet state of alertness' trigger and advance the paths of purification and conversion, and afford visions of the Absolute, the supreme value. The ecstatic feelings evoked by an overwhelming mystical event are so intense that they remain forever engrained in memory.

It is important to state at this point that the domain of ecstatic experience and/or the phenomenological condition of the 'ecstatic consciousness' elude psychological investigation to a large extent.

---

189 [Note: The view that the ultimate mystical experience occurs within the 'ecstatic consciousness' is contentious, and likely to be questioned by scholars in the field of religious studies. Though it is true that in the most Christian and non-Christian theistic traditions, the experience of mystical union (*unio mystica*) is linked to the state of ecstasy, and valued as the most highly treasured and ultimate gift of God, this claim does not apply to all mystics, and obviously not to mystics of monistic traditions. Meister Eckhart and other Christian representatives of 'negative theology' (from Pseudo-Dionysius through the author the *Cloud of Unknowing*, Walter Hilton, Johannes Tauler in the 14th c., through the Quietists and Giovanni B. Scaramelli in the 17th and 18th centuries, to Thomas Merton in the 20th c.), suggest that the ultimate mystical state is only attained beyond or after the state of ecstasy: The perfect and ineffable union with the Godhead is considered by them as a transecstatic experience, because all feelings have been extinguished temporarily in the perceiver, when he/she is 'oned' with the Divine. The ultimate mystical experience, then, is a transecstatic state, experienced beyond the state of mystical rapture. – In (monistic) Buddhist traditions ecstasy is likewise seen as a state of consciousness that must be overcome before the mystic's self can enter the perfectly tranquil and serene 'state of no-consciousness' (*nirvana*). – FW.]

The main reasons for this deficiency are methodological and the perceptual impasse: For when the state of ecstasy reaches its climax, there is inevitably an experiential 'hiatus', i.e. there is inevitably an 'awareness gap' in the 'ecstatic state of consciousness' [when the subject-object split is suspended]. In such a liminal event empirical psychology can only elucidate the structure of consciousness before and after the [climactic] state of ecstasy, but even that only fragmentarily. Empirical psychology can thus never recapture the phenomenological structure of the 'ecstatic consciousness'. Even so it is possible to infer from the vantage point of the 'quiet state of alertness' [i.e. on the basis of the records spoken by subjects when transported into the incipient stage of ecstasy] that the state of mystical ecstasy involves the complete loss of self-awareness [i.e. the loss of any awareness of the perceiver functioning as 'experiencing I']: For example, the sense of being overwhelmed by the 'arrival' of the [loving] 'Thou' evokes an eruption of ardent feelings of love, which transcend anything previously experienced. And the ineffability of the loving bliss aroused by such an experience accounts for the high value the mystic attributes to an ecstatic mystical experience; in fact mystical ecstasy is valued as the most hallowed and ultimate state of being. The culminating event of [ecstatic] 'mystical union' remains forever engrained in memory and has enduring after-effects on the mystic and on his/her future existence.

The aim of this psychological study was to provide a systematic phenomenology of the structure of several states of consciousness, including states of mystical experience. The content of individual mystical experiences has been considered only in so far as the content-related aspects have been considered relevant for outlining the formal features and varieties of mystical experience. The history of mysticism can be traced through thousands of years; it thus provides persuasive evidence that mysticism has been a never-ending, perennial stream that has become manifest in all cultures of humanity. Numerous eminent personalities have been gratified with mystical experiences, which resulted in a life inspired by mystical intuitions and a living relationship to a mystical 'Otherness'. Amongst these individuals were personages of a highly individualistic mould, as well as human beings bestowed with a wealth of religious experiences, which, in their entirety, can never be subjected to, let alone recaptured by, a formal [scientific, psycho-phenomenological] analysis. Every mystic aspires, in his/her own special way, towards a direct encounter with 'the All-encompassing', which to him/her is the highest value in life, and at which all his/her intentions, actions and consciousness are oriented. If we call such a person a 'mystic', we do not mean a person devoting several hours per day to the practice of 'introversion' (or spiritual prayer and other meditational practices), just to become immersed in the 'quiet state of alertness' and thus alert and receptive to intimations of 'the All-encompassing'. We only contend that a mystic is a person who has been gratified with a direct encounter with 'the All-encompassing' while absorbed in the 'quiet state of alertness', and that such an event has (once, or on several occasions) been an experience which has positively transformed his/her existence. It goes without saying, however, that a mystic may consider religious experiences of an entirely different kind more valuable and more beneficial [than the empirical encounter with the 'All-encompassing' in the 'quiet state of alertness']. Thus the desire to die as a martyr, or the wish to live a life devoted to acts of charity, or to times of prayer, are all varieties of religious experience which may be more highly esteemed by a mystic than the [direct mystical encounter with 'the All-encompassing'] 'arriving' in the 'quiet state of alertness'. In empirical reality we may encounter a wide variety of different human beings, who share – irrespective of striking differences in character – a unifying common core, which is why it would be imprudent and improper to impose the same psychological pattern on all of them when assessing their mystical experiences individually. Nothing is more highly treasured by a mystic than the awe-inspiring, overwhelming and life-transforming experience of 'ecstatic union'. For the psychologist, however, the state of ecstasy is a borderline phenomenon since it transgresses the confines of the 'quiet state of alertness' and is thus, methodologically, largely beyond psycho-phenomenological enquiry. The few insights that can be derived from the analysis of the pre-ecstatic condition of the 'quiet state of alertness' when facing 'the All-encompassing' is all that can be said from the perspective of empirical psychology about the nature of the 'ecstatic consciousness'; the domain of the 'ecstatic consciousness' of 'ecstasy' thus largely eludes phenomenological analysis by empirical psychology. One thing, however, is certain: Every discerning mystic knows that mystical ecstasy is a rare, liminal state of consciousness, albeit the one most highly valued, and seen as the ultimate climactic event in his/her life; however, every genuine mystic is also aware, and willing to acknowledge, that the [non-ecstatic mystical] experiences encountered in the 'quiet state of alertness' are indispensable and most significant for advancing spiritual growth. The fact that the 'state of ecstasy' has been acclaimed the ultimate goal and culmination in the life of a mystic, and as a proof that he/she has reached the state of 'perfection', may explain why the ecstatic state is ranked highest in a mystic's hierarchy of values. Hence the 'state of ecstasy' is the highest aspiration of a seeker in (most) mystical traditions. The exceptional status of ecstasy in the life of a mystic has to some extent misled psychologists in their critical assessment of mystical experience in general, and of both 'ecstatic states' and non-ecstatic mystical encounters in particular. This kind of flawed assessment of diverse mystical experiences is the reason why I think that the psychological concept of mysticism must not be developed from, or hinge on ecstatic mystical experience, but must rather be derived from (non-ecstatic) mystical encounters and mystical events that have been recurrent and typical experiences in the lives of mystics. It is only by applying a methodological approach like the one taken in this study that the trite and widespread misconception can be dispelled that mystical experience is equated with a blurred or drowsy state of consciousness, hence as an experience occurring in a mental state of reduced clarity and diminished alertness. The empirical evidence provided in this study has demonstrated persuasively that the very opposite is true: [Genuine] mystical experience occurs prominently, and can most clearly identified as such, in the most lucid, tranquil, most clearly structured and, inwardly, most highly alert state of consciousness available to man. Though it is true that we may encounter in the lives of several mystics also experiences and psychic phenomena that must be classified or diagnosed as spurious and pathological, hence as occurring in a blurred and hypo-lucid mental state, this does not falsify the claim that [the core of genuine] mystical experience is a coherently structured experience, perceived with utmost clarity in the 'vista of inner sight' in a vacated, serene, highly lucid 'quiet state of alertness'. Any attempt to develop the concept of mysticism on the basis of pathological or spurious psychological phenomena must therefore be dismissed as abortive and flawed. Such an attempt would be just as absurd as, for instance, the endeavour to trace to a pathological mental state the phenomena emerging in the consciousness of an artist when absorbed in composing music, or writing poetry. Thus we can seriously approach the personality of a mystic through psychology only on the basis of a sound, scientific concept of mysticism, which is informed by ample, solid and reliable empirical data. Only when these epistemological premises are given are we furnished with the methodological requirements and the criteria that enable us to discern genuine mystical phenomena from pathological and/or spurious [pseudo-mystical] ones. It is only when we are prepared to provide these epistemological preconditions that we give due respect and reverence to the mystics and their experiences; it is only when these requirements are granted as well as heeded that we may dare to subject the lives and experiences of great mystics and saints to psychological enquiry.

The Concept of Mysticism

To begin with we will distinguish between a 'narrow' and a 'broad' concept of mysticism. It is inevitable to introduce this differentiation as we have excluded the domain of ecstatic experience and/or the 'ecstatic consciousness' from our psychological and phenomenological enquiries into the nature of mysticism, and along with it, we have eliminated bogus phenomena featuring in received popular notions of mysticism. Thus the 'narrow' concept of mysticism is based on the strictly scientific and methodological principles of our empirical enquiry. The reasons why we have opted for the 'narrow' definition rather than the 'broad' concept of mysticism in this study are the following:

1. The core of ecstatic experience entails the complete extinction of the 'subject-object split'. This means that the ecstatic consciousness remains inevitably beyond the reach of an introspective

empirical research, since the 'experiencing I' will lose any awareness of him-herself in the process, and thus the capacity to perceive an 'object arriving' in 'inner sight'. It is only the incipient state of ecstasy, in which the 'subject-object split' is not yet fully eroded, that is accessible to a limited extent to psychological analysis. However, even in this case the insights can only be inferred by way of analogy by comparing the budding ecstatic mystical experience to the features inherent in a mystical experience encountered in the 'quiet state of alertness'. This means that the only feasible scientific methodological approach to explore ecstatic mystical experience is by way of comparison with varieties encountered in the 'quiet state of alertness'.

2. The 'broad' or 'extended concept' of mysticism is deficient in coherence and homogeneity, because it is enlarged to include phenomena pertaining to two contiguous states of consciousness: the 'quiet state of alertness' and the 'ecstatic consciousness'. However, if we concede that mysticism does not only embrace the experience of 'the All-encompassing' in the 'quiet state of alertness', but also that of the 'ecstatic consciousness', we are faced with the problem of why religious and/or numinous experiences, which may occur in the 'waking consciousness' as well, are not to be classified as 'mystical', or else, why 'somnambulist states' are excluded from the category of mystical experiences, since somnambulist states may evoke events in which the 'I', fluctuating between different altered mental states, may acquire the quality of 'the All-encompassing'.

In the field of psychological phenomenology only the 'narrow concept' of mysticism can be applied, because it is, from a scientific point of view, the concept that is more precise and more stringent [than the broader concept]. *The 'narrow concept' comprises the primeval mystical phenomenon* [i.e. Ur-phenomenon]. *This concept depends on two necessary conditions:* [the givenness of] *'the All-encompassing' and the 'quiet state of alertness'. We may thus define the 'narrow' concept of mysticism as follows:* **Mysticism is the 'arriving' of an 'All-encompassing' in the 'quiet state of alertness'.**

The 'broad' or 'extended concept' of mysticism has likewise two necessary preconditions, although the second one offers two options: The first condition is that 'the All-encompassing' appears and is perceived in a genuine empirical encounter; the second condition is that the experience occurs in a specifically structured state of consciousness, which can be either the 'quiet state of alertness' or the 'ecstatic consciousness'. *The 'extended concept' of mysticism can thus be formulated: Mysticism is both the experience of an 'All-encompassing' 'arriving' in the 'quiet state of alertness', and the 'ecstatic' experience of an 'All-encompassing'.*

Although the 'quiet state of alertness' in which a mystical experience is occurring, and the mystical state of the 'ecstatic consciousness', can phenomenologically, hence theoretically, be clearly distinguished, we have to concede that in empirical reality the 'state of ecstasy' is often the ultimate state of a mystical experience that has begun in the 'quiet state of alertness'. This may explain why non-ecstatic mystical experiences and ecstatic mystical states are not differentiated in common usage of the term mysticism.

Epilogue

The aim of this study had been to open up a scientific avenue of research to the phenomenon of mysticism; more specifically, the study has tried to develop an innovative empirical approach to mystical consciousness, one that could claim to provide a comprehensive systematic phenomenology of mystical consciousness on the basis of reliable empirical data. Before starting this investigation, only the methodology had been established and reflected on; the results of the practical analysis, however, were gained consecutively, piece by piece, as the empirical investigations continued to progress. Therefore the findings and the final results could only be presented and summarized after the enquiries had ended, i.e. in the third and final part of this study. Now that the results have been provided and the methodological approach explained, the final question that needs to be considered is if the method of describing states of consciousness in strictly psychological-phenomenological terms is at all adequate and appropriate to mysticism.[190]

---

190 Fundamental objections of this kind have been raised by Gerhard Krüger. [Note: Albrecht does not further explain the nature of his dispute with Krüger, nor does he give any bibliographical reference. – Gerhard Krüger (1902-1972) was a German philosopher and convert to Catholicism. He held a chair in philosophy at several German universities, including Münster and Frankfurt/Main, where he succeeded Gadamer in 1952. Cf. Schaeffler, Richard. "Krüger, Gerhard." *Neue Deutsche Biographie*, vol. 13. Berlin: Duncker & Humblot, 1982. 104. Online source: https://www.deutsche-biographie.de/gnd118724703.html#ndbcontent. – Albrecht's daughter Adelheid Haas has supplied the information (e-mail message dated 12 Nov. 2016) that Krüger was a frequent visitor in the home of the Albrecht family; in the late 1940s and early 1950s Albrecht often hosted philosophical debates in his home, in which Krüger and other eminent scholars were invited as speakers. – FW.]

Psychological phenomenology can of course not explore the entire phenomenon of mysticism, but may only investigate the [limited] domain of mystical experience that is accessible to an approach through introspective empirical psychology. When engaging in empirical research in the field of mysticism, we are, moreover, inevitably faced with the dilemma between, on the one hand, the researcher's endeavour to capture as much of the phenomenological structure of as many varieties of mystical experience as possible, and, on the other hand, the demand for scientific coherence, clarity as well as precision in defining concepts and phenomena, and the need to corroborate the data empirically, and to arrange them systematically. The discrepancy between these requirements inevitably calls for limitation and differentiation. This predicament becomes apparent in this book whenever the perspective is shifted to the mystic's way of thinking. The thinking of a mystic is informed and governed by ethical and metaphysical categories. To a mystic, any psychological method that is guided by scientific principles rather than an established hierarchy of values, and which is, over and beyond this, confined to the area of the psychology of consciousness, will surely be inadequate or even inappropriate, not least because his/her entire existence is firmly rooted in the framework of cherished values. We have to admit that our study is open to such criticism. We frankly wish to acknowledge the problematic issues of our investigation, in the following apologetic considerations:

1. The [mystical and non-mystical] experiences reported in the subjects' testimonials, which were examined in our enquiry, can be claimed to have occurred in the clear, homogeneous and 'quiet state of alertness'. The records include a wide variety of diverse [mystical and non-mystical] experiences, such as narratives of improved performance, accounts in which 'split-off' items of the unconscious are described, as well as experiences of self-transformation and spiritual growth, and testimonies of mystical encounters, in which 'the All-encompassing' is perceived as a Persona or as a numinous 'wholeness' experienced in entirely a-personal terms. This array of experiences is, seen from the perspective of the mystic, a rather diverse and confusing compilation of often incongruous phenomena. The 'quiet state of alertness' is a purely formal concept of consciousness, in which

several other states of consciousness are contained; the stages encompassed by the process of 'introversion', and the consciousness of the 'quiet state of alertness' have been empirically explored, and its phenomenological features been systematically arranged and classified psychologically. However, because of the constraints imposed by the strictly psychological conception of the 'quiet state of alertness', it was imperative to exclude any potentially mystical phenomenon that might emerge in consciousness from the category of mystical phenomena, unless it became manifest in the hyper-lucid, emptied and 'quiet state of alertness'. Thus mystical experiences which occurred in a mental condition outside the 'quiet state of alertness', for instance, during spiritual prayer, were not included. Moreover, records describing experiences of 'the All-encompassing' that have the hallmarks of a genuine mystical phenomenon are placed side by side in this study with descriptions of encounters with such non-mystical phenomena as 'improved proficiency performance', or with phenomena identified as 'split-off' items of the unconscious, and phenomena surfacing from the unconscious 'mechanically'. Over and beyond this, the methodology applied in generating the process of 'introversion' and advancing the 'quiet state of alertness' might (at first glance) be misunderstood and erroneously be seen as a mind-transforming technique akin to hypnosis, which it is definitely not. Another shortcoming of our enquiry has been that we have not elaborated clearly enough criteria for distinguishing between a religious state of consciousness and psychotherapeutic mental conditions. This aspect has not sufficiently clearly been brought into focus. Though it is possible to attribute religious notions and experiences such as sin/guilt, purgatory, or the path of preparation to both experiences of 'split-off' items of the unconscious and to genuine mystical experiences – (I have indeed gathered a series of records spoken by subjects during the 'quiet state of alertness' in which such a development is documented) – it goes without saying that the distance between the phenomenon of 'improved proficiency performance' and the experience of an 'All-encompassing' 'arriving' in the vista of 'inner sight' is too big to be bridged by accounting for all these phenomena in a study of this kind. And, obviously, in a scientific study the categories of empirical psychology cannot be reconciled let alone identified with the metaphysical, religious and ethical categories addressed in the records examined.

2. Our methodological approach relies, amongst other received notions, on the concept of the 'subject-object split'. For this reason mysticism was explored from this particular premise and perspective, meaning that only mystical experiences in which the 'subject-object split' is maintained could be examined. We have already addressed the different views held in this study relating to the high value that some mystics attribute to the experience of 'mystical union' and the assessment of this liminal ecstatic state in mystical traditions. The mystic demands that the phenomenon of mysticism must be explored (if at all) by a method that does not rely on the notion of the 'emancipation of human consciousness', nor on the isolation of the 'I', nor on a method that is focused more on the formal structure of consciousness than on its 'content'. The mystic, in other words, calls for a methodology in which the 'mystical object' has come into view before assessing and dealing with the impact and after-effects caused by it. This critical objection results from the fundamental philosophical question, if it is possible in empirical reality for a subject to vacate the mind so radically from any content that nothing but the formal framework of an empty, hyper-lucid 'quiet and alert state' of consciousness remains. Yet it is imperative for methodological reasons to maintain the strict dichotomy between the formal structure of consciousness and its content. The dichotomy between form and content is, in other words, the result of the methodological stricture not to transgress the confines of the psychology of consciousness at any stage of this empirical investigation. From a philosophical point of view, however, our method, and the way it has been applied, is likely to provoke criticism, particularly as it is admittedly impaired by the following *aporias*: The mind-body problem; the impossibility of sustaining a clear-cut distinction between understanding and explaining; and the problem of how to assess the influence of the unconscious on consciousness at large. But as the explicit focus of this empirical investigation has been on the psychological analysis of phenomena of consciousness, some important questions have been considered that go beyond this study's scope, or not been treated exhaustively: For instance, the question if or why the confirmed somatic changes can

be claimed to be after-effects of experiences occurring in the 'quiet state of alertness'; moreover, the question as to whether these somatic changes are significant enough to be assessed as effects triggered by the 'quiet state of alertness', or if they are to be attributed to a special state within other mental states, notably the 'waking consciousness' or the 'dream consciousness'.

3. The scientific method chosen in this enquiry has inalienably had consequences on its results, not least because certain phenomena of a particular state of consciousness have been given more attention over other phenomena and mental states. This shortcoming is evident and has posed the following problem: In order to be able to elucidate phenomenologically the empirical structure of the 'quiet state of alertness', we do require a psycho-phenomenological description of the consciousness of 'introversion', and juxtaposed to it, of the 'waking consciousness'. In doing so, the focus of the enquiry is shifted from the phenomena elicited by the process of 'introversion' to the characteristics of the mental practice itself. It is possible that there are periods in the life of a mystic in which he/she will learn how to practice a [particular] method of meditation viz. 'method of introversion', but more often the practice of 'introversion' (viz. 'meditation') is an integral part of an ongoing [spiritual] development. Such a development can be inferred from, or equated with, the stages of 'purification' and 'preparation' that the seeker has passed through on the mystical path. Moreover, the 'mystical state of quiet alertness' develops (usually) gradually from the 'waking consciousness', after shifting to the 'quiet state of alertness'. Vocal prayer may change over to meditational prayer, which again may be replaced by the 'state of contemplation', which is already a 'mystical state of quiet alertness'. The stages of consciousness passed through by path of *'mystical introversion'* may include items of 'content', which we have not come across in our records and in our phenomenological enquiry. For example, there are disruptions a mystic or seeker may be faced with in the process of 'introversion' that are assumed to be the result of a flawed process of 'emptying' the mind, but the failure to silence the active functions of the 'I' can also be seen as a means imposed by God for the purpose of purifying the ego or advancing the seeker's humility in order to become worthy of the special gift of

grace, and thus for the encounter with the [Divine] 'Thou'. That is to say, there are admittedly several ways in which the transfer from the 'waking consciousness' to the 'quiet state of alertness' may be achieved by individual practitioners, which have not been considered in our conception of 'introversion'.

These apologetic remarks can answer only some, though not all the critical objections to our research method and its findings. In particular, the pivotal question as to whether the phenomenon of mysticism can be appropriately investigated by an approach through the science of psychology will remain open to critical controversy. The method of psychological phenomenology can, admittedly, offer access only to a limited and fragmented range of phenomena germane to mystical experience, but it cannot recapture the entire phenomenon, and thus the approach taken can be claimed to be only adequate to a limited extent. In retrospect, we have to admit that several of the critical objections that are likely to be raised are justified: The mystical experience, esteemed most highly in Western mystical tradition and termed 'mystical union' (*unio mystica*), has not been the focus of our enquiry, but was deliberately and for methodological reasons removed to the periphery. – The process of 'introversion' has been outlined mainly by reference to the topic of its advance determination, i.e. the role of 'predetermined dispositions' generated in the preceding 'waking consciousness'. – The considerations relating to the process of 'introversion' have been unduly overemphasized. – The multifarious 'objects' that may 'arrive' in and supply the 'content' of the 'quiet state of alertness' have not been explored in the wider context of their 'inner coherence', but have merely been examined in view of their *formal* characteristics. – Finally, there is the critical objection that the phenomena relating to the framework of the 'quiet state of alertness' have been considered only in juxtaposition to the 'waking consciousness'. Thus the main focus has been on the description of 'introversion', understood as a process that is governed by the will, at the expense of autonomous, self-determined, or free-floating processes of consciousness. It is true that we may find the latter in the 'waking consciousness' as well, and that free-floating processes can also be an integral part of acts of the 'I'.

Although I have been clearly aware of these deficiencies and controversial issues when embarking on this investigation, I have nevertheless decided to employ the method of psychological phenomenology for exploring the phenomenon of mysticism throughout in this study. Making a choice was indispensable, not least because the disciplines of modern science have split up into many different fields and sub-disciplines, which rely on rather divergent [epistemological] premises and often incongruous principles. Hence choosing a particular method from a single scientific discipline was imperative right from the beginning of this enquiry. From amongst the various methodological options available for the purposes of this empirical investigation, the method of psychological phenomenology appeared to be the one best suited for achieving the intended goal of providing a comprehensive, systematic phenomenology of mysticism on the basis of empirical data. As mysticism has become a rather fuzzy and distorted term today in common parlance, it is particularly pertinent to define the concept clearly and persuasively. Therefore it has been my endeavour to elucidate the phenomenon by showing that the 'mystical state of quiet alertness' is a real empirical mental state, one that is perfectly sane and based on an experience of highest clarity. Moreover, the concept of 'inner sight' and the fundamental difference between an 'object arriving' from within the 'sphere of the self', and an 'object arriving' from beyond the 'sphere of the self' perceived as 'All-encompassing', had to be evolved in detail in order to provide a [tangible scientific] foundation of the nature of mysticism, and a basis for future philosophical considerations, whether epistemological, metaphysical or both.

BIBLIOGRAPHY

1. PRIMARY WORKS

ALBRECHT, Carl. *Das Mystische Erkennen. Gnoseologie und Philosophische Relevanz der Mystischen Relation.* 1958. Bremen: Grünewald, 1982.

ALBRECHT, Carl. *Das Mystische Wort. Erleben und Sprechen in Versunkenheit.* Ed. Hans A. Fischer-Barnicol. Preface by Karl Rahner. Mainz: Grünewald, 1974. (Reprinted 1986).

ALBRECHT, Carl. *Psychologie des Mystischen Bewußtseins.* 1951. Bremen: Grünewald, 1976. (2nd rpt. 1990). (Henceforth abbreviated *PMB*).

2. WORKS CITED by ALBRECHT

(Books and Articles listed in the "Literaturverzeichnis" [i.e. Works Cited] in *PMB*)

ACH, Narziss. "Über den Begriff des Unbewußten in der Psychologie der Gegenwart." *Zeitschrift für Psychologie* 129 (1933): 223-245.

ACH, Narziss. *Analyse des Willens.* Berlin: Urban & Schwarzenberg, 1935.

BENDER, Hans. "Zum Problem der Außersinnlichen Wahrnehmung. Ein Beitrag zur Unter-suchung des 'räumlichen Hellsehens' mit Laboratoriumsmethoden." *Zeitschrift für Psychologie* 135 (1935): 20-130.

BERGSON, Henri. *Denken und Schöpferisches Werden.* Meisenheim am Glan: Westkulturverlag, 1948.

BINSWANGER, Ludwig. *Ausgewählte Vorträge und Aufsätze.* 2 vols. Bern: Francke, 1947.

BÖHME, Jakob. *Schriften.* Leipzig: Insel-Verlag, 1923.

BRENTANO, Franz. *Untersuchungen zur Sinnespsychologie.* Leipzig: Duncker & Humblot, 1907.

BUBER, Martin. *Ekstatische Konfessionen.* 1909. Leipzig: Insel, 1923.

DAVID-NEEL, Alexandra. *Heilige und Hexer. Glaube und Aberglaube im Lande d. Lamaismus / Nacheigenen Erlebnissen dargestellt von Alexandra David-Neel.* [Aus d. Franz. v. Ada Ditzen]. Leipzig: Brockhaus, 1931.

ECKHART, Meister. *Schriften und Predigten.* Ed. H. Büttner. 2 vols. Jena: Diederichs, 1917.

EILKS, Hans. "Das Vorgestalterlebnis unter Typologischem Gesichtspunkt." *Zeitschrift für Psychologie* 143 (1938): 19-79.

ELSENHANS, Theodor. *Lehrbuch der Psychologie*. 1912. 3rd ed. Tübingen: Mohr, 1939.

GIRGENSOHN, Karl. *Der Seelische Aufbau des Religiösen Lebens: Eine Religionspsychologische Unter-suchung auf Experimenteller Grundlage*. Leipzig: Hirzel, 1921.

GRUEHN, Werner. *Das Werterlebnis*. Leipzig: Hirzel, 1924.

GRUHLE, Hans W. *Verstehende Psychologie (Erlebnislehre). Ein Lehrbuch*. Stuttgart: Thieme, 1948.

HARTMANN, Nicolai. *Grundzüge einer Metaphysik der Erkenntnis*. 2nd ed. Berlin: de Gruyter, 1925.

HARTMANN, Nicolai. *Philosophie der Natur: Abriss der Speziellen Kategorienlehre*. Berlin: de Gruyter, 1950.

HAERING, Theodor. *Untersuchungen zur Psychologie der Wertung (auf Experimenteller Grundlage) Mit Besonderer Berücksichtigung der Methodologischen Fragen*. Leipzig: Engelmann, 1920.

HAUER, Jakob W. *Der Joga als Heilsweg. Nach Indischen Quellen Dargestellt*. Stuttgart: Kholhammer, 1932.

HECK, Philip. *Begriffsbildung und Interessenjurisprudenz*. Tubingen: J.C.B. Mohr, 1939.

HEIDEGGER, Martin. *Sein und Zeit*. 1927. 2nd ed. Halle: Niemeyer, 1929.

HEILER, Friedrich. *Die Buddhistische Versenkung*. 1918. Munich: Reinhardt, 1922.

HEYER, Gustav R. *Der Organismus der Seele: Eine Einführung in die Analytische Seelenheilkunde*. Munich: Lehmanns, 1932.

HUMBOLDT, Wilhelm Freiherr von. *Über die Kawi-Sprache auf der Insel Java, Nebst einer Einleitung über die Verschiedenheit des Menschlichen Sprachbaues und Ihren Einfluss auf die Geistige Entwicklung des Menschengeschlechts*. Vol. 1. Berlin: Königliche Akademie der Wissenschaften, 1836.

JAENSCH, Erich R. *Über den Aufbau der Wahrnehmungswelt*. Leipzig: Barth, 1923.

JAENSCH, Erich R., and H. RUPPERT. *Über den Aufbau des Bewußtseins*. Leipzig: Barth, 1930/31.

JASPERS, Karl. *Allgemeine Psychopathologie. Ein Leitfaden für Studierende, Ärzte und Psychologen*. 1913. 5th ed. Berlin and Heidelberg: Springer, 1948.

JASPERS, Karl. *Psychologie der Weltanschauungen*. 1919. 3rd ed. Berlin: Springer, 1925.

[Note: in *PMB* the reference is to the 2nd ed. which seems to be an error – since the 2nd ed. was published in 1922 – only the 3rd ed. was published in 1925.

See http://www.jaspers-stiftung.ch/fileadmin/media/pdf/jaspers-primaerbibliographie-neuauflage-2014-final-mit-titelei-140218.pdf]

JASPERS, Karl. *Vernunft und Existenz: Five Lectures.* Bremen: Storm, 1947.

JUNG, Carl Gustav. *Psychologische Typen.* Zurich: Rascher, 1925.

JUNG, Carl Gustav. *Über die Psychologie des Unbewußten.* 6th ed. Zurich: Rascher, 1948.

JUNG, Carl Gustav. *Wandlungen und Symbole der Libido.* 3rd ed. Leipzig and Vienna: Deuticke, 1938.

KIERKEGAARD, Søren. *Der Begriff Angst.* 1844. Jena: Diederichs, 1923.

KLAGES, Ludwig. *Der Geist als Widersacher der Seele.* 4 vols. Leipzig: Johann A. Barth, 1929-1932.

KRETSCHMER, Ernst. *Medizinische Psychologie.* 9th ed. Stuttgart: Thieme, 1947.

KRUEGER, Felix. *Der Begriff des Absolut Wertvollen als Grundbegriff der Moralphilosophie.* Leipzig: Teubner, 1898.

KRUEGER, Felix. *Das Wesen der Gefühle: Entwurf einer Systematischen Theorie.* Leipzig: Akademische Verlagsgesellschaft, 1930.

KRUEGER, Felix. *Die Tiefendimension und die Gegensätzlichkeit des Gefühlslebens.* Munich: Beck, 1931.

LERSCH, Philipp. *Der Aufbau des Charakters.* 3rd ed. Leipzig: Barth, 1948.

LIEBRUCKS, Bruno. "Über das Wesen der Sprache. Vorbereitende Betrachtungen." *Zeitschrift für Philosophische Forschung* 5.4 (1950): 465-484.
[The bibliographical reference in *PMB* does not specify the source as given above, but refers to the paper read by Liebrucks at the Third Congress of German Philosophy in Bremen in 1950. – FW.]

McDOUGALL, William. *Aufbaukräfte der Seele. Grundriß einer Dynamischen Psychologie.* Trans. Fr. Becker and H. Bender. Leipzig: Thieme, 1937.

MEINERTZ, Josef. *Moderne Seinsprobleme in Ihrer Bedeutung für die Psychologie.* Heidelberg: Schneider, 1948.

MESSER, August. *Psychologie.* 1911. 5th ed. Leipzig: Meiner, 1934.

MESSER, August. "Zur Wertpsychologie." *Archiv für die Gesamte Psychologie* 34 (1915): 157-188.

MOSER, Fanny. *Der Okkultismus.* 2 vols. Munich: Reinhardt, 1935.

OTTO, Rudolf. *Das Heilige. Über das Irrationale in der Idee des Göttlichen und sein Verhältnis zum Rationalen.* 1917. 5th ed. Breslau: Trewendt & Graniers, 1921.

PLOTINUS. *Die Enneaden des Plotin.* Trans. Hermann F. Müller. Berlin: Weidmannsche Buchhandlung, 1878.

POLLAK, Franz. "Die Stellung des Vegetativen Nervensystems im Psychocerebralen Bauplan." *Zeitschrift für die Gesamte Neurologie und Psychiatrie* 137 (1931): 339-353.

ROHRACHER, Hubert. *Einführung in die Psychologie.* 3rd ed. Vienna: Urban & Schwarzenberg, 1948.

ROTHACKER, Erich. *Die Schichten der Persönlichkeit.* 4th ed. Bonn: Bouvier, 1948.

SAUERBRUCH, Ferdinand, and Hans WENKE. *Wesen und Bedeutung des Schmerzes.* Berlin: Junke & Dunnhaupt, 1936.

SCHILDER, Paul, and Otto KAUDERS. *Lehrbuch der Hypnose.* Vienna: Springer, 1936.

SCHULTZ, I. H. *Das Autogene Training. Versuch einer Klinisch-Praktischen Darstellung.* Leipzig: Thieme, 1932.

STARBUCK, Edwin Diller. *Religionspsychologie. Empirische Entwicklungsstudie Religiösen Bewußtseins.* Trans. Friedrich Beta. 2 vols. Leipzig: Klinkhardt, 1909.

STERN, Erich. "Beiträge zur Psychologie der Wertungen." Diss. Strassburg, 1917.

STÖRRING, Gustav E. *Über Grundfragen der Medizinischen Psychologie.* Düsseldorf: Renaissance-Verlag, 1948.

STROHAL, Richard. "Untersuchungen zur Deskriptiven Psychologie der Einstellung." *Zeitschrift für Psychologie* 130 (1933): 1-27.

STRUNZ, Kurt. "Über die 'Vertikale' Ordnung der Seelischen Dispositionen. Ein Beitrag zur Psychologischen Schichttheorie." *Zeitschrift für Psychologie* 154 (1943): 103-202.

TAULER, Johannes. *Predigten.* Transl. and Introd. Leopold Naumann. Leipzig: Insel, 1923.

THOMAE, Hans. *Bewußtsein und Leben: Versuch einer Systematisierung des Bewußtseinsproblems.* Bonn. Phil. Diss. Leipzig: Akad. Verlagsgesellschaft, 1940. (Archiv f. d. ges. Psychologie, 105).

TRÖMNER, Ernst. "Steigerung der Leistungsfähigkeit im Hypnotischen Zustand." *Journal für Psychologie und Neurologie* 20.2 (1913): 181-184.

VOLKELT, Johannes. *Versuch über Fühlen und Wollen.* Munich: Beck, 1930.

WALTHER, Gerda. *Zur Phänomenologie der Mystik.* Halle a. S.: Niemeyer, 1923.

WINTERSTEIN, Alfred Freiherr von. *Telepathie und Hellsehen im Lichte der Modernen Forschung und Wissenschaftlichen Kritik.* Leipzig: Leo, 1937.

3. WORKS CITED IN THE PREFACES, THE GENERAL INTRODUCTION AND ANNOTATIONS

ALPER, Matthew. *The 'God' Part of the Brain: A Scientific Interpretation of Human Spirituality & God.* 1996. New York: Rogue, 2009.

ANDRESEN, Jensine, ed. *Religion in Mind: Cognitive Perspectives in Religious Belief, Ritual, Experience.* Cambridge: Cambridge UP, 2000.

AUSTIN, James H. *Selfless Insight: Zen and the Meditative Transformations of Consciousness.* Cambridge, MA: MIT Press, 2011.

BAATZ, Ursula. Hugo *Makibi Enomiya-Lassalle. Mittler Zwischen Buddhismus und Christentum.* Ratisbon: Topos Plus, 2017. (e-book)

BECKER, D. and Dean SHAPIRO. "Physiological Responses to Clicks During Zen, Yoga and TM Meditation." *Psychophysiology* 18 (1981): 694-99.

BEHN, Irene. *Spanische Mystik. Darstellung und Deutung.* Düsseldorf: Patmos, 1957.

BENSON, H., M. S. MALHOTRA, et al. "Three Case Reports of the Metabolic and Electro-encephalographic Changes During Advanced Buddhist Meditation Techniques." *Behavioral Medicine* 16 (1990): 90–95.

BLOCK, Ned, Owen FLANAGAN, and Güven GÜZELDERE, eds. *The Nature of Consciousness. Philosophical Debates.* Cambridge, MA: MIT Press, 1997.

BOCK, Eleonore. *Die Mystik in den Religionen der Welt.* 1991. Münster: Principal, 2009.

BÖHME, Wolfgang, and Josef SUDBRACK, eds. *Der Christ von Morgen – Ein Mystiker?* Würzburg: Echter, 1989.

BORCHERT, Bruno. *Mysticism: Its History and Challenge.* York Beach, ME: Weiser, 1994.

BRUSATI, Celeste, Karl A. ENENEKEL and Walter S. MELION, eds. *The Authority of the Word. Reflecting on Image and Text in Northern Europe, 1400-1700.* Leiden and Boston: Brill, 2012.

BRUZINA, Ronald. *Edmund Husserl and Eugen Fink: Beginnings and Ends in Phenomenology 1928-1938.* New Haven: Yale UP, 2004. (Yale Studies in Hermeneutics).

BUBER, Martin. *Ich und Du.* Leipzig: Insel, 1923.

BUBER, Martin. *I and Thou.* 1923. Trans. Ronald G. Smith. Edinburgh: Clark, 1937.

BUCKE, Richard M. *Cosmic Consciousness: A Study in the Evolution of the Human Mind.* Philadelphia, PA: Innes, 1905.

BULYGIN, Eugenio. *Essays in Legal Philosophy*. Ed. Carlos Bernal et al. Oxford: OUP, 2015.

CARMODY, Denise L., and John Tully CARMODY. *Mysticism: Holiness East and West*. New York: Oxford UP, 1996.

CONZE, Edward. *Buddhism: Its Essence and Development*. New York: Harper, 1959.

CONZE, Edward. *Buddhist Meditation*. London: Unwin, 1972.

DAWKINS, Richard. *The God Delusion*. London: Bantam, 2006.

DEIKMAN, Arthur. "De-automatization and the Mystic Experience." *Psychiatry* 29 (1966): 329-343.

DINZELBACHER, Peter. *Christliche Mystik im Abendland*. Paderborn: Schöningh, 1994.

DOOLEY, Christopher. "The Impact of Meditative Practices on Physiology and Neurology: A Review of the Literature." *Scientia Discipulorum* (SUNY Plattsburgh) 4 (2009): 35-59.

EGAN, Harvey, S.J. *Christian Mysticism: The Future of a Tradition*. New York: Pueblo, 1984.

ENOMIYA-LASSALLE, Hugo, S.J. *Der Versenkungsweg. Zen-Meditation und Christliche Mystik*. Munich: Herder, 1999.

ENOMIYA-LASSALLE, Hugo, S.J. *Meditation als Weg zur Gotteserfahrung. Eine Anleitung zum Mystischen Gebet*. Mainz: Grünewald, 1972.

FISCHER, Roland. "A Cartography of the Ecstatic and Meditative States." Ed. Woods, Richard. *Understanding Mysticism*. London: Athlone, 1981. 286-305.

FISCHER, Roland. "State-Bound Knowledge: 'I Can't Remember What I Said Last Night, but It Must Have Been Good.'" Ed. Woods, Richard. *Understanding Mysticism*. London: Athlone, 1981. 306-311.

FOLEY, Edward, gen. ed. *A Commentary on the Order of Mass of The Roman Missal*. Collegeville, MN: Liturgical Press, 2011.

FORMAN, Robert K. C. *Mysticism. Mind. Consciousness*. Albany, NY: State U of New York P, 2004.

GALLAHER, Shaun. *How the Body Shapes the Mind*. Oxford: Clarendon, 2006.

GRANQVISTA, Pehr, et al. "Sensed Presence and Mystical Experiences Are Predicted by Suggestibility, Not by the Application of Transcranial Weak Complex Magnetic Fields." *Neuroscience Letters* 379 (2005): 1-6.

HALIK, Tomas. "Religion und der Geistlich Suchende Mensch." GRUEN, Anselm, Tomas HALIK, and Winfried NONHOFFF. *Gott Los Werden? Wenn Glaube und Unglaube Sich Umarmen*. Münster-schwarzach: Vier-Türme-Verlag, 2016. 93–106.

HALIK, Tomáš and Winfried NONHOFF. *Gott Los Werden? Wenn Glaube und Unglaube Sich Umarmen.* Münsterschwarzach: Vier-Türme-Verlag, 2016. 93-106.

HAMER, Dean. *The God Gene: How Faith Is Hardwired into Our Genes.* New York: Anchor, 2010.

HARDY, Sir Alister. *The Spiritual Nature of Man: A Study of Contemporary Religious Experience.* Oxford: Oxford UP, 1978.

HEAD, Henry, and G. M. HOLMES. "Sensory Disturbances from Cerebral Lesions." *Brain* 34 (1911): 102-254.

HEIDEGGER, Martin. *Holzwege. Gesamtausgabe*, vol. 5. Frankfurt a. M.: Kolstermann, 1950.

HILTON, Walter. *The Scale of Perfection.* Ed. and trans. John P. H. Clark and Rosemary Dorward. New York: Paulist, 1991.

JAMES, William. *The Varieties of Religious Experience.* London: Longmans, 1902.

JOHNSTON, William. *The Inner Eye of Love: Mysticism and Religion.* London: Collins, 1974.

KATZ, Steven T. "Language, Epistemology and Mysticism." *Mysticism and Philosophical Analysis.* Ed. Steven T. Katz. London: Oxford UP, 1978. 22-74.

KIMMEL, Monica. *Interpreting Mysticism: An Evaluation of Steven T. Katz's Argument Against a Common Core in Mysticism and Mystical Experience.* Saarbrücken: VDM, 2010.

KROIS, John M. *Bildkörper und Körperschema: Schriften zur Verkörperungstheorie Ikonischer Formen.* Ed. Horst Bredekamp and Marion Lauschke. Berlin: Akademie Verlag, 2011.

LANCASTER, Brian. *Approaches to Consciousness: The Marriage of Science and Mysticism.* Basingstoke: Palgrave, 2004.

LEUBA, James H. *The Psychology of Religious Mysticism.* New York: Harcourt, 1925.

MAHESH, Mehta. "Ineffability Reconsidered." Ed. Coward, Harold. *'Language' in Indian Philosophy and Religion.* Calgary: Calgary UP, 1976. 63-82.

McGINN, Bernard. *The Foundations of Mysticism.* Vol. 1, *The Presence of God: A History of Western Christian Mysticism.* London: SCM Press, 1992.

McGINN, Bernard. "Mystical Consciousness: A Modest Proposal." *Spiritus: A Journal of Christian Spirituality* 8 (2008): 44-63.

MILLER, Lisa, ed. *The Oxford Handbook of Psychology and Spirituality.* New York: OUP, 2012.

MINNIS, Alastair J. *Medieval Theory of Authorship: Scholastic Literary Attitudes in the Later Middle Ages.* 2nd ed. Aldershot: Gower, 1984.

MOHR, Arno. *Sozialwissenschaftliches Wörterbuch: English-Deutsch, Deutsch-English*. Oldenbourg: de Gruyter, 2001.

NELSON, Kevin. *The God Impulse: Is Religion Hardwired into the Brain?* London: Simon & Schuster, 2011.

NEWBERG, Andrew, Eugene D'AQUILI and Vince RAUSE. *Why God Won't Go Away*. New York: Ballantine, 2002.

NEWBERG, Andrew. "Transformation of Brain Structure and Spiritual Experience." *The Oxford Handbook of Psychology and Spirituality*. Ed. Lisa Miller. New York: OUP, 2012. 489-499.

NEWBERG, Andrew, and Mark Robert WALDMAN. *How God Changes Your Brain: Breakthrough Findings from a Leading Neuroscientist*. New York: Ballantine, 2010.

ORNSTEIN, Robert. *The Psychology of Consciousness*. New York: Freeman, 1973.

OTTO, Rudolf. *Das Heilige. Über das Irrationale in der Idee des Göttlichen und Sein Verhältnis zum Rationalen*. Breslau: Trewendt, 1921.

PALOUTZIAN, Raymond F., and Crystal L. PARK, eds. *Handbook of the Psychology of Religion and Spirituality*. 2nd ed. New York: Guilford Press, 2015.

PAULSON, Steve. *Atoms & Eden: Conversations on Religion & Science*. New York: Oxford UP, 2011.

PENG-KELLER, Simon. *Gottespassion in Versunkenheit. Die Psychologische Mystikforschung Carl Albrechts aus Theologischer Perspektive*. Würzburg: Echter, 2003. (Studien zur Systematischen und Spirituellen Theologie, 39.)

PENG-KELLER, Simon. "Präsenzschau in Versunkenheit und Ekstase. Carl Albrechts Phänomenologie der Mystik." *Zeitschrift für Missionswissenschaft und Religionswissenschaft* (Freiburg) 90 (2006): 90-102.

RAHNER, Karl. "Frömmigkeit Früher und Heute." *Schriften zur Theologie VII*. Einsiedeln: Benziger, 1966. 11-31.

RAHNER, Karl. "Mystik – Weg des Glaubens zu Gott." *Horizonte der Religiosität. Kleine Aufsätze*. Ed. Georg Sporschill. Vienna: Herold, 1984. 11-24.

RAHNER, Karl. "Vorwort." ALBRECHT, Carl. *Das Mystische Wort. Erleben und Sprechen in Versunkenheit*. Ed. and Notes by Hans A. Fischer-Barnicol. Mainz: Grünewald, 1976. vii-xiv.

RAHNER, Karl. "Transzendenzerfahrung aus Katholisch-Dogmatischer Sicht." *Schriften zur Theologie XIII*. Zurich: Benziger, 1978. 207-225.

RAUB, James A. "Psychophysiologic Effects of Hatha Yoga on Musculoskeletal and Cardiopulmonary Function: A Literature Review." *Journal of Alternative and Complementary Medicine* (New York) 8 (2002): 797-812.

ROHR, Richard. *The Naked Now. Learning to See as the Mystics See.* New York: Crossroad, 2009.

RUH, Kurt. *Meister Eckhart. Theologe, Prediger, Mystiker.* 2nd ed. Munich: Beck, 1989.

SAKAGUCHI, Alicja. *Sprechakte der Mystischen Erfahrung: Eine Komparative Studie zum Sprachlichen Ausdruck von Offenbarung und Prophetie.* Freiburg i. Br.: Alber, 2015.

SAGAN, Samuel. *Awakening the Third Eye.* 3rd ed. Roseville, N.S.W.: Clairvision, 2007.

SCARAMELLI, Giovanni B., S.J. *Il Direttorio Mistico.* 1756. Trans. Wilhelm Schamoni. *Anleitung in der Mystischen Theologie.* 1855-56. 2 vols. Hildesheim: Olms, 1972.

SCHILPP, Paul Arthur. *The Philosophy of Karl Jaspers.* New York: Tudor, 1957.

SHELDRAKE, Philip, ed. *The New Westminster Dictionary of Christian Spirituality.* Louisville, KY: John Knox Press, 2005.

STAAL, Frits. *Exploring Mysticism.* Harmondworth: Penguin, 1975.

STACE, Walter T. *Mysticism and Philosophy.* London: Macmillan, 1961.

STARBUCK, Edwin Diller. *The Psychology of Religion. An Empirical Study of the Growth of Religious Consiousness.* London: Scott, and New York: Scribner, 1899.

STEINBOCK, Anthony J. *Phenomenology and Mysticism. The Verticality of Religious Experience.* Bloomington: Indiana UP, 2009.

STEINER, Rudolf. "Meister Eckhart." *Mysticism at the Dawn of the Modern Age.* Trans. Karl E. Zimmer. Englewood, N.J.: Rudolf Steiner Publications, 1960.

STOLZ, Anselm, O.S.B. *The Doctrine of Spiritual Perfection.* Trans. Aidan Williams, O.S.B. Eugene, OR: Wipf and Stock, 2013.

STRUVE, Wolfgang. *Homo Mysticus. Three Lectures.* 1983, 1986. Transl. George Wald. Lanham, MD: UP of America, 2015.

SUDBRACK, Josef. "Der Christ von Morgen – ein Mystiker? Karl Rahners Wort als Mahnung, Aufgabe und Prophezeiung." BÖHME, Wolfgang, and Josef SUDBRACK, eds. *Der Christ von Morgen – Ein Mystiker?* Würzburg: Echter, 1989. 99-136.

SUDBRACK, Josef. *Mystische Spuren. Auf der Suche nach der Christlichen Lebensgestalt.* Würzburg: Echter, 1990.

SUZUKI, Daisetz T. *Mysticism. Christian and Buddhist.* Surrey, B.C.: Eremitical Press, 1957.

TART, Charles T. *States of Consciousness.* New York: Dutton, 1975.

UNDERHILL, Evelyn. *Mysticism: A Study in the Nature and Development of Man's Spiritual Consciousness*. London: Methuen, 1911.

WAAJMAN, Kees. "Toward a Phenomenological Definition of Spirituality." *Studies in Spirituality* 3 (1993): 5-57.

WAINWRIGHT, William J. *Mysticism: A Study of Its Nature, Cognitive Value and Moral Implications*. Madison: Wisconsin UP, 1981.

WEST, Michael A., ed. *The Psychology of Meditation*. New York: Oxford UP, 1987.

WILBER, Ken. *The Spectrum of Consciousness*. Wheaton, IL: Theosophical Publishing House, 1985.

WILMS, Hieronymus, O.P. "Das Seelenfünklein in der Deutschen Mystik." *Zeitschrift für Aszese und Mystik* 12 (1937): 157-166.

WÖHRER, Franz. *"The Cloud of Unknowing*: A Late Medieval Example of Apophatic Spiritual Guidance." *Studies in Spirituality* 7 (1997): 113-144.

WÖHRER, Franz. *Phänomenologie Mystischer Erfahrung in der Religiösen Lyrik Englands im 17. Jahrhundert*. Frankfurt a. M.: Lang, 2003.

WOODS, Richard, ed. *Understanding Mysticism: Its Meaning, Its Methodology, Interpretation in World Religions, Psychological Evaluations, Philosophical and Theological Appraisals*. London: Athlone, 1981.

WOODWARD, F., Trans. *The Book of the Kindred Sayings (Samyutta Nikaya)*. Vol. 4. London: Pali Text Society, 1927.

ZAEHNER, R. C. *Mysticism, Sacred and Profane: An Inquiry into Some Praeternatural Experience*. Oxford: Clarendon, 1957.

4. ELECTRONIC SOURCES

"Ferdinand Tonnies". *Encyclopædia Britannica. Encyclopædia Britannica Online*. Encyclopædia Britannica Inc., 2016. Web. 25 Jän. 2016. http://www.britannica.com/biography/Ferdinand-Julius-Tonnies.

Lexikon der Psychologie, 17th ed. Web. 26 Nov. 2015. https://portal.hogrefe.com/dorsch/de/ startseite/.

MULLER, Charles A. *Digital Dictionary of Buddhism*. Web. 2 Mar. 2010. http://www.buddhism-dict.net/ddb/.

SCHAEFFLER, Richard. "Krüger, Gerhard." *Neue Deutsche Biographie*, vol. 13. Berlin: Duncker & Humblot, 1982. 104. Web. 14 Oct. 2016. https://www.deutsche-biographie.de/gnd118724703.html#ndbcontent.

THORNHILL, Chris. "Karl Jaspers." *The Stanford Encyclopedia of Philosophy* (Spring 2011 Edition), Ed. Edward N. Zalta. Web. 15 April 2017. http://plato.stanford.edu/archives/spr2011/entries/jaspers/.

INDEX

A

'All-encompassing, the', ("Das Umfassende"), xvi, xvii, xxii, 9, 13–16, 17, 18, 20, 21, 25, 274, 306, 309–324, 325–364, 372–375
    Buddhism, and, 329–337. *See also* Buddhism
    calmness, perceived as, 201, 202, 324–336, 337, 338, 339, 341, 342, 344–345, 352, 358
    definition, 318–320, 341
    direction of 'arrival', 319
    emotions, responding to, 330, 356–357
    'forms of arriving' in consciousness, of, 307–364, 372
    intellectual awareness, of, 359–360
    'Light', perceived as. *See* 'Light'
    metaphoric manifestation, of, 356
    Nothingness, perceived as, 337, 338–339
    numinous quality, of, 322, 323–324
    Persona, non-visual, perceived as, 353–358, 359, 360, 363, 367–368, 369. *See also* 'arriving', forms of
    personal v. a-personal, awareness of, 314, 322–323, 329, 336–337, 353, 358, 360
    psychological v. philosophical conception of, 314–318
    'Ur-love', perceived as. *See* 'Ur-love'
    values, affected by, 356–357. *See also* evaluation, acts of
    varieties of experiencing, 311–312, 338–341, 346–350, 354–357
archetype, 240, 267
'arriving', (of phenomena in 'inner sight'), 16, 205, 232, 234–247, 261, 264, 268–269, 270–282, 286, 287, 294, 304, 309, 320, 321, 322, 338, 341, 346, 358–364, 372–374
    composite, forms of, 270, 273, 282–283, 286, 287, 288, 300, 305, 341, 363–364
    emotional response, as a form of, 108, 132, 133, 134, 137–138, 140, 143, 149, 182, 196, 233, 249, 251–252, 255, 270, 291, 330, 346, 353, 356
    hearing, inner, as a form of, 16, 157, 279, 360–361, 363
    intuition, as a form of. *See* intuition
    language (words, word-sequences), as a form of, 220, 279–281, 286–288, 295, 309, 341
    metaphoric form of, 269–270, 274, 281, 358
    non-visual awareness of the presence of 'the All-encompassing' as a Persona, as a form of, 15, 324, 343, 359–360, 363
    reel-like pictures/images from memory, as a form of, 93, 118, 149, 153, 160, 166, 182, 185, 191, 197, 208, 221–223, 236, 243–244, 249–251, 258–261, 266, 271, 281, 287, 321, 366

self-understanding (self-knowledge), as a form of, 242, 244, 246, 258, 259–270, 272, 275, 279, 281, 282, 302, 321
somatic response to 'the All-encompassing', as a form of, 346, 361–362 somatic seizure, as a form of, 255–257, 259, 279, 281, 346, 353, 361, 362, 367, 379
split-off-item from the unconscious, as a form of, 236–270, 274, 281, 288, 305, 309, 311–312, 314, 321–322, 347, 350, 360–362, 376, 377
symbol, as a form of, 252–255, 261, 269, 270, 281, 358
attentiveness, 110–113
Autogenic Training, 3, 4, 5, 20, 97, 170, 172, 173–177, 186, 207–209, 221. *See also* Schultz, I. H.
   change of consciousness, effected by 175–177. *See also* 'introversion', process of
   defined, 174–175
automatic writing, 310, 348–349
awareness, ("Bewußtheit"), 6, 15, 18, 19, 21, 25, 42, 44, 49, 51, 70, 82, 94, 102, 109, 112–118, 120, 125, 128, 147, 158–159, 180, 186, 193–194, 201, 224–226, 235, 258, 274, 287, 318–320, 322, 324, 331, 339, 341–342, 357, 359, 362, 373
   awareness-gap, 369
   definition of, 153–156
   degrees of, 243–246, 288–289, 369, 373

B

Bergson, Henri, intuition, 278
Binswanger, Ludwig, 239
body
   experience of, 55–56, 60, 62

perception of environment, 45–49
reposing, condition of, 59, 61, 62, 64, 79, 174
sensory perception, 45–47
vital functions, 49–55
Böhme, Jakob, 26, 343
Buber, Martin, 135, 324
Buddhism 18, 23, 24, 329, 332, 333. *See also* Zen
   Pali canon, 18, 332
   Theravada, tradition of, 18
   jhâna, states of, 18–19, 332–335, 336
   nirvana, 291, 329–336, 368

C

calmness, inner, xvi, xviii, 5, 6, 14, 18, 22, 31, 47, 48, 53–55, 58–62, 70, 71, 79, 80, 82, 85–86, 101, 102–103, 107, 112, 115, 118, 121, 125–126, 130, 132, 134, 136–139, 141, 144, 146–149, 151–152, 155, 162, 171, 183, 192–194, 196–200, 209, 211, 253, 255, 272, 301, 303–304, 362, 367
   experienced as 'all-encompassing', 323, 324–336, 338. *See also*, all-encompassing, calmness
   object-like quality of, 85–86, 112, 144, 155–156, 200
   visual imagery, emerging in, 150, 211
Cloud of Unknowing, The, 368
cognitio Dei experimentalis, xxi, 26, 75
concentration, 162–164
   defined, 162–163
   introversion, difference from, 163
consciousness, 39–41, 126
   clarity (lucidity) of, 18, 39, 111, 113–115, 119, 123, 142, 157, 167–168, 213. *See also* hyper-lucidity
   dispositions in, 119–121, 60–62,

177–178
dreaming, 114–117, 165, 181. *See also* 'dream consciousness'
ecstatic state of, 288–295, 305–306, 368–371, 372–374. *See also* 'All-encompassing, the'
  and language, 293–295
  and emotions, 291–292
  and quiet state of alertness ("Versunkenheit"). *See* quiet state of alertness
  feelings in, 126–146
  limitations of psychological enquiry of, 372–373
  mystical c. *See* mystical experience, mysticism
  psychological characteristics of, 373, 368–369
  quiet state of alertness, transition from, 292, 320, 340
  somnambulistic c. *See* somnambulism
  speaking in diverse states of, 216–220. *See also* language, locutions,
  states of, 55–56, 63, 65, 74, 77, 80–81, 82, 93–94, 113–114, 117–118, 121–126, 128–129, 143–144
  stream of, 121–125, 155
  subject-object split, suspended in. *See* subject-object-division
  waking state, compared to. *See* waking consciousness
contemplation, xvii, 20, 23, 75, 230, 379

D

dispositions, 117, 119–121, 212
  defined, 119
  drives, and, 66–67, 70

emotional, 60–62
'introversion', and, 54, 65, 71, 79, 85, 92, 120–121
'the quiet state of alertness', and, 57, 65, 71, 92, 94, 102–103, 120, 192
'divine spark', ("Seelenfünklein"), 9
Divine, the, 13, 21, 26, 75, 325, 352, 356, 365, 368, 380
'dream consciousness' 88, 89, 114, 116–117, 150, 151, 165–167, 181, 216, 226, 256, 264, 266–268, 379
drives, 51, 53, 57, 58, 61, 64–71
  (defined), 72, 79, 80, 85, 92, 94, 102–103, 117, 129, 155, 169, 179, 182, 213, 262, 272, 273, 296
  hierarchy of, 67–68
  feelings, and, 51, 57, 58, 60–61, 79–80, 85

E

Eckhart, Meister 11, 21, 201, 329, 365, 368
Eilks, Hans, *Das Vorgestalterlebnis unter Typologischem Gesichtspunkt*, 282–283
emotions, 60–62, 79–80, 105, 123, 126–154. *See also* feelings
  calmness. *See* calmness, inner
  emerging in 'introversion', 61–62, 77, 79, 83, 85, 102–103, 117–118, 126–154
    angst, 140–141, 143, 144–146, 179, 196, 349–350
    awe, 128, 143, 152, 248, 275, 286, 287, 342–343, 347, 351, 370
    bliss, 56, 143, 292, 294, 324, 335, 347, 357, 358, 369
    desire, 9, 10, 51–53, 74, 151, 171, 197, 213, 274, 296, 311, 344, 365

desire to surrender, 70, 71, 121, 273, 291
longing for transcendence/union, 70, 84, 149, 273, 277, 313, 347
disquiet, 130, 232, 301
fear (compared to angst), 51, 124, 128, 129–130, 132, 137, 140–141, 171, 196, 209, 232, 248, 249, 250, 252, 273, 275, 281, 286, 301, 302, 311, 312, 342, 350
grief, 128, 132, 135, 140–143, 179, 275
joy, 85, 128–130, 135, 137, 138, 143, 179, 301, 334–336, 347, 357
melancholy/sadness, 79, 136, 138, 142, 143, 179
sorrow, 19, 52, 79, 124, 130, 131, 132, 138, 292, 340
Enomiya-Lassalle, Hugo, S.J., xi, xii, 22–23
evaluation, acts of (released in the 'quiet state of alertness'), 295–302. *See also* value judgements
experience, mystical, vi, xi, xii, xv, xvi, xx, xxii, xxvi, 2–5, 7–12, 14–17 (defined), 24–26, 31–32, 34, 60, 202–204, 240, 271, 283, 285, 288, 294, 303, 306, 310, 320, 325, 331, 338, 341, 344, 348, 354–355, 363, 368–373, 375–376, 380–381
  after-effects, triggered by, 10, 23, 63, 97, 120, 204–205, 207–208, 223, 255, 265, 274, 353, 355–356, 365, 367, 369, 378–379
  and telepathy, telepathic, 230–232, 234, 319
  compared to epileptic seizure, 10–11, 256, 290
  composite forms of, 273–274, 286–287, 363
  ecstatic, 6, 14, 289, 292–293, 331, 344, 347, 348, 351, 357, 368, 272–373
  ineffability of, 19, 290, 294, 312, 314, 336, 342, 358, 368, 369
  monistic v. theistic, 16–24, 328–336, 339
  paranormal, 4, 10, 166, 296, 362, 363
  personal growth, and, 263, 266, 273, 285, 356, 367
  pseudo-mystical. *See also* pseudo-mysticism and seeming varieties, of
  revelation, psychological sense of, elicited by, 10, 15, 284,, 285, 321–322 (definition), 323, 330, 338, 352, 354, 356, 358, 361
  seeming varieties of, 4, 7, 11, 16, 41, 43, 45–47, 52, 54–57 (defined), 59–60, 70, 85, 88, 91, 94, 97, 103, 105, 107–109, 118–119, 121–129, 130, 134–139, 143, 144, 149, 152, 156–160, 180–181, 183, 199, 203, 208–210, 212, 218, 226, 230, 237, 241, 244, 249, 256, 264, 266, 267–269, 271, 274, 299–302, 305, 311, 319
  somatic, varieties of, 42–43, 46, 50, 54, 83, 97, 142, 146, 161, 169, 172–177, 185, 199, 205–208, 249, 253, 255–256, 259, 277, 279, 281, 327, 346, 353, 356, 361, 362, 367, 379

F

feelings, 126–133. *See also* emotions
defined, 126–154
emerging in 'introversion'. *See* 'introversion'
emerging in 'the quiet state of alertness'. *See* 'quiet state of alertness'

emerging in the 'ecstatic consciousness'. *See* consciousness, ecstatic
non-object related, 55, 139–147
pointed feelings, 107–108, 133–139, 155, 195
Fischer, Roland 5, 6, 30

G

Gestalt, concept of, 41, 227–229, 234, 282
  psychology of, 227–229, 231
Giergensohn, Karl, 298
God, xix, xxi, xxii, 8–9, 10–11, 12, 13, 25, 26, 27, 75, 206, 252, 276, 302, 321, 324, 325, 329, 351, 360–361, 365, 368, 379
Godhead, the, xix, 21, 329, 368
God gene, the, 8–9
Gruhle, Hans, 39, 43, 72, 86, 111–113, 277
Guyon, Madame, 329, 359, 360

H

Hamer, Dean, *The God Gene: How Faith Is Hardwired in Our Genes* 8–9
Hartman, Nicolai, 278
Heidegger, Martin, 140, 144, 217, *Sein und Zeit* 144, *Holzwege* 217
Heiler, Friedrich, *Die Buddhistische Versenkung* 18, 329, 332, 334–336
Humboldt, Wilhelm, Freiherr von, 217, 309
Husserl, Edmund, 36, 105
hyper-lucid condition of consciousness, 110, 117, 119, 159, 166–167, 185, 186, 304
hypnosis, 168–172
  definition of, 168
  'introversion', compared with, 170
  'quiet state of alertness', compared with, 172, 177
  rapport, 168–172, 176
  state of, 169–170
  will, and, 170–171

I

'I', the ("Das Ich"), 103–109
  defined, 103
'inner eye', term and function of, 138, 156, 333, 360. *See also* 'inner sight'
'inner sight', ("Innenschau"), 42, 156–160, 181, 199–200, 204–205, 214, 224–225, 271–272, 295
  See also 'inner eye' and 'arriving'
  auditory phenomena, appearing in, 16, 88, 279, 286, 360–361. *See also* hearing, inner
  defined, 157–158
  hyper-lucidity, in, 159–160. *See also* clarity of consciousness
intuitions, arriving in, 15, 105, 150, 235, 277–279 (concept defined), 286, 295, 321, 341, 358, 369. *See also* 'arriving'
  'inwardness', distinguished from, 157, 159
  non-visual phenomena, perceived in, 15, 88, 279, 286, 324, 343, 359, 360
  mental prerequisites, for functioning of, 157–158
  'quiet state of alertness', as ideal mental condition. *See* 'quiet state of alertness'
  sensory perception, in, 160
  visual phenomena, appearing in, 16, 88, 258, 264, 344, 348
'introversion', ("Versenkungsvorgang"), psychology of, 39–187
  advanced stage, of, 40, 45, 51, 52, 61–62, 65, 69, 75–77, 84–85, 91–94, 108, 100–101, 112, 117, 118, 131–132, 147–154, 161–162, 191–194, 211, 325–326
  changes in consciousness, effected

by, 63, 68, 70, 76–77, 79,
80–81, 91, 104–105, 106, 108,
109, 110, 116, 123, 129, 136,
169–170, 183–187
defined, 63, 69, 70, 161–162,
300–301
'dream consciousness', distinction
from, 117
emptying the mind, process of, 54,
63, 109, 118, 155, 167–168,
185, 193, 198–200, 211, 379
incipient stage, of, 40, 50, 51, 52,
54, 65, 68, 69, 74, 75, 77, 78,
84–85, 92, 93–95, 100–101,
107, 108, 112, 121, 124, 131–
132, 142, 192
intended goal, of, 65–66, 76, 85,
93, 101–103, 107, 121, 134,
147, 155, 171, 191–192, 194,
198, 200, 326, 332. *See also*
'quiet state of alertness'
sense of time, changed during, 123,
125, 328
surrender, desire for, evoked in,
69–71, 74, 76, 79, 92, 94, 121,
142, 148, 149, 171, 230, 273,
285, 286, 340, 347, 357
thinking, transformed in, 90–94
vital functions, changed in, 49–54
will, role of, 72–85, 170–171
'inwardness', 42–44, 108–109, 137
defined, 126
'inner sight', distinguished from,
157, 159
self-reflection, contrasted to, 44
thinking, compared to, 44
intuition, as a 'form of arriving', 15,
105, 150, 235, 277–279 (defined),
281, 286, 295, 321, 341, 358, 369

J

James, William, *Varieties of Religious Experience* xx, 224

Jaspers, Karl,
'basic knowledge', concept of,
261–262, 284, 292–293
'The All-comprising', distinguished
from 'the All-encompassing',
314–318
Jung, C. G., 264, 266–267, 277, 295,
302
archetypes, 240, 267
symbols, 267–268

K

Kierkegaard, Søren, *Der Begriff Angst*
140, 144
Klages, Ludwig, 123
Kretschmer, Erich, 116

L

Lersch, Phillip, *Der Aufbau des
Charakters* ('The Structure of the
Character') 133, 144–145, 179
'Light', as a variety of mystical
experience, 273, 276, 287, 302, 323,
345, 347–348, 350, 351
locution, as a phenomenon 'arriving',
15, 16–17, 26, 301, 310, 361. *See
also* speaking in the
'quiet state of alertness', and
mystical experience
Logos, 26
Love, as a variety of mystical
experience, 21, 25, 323, 324
personal and a–personal varieties,
of experiencing, 344–354, 355,
357, 358
See also Ur-love

INDEX

M

McGinn, Bernard, 27, 28
meditation, xii–xiv, 3, 5, 17, 18–19, 20, 22, 23, 30, 94–98, 123, 192, 197, 206, 211
    and thinking, 96–98
    defined, 95–96, 373
    dissolving disturbances, 53, 86, 95–96, 99–100
    emotions, in, 97. *See also* emotions, feelings
    'introversion', stages of, compared to. *See* 'introversion'
    judgements, and, 96–97
    mental clarity, in. *See* consciousness, clarity of, lucidity, and hyper-lucidity
    techniques of, xvii, 4, 5, 11, 23, 53, 80, 110, 142, 162, 176, 206–207, 209–210, 331, 333–336, 341, 379
    visual imagery, encountered in, 208–210
mood, basic ("Grundgestimmtheit"), 60–61
mysticism, 238, 372–374
    Buddhist traditions of. *See* Buddhism
    Christian traditions of, 24, 26, 27, 75, 156, 325, 329, 356, 360, 361, 368
    broad definition of, 373–374
    conversion, and, 364–372
    narrow definition of, 372–373
    path of preparation, for, 364–372
    phenomenological characteristics of. *See* experience, mystical
    psychology and, 240–241, 369–371, 372–373

N

'Negative Theology', tradition of, 21, 365, 368

Nelson, Kevin, *The God Impulse: Is Religion Hardwired in the Brain* 2, 10–11
nirvana, *see* Buddhism
neurotheology, 2, 11
Newberg, Andrew, *How God Changes Your Brain* 2, 8, 11–12, 206
Nothingness, as an a-personal variety of mystical experience, 18, 19–21, 143, 145, 201, 286, 287, 323, 324, 328–329, 331, 334, 336–339, 340, 345, 354, 355
numinous experience, 10, 313, 322–323, 330, 331, 342, 346, 373
    mysterium fascinosum, 15, 313, 331, 342
    mysterium tremendum, 15, 313, 331, 342, 346

O

'object arriving' (in 'inner sight'), ("das Ankommende"), 158–159, 185, 204–205, 223–230, 266, 269, 288–295, 304–305, 306, 311, 312–314, 338, 341, 350, 356. *See also* 'inner sight', 'arriving', and 'All-encompassing, the'
    associations, 221–224, 236
    auditory phenomena, as, 360–361. *See also* hearing, inner
    defined, 224
    dispositions, 252–252
    emotions, 233, 243–244, 270, 272, 281, 286, 291–292, 322
    'forms of arriving'. *See* 'arriving', forms of
    'experiencing I', 225, 229, 237, 285, 287, 289, 341
    intuition, as, 277–279, 281, 358
    language, as, 279–281, 286–287
    memories, as, 236–237, 239, 249
    metaphor, as, 264–265, 269, 270–271, 273–275, 279, 287, 358

400 INDEX

mysticism, relationship to, 306
'partial I' and, 245–246, 251, 254, 288
responding feelings, as, 275, 281
self-knowledge, as, 272, 281
sense perceptions, distinguished from, 230
split-off items from 'the self', as 236–261, 264, 305, 313–314, 321–322, 350, 366
telepathic state, distinguished from, 230–234

Otto, Rudolf. *Das Heilige* 15, 313, 330

P

Paulson, Steve 12
personality, layer theory of, 73, 103, 177–182, 237, 241
    'introversion' and, 180–181
    'quiet state of alertness' and, 182
phenomenology, psychological, 2, 3, 12, 17, 27, 35, 36, 65, 159, 161, 170, 191, 203, 224, 230, 234, 240, 241, 305–306, 332, 337, 369, 373, 375, 380–381
    method, defined, 36
Plotinus, *Enneads* 11, 353
presence, awareness/sense of, 15, 46, 185, 224, 226
    of God, xxi, 12, 27, 325
    of a non-visual Persona, 15, 323–324, 359–360, 363
Pseudo-Dionysius, Areopagite, the, 21, 365, 368
pseudo-mysticism / pseudo-mystical phenomena, vi, 4, 10, 160, 184, 258, 302, 361, 363, 372

Q

'quiet state of alertness, the', ("Versunkenheit"), 154–156, 303–306. *See also* introversion, advanced stage of

associating in, 221–224
calmness, as the basic mood, 55–56, 61–62, 85, 103, 118–119, 125–126, 130–131, 155–156
clarity, 113, 117, 118–119, 155, 213, 288. *See also* lucidity, hyper-lucidity
compared to other states of consciousness, 143–146, 148, 149, 157–159, 161–163, 191–202, 210–212, 213–216, 219–224, 225–230, 303–304, 373–374
defined, 162, 303
detachment, from external world, in, 45, 47–49, 52, 56, 63, 70, 285, 334
dispositions, sustained in, 94, 102–103, 120–121, 192, 198–199, 208, 212, 223, 304
drives, transformed in, 57, 61, 64–71
emptiness of content, in, 6, 20, 118, 142, 143–144, 155, 171, 198–200 (defined), 212–213, 215, 218, 220, 227, 303, 327, 328, 378
enhanced proficiency, achieved in, 185–186, 205–208, 213, 214, 219–220, 221, 222, 236
experiences, occurring in, 203–215, 247–261, 271–277, 284–288, 293–295, 302, 311–312, 368
feelings in, 57, 58, 61–62, 103, 130–131, 126–146, 155, 199, 248–249, 251–252, 327
'inner sight', capacity of, opened up in, 156–157, 199–200, 204–205, 224, 271–272, 304
'introversion', distinction from, 65, 155
'inwardness', 109, 130–131
memory, in, 166–167, 222, 223,

366–367
music and, 229–230
originating from the 'waking state', 182, 194, 197–198
pain, and, 52, 54
poetic imagery, in, 59
receptive condition of, 14, 20, 31, 79, 109, 144, 148, 158, 159, 167, 171, 183, 186, 198–199, 214, 229, 241, 255, 260, 264, 275, 367, 370
self-realization, elicited in, 273–274, 285
sense perception, transformed in, 40, 46, 48, 49, 51, 55
speaking in, 216–220, 309–310
surrender, desire for, evoked in, 71
termination, of, 82–83
thinking in, 84, 85, 90–94, 195, 210–215, 215
time, subjective experience in, 125, 155
value judgments, in, 298–301, 366–367
visual imagery, surfacing in, 47, 102, 155, 367
'waking consciousness', compared to. *See* 'waking consciousness'
will, transformed in, 74–75, 76, 80, 83, 212

R

Rahner, Karl, S.J., xxii, 23, 27
recollecting, 162–164
  defined, 163–164
  introversion, affinity with, 163–164
research methodology, psycho-phenomenological, 29–36, 375–381
  revelation, psychological concept of, 10, 15, 284, 285–286 (defined), 321, 322, 330, 338, 345, 352, 354, 356, 358, 361

Rothacker, Erich, *Die Schichten der Persönlichkeit*, 178. *See also* personality, layer theory, of

S

Sakaguchi, Alicja, *Sprechakte der Mystischen Erfahrung* 25–26
sancta indifferentia, 329
Schultz, I. H., *Das Autogene Training (Autogenic Training)* 97, 173–177
'self, the', 261–263. *See also* 'object arriving'
  arriving, 264, 265
  defined, 265
  ideas and, 262
  'sphere of the self', ("Selbstsphäre"), 6, 105, 125, 137, 138, 144, 146, 265, 266, 271, 274–275, 285, 293, 294, 305, 312, 314, 319, 321–322, 337–338, 340, 342, 345, 381
  split-off items from personality, 236–270
  symbols of, arriving in consciousness, 261–270
self-observation, 44, 50, 55
sense perceptions, 41–55, 172–177, 207–208
  defined, 41–41
  detachment, from. *See* detachment
  imagination, 41–42, 87
  in 'introversion', 46–47, 51, 54, 94–95, 117–118, 124, 138, 148
  in 'the quiet state of alertness', 40, 48, 55
  thoughts, and, 98, 131
'somnambulistic consciousness', 5, 6, 90, 164–168 (defined), 172, 191, 203, 216, 218, 221, 231, 233, 245, 246–252, 254, 255, 266–268, 286, 304, 310, 350, 373
  compared to 'the quiet state of alertness', 166–167, 203–204

lucidity, missing from, 167
'the experiencing I' and, 165, 166
memory, capacity of, in, 165, 166, 167–168
sense perceptions, in 165
split personality, and, 166
'waking state', interspersed in, 165, 166, 167
Steiner, Rudolf, 365
'sub-consciousness', ("Mit-Bewußtsein"), 116, 120, 126, 238
subject-object-division, (subject-object-split), 14, 108, 109, 157, 159, 201, 288, 289, 291, 292–293, 305, 320, 331, 335–336, 346–347, 357, 369, 372, 373, 378
surrender, desire for, 69–71, 74, 76, 78, 79, 92, 94, 121, 148–149, 151, 171, 230, 260, 273, 285, 286, 347, 350, 357

T

Tauler, Johannes, 21, 201, 329, 368
telepathy (telepathic experience), 230–234, 237, 247, 319
Teresa of Avila, xiii, xxi, 11
thinking, 86–103
    and 'introversion', 54, 79, 90–103, 112, 118, 124, 131. *See also* 'introversion'
        and the imagination, 87
        associations, 98–103
        concepts, and, 88
        elimination, of, 63–64
        emotions, and, 79, 108
        focused observation, 75, 118
        judgement, and, 89
        meditation, and, 97
        words, and, 88, 94

U

'ultimate phenomenon', ("Phänomenletztheit"), 72, 86–87 (defined), 103, 104, 111, 141, 220
'Unconscious, the', ("Das Unbewußte"), 236–261
    split-off items, from, 236–261
Underhill, Evelyn, xx
union, mystical, (*unio mystica*), 25, 26, 70, 293, 305, 336, 365, 368, 369, 370, 378, 380
'Ur, the', 336–344
    a-personal, experience of, 342
    distinguished from 'All-encompassing calmness', 342
    ecstatic response to, 343–344, 348
Ur-love, 344–353
    a-personal experience of, 351–352
    gift of a hidden transcendental Being, perceived as, 351–352

V

value judgements, 295–302
    'experiencing I', and, 298, 300
    Gruen, Werner, referring to Girgensohn, Karl, 298
    Haering, Theodor, 296
    human beings, types of, 297–298
    Krueger, Felix, 296
    'quiet state of alertness', and, 298–301
    Rohracher, Hubert, 296
vital functions, 49–54, 57
    feelings linked to, 57, 60
    perception of ("Vitalwahrnehmung"), 48–49, 55
Volkelt, Johannes, *Versuch über Fühlen und Wollen (An Attempt [at a Study] on Feelings and the Will)*, 127–128

W

'waking consciousness', xviii, 5, 7, 17, 31–33, 35, 39–40, 45, 47, 51–54, 63, 65, 68, 70, 73, 75–77, 89, 90–93, 96, 102, 104, 106–109, 112–117, 121–124, 126, 177, 179–180, 186, 202,

208, 210, 219, 243, 245, 246, 249, 253, 260, 264, 268–269, 271–272, 280, 287, 290, 292, 300–304, 316, 330, 333, 343, 349, 350, 353, 357, 364, 367, 373, 379, 380
  clarity, changing degrees in, 113–114, 115–116, 117, 213. *See also* lucidity
  compared to consciousness of 'introversion', 143–146, 148, 149, 157–159
  compared to 'dream consciousness', 116–117, 165, 181
  compared to hypnotic state, 168–172
  compared to the 'quiet state of alertness', 161–163, 210–212, 213–216, 219–224, 225–230
  compared to the 'somnambulistic consciousness', 164–168. *See also* 'somnambulist consciousness'
  dispositions, in 196–197, 202, 212
  distinctive features, of, 112–117, 121–124, 197–198, 243–249
  feelings in, 77, 129, 131–132, 134, 136, 141, 146
  governed by 'the I', 104, 106–107, 109, 197
  memory, and, 221–223, 236–237, 249–250, 287
  restlessness, in, 51, 130, 132, 140, 143–144, 146–147, 272
  self-knowledge, in, 271–272
  shifting from/to other mental states, 65, 68, 77–79, 80–83, 117, 144, 161–162, 182, 208, 210, 229–230, 274, 280
  subject-object-split, experienced in, 292. *See also* subject-object-division
  thinking, in, 90, 91–92, 96, 114, 123–125, 131, 210–211, 214

  will and, 73, 75, 114, 182, 197–198, 272–273
Weinberg, A., 176
will, (capacity of volition), 41, 52, 54, 64, 72–86, 90, 91, 106, 111–112, 114, 163, 170, 212, 214, 229, 259, 272, 281
words, as objects of inner perception, xvii, 16, 26, 214, 220, 247, 279–280, 309, 310, 341, 360–361. *See also* 'arriving', language

Z

Zen, xi, 20, 22–24, 30, 206

www.ingramcontent.com/pod-product-compliance
Lightning Source LLC
Chambersburg PA
CBHW030104010526
44116CB00005B/86